NEW REVISED

Webster's
Classic
Reference
Library

Over
6 million
in print!

DICTIONARY

© 1999 Landoll, Inc.
Ashland, Ohio 44805
® The Landoll Apple Logo is a trademark owned by Landoll, Inc.
and is registered with the U.S. Patent and Trademark Office.
No part of this book may be reproduced or copied.
All Rights Reserved. Manufactured in the U.S.A.

00705-1591

This is an abridged dictionary, containing a selection of the many words and definitions that make up the English language. In the interest of convenience, we have made this volume as comprehensive as space permits, choosing words and definitions for both reliability and versatility. In this manner, we have excluded place names, proper names, and historical events, which are best researched in more expansive dictionaries. An abridged dictionary like this one offers the reader a reliable listing of everyday words in a compact, convenient format.

ABBREVIATIONS

abbr.-abbreviation

adj.-adjective

adv.-adverb

coll. n.-collective noun

conj.-conjunction

contr.-contraction

ind. art.-indefinite article

interj.-interjection

meta.-metaphor

n.-noun

pl.-plural

prep.-preposition

pron.-pronoun

var.-variant

v.-verb

A

A, a The first letter of the English alphabet; the highest grade, meaning excellent or best; in music, the sixth note of the C major scale. *art.* A singular unspecified referent; one, any.

aard•vark *n.* A large burrowing insect-eating mammal resembling the anteater, native to sub-Saharan Africa.

a•back *adv.* Unexpectedly; by surprise; startled.

a•ba•cus *n.* A frame holding parallel rods with beads, used for manual computation, especially by the Chinese.

a•ban•don *vt.* To yield utterly; to desert, forsake, or withdraw protection, support, or help from. **abandonment** *n.*

a•bate *v.* To diminish or decrease in strength, value, or intensity; to wane or ebb. **abater** *n.*, **abated** *adj.*

ab•bess *n.* The female superior of a convent of nuns, possessing the same authority as an abbot.

ab•bey *n.* An abbey church, monastery, or convent, run by an abbot or abbess.

ab•bot *n.* The male superior of the monastery.

ab•bre•vi•ate *v.* To make briefer; to abridge; to shorten; to reduce to a briefer form, as a word or phrase.

ab•bre•vi•a•tion *n.* A shortened form of a word or phrase, used to represent the full form.

ab•do•men *n.* That part of the human body that lies between the thorax and the pelvis and contains the stomach, spleen, liver, kidneys, bladder, pancreas, and intestines. **abdominal** *adj.*, **abdominally** *adv.*

ab•duct *v.* To carry away wrongfully, as by force or fraud; to kidnap; to draw aside or away. **abductor, abduction** *n.*

abide *v.* To tolerate; to bear; to remain; to last; [with *by*] to conform to; to comply with.

a•bid•ing *adj.* Enduring, long-lasting, deep-rooted.

a•bil•i•ty *n.* State of being able; possession of necessary qualities; competence; skill; talent; physical or mental prerequisite.

a•blaze *adv.* On fire; brilliantly lighted up; *meta.* Very excited; angry.

a•ble *adj.* Having sufficient ability; capable or talented. **ableness** *n.*, **ably** *adv.*

a•ble-bod•ied *adj.* Having a sound, strong body; competent for physical service.

a•bloom *adj.* In the state of flowering, especially of plants with multiple flowers; blooming; *meta.* Opening, as a flower.

ab•ly *adv.* Done in an able manner; capably.

ab•nor•mal *adj.* Not normal; irregular; unnatural. **abnormality** *n.*, **abnormally** *adv.*

a•board *adv.* On board a ship or other vehicle.

a•bode *n.* Dwelling place; home; place of residence; habitation.

a•boil *adj.* Boiling; heated to the point where a fluid turns into a gas; *meta.* Angry, fuming, about to erupt.

a•bol•ish *v.* To put an end to; to annul, especially a tenet or law. **abolition** *n.*

ab•o•li•tion *n.* The principle or belief that a political policy should be abandoned; specifically, the effort to end slavery; the state of being abolished. **abolitionary** *adj.*

a•bom•i•na•ble *adj.* Detestable; loathsome, extremely disagreeable. **abominably** *adv.*

ab•o•rig•i•ne *n.* Earliest inhabitant of a region, especially after invasion and colonization by others; *cap.* One of an indigenous people of Australia.

a•bort *v.* To terminate or cause to terminate an operation or procedure before completion; to miscarry in giving birth; to cancel a mission or flight before completion of its goal.

a•bor•tion *n.* Induced termination of pregnancy before the fetus can survive; something malformed.

a•bound *v.* To have plenty; to exist in large numbers; to multiply and expand to or past bounds.

a•bout *adv.* Approximately; near to; out, here and there. *prep.* Regarding; pertaining to; throughout.

a•bout-face *n.* In military, a marching maneuver reversing the direction of the troops; *meta.* The abrupt reversal of one's point of view or attitude.

a•bove *adv.* Higher or greater than; in or at a higher place.

a•bove all *adv.* Before all other considerations.

a•bove•board *adv.* In a straightforward manner; open, fully revealed to all parties.

a•bove•ground *adj.* Located or positioned above the level or surface of the ground; legitimate.

a•bra•sion *n.* The act of grinding, as a surface, with the use of friction; a shallow skin injury caused by abrading.

a•bra•sive *adj.* Abrading; capable of increasing abrasion; of behavior, coarse or offensive, causing irritation and friction.

a•breast *adv.* or *adj.* Side by side, as bodies in line; up to date on current trends and events.

a•bridge *v.* To make smaller, fewer, or shorter while maintaining essential contents. **abridgment** or **abridgement** *n.*

a•broad *adv.* Widely; in many places; outside one's country; at large; in the open air.

a•brupt *adj.* Happening or coming suddenly without warning; terse or short of patience in discourse; rudely brief. **abruptness** *n.*, **abruptly** *adv.*

ab•scess *n.* A locally infected place in the body, characterized by pus surrounded by sore and swollen inflamed tissue. **abscessed** *adj.*

ab•sence *n.* Failure to attend; not present; time not in attendance; the state of being not in one's presence; inattention, lack of mental focus; not in existence, as in a diagnostic analysis. **absent** *adj.*, **absently** *adv.*

ab•sen•tee *n.* An absent person.

ab•sent-mind•ed *adj.* Forgetful; preoccupied with thoughts other than the present; tending to forget or lose concentration.

ab•sent with•out leave *adj.* In military, absent without permission from the place of duty.

ab•so•lute *adj.* Unconditional; without restraint or qualification; perfect. **absoluteness** *n.*, **absolutely** *adv.*

ab•solve *v.* To free or release from responsibility, guilt, or penalty; to perform absolution. **absolver** *n.*, **absolvable** *adj.*

ab•sorb *v.* To take in; to incorporate into an existing form; to engage one's whole attention; in physics, to transform energy or store one substance inside another. **absorbability** *n.*

ab•sor•ben•cy *n.* The act or state of being absorbent; a measure of capacity to absorb.

ab•sor•bent *adj.* Able to absorb something.

ab•stain *v.* To refrain; to avoid on principle; to deny by self-discipline; to choose neither side, as in a vote. **abstainer** *n.*

ab•stract *v.* To remove from, reduce, or summarize; to separate from the specific instance. **abstractedness** *n.*

ab•stract *adj.* Nonrepresentational; theoretical or nonpractical; not based in pragmatism or reality; apart from applicability or practicality.

ab•stract *n.* A summary of a larger document; a painting or other work of art based on nonrepresentational principles.

ab•strac•tion *n.* The process or product of abstract thinking or creating. **abstractive** *adj.*

ab•surd *adj.* Contrary to reason; unreasonable beyond consideration; logically contradictory; meaningless. **absurdity**, **absurdness** *n.*

ab•surd•ism *n.* A philosophy based on the idea that humanity has been thrown into a meaningless universe where order is an illusion, and any search for purpose will conflict with the irrationality of the universe itself. **absurdist** *adj.* or *n.*

a•bun•dance *n.* Ample supply; plenty; amount more than enough. **abundant** *adj.*, **abundantly** *adv.*

a•buse *v.* To use in an improper or wrong way; to mistreat, especially physically. *n.* Improper treatment; injury or damage resulting from mistreatment.

a•bu•sive *adj.* Injurious or damaging to another. **abusiveness** *n.*

a•bys•mal *adj.* Immeasurably deep or low; extremely poor; fathomless.

a•byss *n.* A deep crack or gap; in mythology, a bottomless cavern to the center of the earth; any unbridgeable distance, especially in space.

ac•a•dem•ic *adj.* Pertaining to or related to an academy.

a•cad•e•my *n.* A private school for special training, as in music, dance, or art; a military or law enforcement training school.

ac•cede *v.* To consent; to agree; to arrive at a certain condition or state; to give in to.

ac•cel•er•ate *v.* To make run or work faster; to increase the speed.

ac•cel•er•a•tion *n.* The process of accelerating something.

ac•cel•er•a•tor *n.* Something that accelerates something else; in engineering, the machine part allowing the operator to increase speed.

ac•cent *n.* In linguistics, a pronunciation that gives one syllable more prominence than the others; the mark indicating such prominence; emphasis; area of concentration; focus of attention.

ac•cept *v.* To take what is offered or given; to believe to be true; to agree; to embrace, as a concept or belief. **accepter, acceptor** *n.*

ac•cept•able *adj.* Satisfactory; proper; good enough; agreeable.

ac•cep•tance *n.* Approval or belief; a condition of being accepted; the receipt of agreed-upon terms or conditions.

ac•cess *n.* Admission, entrance; permission or power to enter; opportunity to communicate or influence. **accessibility** *n.*, **accessible** *adj.*

ac•cess *v.* In computers, to open files and obtain data from electronic storage.

ac•ces•so•ry *n.* Aid or contributor to an action or state; a detail accompanying a visual display, especially a wardrobe. **accessories,** *pl.*

ac•ci•dent *n.* An unplanned or unexpected event; a collision of vehicles; injury or damage to persons or property caused by unavoidable circumstances; an unintentional variation in a work of art. **accidental** *adj.*, **accidentally** *adv.*

ac•claim *v.* To greet with strong approval or loud applause; to hail or cheer. *n.* Strong regard, recognition; public acknowledgment of accomplishment.

ac•com•mo•date *v.* To give room or lodging; to make fit; to adjust to new conditions. **accommodation** *n.*

ac•com•mo•dat•ing *adj.* Ready to help; willing to please; obliging.

ac•com•pa•ni•ment *n.* Something that shares or supports; a companion dish to the main course; in music, the instrumental support to singing or recitation; the harmonic addition to melody.

ac•com•pa•nist *n.* A person who plays a musical accompaniment.

ac•com•pa•ny *v.* To be together with; to go along with on a journey.

ac•com•plice *n.* Companion who helps another, especially in an illegal act.

ac•com•plish *v.* To perform; to carry out; to complete through effort; to do. **accomplisher** *n.*, **accomplishable** *adj.*

ac•com•plish•ment *n.* A finished task; completion of effort, especially admirable or noteworthy.

ac•cord *n.* Harmony; agreement; formal treaty between opposing factions. *v.* To grant or award. **accordance** *n.*

ac•cord•ing•ly *adv.* In a way that is proper and fitting.

ac•cor•di•on *n.* A musical instrument fitted with bellows and button keyboards, played by pulling out and pressing together the bellows to force air through reeds; a shape or configuration folded like an accordion.

ac•cor•di•on•ist *n.* An accordion player.

ac•count *n.* A description of an event or experience; a statement of debts and credits in money transactions; a record; a report. **accounts** *pl.* The bookkeeping records of a company or enterprise.

ac•count *v.* [with *for*] To explain; to justify, especially amounts or actions.

ac•count•a•ble *adj.* Liable to be held responsible; able to be explained. **accountableness** *n.*, **accountably** *adv.*

ac•count•ant *n.* One who keeps accounts; the position of responsibility in public or private accounting.

ac•count•ing *n.* A report on how accounts have been balanced; the system of keeping business records or accounts.

ac•cu•ra•cy *n.* Exactness; precision; the fact of being accurate or without mistakes. **accuracies** *pl.*

ac•cu•rate *adj.* Without mistakes or errors; careful and exact; correct; precise in detail; true.

ac•cu•sa•tion *n.* A charge that a person is guilty, especially of breaking the law.

ac•cuse *v.* To find fault with; to blame; to charge someone with doing wrong or breaking the law. **accuser** *n.*

ace *n.* The face of a playing card, die, or domino marked with one spot; an expert in an event, especially flight combat; in tennis, a score made by an unreturned serve.

a•cet•y•lene *n.* A highly inflammable, poisonous, colorless gas that burns brightly with a hot flame, used in blowtorches for cutting metal, welding, and soldering.

ache *v.* To give or have a dull, steady pain; to want very much; to experience longing or yearning; to long for. **achy** *adj.*, **achiness** *n.*

ache *n.* A dull, continuous pain.

a•chieve *v.* To set or reach by trying hard; to do; to succeed in doing; to accomplish. **achiever** *n.*, **achievable** *adj.*

a•chieve•ment *n.* Something achieved by work, courage, or skill.

ac•id *n.* A chemical compound containing hydrogen that forms a salt when combined with a base; a substance with less than pH 7. *slang* The drug LSD. **acid** *adj.*

a•cid•i•ty *n.* Condition or quality of being acid.

ac•knowl•edge *v.* To admit the truth, existence or reality of; to publicly credit; to respond to a gesture. **acknowledgment** *n.*, **acknowledgeable** *adj.*

ac•ne *n.* A common skin disorder of young people in which minor inflammation of glands and follicles continue to appear on the body, especially the face.

a•corn *n.* The nut of an oak; the distinctive shape of an acorn.

a•cous•tic *adj.* Pertaining to sound or the sense of hearing; the sense of sound; absorbing sound. **acoustical** *adj.*, **acoustically** *adv.*

ac•quaint *v.* To make familiar; to let know; to make aware; to inform.

ac•quain•tance *n.* A person known casually or briefly but not as a close friend; [with *with*] a superficial knowledge of a subject or topic. **acquaintanceship** *n.*

ac•quire *v.* To secure control or possession; to become the owner; to get.

ac•qui•si•tion *n.* Something acquired; the act of acquiring; a purchase.

ac•quit *v.* To rule that a person accused of something is not guilty; to conduct oneself in a manner that removes doubts or reservations in others. **acquittal** *n.*

a•cre *n.* A measurement of land that, in U.S. and England, equals 43,560 square feet. **acres** *pl.*

a•cre•age *n.* The total number of acres in a section of land.

ac•rid *adj.* Having a sharp, bitter, pungent, or irritating taste or smell. **acridity**, **acridness** *n.*, **acridly** *adv.*

ac•ro•bat *n.* One skilled in gymnastic feats; a physically nimble or flexible performer. **acrobatic** *adj.*

ac•ro•bat•ics *n.* The art, sport, or

performance of an acrobat.

a•cross *prep.* From side to side; to one side from the other; on the other side of.

act *n.* A thing done; deed; an action; one of the main parts of a play or opera; a law; decree; **actability** *n.*, **actable** *adj.*

act *v.* To perform in a play or mimesis; to feign an emotion or reaction that is not real or true; to take action; [with *on*] to produce an effect or result.

act•ing *adj.* In the temporary state of performing the duties, services, or functions of another person. *n.* The art or practice of mimesis.

ac•tion *n.* The process of doing or acting; an effect produced by something; a lawsuit.

ac•ti•vate *v.* To put into action; to begin or make active; to bring into motion. **activation** *n.*

ac•tive *adj.* Working; full of action; busy; lively; quick. **activeness** *n.*, **actively** *adv.*

ac•tiv•ism *n.* A practice based on direct action to affect changes in government and social conditions.

ac•tiv•i•ty *n.* An event or action, with a series of steps, usually ordered and benign; the normal process of a living being.

ac•tor *n.* A person of either gender who acts in films, plays, television shows, and other media, usually in fictive, mimetic roles.

ac•tress *n.* [Obsolete] A female actor.

ac•tu•al *adj.* Acting or existing in fact or reality; as it really is; true; real; not theoretical. **actuality** *n.*, **actually** *adv.*

ac•u•punc•ture *n.* A traditional Chinese means of treating some illnesses or lessening pain by inserting thin needles into certain parts of the body.

a•cute *adj.* Extremely sensitive; sharp and quick, as pain; shrewd; serious; pivotal to result. **acuteness** *n.*, **acutely** *adv.*

ad•age *n.* A proverb; a wise or true saying; a metaphor or analogy embracing a universal observation.

a•dapt *v.* To fit or suit; to change oneself as to adjust to new conditions; to alter one's behavior to surroundings; in biology, to alter genetic makeup by natural selection in response to environment. **adaptability** *n.*, **adaptable** *adj.*

ad•ap•ta•tion *n.* Variation from original; an act of changing so as to fit or become suitable; a creative work restructured from the original genre or source.

add *v.* To join or put together with another; to cause an increase; to perform mathematical addition; to include into a group.

ad•den•dum *n.* An addition to a formal document, usually at the end; supplement attached to the main body of a discourse. **addenda** *pl.*

ad•der *n.* A common venomous viper found in North America and Europe.

ad•dict *n.* A person with a habit so strong that it cannot easily be broken; one with chemical or psychological dependency on a substance. **addiction** *n.*, **addicted** *v.*

ad•di•tion *n.* An adding of numbers to find their total; the act of joining one thing to another; the mathematical process of combining numbers; a part of a house or building attached to the original structure.

ad•di•tion•al *adj.* Extra; added onto; more than the original amount; supplemental. **additionally** *adv.*

ad•di•tive *n.* A substance added to another in small amounts to alter or improve its performance or properties.

ad•dress *v.* To direct or aim; to speak to; to give attention to; *n.* The location to which mail or goods can be sent to a person; in computers, one's identifying electronic code allowing access to an internet.

ad•dress•ee *n.* The person to whom a letter or package is addressed.

a•dept *adj.* Highly skilled; expert; proficient. **adeptly** *adv.*, **adeptness** *n.*

a•dept *n.* A person learned in the arts, especially of magic or alchemy.

ad•e•qua•cy *n.* The state of being good enough; sufficiency; acceptability.

ad·e·quate *adj.* Sufficient; good enough for what is needed; meeting the minimum requirements; capable. **adequateness** *n.*, **adequately** *adv.*

ad·here *v.* To stay attached; to stick and not come loose; to stay firm in support.

ad·he·sive *adj.* Tending to stick and not come loose; clinging; having a sticky surface. **adhesion** *n.*, **adhesively** *adv.*

ad·ja·cent *adj.* Close or nearby; touching; next to each other. **ad·ja·cen·cy** *n.*

ad·jec·tive *n.* A descriptive word used to modify a noun or pronoun, denoting quality, quantity, extent, and the like.

ad·just *v.* To arrange or change; to make work correctly; to regulate; to change settings for best result. **adjustability** *n.*

ad·just·a·ble *adj.* Capable of adjustment; variable by choice.

ad·just·ed *adj.* Altered to attain or achieve a harmonious relationship; regulated; changed to suit a particular circumstance or environment.

ad·just·ment *n.* The act or process of changing; a settlement of a suit or claim.

ad·min·is·tra·tion *n.* The organizational structure of a school, company, or bureau; collectively, the persons who operate the structure.

ad·min·is·tra·tor *n.* A person who administers or directs; an executive; a manager.

ad·mi·ra·ble *adj.* Worthy of being admired or praised; excellent.

ad·mi·ral *n.* The highest rank for a naval officer; the commanding officer of a navy.

ad·mi·ral·ty *n.* The department of the British navy; the court and law dealing with ships and shipping.

ad·mire *v.* To hold a high opinion; to regard with wonder, delight, and pleased approval. **admiringly** *adv.*

ad·mir·er *n.* One who admires; a romantic suitor in the early stage of courtship.

ad·mis·si·ble *adj.* Capable of being admitted, accepted or allowed.

ad·mis·sion *n.* The right or act of being admitted; an admitting of the truth of something; a confession.

ad·mit *v.* To take or accept as being the truth; to permit or give the right to enter. **admittedly** *adv.*

ad·mit·tance *n.* Permission to enter; successful entry.

ad·mit·ted·ly *adv.* By one's own admission or confession.

ad·o·les·cent *n.* A person in the transitional period between childhood and adulthood.

a·dopt *v.* To take into one's family legally and raise as one's own; to accept as a process; to take up formally; to choose as a source or method. **adoption** *n.*

a·dor·a·ble *adj.* Very likable; charming; worthy of deep admiration. **adorably** *adv.*, **adorableness** *n.*

a·dore *v.* To love greatly; to worship or honor highly; to like very much; to venerate as a deity. **adoration** *n.*

a·dorn *v.* To add splendor or beauty; to embellish; to wear as decoration.

a·drift *adv.* Drifting; floating freely without being steered; having no clear purpose or aim; lost or directionless.

a·dult *n.* A fully grown man or woman; a mature person. *adj.* Having reached full size and strength; appropriate for grown persons. **adulthood** *n.*

ad·vance *v.* To move ahead; to make or become higher; to increase in value or price.

ad·vance *n.* An improvement or progression; payment of wages or compensation before completion of a task; proposition or suggestion, especially romantic.

ad·vanced *adj.* Ahead in time; beyond beginning status; precocious or educated past one's age.

ad·van·tage *n.* A better chance or more forcible position; a condition, thing or event that can help or benefit; in tennis, the first point after deuce.

ad·van·ta·geous *adj.* Giving advantage; favorable.

ad·ven·ture *n.* An exciting, dangerous or unusual experience; a series of events offering new experiences. **adventure** v.

ad·ven·tur·er n. A person who engages in unusual or experiential activities; one who seeks wealth and social position. **adventurous** adj.

ad·verb n. A word which modifies a verb, adjective, or another adverb signifying condition or manner, as when, where, how, what kind, or how much. **adverbial** adj., **adverbially** adv.

ad·ver·tise v. To draw public attention to a product for sale; to disseminate information about, as a job or opportunity. **advertiser** n.

ad·ver·tise·ment n. A public notice stating the qualities of a commodity, conditions of sale, and methods for purchase.

ad·ver·tis·ing n. The profession of preparing advertisements for publication or broadcast; the act of promoting for sale.

ad·vice n. Suggestion or recommendation regarding a course of action or decision; expert opinion, especially legal, used in decision making.

ad·vis·a·ble adj. Fit to be done or advised; recommended; capable of being suggested as a course of action. **advisability** n.

ad·vis·ed·ly adv. Deliberately; with consideration; carefully.

ad·vis·er n. A person who gives an opinion or advises; one who helps prepare academic schedules.

ad·vis·o·ry adj. Exercising or having the power to advise; giving or containing advice, without actual legislative power.

aer·i·al adj. Of or in the air; pertaining to aircraft. n. An antenna for television or radio. **aerially** adv.

af·fa·ble adj. Good-natured; easy to talk to; friendly. **affably** adv.

af·fair n. An event or occurrence; matters of business or public concern; a romantic relationship outside marriage.

af·fect v. To move emotionally; to feel sympathetic or sad; to bring about a change in. **affecting, affected** adj.

af·fect n. Emotional element; subjective response aside from physical or logical conditions.

af·fec·tion n. A tender or fond feeling toward another.

af·fec·tion·ate adj. Loving and gentle; feeling deeply. **affectionately** adv.

af·firm v. To declare positively; to stand by the truth; to state in positive terms. **affirmation** n.

af·flict v. To cause suffering or pain; to cause mental suffering. **affliction** n.

af·ford v. To be able to provide; to have enough money to spare.

a·fire adv. Burning; on fire; full of energy and purpose.

a·flame adj. Burning; in flames; glowing.

a·float adv. Floating on the surface of water; circulating or moving freely.

a·fraid adj. Hesitant; filled with fear; reluctant.

a·fresh adj. Once more; again; begun anew.

Af·ri·can A·mer·i·can n. An American citizen of African or Negroid descent. **African-American** adj.

af·ter adv. In the rear; behind. prep. Following spatially or temporally; subsequent in order to.

af·ter·math n. State or condition after an event; consequence; result; subsequent environment.

af·ter·thought n. An idea occurring later; idea added after.

a·gain adv. Moreover; another time; once more; on the other hand; yet; in addition.

a·gainst prep. In opposition to or in combat with; in contrast with; in exchange for; in preparation for; counter to.

ag·ate n. Quartz chalcedony containing bands or patterns of colors; a playing marble made of agate; in typesetting, a type size of about 5 1/2 points.

age n. The length of time from beginning to a certain date; [with of] the time of life when a person has full legal rights; v. To grow or become old; to mature; to rest until fruition, as wine or cheese. **aged** adj., **agedness** n., **agedly** adv.

aged

ag•ed *n.* Very old; venerably advanced in years; ancient.

age•ism *n.* In law, discrimination, prejudice, or bias based on age.

age•less *adj.* Existing forever; never seems to grow old.

a•gen•cy *n.* A business or service that acts for others; a subdivision of a bureaucratic structure; action; active influence; power.

a•gen•da *n.* Program or list of things to be done; formal order of discussion topics; aim or goal.

a•gent *n.* One who acts as the representative of another; that which acts or exerts power; the active or precipitating ingredient in a reaction. **agency** *n.*

ag•gra•vate *v.* To annoy; to make worse; to reinjure or damage again; to cause a reaction to.

ag•gres•sion *n.* Hostile action or behavior; an unprovoked assault; anger manifested in attack or confrontation.

ag•gres•sive *adj.* Offensively and combatively active; tending to initiate confrontation; pushy; proactive and deliberate. **aggressiveness** *n.*

a•ghast *adj.* Appalled; struck with amazement; taken aback; momentarily breathless.

ag•ile *adj.* Marked by the ability to move quickly and easily; nimble or flexible; capable of complex movement. **agility** *n.*

a•go *adj or adv.* In the past; gone by; earlier than now.

ag•o•nize *v.* To afflict with great anguish or suffering; [with *over* or *about*] to worry excessively; to fret painfully; to suffer regarding a decision or course of action. **agonized, agonizing** *adj.*

ag•o•ny *n.* Intense mental distress or physical pain; anguish; suffering caused by internal conflict. **agonies,** *pl.*

a•gree *v.* To give assent; to consent; to share an understanding or opinion; to be beneficial or suitable; to correspond.

a•gree•a•ble *adj.* Pleasant; pleasing; willing; ready to consent. **agreeableness** *n.*, **agreeably** *adv.*

a•gree•ment *n.* Harmony; concord; state or act of agreeing; coincidence of mathematical or scientific results.

ag•ri•cul•ture *n.* The science and occupation of raising livestock, crops, or other consumable products grown on land. **agriculturalist, agriculturist** *n.*

a•ground *adv. or adj.* Stranded; on the ground; stopped by contact with the floor of a body of water; run ashore; beached.

a•head *adv.* Before; in advance; to or at the front; successfully or progressively.

aid *v.* To give help or assistance.

AIDS *abbr.* Acquired Immune Deficiency Syndrome; a disease in men and women, transmitted by exchange of bodily fluids, that destroys the body's immunological system, especially the ability to produce helper T cells.

ail *v.* To feel sick; to make ill or uneasy.

ail•ment *n.* Mild illness; chronic disorder.

aim *v.* To direct a weapon; to direct purpose. *n.* Intention; goal.

aim•less *adj.* Lacking of purpose; without direction or motive.

ain't *contr.* [Lit.] Are not; *slang* am not, is not, has not, or have not; do not, does not, did not.

air *n.* An odorless, tasteless, colorless, gaseous mixture, primarily composed of nitrogen (78%) and oxygen (21%); the sky; a breeze; [with *on the*] broadcast medium; a melody.

air•borne *adj.* Borne by or carried through or by the air.

air•brush *n.* Machine using compressed air to spray paint and other liquids on a surface.

air con•di•tion•er *n.* Equipment used to lower the temperature and humidity of an enclosure.

air•craft *n.* A machine that flies, such as a helicopter, airplane, or glider.

air•craft car•ri•er *n.* A large ship on which airplanes can be transported, stored, launched, and landed.

air•field *n.* Paved runways at an airport; landing strip.

air·line *n.* An air transportation company.

air·lin·er *n.* A large passenger aircraft.

air·mail or **air mail** *n.* Mail sent by means of air.

air·plane *n.* A fixed-wing vehicle capable of flight, heavier than air, commonly propelled by jet engine or propeller.

air·port *n.* A terminal station where aircraft take off, land, board and discharge passengers; usually attached to storage and maintenance facilities.

air·y *adj.* Open to the air; breezy; light as air; graceful. **airiness** *n.*, **airily** *adv.*

aisle *n.* Passageway between rows of seats, as in a church, auditorium, or airplane. **aisled** *adj.*

a·jar *adv.* or *adj.* Partially opened; not tightly closed.

a·larm *n.* A warning of danger; sudden feeling of fear; the bell or buzzer of a clock. *v.* To frighten or warn by an alarm. **alarming** *adj.*, **alarmingly** *adv.*

al·ba·tross *n.* Large, web-footed, long-winged sea bird.

al·bum *n.* A bound book with pages or receptacles for photographs, autographs, stamps, or other small flat items; a book of collections; a collection of songs, music, or other recordings marketed in one package.

al·co·hol *n.* Hydroxyl derivatives of hydrocarbons; a series of related organic compounds; intoxicating liquor containing alcohol; ethanol

al·co·hol·ic *adj.* Resulting from alcohol; containing or preserved in alcohol; suffering from alcoholism. **alcoholic** *n.*

al·co·hol·ism *n.* Excessive alcohol consumption; a habit or addiction.

al·cove *n.* Recess or partly enclosed extension of a room.

ale *n.* Beverage similar to, but more bitter than beer, made from malt by fermentation.

a·lert *adj.* Vigilant; brisk; watchful; active. *n.* A signal by siren of air attack. *v.* Bring attention to, make noticeable. **alertly** *adv.*, **alertness** *n.*

al·ge·bra *n.* A procedure of mathematics in which symbols, especially letters, represent members of a specified set of numbers and are related by operations that hold for all numbers in the set. **algebraic** *adj.* **algebraically** *adv.*

al·i·bi *n.* In law, a form of defense by which the accused shows the physical impossibility of having committed a crime; an attempt by a defendant to prove absence from a crime scene; an excuse.

a·li·en *adj.* Unfamiliar; outside of one's natural environment; not in residence at the place of one's allegiance; *n.* A member of another region or country; a stranger; a foreigner; a non-native.

a·lign *v.* To arrange in a line; to position in a straight line; to take one side of an argument or cause. **aline** *v.*

a·like *adj.* Similar in all essentials; parallel and equal; having very close resemblance. *adv.* In the same manner, way, or degree.

a·live *adj.* Living; having life; able to sustain life processes; in existence or effect; viable; full of life. **aliveness** *n.*

all *adj.* Total extent or total entity; being a whole number, amount, or quantity; every.

all-a·round or **all-round** *adj.* Total; in full spectrum; comprehensive; in every aspect.

al·le·giance *n.* Loyalty to one's nation, cause, or sovereign; faithfulness and commitment to an ideology; obligations of a vassal to an overlord. **allegiant** *adj.*

al·ler·gic *adj.* Causing a reaction; hypersensitive, especially to a substance; responsive or reactive to an allergen.

al·ler·gist *n.* A doctor specializing in allergies.

al·ler·gy *n.* Pathological or abnormal reaction to environmental substances, as foods, dust, pollens, or microorganisms. **allergic** *adj.*, **allergies** *pl.*

al·ley *n.* Narrow roadway, lane, or passageway between or behind buildings; a bowling lane. **alleys** *pl.*

al·li·ance *n.* A union, relationship, or connection by kinship, marriage, or common interest; a confederation of nations by a formal treaty; an affinity.

al•li•ga•tor *n.* Large amphibious reptile with very sharp teeth, powerful jaws, and a shorter snout than the related crocodile.

al•lot *v.* To distribute or set aside as a share of something. **allotment, allotter** *n.*

all out *adv.* With every possible effort or resource; leaving no reserve.

al•low *v.* To make a provision for, to permit; to permit to have; to admit; to concede. **allowable** *adj.*, **allowably** *adv.*

al•low•ance *n.* The amount allowed or set aside; the permissible degree of refinement or calibration; the act of allowing something; a periodic payment for regular duties or compliances; a price discount.

al•loy *n.* Something added to; an item reduced in purity or value; a mixture or combination of two or more pure elements, especially in metallurgy.

all right *adj.* Meets satisfaction, certainly. *adv.* Satisfactory; correct; unhurt. *adj.*, *slang* Good; of sound character.

all-round *adj.* Total; versatile; including all aspects.

all-star *n.* An exemplary player or performer; one chosen to perform among other superior players; composed entirely of star performers.

al•ly *v.* To connect or unite in a formal or close relationship or bond; to claim an affinity for or agreement with. *n.* One united with another in a formal or personal relationship; one who agrees; a force or power on the same side in a conflict.

al•ma•nac *n.* Annual publication of meteorological, agricultural, astronomical, and geological cyclic information, containing calendars with weather forecasts, natural phenomenal information, and other facts.

al•might•y *adj.* Having absolute power; possessing the highest authority. **almighty** *n.* [cap., with *the*] Almighty God.

al•mond *n.* An oval, edible nut with a soft, light-brown shell; tree bearing such nuts; the wood from this plant.

al•most *adv.* Not quite; slightly short of; nearly.

alms *n.* Goods or money given to the poor in charity.

a•loft *adv.* Toward the upper rigging of a ship; in or into a high place; in the air.

a•lone *adj.* or *adv.* Away from other people; single; solitary; excluding anyone or anything else; with nothing further; sole; by oneself; only. **alone** *adv.*

a•long *adv.* In a line with; on the length or path; in association; together; as a companion; following shortly.

a•long•side *adv.* Along, at, near, or to the side of; side by side with; nautically, touching at the beam.

a•loof *adj.* Indifferent; distant; haughty; above in class or quality; uninvolved. **aloofness** *n.*, **aloofly** *adv.*

a•loud *adv.* Orally; audibly; with the result of making a sound.

al•pha•bet *n.* The letters of a language, arranged in an order fixed by custom.

al•pha•bet•i•cal *adj.* Arranged in the traditional order of the letters of a language. **alphabetically** *adv.*

al•pha•bet•ize *v.* To arrange in alphabetical order.

al•read•y *adv.* By this or a specified time; previously to now.

al•so *adv.* Likewise; besides; in addition.

al•tar *n.* An elevated structure for raising or isolating a religious or sacrificial ceremony.

al•ter *v.* To make change or become different; to modify; to castrate or spay, as an animal. **alterability** *n.*

al•ter•a•tion *n.* A change in structure or specification after manufacture. *pl.* Cutting and sewing done to a garment for improved fit, after manufacture.

al•ter•nate *v.* To happen or follow in turn; to occur in successive turns. **alternately** *adv.*, **alternation** *n.*

al•ter•nate *n.* Substitute; second choice; deputy; person selected to replace first choice.

al•ter•na•tive *n.* A choice between to or more possibilities; one of the possibilities to be chosen. **alternatively** *adv.*

al·ter·na·tive *adj.*

al·though *conj.* Even though; despite the fact that.

al·ti·tude *n.* The height of a thing above a reference level; distance above the earth's surface, usually in feet; flying space; distance above sea level.

al·to *n.* [Italian] High. Lower of two female singing voices in a four-part chorus; the range between soprano and tenor.

al·to·geth·er *adv.* Entirely; with all included or counted; taken as a whole.

alu·mi·num *n.* A silvery-white, ductile metallic element used to form many hard, light, corrosion-resistant alloys.

al·ways *adv.* Continuously; forever; on every occasion; at all times.

am *v.* First person, singular, present tense of *be*.

am·a·teur *n.* One who engages in an activity for enjoyment rather than profit; one outside the profession; one who lacks expertise; dilettante. *adj.* Not up to professional standards; not engaged in as a profession. **amateurish** *adj.*, **amateurism** *n.*

a·maze *v.* To astound; to affect with surprise or wonder; to confound as in a maze. **amazingly** *adv.*, **amazedness, amaze** *n.*, **amazing** *adj.*

am·bass·a·dor *n.* Official representative of the highest rank, accredited by one government to another; chief executive of an embassy; an envoy or courier, especially of good will. **ambassadorial** *adj.*, **ambassadorship** *n.*

am·ber *n.* A hard, translucent, yellow, brownish-yellow, or orange fossil resin, used for jewelry and ornament. *adj.* Medium to dark orange yellow in color.

am·bi·tion *n.* Strong desire to achieve; will to succeed; the goal or object desired.

am·bi·tious *adj.* Challenging; complex and demanding; desirous of achievement or advancement. **ambitiousness** *n.*, **ambitiously** *adv.*

am·ble *v.* To move at a leisurely pace; to walk with a leisurely gait; to stroll aimlessly; to saunter.

am·bu·lance *n.* Vehicle equipped to transport the injured or sick.

am·bush *n.* Surprise attack made from a hidden position.

a·mend *v.* To correct; to improve; to rectify; to add to or change, as a statute or law. **amendable** *adj.*

a·mend·ment *n.* Correction, reformation or improvement; added alteration or refinement; the parliamentary procedure where such alteration is made.

a·mends *pl. n.* Compensation for insult or injury, usually informal; a balancing gesture or action to rectify an earlier wrong.

a·mi·a·ble *adj.* Friendly and pleasant; likeable; willing to treat hospitably. **amiability** *n.*, **amiably** *adv.*

a·miss *adj.* Out of order or place; in an improper or wrong way; not right; suspiciously different.

am·mu·ni·tion *coll. n.* A supply of projectiles containing explosive material, propelled or discharged from guns; bullets; any means of offense. *meta.* Fact or evidence in support of an argument.

am·ne·sia *n.* The loss of memory; a mental disorder preventing recollection of past events.

am·nes·ty *n.* Pardon for political offenders; a general policy of nonreprisal or forgiveness.

a·moe·ba *n.* Any of various minute one-celled organisms having an indefinite, changeable form, and lacking structural stability. **ameba** *var.*, **amoebas** or **amoebae** *pl.*

a·mong *prep.* In or through the midst of; with others; considered as a group.

am·o·rous *adj.* Inclined to or indicative of sexual love; romantic; receptive to or inviting love. **amorousness** *n.*

a·mount *n.* Aggregate, sum, or total quantity; the measurable equivalency; a measure of mass or collectives.

am·phib·i·an *n.* An organism, as a frog or toad, developing from an aquatic state into an air-breathing state; vehicle, especially an aircraft, that can take off and land on land or water.

am·ple *adj.* Sufficient; abundant; large; full past need. **ampleness** *n.*, **amply** *adv.*

a·muse *v.* To entertain in an agreeable, pleasing way; to make mildly or temporarily happy. **amusable, amused** *adj.*

a·muse·ment *n.* A diversion; a pleasant activity; a diverting event holding one's temporary attention.

an *ind. art.* One; a (used before words beginning with a vowel or with an unpronounced *h*); one sort of; each.

a·nal·o·gy *n.* Connection between things that are otherwise dissimilar; an illustration of an abstract principle or idea by concrete parallel example; a conclusion or opinion that if two things are alike in some respects they must be alike in others.

a·nal·y·sis *n.* The disassembly or separation of elements for identification; an examination of relationships among parts of a whole; a detailed inventory of interconnected elements. **analytical** *adj.*

an·a·lyst *n.* A person who analyzes or who is skilled in analysis.

an·a·lyze *v.* To make an analysis of; to examine for cause.

an·ar·chy *n.* The absence of recognized political authority; the dissolution of order, purpose, or standard; the absence of external or artificial constraints.

a·nat·o·my *n.* Structure of an organ or organism; a detailed analysis of such a structure; analysis of the interrelationship among living parts. **anatomical, anatomic** *adj.*

an·ces·tor *n.* A person who comes before one in a family line; someone earlier than a grandparent; forefather or foremother. **ancestral** *adj.*

an·ces·try *n.* Line of descent; lineage; ancestors collectively. **ancestries** *pl.*

an·chor *n.* Heavy metal device lowered into the water by a chain or line, whose weight and configuration prevent stopped ships from drifting relative to the bottom.

v. To attach or fix firmly.

an·chor·age *n.* A shallow protected place for anchoring a ship; a strong support that keeps something steady; a harbor offering moorage rather than dockage.

an·cient *adj.* Very old; from a time long past; belonging to the early history of people. *n.* An extremely elderly person in a position of wisdom or authority. **ancientness** *n.*, **anciently** *adv.*

and *conj.* Together with; along with; as well as; added to; as a result; plus; also.

an·ec·dote *n.* Story; brief fictive or factual account, usually illustrative of an argumentative point. **anecdotal** *adj.*

an·gel *n.* An immortal being attendant upon God; a very kind and lovable person; a helping or guiding spirit; one lacking inclination or ability to do evil; a backer or supporter of a creative enterprise. **angelic** *adj.*

an·ger *n.* Feeling of extreme hostility; rage; intense emotional displeasure; aggressive reaction to wrongdoing or injustice.

an·gle *n.* A shape made by two straight lines meeting in a point, or two surfaces meeting along a line; a sharp change in planar configuration. *v.* To make an angle; to move in an angular path; to persuade by distorting argument.

an·gler *n.* A fisherman; one who fishes, especially by casting with pole and hook. **angling** *n.*

an·gry *adj.* Feeling or showing anger; having a menacing aspect; inflamed.

an·guish *n.* Great suffering, from worry, grief, or pain; agony.

an·gu·lar *adj.* Having angles or sharp corners; measured by an angle or degrees of an arc; gaunt; bony; lean. **angularity** *n.*, **angularly** *adv.*

an·i·mal *n.* Any being other than a human being; any four-footed creature; beast.

an·i·mate *v.* To give liveliness, life or spirit to; to cause to act; to inspire. **animatedly** *adv.*

an·i·ma·tion *n.* The process of bringing

to life; an art form in which movement is simulated by a rapidly visualized series of subtly changing still figures.

an•kle *n.* Joint that connects the foot with the leg; slender section of the leg immediately above this joint.

an•nex *v.* To add or join a smaller thing to a larger one; *n.* a structure added to another. **annexation** *n.*

an•ni•hi•late *v.* To destroy completely; to raze to the ground; to cause to cease to exist; to bring into nothingness.

an•ni•ver•sa•ry *n. pl.* **-ries** The date on which something happened at an earlier time; this event, especially a marriage, celebrated on this date each year.

an•nounce *v.* To proclaim; to give notice; to state publicly. **announcement** *n.*

an•nounc•er *n.* A performer on radio or television who provides program continuity and gives commercial and other points of interest.

an•noy *v.* To bother; to irritate; to make slightly angry. **annoying** *adj.,* **annoyingly** *adv.*

an•noy•ance *n.* A nuisance; irritation; act of annoying.

an•nu•al *adj.* Yearly; recurring or done at the same time each year. *n.* A yearly publication, as a yearbook. **annually** *adv.*

a•noint *v.* To apply oil in a religious ceremony. **anointer** *n.*

a•non•y•mous *adj.* Unknown; without a name; not identified or credited; of unknown origin or authorship. **anonymity** *n.,* **anonymously** *adv.*

an•oth•er *adj.* Additional; one more; different, but of the same character; the other.

an•swer *n.* A written or spoken reply, as to a question; a result or solution, as to a problem; a response. *v.* To respond; to be responsible for.

ant *n.* A small insect, usually without wings, which lives in or on the ground, or in wood in large colonies.

ant•eat•er *n.* Mammal with a long snout and a long, sticky tongue, indigenous to the New World, feeding mainly on ants and termites; aardvark.

an•ten•na *n.* Slender feelers on the head of an insect, lobster, crab, and other crustaceans; wire or other device used in radio and television to send and receive signals.

an•them *n.* Hymn of praise or loyalty; an official song of a country, school, or other organization.

an•thol•o•gy *n.* A collection of stories, poems, or other writings.

an•tic *n.* Mischievous caper or act; a clownish acrobat. *pl.* Misbehavior, erratic actions.

an•tic•i•pate *v.* To look forward to; to act in advance of; to foresee; to act as a preventive to. **anticipation, anticipator** *n.*

an•ti•dote *n.* A substance that counteracts an injury or poison.

an•ti•freeze *n.* Substance, as ethylene glycol, mixed with water or other liquid to lower the freezing point.

an•tique *adj.* Belonging to or of ancient times; very old.

an•tique *n.* An object, customarily over 100 years old, whose value lies in its rarity and example of lost skills and crafts; collectibles of a certain age. *v.* To seek antiques; to shop for or trade in old and rare items, especially furniture, artwork, and household objects.

an•ti•qui•ties *coll. n.* Objects from ancient times, especially other cultures; movable items of cultural value to a country, classified as not exportable without special license.

an•ti•qui•ty *n.* Quality of being ancient or old.

ant•ler *n.* One of a pair of bony growths on the head of a member of the deer family.

an•to•nym *n.* A word opposite in meaning to another word.

an•vil *n.* A heavy block of steel or iron on which metal is formed.

anx•i•e•ty *n.* A state of uncertainty; disturbance of the mind regarding uncertain events; uneasiness caused by indecision or the failure of events to reconcile

anxious

themselves.

anx·ious *adj.* Troubled in mind or worried about some uncertain matter or event. **anxiousness** *n.*, **anxiously** *adv.*

an·y *adj.* One of some; no matter which; some; every; an unqualified quantity or part.

an·y·bod·y *pron.* Anyone; any person.

an·y·how *adv.* By any means; in any way; whatever.

an·y·more *adv.* At present and from now on.

an·y·one *pron.* Any person; anybody.

an·y·place *adv.* Anywhere.

an·y·thing *pron.* Any occurrence, object or matter.

an·y·time *adv.* At any time whatever.

an·y·way *adv.* Nevertheless; anyhow; in any manner; regardless of outcome.

an·y·where *adv.* In, at, or to any place, regardless of location; to any extent.

a·or·ta *n.* The main artery that carries blood away from the heart and distributes blood to all of the body except the lungs. **aortal, aortic** *adj.*

a·part *adv.* Separate or at a distance; in pieces; to pieces; set aside.

a·part·heid *n.* In the Republic of South Africa, an abandoned official policy of political, social, and economic discrimination and segregation against nonwhites.

a·part·ment *n.* A suite or room in a building, sharing walls, floor, or ceiling with others, equipped for individual living.

ap·a·thy *n.* The lack of emotions or feelings; indifference; absence of emotional involvement or reaction.

ape *n.* A large mammal of the hominid group, such as a gorilla, chimpanzee, or monkey; a very clumsy, coarse person.

ape *v.* To mimic or copy; to imitate in a comic way; to follow faithfully in action or behavior.

a·piece *adv.* For or to each one; each; singly.

a·pol·o·get·ic *adj.* Making an expression of apology. **apologetically** *adv.*

a·pol·o·gize *v.* To make an apology.

a·pol·o·gy *n.* A statement expressing regret for an action or fault; a formal justification or defense; a protracted explanation in response to criticism.

a·pos·tro·phe *n.* The mark used to indicate the removal of letters or figures, the plural of letters or figures, and the possessive case; the act of turning away; addressing the usually absent person or a usually personified thing rhetorically.

ap·pa·ra·tus *n.* Appliance or instrument designed and used for a specific operation. **apparatus** or **apparatuses** *pl.*

ap·par·el *v.* To dress or put on clothing; to adorn or embellish. *n.* Clothing; decoration or ornament, especially of fabric.

ap·par·ent *adj.* Clear and opened to the eye and mind; open to view, visible; on the surface; according to the immediate evidence of the senses. **apparently** *adv.*

ap·peal *n.* Power to arouse a sympathetic response; an earnest plea; a legal proceeding where a case is brought from a lower court to a higher court for a rehearing. *v.* To make a request; to ask another person for corroboration, vindication, or decision on a matter of importance; to beg or ask formally but vigorously. **appealable** *adj.*

ap·peal·ing *adj.* Attractive, personable, desirable, or pleasant; having acceptable or agreeable properties; having elements in favor of adoption. **appealingly** *adv.*

ap·pear *v.* To come into sight or existence; to come into public view; to come formally before an authorized person; to give ocular evidence; to seem; to be apparent.

ap·pear·ance *n.* The action or process of appearing; an outward indication or showing; presence at an event.

ap·pend·age *n.* Something added to something more important or larger; a subordinate or a dependent person; a part attached but clearly outlined; a partially detached but still connected section of a body, as an arm.

ap·pen·dec·to·my *n.* The surgical removal of the appendix.

ap·pen·dix *n.* Supplementary material

usually found at the end of a written work; any addition after the main body; in medicine, the vermiform appendix, a vestigial organ attached to the large intestine and abdominal wall by mesenteries.

ap•pe•tite *n.* The craving or desire for food or other need; a desire to consume.

ap•pe•tiz•er *n.* Food or drink served before a meal to stimulate the appetite; an aperitif.

ap•plaud *v.* To express or show approval by clapping the hands; to congratulate, as an accomplishment; to encourage by acknowledging previous effort.

ap•plause *n.* The expression of public approval. **applausive** *adj.*

ap•ple *n.* The round, red, yellow, or green edible fruit of a tree.

ap•plet *n.* A task-specific small program in Java computer language.

ap•pli•ance *n.* A piece of equipment or device designed for a particular use; a kitchen or household device, usually electrical or gas-powered, to ameliorate housework.

ap•li•ca•ble *adj.* Appropriate; suitable; capable of being applied; germane to the task at hand. **applicability** *n.*

ap•pli•cant *n.* A person applying for a job, position, membership, or other entry.

ap•pli•ca•tion *n.* The act of putting something to use; the act of superposing or administering; request or petition; a form used to make a request. **apply** *v.*

ap•plied *adj.* Put to practical use to solve definite problems.

ap•ply *v.* To make a request in the form of a written application; to put into use for a practical purpose or reason; to put into operation or to bring into action; to employ with close attention.

ap•point *v.* To arrange something; to fix or set officially; to place into office or position without election. **appointable** *adj.*, **appointer** *n.*

ap•point•ment *n.* The act of appointing or designating; arrangement for or time of a meeting; a nonelective position or office;

engagement or meeting.

ap•prais•al *n.* The evaluation of property by an authorized person; the act of placing value on an action or plan.

ap•praise *v.* To estimate the value, worth, or status of a particular item or action. **appraiser** *n.*, **appraising** *adj.*

ap•pre•ci•a•ble *adj.* Measurable; able to be perceived, noticed, or estimated; considerable. **appreciably** *adv.*

ap•pre•ci•ate *v.* To recognize the worth, quality, or significance; to value very highly; to realize; to acknowledge the value of; to increase in price or value over time. **ap•pre•ci•a•tion** *n.*, **ap•pre•cia•tive** *adj.*

ap•pren•tice *n.* A person learning a trade, art, or occupation under a skilled worker for a prescribed period of time; someone learning a task by performing its simpler aspects. *v.* To work as an apprentice under the supervision of a skilled worker. **apprenticeship** *n.*

ap•proach *v.* To come near to or draw closer; to be close in appearance. *n.* Access or entrance to a place; a method for analysis; the first stage of an act, especially landing an aircraft. **approachable** *adj.*

ap•pro•pri•ate *v.* To take possession of; to take by authority, with or without permission; to attach by bonds of ownership.

ap•pro•pri•ate *adj.* Suitable for a use or occasion; fitting; measured in a like manner or amount. **appropriately** *adv.*, **appropriateness** *n.*

ap•prov•al *n.* The act of approving; the right of acceptance or refusal; blessing or permission from higher authority.

ap•prove *v.* To regard or express a favorable opinion; to give formal or official permission; to acknowledge as satisfactory; to warrant the meeting of standards. **approvingly** *adv.*

ap•prox•i•mate *adj.* Located close together; almost accurate or exact; near. *v.* To bring close or near to; to approach; to estimate; to be near the same. **approximately** *adv.*

ap•ron *n.* A garment, easily worn and removed, used to protect clothing; the area of a proscenium stage in front of the curtain line; paved area around an airport terminal building or airport hangar; waterfront edge of a wharf or pier.

apt *adj.* Unusually qualified or fitting; appropriate; having a tendency; suitable; capable, intelligent, or quick to understand. **aptly** *adv.*, **aptness** *n.*

ap•ti•tude *n.* A natural talent, skill, or ability; a tendency to excel; quickness in learning or understanding.

a•quar•i•um *n.* An artificial pond where living plants and aquatic animals are maintained and exhibited.

a•quat•ic *adj.* Occurring on or in the water; viable in water; related to water.

a•rach•nid *n.* Arthropods, including spiders, scorpions, and ticks, that are mostly air-breathing, with two major body segments, having four pairs of legs but no antennae.

ar•bi•trar•y *adj.* Based on a whim or impulse; ungoverned or unregulated by law or tradition; illogical; coming about at random; not predictable. **arbitrarily** *adv.*, **arbitrariness** *n.*

ar•bor *n.* A garden shelter from the sun or weather, covered with or made of broadleafed climbing plants; an axle or rotating shaft on a tooling machine. **arborous** *adj.*

arc *n.* A shape or structure that is curved or arched; a continuous curved line, especially part of a circle; the measurement of such a curve; the luminous discharge of electric current across a gap of two electrodes.

ar•cade *n.* An arched covered passageway supported by columns; a long arched gallery or building, sometimes having shops and stores; a shopping mall; an amusement facility, usually indoors, offering coin-operated games of chance and skill. **arcaded** *adj.*

arch *n.* A structure that spans over an open area and gives support. **archly** *adv.*,

archness *n.*

ar•chae•ol•o•gy *n.* Scientific study of ancient times and ancient peoples by analysis of artifacts, remains, gravesites, monuments, and antiquities. **archaeological** *adj.*, **archaeologist** *n.*

ar•cha•ic *adj.* Belonging to an earlier time; old past value or currency; characteristic of an earlier language or expression, now used only in special cases. **archaism**, **archaist** *n.*

arch•er *n.* A person trained in the skills of the bow and arrow.

ar•cher•y *n.* The practice or art of shooting with a bow and arrow; the equipment used by an archer.

ar•chi•tect *n.* A person who designs and supervises the preparation for and construction of large structures, especially those requiring knowledge of physical principles.

ar•chi•tec•ture *n.* The art or science of designing and building structures; the method or style of construction or building; architectonics. **architectural** *adj.*

ar•chive *n.* To catalog, taxonomize, store, and retrieve documents or objects for study or long-term preservation. *pl. n.* Public documents or records; the place where archives are kept.

arch•way *n.* A passage or way under an arch; an arch over a passage.

arc•tic *adj.* Extremely cold or frigid; relating to the territory north of the Arctic Circle. *n.* A waterproof boot that covers or comes just above the ankle.

are *v.* First, second, and third person plural and second person singular of the verb *to be*.

ar•e•a *n.* A flat or level piece of ground; the product of length and width; field of study; the scope of a concept, activity or operation; region, especially geographical.

ar•e•a code *n.* The three-digit number assigned to each telephone area, and used to call another area, in the U.S. or Canada.

a•re•na *n.* Enclosed area for public entertainment, such as football games, or concerts; a place of combat or confrontation; area of concentration or attention.

ar•gu•a•ble *adj.* Open to argument; questionable; capable of being supported by evidence; separable by point of view. **arguably** *adv.*

ar•gue *v.* To debate, to offer reason for or against; to dispute or quarrel; to persuade or influence; to state evidence for in a court or deliberative body. **arguer** *n.*

ar•gu•ment *n.* A quarrel or dispute; a reasoned statement of a point of view or opinion; the body or summary plot of a literary work; a formal presentation of evidence.

ar•id *adj.* Experiencing little or insufficient rain; dry; climatologically low in total rainfall; lacking in interest or feeling; dull; aloof and unemotional in demeanor.

a•rise *v.* To come up; to rise; to come to one's attention; to come into view; to mount; to move to a higher place; to get out of bed.

ar•is•toc•ra•cy *n.* A government by a small privileged class of hereditarily superior individuals or families; class or group viewed as superior; the hereditary privileged ruling nobility or class. **aristocrat** *n.*, **aristocratic** *adj.*

a•rith•me•tic *adj.* Branch of mathematics dealing with addition, subtraction, multiplication, division.

ark *n.* Any large vessel whose cargo provides the means for survival and proliferation; the ship Noah built during the Great Flood; the chest containing the Ten Commandments or covenant on stone tables, carried by the Jews; something that gives protection.

arm *n.* The body part between the shoulder and the wrist; upper limb of the human body. *v.* To furnish with protection against danger; to provide weapons to; to load or activate in preparation for use.

ar•mi•stice *n.* The temporary suspension of combat by mutual agreement; truce between warring factions; the document declaring such an agreement.

ar•mor *n.* Covering used in combat to protect the body or a piece of machinery, made of metal or other impenetrable material; fleet of vehicles with such covering, as tanks and heavy transports. **armor** *v.*, **armored** *adj.*

ar•my *n.* A group of persons organized for a country's protection; the land forces of a country. **armies** *pl.*

a•ro•ma *n.* A distinctive fragrance or pleasant odor; pleasing smell, especially of food. **aromatical, aromatic** *adj.*

a•round *adv.* To or on all sides; in succession or rotation; from one place to another; in a circle or circular movement; near; in the vicinity of; occasionally seen.

a•rouse *v.* To wake up from a sleep; to stir; to excite. **arousal** *n.*

ar•range *v.* To put in correct order or proper sequence; to prepare for something; to take steps to organize something; to bring about an understanding or an agreement. **arrangement** *n.*

ar•rest *v.* To stop or to bring an end to; to capture; to seize; to hold in custody by the authority of law. *n.* The act of bringing into custody; the legal recording of such acts.

ar•riv•al *n.* The act of arriving.

ar•rive *v.* To reach or get to a destination; to succeed into public attention; to attain a sum or answer.

ar•ro•gance *n.* An overbearing manner, intolerable presumption; an insolent pride. **arrogant, arrogantly** *adv.*

ar•row *n.* The shaft shot as a weapon or projectile from a bow; a sign or mark to show direction; a pointed missile designed to penetrate the target.

ar•row•head *n.* The striking end of an arrow, usually shaped like a wedge; the archeological remains of primitive projectile weaponry, especially those found in open spaces.

ar•son *n.* The fraudulent burning of property; the crime of destruction by fire. **arsonist** *n.*, **arsonous** *adj.*

art *n.* A human skill of expression of other

objects by painting, drawing, sculpture, etc.; a branch of learning.

ar•ter•y *n.* A blood vessel that carries blood from the heart to the other parts of the body; a major means for transportation or transport. **arterial** *adj.*

ar•thro•pod *n.* Member of phylum Arthropoda; invertebrate animal with jointed limbs and segmented body, including insects, crustaceans, and arachnids.

ar•ti•cle *n.* A term or clause in a contract; a paragraph or section; a condition or rule; an object, item or commodity; a grammatical signifier of the presence of a noun.

ar•ti•fi•cial *adj.* Not genuine; made by man; not found in nature; following the design of, but without the genuineness of, a natural occurrence. **artificially** *adv.*

art•ist *n.* A person practicing the fine arts of painting, sculpture, architecture, literature, music, dance, or theater.

ar•tis•tic *adj.* Relating to the characteristic of an artist or art; creative; answering to aesthetic rather than practical criteria. **artistically** *adv.*

art•work *n.* The artistic work of an artist; the product, usually collective, of the graphic element in a print layout.

as *adv.* In the manner like; of the same degree or amount; similar to. *conj.* At the same time when; since; given the fact that.

as•bes•tos *n.* A noncombustible, fibrous, mineral form of magnesium silicate once used in fireproofing, but since linked to some forms of cancer.

as•cend *v.* To rise up from a lower level; to climb; to mount; to walk up.

as•cent *n.* A way up; a slope; the act of rising; a journey to the summit.

as•cer•tain *v.* To find out for certain; to make sure; verify by evidence.

ASCII *abbr.* American Standard Code for Information Interchange; type of text file without binary characters.

a•shamed *adj.* Feeling guilt, disgrace, or shame; feeling unworthy or inferior; emotionally acknowledging wrongdoing, sin, or guilt.

a•shore *adv.* On or to the shore.

a•side *adv.* Out of the way; to a side; to one side. *n.* Something said in an undertone and not meant to be heard by someone; a theatrical device for informing the audience of a character's thoughts or reactions without revealing them to other characters on stage.

as if *conj.* As it would be if; like; that; acting despite the unlikelihood that.

ask *v.* To request permission; to require or seek information; to pose a question or request. **asker** *n.*

a•sleep *adv.* In a state of sleep; lacking sensation; numb; not alert.

as•pect *n.* The situation, position, view, or appearance; an area of interest in a study or problem.

as•phalt *n.* A sticky, thick, blackish-brown residue of petroleum manufacture, used in paving roads and roofing buildings.

as•phyx•i•ate *v.* To suffocate, to prevent from breathing; to close off or reduce air to. **asphyxiation** *n.*

as•pi•rin *n.* Medication containing a derivative of salicylic acid, used for the relief of pain and fever.

ass *n.* A hoofed animal; a donkey; a stupid or foolish person.

as•sail *v.* To attack violently with words or blows. **assailant** *n.*

as•sas•sin *n.* Murderer, especially of a politically or ideologically important person, either from fanatical beliefs or for hire; a hired killer used by others to change the course of events.

as•sas•si•nate *v.* To murder a prominent person by secret or sudden attack. **assassination** *n.*

as•sault *n.* A violent physical or verbal attack on a person; a valiant attempt at conquering or completing something.

as•sem•ble *v.* To put together the parts of something; to come together as a group. **assembly** *n.*

as•sign *v.* To designate as to duty; to give or allot; to attribute. **assignable** *adj.*

as•sign•ment *n.* A given amount of work or task to undertake, allotted by a superior; a post, position, or office to which one is assigned.

as•sist *v.* To give support, to aid, to give help. **assistance, assistant** *n.*

as•so•ci•ate *v.* To connect or join together; to accompany socially; to find relationships between. *n.* A partner, colleague, or companion; one with whom another works or does business.

as•so•ci•a•tion *n.* An organized body of persons or professions having a common interest; a society; the act of making mental connections among disparate ideas or facts. **associational** *adj.*

as•sort•ed *adj.* Made up of different or various kinds; intentionally mixed as a sample of possibilities; miscellaneous. **assortment** *n.*

as•sume *v.* To accept as fact; to take upon oneself to complete a job or duty; to take responsibility for; to take for granted.

as•sump•tion *n.* An idea or statement believed to be true without proof; the taking on of, laying claim to, or otherwise possessing by authority.

as•sur•ance *n.* A statement made to inspire confidence of mind or manner; freedom from uncertainty; guarantee.

as•sure *v.* To give the feeling of confidence; to make sure or certain; to guarantee by self-reputation. **assurer** *n.*

as•sured *adj.* Satisfied as to the truth or certainty; confident; sure of. **assuredly** *adv.*

as•ter•isk *n.* The character used to indicate letters omitted or as a reference to a footnote.

as•ter•oid *n.* One of thousands of small planetary fragments in solar orbit between Jupiter and Mars.

as though *conj.* As it may be; acting on the likelihood that.

as•ton•ish *v.* To strike with sudden fear, wonder, or surprise; to amaze, confound, or momentarily disorient. **astonishing** *adj.* **astonishingly** *adv.* **astonishment** *n.*

as•tound *v.* To fill with wonder and bewilderment. **astounding** *adj.*, **astoundingly** *adv.*

a•stride *prep.* One leg on either side of something; placed or lying on both sides of; extending across or over.

as•tro•nom•i•cal *adj.* Relating to astronomy; something inconceivable or enormously large. **astronomically** *adv.*

as•tron•o•my *n.* The science of the celestial bodies and their motion, magnitudes, and constitution. **astronomer** *n.*

a•sy•lum *n.* A refuge or institution for the care of the needy or sick; a place of security and retreat; the granting of political protection to a noncitizen; an institution providing care for the destitute or insane.

at *prep.* Next to; in the same place as; indicative of presence, occurrence, or condition; in congruence with the time of.

ath•lete *n.* A physically skilled and trained person who participates in competitions and sports.

ath•let•ic *adj.* Relating to athletes; physically strong and active.

at•las *n.* A collection or book of maps; *cap.* Greek titan said to hold up the world on his shoulders.

at•mos•phere *n.* A gaseous mass that surrounds a celestial body, as the earth; a predominant mood or feeling.

at•om *n.* A tiny particle; the smallest unit of an element; the basic building block of matter, consisting of a nucleus and electrons in erratic orbit.

at•om bomb or **a•tom•ic bomb** *n.* A bomb that explodes violently due to the sudden release of atomic energy, occurring from the splitting of nuclei of a heavy chemical element.

at•om•ic en•er•gy *n.* Energy released by changes in the nucleus of an atom.

at•tach *v.* To bring together; to fasten or become fastened; to bind by personal attachments. **attachable, attached** *adj.*

at•tach•ment *n.* The state of being attached; a tie of affection or loyalty; the supplementary part of something; a document added to a direct communication.

at•tack *v.* To initiate the offensive; to apply force, to assault; to work on with vigor.

at•tain *v.* To arrive at or reach a goal; to achieve by effort. **attainable** *adj.*

at•tempt *v.* To make an effort to do something; to try.

at•tend *v.* To be present; to take charge of or to look after; to listen with attention.

at•ten•dance *n.* The fact or act of attending; the number of times a person attends; the number of persons present at an event.

at•ten•dant *n.* One who provides a service for another; a helper or assistant in a specific act; one who accompanies the main participant in a ceremony.

at•ten•tion *n.* Observation, notice, or mental concentration; a military condition or command of extreme readiness.

at•tic *n.* The space directly below the roof of a building.

at•tire *n.* A person's dress or clothing. *v.* To clothe; to dress.

at•ti•tude *n.* A mental position; a predisposition or assumption at the start of a communication; the feeling one has for oneself; the position, especially regarding levelness, of a vessel.

at•tor•ney *n.* A person with legal training appointed to transact business or represent another in litigation; a lawyer. **attorneys** *pl.*

at•tract *v.* To draw by appeal; to cause to draw near.

at•trac•tion *n.* The capability of attracting; something that attracts or is meant to attract; a popular site or event.

at•trac•tive *adj.* Having the power of charming, or quality of attracting. **attractively** *adv.*, **attractiveness** *n.*

auc•tion *n.* A public sale of merchandise, property, or rights to the highest bidder. *v.* To offer for sale by the auction process.

auc•tion•eer *n.* One who conducts an auction, describing the item and regulating the bidding.

au•di•ble *adj.* Capable of being heard; within the range of human auditory perception.

au•di•ence *n.* A group of listeners; those in attendance at an event or performance; the opportunity to express views; a formal hearing or conference.

au•di•tion *n.* A trial performance given by an entertainer to demonstrate ability or suitability; a tryout.

au•di•to•ri•um *n.* A hearing place; a large room in a public building or a school that holds many people.

aunt *n.* A sister of one's father or mother; the wife of one's uncle; a close, older female family friend not literally an aunt.

au•then•tic *adj.* Real; genuine; worthy of acceptance.

au•thor *n.* A person who writes an original literary work; the creator of anything; the source or fountain. **author** *v.*

au•thor•i•ty *n.* A group or person with power; a government; an expert. **authorities** *pl.*

au•thor•i•za•tion *n.* Authorizing something; permission; legal right; the process of gaining authority. **au•thor•ize** *v.*

au•to•bi•og•ra•phy *n.* The life story of a person, written by that person. **autobiographer** *n.*

au•to•graph *n.* A handwritten signature. *v.* To sign with one's signature.

au•to•mat•ic *adj.* Operating with little control; self-regulating; without thought or premeditation. **automatically** *adv.*

au•to•mo•bile *n.* A four-wheeled passenger vehicle commonly propelled by an internal combustion engine; a car.

au•tumn *n.* The season between summer and winter; the fall; the waning years of a cycle. **autumnal** *adj.*

aux•il•ia•ry *adj.* Providing help or assistance to someone; giving support; additional or extra; acting as an emergency replacement or supplement to.

a•vail•a•bil•i•ty *n.* The state of being available; handiness or readiness to use; the state of being accessible or attainable.

a•vail•a•ble *adj.* Ready for immediate use.

av·a·lanche *n.* A large amount of rock, snow, or other mass that slides down a mountainside; any overwhelming amount suddenly present.

av·e·nue *n.* A street lined with trees; a wide thoroughfare in a city or residential area; a strategy for achieving something.

av·er·age *adj.* Typical or usual; not exceptional; common; expressive of the normal. *n.* The number that summarizes a set of unequalities; the expression of the arithmetic mean; the expected or previously determined or experienced amount.

a·vi·a·tion *n.* The operation of planes and other crafts of flight.

a·vi·a·tor *n.* Operator or navigator of an aircraft; a pilot.

av·id *adj.* Eager; enthusiastic; vigorously or inordinately desirous.

a·void *v.* To stay away from; to shun; to prevent or keep from happening. **avoidable** *adj.*, **avoidably** *adv.*, **avoidance** *n.*

a·wait *v.* To wait for something; to watch in anticipation.

a·wake *v.* To wake up; to be or make alert or watchful. **awaken** *v.*

a·ward *v.* To give or confer as being needed or merited; to give in favorable judgment of. *n.* A judgment or decision; a prize; a recognition of accomplishment.

a·ware *adj.* Being conscious or mindful of something. **awareness** *n.*

a·wash *adj.* Flooded; afloat; washed by water.

a·way *adv.* At a distance; apart from; gone; not available for communication.

awe *n.* A feeling of wonder mixed with reverence; astonishment in response to splendor or excellence. *v.* To give such a feeling to another.

awe·some *adj.* Impressive, outstanding; causing astonishment or wonder; expressive of awe. **awesomely** *adv.*, **awesomeness** *n.*

aw·ful *adj.* Very unpleasant or dreadful; very poor; below the lowest minimum standard; so powerful as to be frightening.

a·while *adv.* For a short time; some time past; since.

awk·ward *adj.* Lacking grace or felicity; clumsy; uncoordinated; socially slightly embarrassing. **awkwardly** *adv.*, **awkwardness** *n.*

ax·le *n.* A spindle or shaft around which a wheel or pair of wheels revolve; a rotating weight-bearing bar or beam.

B

B, b The second letter of the English alphabet; a student's grade rating of good, but not excellent.

bab·ble *v.* To reveal secrets; to chatter senselessly; to talk foolishly.

babe *n.* A very young child or infant; a baby.

ba·boon *n.* A species of primate of Africa and southwestern Asia, with large canine teeth and distinctive muzzle features.

ba·by *n.* A young child; infant. **babyish** *adj.*, **babies** *pl.*

ba·by boom *n.* A statistically measurable rise in the U.S. birth rate immediately after the end of World War II.

bach·e·lor *n.* An unmarried male; the first degree from a four-year university.

back *n.* The rear part of a structure or object; the human body from the neck to the end of the spine; the rear part of an animal; a position in the game of football. *adv.* At the rear of, to or toward the rear; in the direction of return.

back·ache *n.* A pain in the back.

back·board *n.* A board that supports when placed under or behind something.

back·bone *n.* The spinal column or spine of the vertebrates; the strongest support, or strength; emotional or moral strength.

back·drop *n.* A flat, curtain, or scene at the back of a stage set.

back·ground *n.* The area or surface behind which objects are represented; conditions leading up to an event; the collection of a person's complete experience.

backing

back•ing *n.* Support or aid; a supply in reserve; support material behind a portrait or picture.

back•pack *n.* A piece of hiking or walking equipment used to carry items on the back, mounted on a lightweight frame, and constructed of nylon or canvas. **backpacker** *n.*

back•rest *n.* A support given to the back.

back•stage *n.* The area behind the visible performing area in a theater.

back•stop *n.* A wall that prevents a ball from being hit out of play.

back•talk *n.* A smart or insolent reply; retort; argument against authority.

back•track *v.* To reverse a policy; to retrace previous steps

back•up *n.* One that serves as an alternative or substitute; an alternative plan of action.

back•ward *adv.* Toward the back; to or at the back. **backwardness** *n.*

back•yard *n.* An area to the rear of a house, usually fenced or enclosed, for recreation or storage.

ba•con *n.* Side and back of a pig, salted and smoked; a breakfast preparation of pork in strips.

bad *adj.* Not good; naughty or disobedient; unfavorable; inferior; poor; spoiled; invalid. **badly** *adv.*, **badness** *n.*

badge *n.* An emblem worn for identification or proof of jurisdiction, especially by enforcement authorities.

bad•ger *n.* A sturdy burrowing mammal. *v.* To harass or trouble persistently.

baf•fle *v.* To puzzle; to perplex or confuse; to impede the progress of. *n.* A device that checks or regulates the flow of gases, liquids, or sound. **baffled, baffling** *adj.*, **bafflingly** adv.

bag *n.* A flexible container used for holding, storing, or carrying; a white canvas square used to mark bases in baseball. *v.* To contain in a bag; to win or capture; to take and keep game, as in hunting. **baggy** *adj.*

ba•gel *n.* A hard, glazed, round doughy roll with a chewy texture and a hole in the middle to augment thorough baking.

bag•gage *n.* The personal belongings of a traveler, usually in canvas or cloth carriers with handles; any excess burden impeding free movement.

bag•gy *adj.* Loose; loose-fitting; containing more than necessary material.

bag•pipe *n.* A musical wind instrument with a leather bag allowing the controlled express of air through a variety of melody pipes, some of which can be fingered to vary notes, and some of which are drones. **bagpiper** *n.*

bail *n.* Security or money given to guarantee the appearance of a person for trial after arraignment. *v.* To remove water from a vessel by dipping and emptying the water overboard.

bait *v.* To lure; to entice; to set a trap with a desirable offering. *n.* Food used to catch or trap an animal, especially in fishing.

bake *v.* To cook in an oven until chemical changes are completed; to harden or dry. **baked** *adj.*, **baker, baking** *n.*

bak•er•y *n.* A store where baked goods are made and sold.

bal•ance *n.* Physical equilibrium; device for determining the weight of something; the agreement of totals in the debit and credit of an account.

bal•ance beam *n.* A narrow wooden beam approximately four feet off the ground used in gymnastics.

bal•co•ny *n.* Gallery or platform projecting from the wall of a building; the high seating area in a theatre or arena.

bald *adj.* Lacking hair on the head; void of growth, as mountaintops above the treeline; bare; obvious; unadorned by artifice. **baldness** *n.*

bald ea•gle *n.* The eagle of North America, dark when young but with a white head and neck feathers when mature.

bale *n.* A large, bound package or bundle, especially of stalks.

balk *v.* To refuse to go on; to stop short of

something; in baseball, a pitcher's false move toward home plate.

ball *n.* A round body or mass; a sphere; a pitched baseball delivered outside of the strike zone.

bal·lad *n.* A narrative story or poem of folk origin; a romantic song of moderate beat. **balladeer** *n.*

bal·last *n.* Heavy material, usually of no intrinsic value, placed in a vehicle, especially a water vessel, to give stability.

ball bear·ing *n.* A sphere or series of spheres of hard material, encased in a metal sheath, to reduce friction by separating the stationary parts from the moving parts of a mechanism.

bal·le·ri·na *n.* A female ballet dancer in a company.

bal·let *n.* An artistic expression of dance by formal choreographic design.

bal·loon *n.* A thin membrane bag or shaped container, inflated with air or a gas lighter than air, which floats in the atmosphere, used as a child's toy; a large air vessel relying on the properties of gases to stay aloft.

bal·lot *n.* A slip of paper used in secret voting; one's right to vote.

ball·park *n.* A stadium where ball games are played.

ball·point *n.* A pen with a small self-inking writing point.

bal·sa *n.* American tree whose wood is very light in weight; the wood of the tree, used in model making.

bam·boo *n.* Tropical, tall grass with hollow, pointed stems; the stalky wood-like material from the plant.

ban *v.* To prohibit; to forbid; to proscribe by formal decree. **ban** *n.*, **banned** *adj.*

ba·nan·a *n.* The crescent-shaped usually yellow, edible fruit of a tropical plant.

band *n.* A strip used to trim, finish, encircle, or bind; the range of a radio wave length; a group of musicians who join together to play their instruments. *v.* To wrap or encircle; to mark with a band.

band·age *n.* A strip of cloth used to protect an injury; any material or activity designed to repair or aid in healing.

band·age *v.* To bind or cover, as a wound, to prevent bleeding and infection.

ban·dan·na *n.* A brightly colored cotton or silk handkerchief, often worn around the neck.

ban·dit *n.* A gangster or robber, especially a member of a marauding or plundering gang. **banditry** *n.*

band·width *n.* Measurement of information-carrying capacity, in bits per second.

bane *n.* A cause of destruction; an ill omen or negative force or influence. **baneful** *adj.*, **banefully** *adv.*

bang *n.* A sudden loud noise, as a gunshot; short hair cut across the forehead.

ban·gle *n.* A bracelet worn around the wrist or ankle; an inexpensive ornament or decoration, often pendant from a bracelet or necklace.

ban·ish *v.* To leave; to drive away; to refuse entry by official declaration. **banished** *adj.*, **banishment** *n.*

ban·is·ter *n.* The handrail on a staircase with its upright supports.

ban·jo *n.* A stringed instrument similar to a guitar. **banjoist** *n.*

bank *n.* A slope of land adjoining water; a slant or obtuse angle, especially to a movement; an establishment that performs financial transactions. **banking** *n.*, **bankable** *adj.*

bank·rupt *adj.* Legally insolvent; in a condition in which remaining property is divided among creditors. **bankrupt** *v.*, **bankruptcy** *n.*

ban·ner *n.* A piece of cloth, such as a flag, used as a standard by a commander or monarch.

ban·quet *n.* An elaborate dinner or feast; a ceremonial meal held for many persons, usually to mark an occasion or honor a prestigious guest.

bar *n.* A rigid piece of material used as a support; an obscured or invisible sedimentary collection of sand or gravel that impedes the progress of a vessel into and out of harbor; a counter where a person can receive drinks. *v.* To prohibit or exclude; to keep out.

bar·bar·i·an *n.* A person or culture thought to be primitive and therefore inferior. **barbarous, barbaric** *adj.*

bar·be·cue *n.* An outdoor fireplace or pit for roasting meat. **barbecue** *v.* To cook on a barbecue pit.

barbed wire *n.* Wire twisted with sharp points, to prevent passage or damage.

bar·bell *n.* A bar with weights at both ends, used for exercise.

bar·ber *n.* A person whose business is cutting and dressing hair and shaving and trimming beards. **bar·ber·shop** *n.*

bard *n.* A poet or oral storyteller, often moving from place to place; a piece of armor for a horse's neck.

bare *adj.* Exposed to view; without coloring or ornament; naked. *v.* To make obvious or self-evident; to expose; to make naked.

bare·back *adv.* or *adj.* Riding a horse without a saddle.

bar·gain *n.* A contract or agreement on the purchase or sale of an item; a purchase made at a favorable or good price. **bargainer** *n.*

barge *n.* A flat-bottomed boat, used for transport of cargo, especially in bulk.

bar·i·tone *n.* The male voice in the range between tenor and bass.

bark *n.* The outer covering of a tree; the abrupt, harsh sound made by a dog; a sailing vessel of three or more masts.

bark·er *n.* A person in a circus who stands at the entrance and advertises the show.

bar·ley *n.* A type of grain used for food and malt products, and for making whiskey and beer.

bam *n.* A farm building used to shelter animals, house equipment, and store products.

bar·na·cle *n.* A marine crustacean with a hard shell at maturity that remains attached to an underwater surface, especially the hulls of ships; a European goose which breeds in the Arctic.

barn dance *n.* A dance gathering, usually in a barn or other large structure, featuring square dancing and a rustic atmosphere.

ba·rom·e·ter *n.* An instrument that records the weight and pressure of the atmosphere. **barometric** *adj.*

bar·racks *coll. n.* Buildings for housing soldiers; residential area of a military base.

bar·rel *n.* A cylindrical container, often of wood, with round, flat ends of equal size and sides that bulge; the elongated hollowed section of a firearm that focuses the force of the explosive and gives direction and rotation to the projectile.

bar·ren *adj.* Lacking vegetation; sterile; infertile; absent of life.

bar·ri·cade *n.* Barrier, especially mobile, that inhibits passage or prevents trespass.

bar·ri·er *n.* A structure that restricts or bars entrance; an impediment to progress.

bar·ri·er reef *n.* A coral reef parallel to shore but separated by a lagoon, which prevents passage from sea to land.

bar·room *n.* A building or room where a person can purchase alcoholic beverages sold at a counter; a tavern; a pub.

bar·tend·er *n.* A person who serves alcoholic drinks at a bar.

bar·ter *v.* To trade something for something else without the exchange of money.

base *n.* The fundamental part; the foundation of an object or process; the bottom; a chemical solution having a pH greater than 7; one of four corners of a baseball infield. **baseless** *adj.*, **basely** *adv.*, **baseness** *n.*

base *v.* To begin with; to build from; to initiate; to establish before continued research or inquiry.

base·ball *n.* A game played with a ball and bat, in which players occupy bases around a diamond; the ball used in a baseball game.

base·board *n.* A molding at the base of a vertical construction that covers the area where the wall meets the floor.

base·ment *n.* The foundation of a

building or home; the cellar formed by the space between the ground and the first floor.

bash v. To smash with a heavy blow; to crush flat; to strike, especially with an object. *slang* An informal party or gathering of some energy and noise. **bashed** *adj.*

bash•ful *adj.* Socially shy; reclusive or nonassertive. **bashfully** *adv.*

ba•sic *adj.* Forming the basis; fundamental. **basically** *adv.*

BASIC *n.* A common computer programming language.

ba•sin *n.* A sink; a washbowl; a round open container used for washing; an area that has been drained by a river system.

ba•sis *n.* The main part; foundation; the initial action or observation from which subsequent activity grows. **bases** *pl.*

bask v. To relax in the warmth of the sun; to enjoy a state of stillness; to savor an accomplishment or acknowledgement.

bas•ket *n.* A container made of woven material, as straw, cane, or other flexible items, open at the top, for carrying goods; in basketball, the hoop with woven strings used as a goal, or the scoring of a point. **basketry** *n.*

bas•ket•ball *n.* A team sport played on a court, each team trying to throw the ball through the hoop at the opponent's end of the court.

bass *n.* A fresh water fish, one of the perch family; the lowest male voice in a quartet; a large stringed musical instrument with a deep range.

bass drum *n.* A large drum with a low booming sound.

bat *n.* A wooden stick made from strong wood; a nocturnal flying mammal. **batter** *n.*

bat boy *n.* A boy who takes care of the equipment of a baseball team.

batch *n.* A quantity (as of cookies) baked or prepared at one time; the total output for a given period of time. *v.* To submit or make available in groups.

bath *n.* The act of washing the body by immersion; hot water or other liquid that is part of an immersion process.

bathe v. To take a bath.

bat•ter v. To beat or strike continuously; to assault. *n.* A cricket or baseball player at bat. **battered** *adj.*

bat•ter•y *n.* A chemical device for generating and storing electrical energy; a group of heavy guns.

bat•tle *n.* A struggle; combat between opposing forces; a prolonged strategic engagement of troops and weapons in warfare. *v.* To engage in a war or battle.

bawl v. To cry very loudly; to weep convulsively and somewhat out of proportion to the cause. **bawling** *n.*

bay *n.* The inlet of a body of water; an inwardly curved portion of the shoreline, allowing some protection from the sea; one of several workstations in a garage or other repair or assembly area.

ba•zaar *n.* A fair where a variety of items are sold as a money-making project for charity, clubs, churches, or other such organizations.

BBS *abbr.* Bulletin board system; a computer system for leaving and retrieving messages and other files.

be v. To exist; used with the present participle of a verb to show action; to occupy a position in space; to occur.

beach *n.* Pebbly or sandy shore of a lake, ocean, sea, or river.

bea•con *n.* A coastal guiding or signaling device.

bead *n.* A small round piece of material with a hole for threading. **beading** *n.*

bea•gle *n.* A small breed of hunting dog with short legs.

beak *n.* The bill of a bird; the horizontally protruding front edge of a cap. **beaked** *adj.*

beak•er *n.* Large, widemouthed cup for drinking; a cylindrical, glass laboratory vessel with a lip for pouring.

beam *n.* Large, oblong piece of wood or metal used as a support element in construction; a ray, especially of light. *v.* To shine or glow.

bean *n.* An edible seed or seed pod of a legume. *v.* To hit on the head.

bear *n.* A large mammal of America and Europe, with shaggy fur and short tail. *v.* To endure; to carry. **bearable** *adj.*

beard *n.* Hair growing on the chin and cheeks.

beast *n.* A four-legged animal.

beast•ly *adj.* In the manner of a beast; uncouth or uncivilized.

beast of bur•den *n.* An animal used to perform heavy work or transport heavy materials.

beat *v.* To strike repeatedly; to defeat; to stir a mix rapidly.

beat *adj.* Exhausted. **beaten** *adj.*

beat *n.* A measure of time in music; a route, territory, or regular path of activity.

beau•ty *n.* Pleasing to the eye; felicity, especially of appearance; graceful or balanced structure; aesthetic perfection. **beautiful** *adj.*, **beautifully** *adv.*

be•cause *conj.* For a reason; since; from the cause that.

beck *n.* A summons, a call.

beck•on *v.* To summon someone with a nod or wave.

be•come *v.* To come, to be, or to grow into existence.

bed *n.* Furniture for sleeping; a piece of planted or cultivated ground; the horizontal base of a truck. **bedding** *n.*

bed•bug *n.* A wingless insect that sucks blood and infests human homes, especially beds.

bee *n.* A hairy-bodied flying insect, often living in hives, with structures for gathering pollen and nectar from flowers.

beef *n.* A cow, steer, or bull that has been fattened for consumption; the flesh of a bovine; a contention or argument. **beefy** *adj.*, **beefs**, **beeves** *pl.*

bee•keep•er *n.* One who raises bees for their honey.

beep *n.* A warning sound from a horn.

beer *n.* An alcoholic beverage made from malt, hops, and other fermented grains.

bees•wax *n.* The wax from bees used for their honeycombs.

beet *n.* The root from a cultivated plant that can be used as a vegetable or a source of sugar.

bee•tle *n.* An insect with modified, horny front wings that cover the membranous back wings when not in flight.

be•fore *adv.* Earlier; previously. *prep.* In front of.

be•friend *v.* To make a friend of someone.

beg *v.* To make a living by asking for charity; to ask for fervently. **beggar** *n.*

be•gan *v.* The past tense of *begin*.

be•gin *v.* To start; to come into being; to commence. **beginner, beginning** *n.*

be•grudge *v.* To envy someone's possessions or enjoyment; to wish ill to one who possesses.

be•gun *v.* The past participle of *begin*.

be•half *n.* The support or interest of another person; in the name of another.

be•have *v.* To function in a certain manner; to act according to set laws, especially physical; to conduct oneself in a proper manner. **behavior, behaviorism** *n.*

be•hind *adv.* To or at the back; late or slow in arriving.

be•hold *v.* To look at; to see; to view with awe.

be•hoove *v.* To benefit or give advantage.

beige *adj.* Light brown-grey in color.

be•ing *n.* One's existence; the physical presence.

be•la•bor *v.* To work on or to discuss beyond the point where it is necessary; to carry to absurd lengths; to emphasize past need.

be•lat•ed *adj.* Tardy; late. **belatedly** *adv.*

bel•fry *n.* A tower housing the bells of a church.

be•lief *n.* Something trusted or believed; a creed or set of axioms by which one makes moral and ethical decisions.

be•lieve *v.* To accept as true or real; to declare as considered subjectively true in hypothesis; to hold onto religious beliefs.

believable *adj.*, **believer** *n.*

be·lit·tle *v.* To think or speak in a slighting manner of someone or something; to make small or trivial.

bell *n.* A metal instrument that gives a metallic sound when struck; any object shaped like a bell; a mechanical or electrical device for announcing one's presence.

bel·low *v.* To make a deep, powerful roar like a bull.

bel·lows *n.* An instrument that produces air in a chamber and expels it through a short tube.

bel·ly The abdomen or the stomach; the innermost chamber.

be·long *v.* To be a part of; to be owned by.

be·long·ings *n.* Articles of ownership; personal effects; one's material goods, especially portable.

be·lov·ed *adj.* Dearly loved; held in deep affection.

be·low *adv.* At a lower level or place; in the lower levels of a vessel. *prep.* In an inferior position to; under.

belt *n.* A band worn around the waist; a zone or region distinctive in a special way; an encircling shape.

belt·way *n.* A highway that encircles an urban area.

be·muse *v.* To bewilder or confuse; to be lost in thought. **bemused** *adj.*

bench *n.* A long seat for more than two people; the seat of the judge in a court.

bend *v.* To arch; to change the direct course; to deflect; to form into a curve or angle.

be·neath *prep.* To or in a lower position; below; underneath.

ben·e·dic·tion *n.* A blessing given at the end of a religious service.

ben·e·fi·ci·ar·y *n.* The person or institution named to receive the estate of another in case of death.

ben·e·fit *n.* Aid; help; an act of kindness; a social event or entertainment to raise money for a person or cause. *v.* To help or ameliorate; to gain advantage.

be·nign *adj.* Having a gentle and kind disposition; gracious; not malignant; entirely curable. **benignly** *adv.*

bent *adj.* Curved, not straight; past tense of *bend.*

be·queath *v.* To give or leave to someone by legal will; to hand down; to teach to the next generation.

ber·ry *n.* An edible fruit, such as a strawberry or blackberry, grown on bushes; the fruit of certain flowering plants.

berth *n.* Space at a wharf for a ship or boat to dock; a built-in bunk or bed on a train or ship; space between moving objects.

be·side *prep.* At the side of; next to.

be·sides *adv.* In addition to; as an extra; preempting or counterindicating a previous statement or argument.

best *adj.* Exceeding all others in quality or excellence; most suitable, desirable, or useful; of the highest degree.

bes·ti·ar·y *n.* A medieval collection of fables about imaginary and real animals, each with a moral; any zoological exhibition.

bet *n.* An amount risked on a stake or wager. *v.* To place a wager.

be·tray *v.* To be disloyal or unfaithful; to indicate or give an outward sign of; to deceive. **betrayal** *n.*

be·trothed *n.* A person to whom one is engaged to marry.

bet·ter *adj.* More suitable, useful, desirable, or higher in quality; the comparative of *good.* *v.* To improve oneself. **betterment** *n.*

be·tween *prep.* In the position or time that separates; in the middle or shared by two; in a place limited by two edges or forms.

be·twixt *prep.* Not knowing which way one should go; between.

bev·er·age *n.* A refreshing liquid for drinking other than water.

bev·y *n.* A collection or group; a flock of birds. **bevies** *pl.*

be·ware *v.* To be cautious; to be on guard; to warn.

be·wil·der *v.* To confuse; to perplex or

puzzle; to confound, as in a maze. **bewilderment** n.

be•witch v. To fascinate or captivate completely; to enchant. **bewitchment** n.

be•yond prep. Outside the reach or scope of; at a farther distance. n. Something past or to the far side; the vague place of the afterlife.

bi•an•nu•al adj. Taking place twice a year; semiannual.

bi•as n. Prejudice or reaction based on previous impressions without fairness. v. To act prejudicially; to slant or weigh rhetorically in one direction. **biased** adj.

bib n. A cloth tied under the chin of small children to protect their clothing; a napkin which ties at the back.

Bi•ble n. The holy book of Christianity, containing the Old and New Testaments. **biblical** adj., **biblically** adv.

bib•li•og•ra•phy n. A list of works by one writer or publisher; a list of sources of information, especially on a specific subject; the reference sources of a study, listed alphabetically by authors' last name. **bibliographer** n.

bick•er v. To quarrel or argue in a small-minded way; to exchange insults in place of sound argument.

bi•cul•tur•al adj. Having, containing, or influenced by two distinct cultures; relating to cross-cultural influences or effects.

bi•cus•pid n. A tooth with two roots.

bi•cy•cle n. A two-wheeled vehicle propelled by pedals, balanced in motion by centripetal inertia, designed for one rider. **bicyclist** n.

bid v. To request something; to offer to pay a certain price; to offer to buy at auction. n. The amount offered in an auction. **bidder** n.

bi•en•ni•al adj. Occurring every two years; lasting for two years. n. The celebration or observance of a two-year event. **biennially** adv.

bi•fo•cals n. Eyeglasses having two focal lengths ground into one lens, to correct both close and distant vision.

big adj. Very large in dimensions, intensity, and extent; grown-up; bountiful; generous in size or effect.

Big Dip•per n. Cluster of seven stars in the northern sky that form a bowl and handle; Ursa Major.

big-heart•ed adj. Habitually generous and kind; open and accessible.

big•horn n. A wild game sheep from the mountainous western part of North America, with heavy curled horns.

big•ot n. One fanatically devoted to one's own group, religion, politics, or race; a hypocrite or intolerant, prejudiced person. **bigoted** adj., **bigotry** n.

big•wig n. slang A person of authority; a superior; an influential person, outside one's own social and economic range.

bike n. A bicycle. **bike** v., **biker** n.

bi•lat•er•al adj. Having or relating to two sides; on both sides of a division. **bilaterally** adv.

bi•lin•gual adj. Able to speak two languages with equal ability.

bill n. Itemized list of fees for services rendered; a document presented containing a formal statement of a case complaint or petition; a government document proposed to a lawmaking body for consideration into law; the beak of a bird.

bill•board n. A place for displaying advertisements, usually outdoors.

bill•fold n. Pocket-sized wallet for holding money and personal information.

bil•liards n. Game played on a table with cushioned edges.

bil•lion n. A thousand million.

bil•lion•aire n. A person whose wealth equals at least one billion dollars.

Bill of Rights n. The first ten amendments to the United States Constitution.

bil•low n. Large swell of water or smoke; wave. v. To puff out or fill with wind. **billowy** adj.

bin n. An enclosed place, sometimes closed at the top, for storage of bulk items.

bind v. To hold with a belt or rope; to bandage; to fasten and enclose pages of a book between covers. **binding** *n.*

bind•er *n.* A notebook for holding paper; payment or written statement legally binding an agreement.

binge *n.* Uncontrollable self-indulgence; a spree; excessive consumption, especially liquor or food.

bin•go *n.* A game of chance in which markers are placed on numbered cards in accordance with numbers drawn by a caller.

bin•oc•u•lars *pl. n.* An optical magnifying device for both eyes at once.

bi•og•ra•pher *n.* A researcher and writer of another person's life story.

bi•og•ra•phy *n.* A researched and accurate report of the life and accomplishments of a prominent or important person, usually chronological, written by another.

bi•o•haz•ard *n.* Biological material that threatens humans or their environment if infective.

bi•o•log•i•cal war•fare *n.* Warfare using organic biocides or disease-producing micro-organisms to destroy crops, livestock, or human life.

bi•ol•o•gy *n.* Science of living organisms and the study of their structure, reproduction, and growth. **biological** *adj.*, **biologist** *n.*

bi•rac•ial *adj.* Composed of or for members of two races.

birch *n.* A tree providing hard, close-grained wood.

bird *n.* A warm-blooded, egg-laying animal, usually capable of flight, whose body is covered by feathers.

bird bath *n.* A shallow basin of water set out for birds.

birth *n.* The beginning of existence; the moment of extraction of an offspring from the womb.

birth con•trol *n.* Any of several techniques used to control or prevent the number of children born by lessening the chances of conception; the practice of controlling the birth rate in a society.

birth•day *n.* The day a person is born and the anniversary of that day.

birth•stone *n.* A gemstone that represents the month in which one was born.

bis•cuit *n.* Small baked quick bread made with baking soda or baking powder; a cookie.

bi•sect *v.* To divide or cut into two equal parts. **bisection** *n.*

bi•sex•u•al *adj.* Relating to both sexes; attracted to persons of either sex. **bisexuality** *n.*

bit *n.* A tiny piece or amount of something; the rotating cutting element of a tool designed for boring or drilling; in computer science, either of two characters, as the binary digits zero and one, of a language that has only two characters; a unit of information; storage capacity, as of computer memory.

bitch *n.* A female dog.

bite *v.* To cut, tear, or crush with the teeth. **bite** *n.*, **bitingly** *adv.*

bit•ter *adj.* Having a sharp, unpleasant taste; not sweet; angry or negative after a defeat or reversal of fortune. **bitterly** *adv.*, **bitterness** *n.*

bi•zarre *adj.* Extremely strange or odd. **bizarrely** *adv.*

blab *v.* To reveal a secret by indiscreet talking; to gossip; to talk incessantly without focus.

blab•ber *v.* To chatter. **blabber** *n.*

black *adj.* Very dark in color; reflecting or transmitting no light; dark and serious in theme.

black•board *n.* Hard, slate-like board written on with chalk.

black box *n.* The damage-proof container protecting the tape recordings of airline pilots from water and fire, normally recoverable in the event of an accident.

black eye *n.* A bruise or discoloration around the eye.

black•list *v.* To make or add a name to a list containing the names of people to be privately and unofficially boycotted.

black•mail *n.* The threat of exposing a past discreditable act or crime; money paid to avoid exposure.

black•smith *n.* One who shapes iron with heat and a hammer, or manufactures beaten metal items; a smithy.

black•top *n.* Asphalt, used to pave or surface roads; a road surfaced with a mixture of asphalt, tar, stone, and other binding materials, poured in a semisolid state and hardening upon cooling and pressing with rollers.

black wid•ow *n.* A poisonous spider of North America, with a distinctive hourglass shape on the female's abdomen.

blade *n.* The cutting part of a knife; the leaf of a plant or a piece of grass; the runner of an ice skate.

blame *v.* To hold someone guilty for something; to find fault; to attribute to as a cause. *n.* The cause of; guilt.

blame•less *adj.* Without blame; not guilty; innocent of effect.

bland *adj.* Lacking taste or style; dull; neutral. **blandly** *adv.*

blank *adj.* Having no markings or writing; empty; confused; at a loss for thought or word. **blankly** *adv.*, **blankness** *n.*

blan•ket *n.* A woven covering used on a bed for warmth. *v.* To cover completely.

blank verse *n.* A poem whose lines adhere to all the conditions of poetry except end rhyme.

blare *v.* To make or cause a loud sound; to shout; to broadcast loudly.

blast *n.* An explosion; a strong gust of air; the sound produced when a horn is blown. *slang* An exciting, active, or unusually enjoyable event. **blasted** *adj.*

blaze *n.* A fire, especially sudden; a sudden outburst of anger; a trail marker; a white mark on an animal's face. *v.* To flare up suddenly; to become full of light.

bleach *v.* To remove the color from a fabric; to become white. *n.* A chemical solution that whitens fabric or cleans stains.

bleach•ers *pl. n.* Rows of plank seating for spectators in a stadium; the cheapest section of seats in an arena.

bleak *adj.* Discouraging and depressing; barren; cold; harsh. **bleakness** *n.*, **bleakly** *adv.*

blear•y *adj.* Dull from lack of sleep; unfocused; blurry.

bleat *n.* The cry of a sheep or goat.

bleed *v.* To lose blood, as from an injury; to extort money; to mix or allow dyes to run together; to leak out slowly.

blend *v.* To mix together smoothly, to obtain a new substance. *n.* A mixture of complementary substances.

blend•er *n.* A kitchen appliance used to blend or liquify food items; any mechanical device for mixing.

bless *v.* To give one's goodwill to; to honor or praise; to confer prosperity or well-being.

bless•ed *adj.* Holy; enjoying happiness; in a state of favor. **blessedly** *adv.*

bless•ing *n.* A short prayer before a meal; approval or permission; a privilege; evidence of good fortune.

blight *n.* A disease of plants causing complete destruction of crop or species.

blimp *n.* A lighter-than-air large aircraft with a nonrigid gas-filled hull; a zeppelin.

blind *adj.* Not having eyesight; not based on facts; unaware of or incapable of perceiving. *n.* A shelter that conceals hunters.

blink *v.* To squint; to open and close the eyes quickly; to take a quick glance; to falter in a mental combat; to weaken.

blink•er *n.* A signaling light that displays a message; a light used to indicate turns.

bliss *n.* The condition of having great happiness or joy; a transcendent state of universal understanding; one's life work or path which gives total satisfaction and happiness. **blissful** *adj.*, **blissfully** *adv.*

blis•ter *n.* The swelling of a thin layer of skin that contains a watery liquid. **blistered** *adj.*

bliz•zard *n.* A severe winter storm characterized by cold temperatures, high wind, and blinding snow.

bloat *v.* To swell or puff out. **bloated** *adj.*

blob *n.* A small shapeless mass.

block *n.* A solid piece of matter; a square or

rectangular piece of wood; a platform used at an auction to display goods to be auctioned; the act of obstructing or hindering something. **blockage** n.

block v. To impede; to prevent from movement or direction; to arrange in blocks.

blond adj. A golden or flaxen color. n. A man or boy with yellow hair.

blonde n. A woman or girl with yellow hair.

blood n. The fluid circulated by the heart throughout the body, carrying oxygen and nutrients to all parts of the body.

blood bank n. A place or institution where blood or plasma is processed, typed, and stored for future needs.

blood•hound n. A breed of tracking dogs with a very keen sense of smell.

blood•stream n. The tubular circulation of blood in the vascular system of arteries and veins.

blood•y adj. Stained with blood; having the characteristics of blood; violent and destructive to participants, as sports.

bloom v. To bear flowers; to flourish; to have a healthy look; to blossom; to mature suddenly from childhood to adulthood. **blooming** adj., **bloomer** n.

blos•som n. A flower or a group of flowers of a plant that bears fruit. v. To flourish; to bloom; to grow. **blossomy** adj.

blot n. A spot or stain. v. To dry with an absorbent material.

blotch n. A discolored area of skin.

blouse n. A loosely fitting shirt or top.

blow v. To express air or wind; to move or be in motion because of a current of air. n. A sudden hit with a hand or fist.

blow•er n. A device, mechanical or electric, for moving objects by air; a motor used to vent an area of contaminated air.

blow-dry v. To dry one's hair with a hand-held hair dryer.

blow•hole n. A hole in the ice that enables aquatic mammals to come up and breathe; the nostril of a whale, located on the top surface of the head.

blow•out n. The sudden deflation of a tire occurring while driving.

blue n. A color the same as the color of a clear sky; the hue between violet and green; the color worn by the Union Army during the Civil War. adj. slang Sad, melancholy.

blue•print n. A reproduction of technical drawings or plans, using white lines on a blue background; any outline or plan of action.

blues pl. n. A style of jazz stemming from African-American post-slavery cultures; a state of depression; the state of being blue.

bluff v. To appear differently from one's actual condition; to deceive or mislead; to intimidate by showing more confidence than the facts can support. n. A steep and ridged cliff.

blun•der n. An error caused by ignorance; an action causing the failure of a project.

blunt adj. Frank and abrupt; without finesse or circumlocution; dull or unsharpened, as an edge.

blur v. To smudge or smear; to become hazy. **blurringly** adv., **blur** n.

blurt v. [with out] To speak impulsively.

blush v. To turn red in the face from embarrassment from modesty or humiliation; to feel ashamed. n. Make-up used to give color to the cheekbones.

blus•ter n. A violent and noisy wind in a storm. v. To speak violently but emptily as a defense against reason.

bo•a n. A large nonvenomous snake of the Boidea family which coils around prey and crushes it; a feathered accessory that wraps around the neck.

board n. A flat piece of sawed lumber; a flat area on which games are played; payment for food in a lodging. v. To receive meals at a lodging, usually for pay; to enter a ship, train, or plane. **boarder** n., **boardlike** adj.

board game n. A game played by moving pieces on a board.

boast v. To brag about one's own accomplishments; to count as one's assets. n. A brag or nonhumble statement of one's accomplishments. **boastful** *adj.*, **boast-fulness** *n.*

boat *n.* A small open craft, capable of being carried by a larger ship; an open gravy holder or similar container.

bob *v.* To cause to move up and down in a quick, jerky movement; to float in water.

bod•y *n.* The main part of something; the physical part of a person; the corporal element of existence, answering to the laws of physics.

boil *v.* To raise the temperature of water or other liquid until the gaseous state; to evaporate; reduce in size by boiling.

boil•er *n.* A vessel containing water, heated for steam power.

bois•ter•ous *adj.* Violent from innocent energy; rough and stormy; undisciplined.

bold *adj.* Courageous; showing courage; distinct and clear; visible from a distance.

bolt *n.* A threaded metal pin designed with a head at one end and a removable nut at the other; a thunderbolt; a large roll of fabric or other material. *v.* To run or move suddenly; to flee from punishment.

bomb *n.* An explosive weapon, sometimes projected or dropped through the air, detonating upon impact, releasing destructive material, gas, and smoke.

bomb•er *n.* A military aircraft that carries and drops bombs; a person who makes or detonates explosive weapons.

bond *n.* Something that fastens or binds together; a duty or binding agreement; an insurance agreement in which the agency guarantees to pay the employer in the event an employee is accused of causing financial loss. **bonded** *adj.*

bond•age *n.* Slavery; servitude; restraint by physical or mental means.

bone *n.* The calcified connecting tissue of the skeleton.

bon•fire *n.* An open outdoor fire for cooking and warmth, made from found onsite combustible materials.

bon•net *n.* A decorative or protective woman's hat with a brim, tying under the chin.

bo•nus *n.* Something given over and above what is expected; extra payment reflecting past overachievement.

book *n.* A group of pages fastened along the left side and bound between a protective cover; literary work written or printed. *v.* To reserve or register a room, facility, or performing act.

book•end *n.* A support for holding a row of books upright.

book•ing *n.* A scheduled engagement; a reservation of talent or space in advance.

book•keep•ing *n.* The business of recording the accounts and transactions of a business; the record-keeping aspect of accounting. **bookkeeper** *n.*

book•mark *n.* Something inserted in a book to mark one's place; in computers, a feature of browsers to allow easy return to a previous web location.

book•mo•bile *n.* A vehicle equipped as a mobile book-lending service, traveling into communities without libraries.

book re•port *n.* A written or oral description, criticism, or analysis of a book, given after reading the book.

book•worm *n.* Various insect larvae that feed on the paste and binding of books; one who reads insatiably, to the neglect of other activities.

boom *n.* A deep, resonant sound; a long pole extending to the top of a derrick giving support to guide lifted objects; the horizontal spar of a sailing vessel; a sudden prosperity.

boo•mer•ang *n.* A carved, flat missile with aerodynamic properties, thrown so that it returns to the thrower.

boost *v.* To increase; to raise or lift by pushing up from below; to support or raise up by encouragement. *n.* An increase in energy, value, or mood.

boost•er *n.* A promoter or supporter of a cause; a supplementary dose of vaccine.

boot *n.* A protective covering for the foot; any protective sheath or covering; in England, the trunk of a vehicle. *v.* In computers, to load a computer with an operating system or other software.

booth *n.* A small enclosed compartment or area; display area at trade shows for displaying merchandise for sale; an area in a restaurant with a table and benches.

bor·der *n.* A surrounding decorative or protective margin or edge; a political or geographic boundary.

bor·der·line *n.* A line or mark indicating a border.

bore *v.* To make a hole through or in something using a drill; to make tired; to become repetitious or dull. **boredom** *n.*

born *adj.* Brought into life or being; having an innate talent.

bor·row *v.* To receive money with the intentions of returning it; to use as one's own with permission.

boss *n.* An employer or supervisor for whom one works; one's superior in a hierarchic structure; a projecting block used in architecture. *v.* To command; to supervise. **bossiness** *n.*, **bossy** *adj.*

bot·a·ny *n.* The science of plants. **botanical** *adj.*, **botanist** *n.*

botch *v.* To ruin something by clumsiness; to repair clumsily.

both *adj.* Two in conjunction with one another; one and another; two as a total.

both·er *v.* To pester, harass, or irritate; to be concerned about something. **bothersome** *adj.*

bot·tle *n.* A receptacle, usually made of glass, with a narrow neck and a top that can be capped or corked; formula or milk fed to a baby from such a container.

bot·tom *n.* The lowest or deepest part of anything; the base; underside; the last; the land below a body of water. **bottomless** *adj.*, **bottomed** *v.*

bough *n.* The large branch of a tree.

boul·der *n.* A large round rock.

boul·e·vard *n.* A broad city street lined with trees and separated by lawn or other barrier to opposing traffic.

bounce *v.* To rebound or cause to rebound; to leap or spring suddenly; to be returned by a bank as being worthless or having no value. **bounce** *n.*

bounc·ing *adj.* Healthy; vigorous; robust; lively and spirited.

bound *n.* A leap or bounce. *v.* To limit; to be tied or restrained; held by an obligation.

bound·a·ry *n.* A limit or border; the edge of an action or right.

bound·less *adj.* Without limits. **boundlessly** *adv.*, **boundlessness** *n.*

boun·ti·ful *adj.* Abundant; plentiful. **bountifully** *adv.*

boun·ty *n.* Generosity; an inducement or reward given for the return of something; a good harvest; the price paid to another to bring a criminal to justice.

bou·quet *n.* A group of cut flowers, held in the hand or arranged in a vessel; the aroma of wine, as when first poured.

bo·vine *n.* A member of the bovid family, with cloven hooves, four-chamber digestive tracts, and pronounced mammary apertures, such as an ox or cow. **bovine** *adj.*

bow *n.* The front section of a boat or ship; bending of the head or waist to express a greeting or courtesy; a weapon made from a curved stave and strung taut to launch arrows; a rod strung with horsehair, used for playing stringed instruments.

bow *v.* To lower one's upper body in homage or respect; to give in to another's wishes; to bend under a burden.

bowl *n.* A hemispherical container for food or liquids; a bowl-shaped part, as of a spoon or ladle; a bowl-shaped stadium. *v.* To roll spherical or cylindrical objects; to participate in the game of bowling.

bow·leg·ged *adj.* Characterized by an outward curvature of the leg at the knee.

bowl·ing *n.* A game in which a person rolls a ball down a wooden alley in order to knock down a triangular group of nine or ten wooden bowling pins; any lawn game involving rolling balls. **bowler** *n.*

bowl·ing al·ley *n.* A building containing alleys for the game of bowling.

box *n.* A small container or chest, usually

with a lid; a special area in a theater that holds a small group of people. *v.* To fight with the fists.

box•car *n.* An enclosed railway car used for the transportation of freight, accessed through sliding side doors on both walls.

box•er *n.* A person who boxes professionally; a German breed of dog with short hair, brownish coat, and a square muzzle.

box•ing *n.* A sport in which two opponents punch each other using padded gloves on their hands, forming fists.

boy *n.* A male youth or child. **boyhood** *n.*

boy•cott *v.* To abstain from dealing with, buying, or using, as a means of organized protest against practices.

boy•friend *n.* A male companion of a mildly romantic relationship with a young person of the opposite sex.

Boy Scout *n.* A boy who belongs to a worldwide organization that emphasizes citizenship and character development.

brace *n.* A device that supports or steadies something; two of a team of work animals. *v.* To support with a brace.

brace•let *n.* An ornamental band for the wrist.

brack•et *n.* A support attached to a vertical surface to hold a shelf or other weight; the typographical marks of enclosure. *v.* To enclose in brackets.

brag *v.* To assert or talk boastfully; to announce one's accomplishments without modesty.

brag•gart *n.* A person who brags.

Brah•man•ism *n.* The religious beliefs and practices of ancient India; strict Hinduism.

braid *v.* To interweave three or more strands of something; to plait. *n.* Fibers or strands that have been braided.

braille *n.* A system of printing for the blind, consisting of six dots, two across and four directly under the first two, with numbers and letters represented by raising certain dots in each group of six.

brain *n.* The large mass of nerve tissue enclosed in the cranium, responsible for the interpretation of sensory impulses, control of the body, and coordination; the center of thought and emotion.

brain•storm *n.* A sudden idea or inspiration. *v.* To think and contribute ideas without censure by reason; to imagine without artificial barriers of practicality.

brake *n.* A device designed to stop or slow the motion of a vehicle or machine; a tool in weaving; a dense covering of shrubbery. **brake** *v.*

branch *n.* An extension from the main trunk of a tree; an offshoot or tributary of a river. **branched** *adj.*

brand *n.* A trademark or label that names a product; a mark of disgrace or shame; a piece of charred or burning wood; a mark made by a hot iron to show ownership. **branded** *adj.*

brand name *n.* A company's verbal trademark, protected by law.

brand-new *adj.* Unused and new; fresh; not introduced before.

bran•dy *n.* An alcoholic liquor distilled from fermented fruit juices or wine.

brass *n.* An alloy of zinc, copper and other metals in lesser amounts.

brat *n.* An ill-mannered child. **brattiness** *n.*, **bratty** *adj.*

brave *adj.* Having or displaying courage; strong in the face of pain; willing to risk harm out of a sense of duty or righteousness. *n.* An honorary term of recognition to a warrior of the Native American tribes.

brav•er•y *n.* The quality of or state of being brave.

brawl *n.* A noisy argument or fight. **brawl** *v.*, **brawler** *n.*

brawn *n.* Well-developed and solid muscles; sturdy. **brawny** *adj.*

bray *v.* To make a loud cry like a donkey. *n.* A donkey's cry.

braze *v.* To solder using a nonferrous alloy that melts at a lower temperature than that of the metals being joined together.

bra•zen *adj.* Made of brass; shameless or impudent.

bread *n.* A leavened food made from a flour or meal mixture, and baked; one's livelihood; the reward for labor.

breadth *n.* The distance or measurement from side to side; width; thickness in a three-dimensional figure.

break *v.* To separate into parts with violence or suddenness; to collapse or give way; to change suddenly; to temporarily cease discussion or activity.

break *n.* A fissure or division in a solid object; in pool, the first stroke that distributes the balls around the table; a stroke of good luck; a chance from which future successes may grow.

break a leg *v.* To be a theatrical success.

break•down *n.* Failure to function; a mental or nervous collapse.

break•er *n.* A wave that breaks into foam.

break ev•en *v.* To make neither a profit or loss in business.

break•fast *n.* The first meal of the day.

break•through *n.* A sudden advance in knowledge or technique; a thrust that goes farther than anticipated or expected.

breast *n.* The milk-producing glandular organs on a woman's chest; the mammary glands; the area of the body from the neck to the abdomen.

breath *n.* The air inhaled and exhaled in breathing; a very slight whisper, fragrance, or breeze.

breathe *v.* To draw air into and expel from the lungs; to inhale and exhale; to allow air or ventilation to surround a thawing or evaporating substance; to take a short rest.

breed *v.* The genetic strain of domestic animals, developed and maintained by mankind. **breeding** *n.*

breeze *n.* A slight gentle wind; a zephyr; something accomplished with very little effort. **breezy** *adj.*

brev•i•ty *n.* A brief duration; conciseness; efficient shortness; briefness.

brew *v.* To make beer from malt and hops by boiling, infusion, and fermentation. **brewer** *n.*

brew•er•y *n.* A building or plant where beer or ale is brewed.

bribe *v.* To influence or induce by giving, illegally or immorally, a token or anything of value for a service. **bribe** *n.*

brib•ery *n.* The practice of giving or receiving a bribe.

brick *n.* A molded block of baked clay, usually rectangular in shape, used for construction and facing.

bri•dal *adj.* Relating to a bride or a nuptial ceremony.

bri•dal wreath *n.* A flower grown for its small white flowers used in bouquets.

bride *n.* A woman just married or about to be married.

bride•groom *n.* A man just married or about to be married.

brides•maid *n.* A woman who attends a bride at her wedding.

bridge *n.* A structure providing passage over two bodies of land, depressions, obstacles, or other rights of way; a contract-bidding card game for four players.

bri•dle *n.* A harness used to restrain or guide a horse. *v.* To restrain or control. **bridler** *n.*

brief *n.* A concise, formal statement of a client's case. *adj.* Short in duration. *v.* To summarize or inform in a short statement. **briefly** *adv.*, **briefness** *n.*

brief•case *n.* A small, flat, flexible case for holding and carrying papers or books.

brief•ly *adv.* For a very short span of time.

bright *adj.* Brilliant in color or light; vivid; shining and emitting or reflecting light; happy; cheerful; lovely; intelligent, quick to learn. **brightness** *n.*

bright•en *v.* To make things brighter. **brightener** *n.*

bril•liant *adj.* Very bright and shiny; sparkling; radiant; extremely intelligent.

brim *n.* The edge or rim of a cup; the top of a cliff or bluff. **brimless** *adj.*

brim•ful *adj.* Completely full.

bring *v.* To carry with oneself to a certain place; to cause, act, or move in a special direction.

brink

brink *n.* The upper edge or margin of a very steep slope; the place past which no return is possible.

brisk *adj.* Moving or acting quickly; being sharp in tone or manner; energetic or invigorating. **briskly** *adv.*, **briskness** *n.*

broad *adj.* Covering a wide area; in proportion measuring from side to side; plain, open, unrefined. **broadly** *adv.*

broad•cast *v.* To transmit a program by radio or television; to make widely known; to scatter or sow seeds. **broadcaster** *n.*

broad•mind•ed *adj.* Tolerant of varied views; liberal; open to the opinions and beliefs of others; not judgmental.

broil•er *n.* A device, usually a part of a stove, used for broiling meat; a young chicken.

broke *adj.* Penniless; completely without money. *v.* Past tense of *break*.

bro•ken *adj.* Separated violently into parts; damaged to the point of inoperability; severed or disconnected; difficult to understand, as speech.

bron•co *n.* A wild horse of western North America.

bronze *n.* An alloy of tin, copper, and zinc; moderate olive brown to yellow in color. **bronze** *v.*, **bronze** *adj.*

Bronze Age *n.* Human culture between the Iron Age and the Stone Age.

brooch *n.* A large decorative pin.

brood *n.* The young offsprings of an animal; a litter. *v.* To produce by incubation; to hatch; to think about at length; to be in a state of deep gloom or meditation.

brook *n.* A small fresh-water stream.

broom *n.* A long-handled implement used for sweeping.

broth *n.* The liquid in which fish, meat, or vegetables have been cooked; cooking stock.

broth•er *n.* A male who shares the same parents as another person; a kindred person by belief or affiliation. **brotherly** *adj.*

broth•er•hood *n.* The state of being brothers; one related to another for a particular purpose; a philanthropic association.

broth•er•in•law *n.* The brother of one's spouse; the husband of one's sister; the husband of one's spouse's sister.

brought *v.* Past tense of *bring*.

brow *n.* The ridge above the eye where the eyebrow grows.

brown *n.* A color between yellow and red; a dark or tanned complexion.

browse *v.* To look over something in a leisurely and casual way; to scan for pertinent information.

bruise *n.* A contusion; an injury that ruptures small blood vessels and discolors the skin without breaking it.

brush *n.* A device consisting of bristles used for applying paint, scrubbing, or grooming the hair; a very dense growth of bushes. *v.* To touch against lightly.

bru•tal *adj.* Very harsh or cruel in treatment; like a brute or animal; violently destructive.

brute *n.* A person characterized by physical power rather than intelligence; one who behaves like an animal. **brutish** *adj.*

bub•ble *n.* A small body of gas contained inside the adhesive surface strength of a liquid; any small round object, usually hollow. *v.* To produce bubbles.

buck *n.* The adult male deer; the lowest grade in the military category. *v.* To move violently in a vertical direction; to throw a rider; to oppose the system.

buck•et *n.* A vessel used to carry liquids or solids; a pail.

buck•eye *n.* A tree with flower clusters and glossy brown nuts.

buck•le *v.* To warp, crumple, or bend under pressure; to fasten with a strap. *n.* Metal clasp for fastening a belt.

bud *n.* Something not developed completely; a small structure that contains flowers or leaves that have not developed; early stage of development. **budding** *adj.*

Bud•dhism *n.* A religion that teaches that suffering is inherited from a previous existence, and that one can be released from it by moral and mental self-purification.

Buddhist *n.* or *adj.*

bud·dy *n.* A companion, partner, or friend; a pal; one who shares in an activity.

budge *v.* To give way to; to cause to move slightly; to change position slightly in response to great exertion.

bud·get *n.* The total amount of money allocated for a certain purpose. *v.* To allot funds or resources carefully in advance of expenditure.

buff *n.* A leather made mostly from skins of buffalo, elk, or oxen having the color of light to moderate yellow. *v.* To polish by rubbing with cloth.

buf·fa·lo *n.* A wild ox with heavy forequarters, short horns, and a large muscular hump; a bison.

buff·er *n.* A tool used to polish or shine; in computer science, a part of the memory used to hold information temporarily while data transfers from one place to another. *v.* To lessen, absorb, or protect against the shock of an impact.

bug *n.* Any small insect or life form; a concealed listening device. *v.* To bother or annoy. **bugged** *adj.*

bug·gy *n.* A small carriage pulled behind a horse; a baby carriage.

bu·gle *n.* A brass wind instrument without keys or valves. *v.* To sound a bugle call. **bugler** *n.*

build *v.* To erect by uniting materials into a composite whole; to fashion or create; to develop or add to; to construct. *n.* The form or structure of a person.

build·er *n.* A person who supervises the construction of a building project.

build·ing *n.* A roofed and walled structure of some size, for permanent use.

bulb *n.* A spherical shape rounded at the bottom, tapering gradually into a point; a rounded underground plant that lies dormant in the winter and blooms in the spring; an incandescent light.

bulge *n.* A swelling of the surface caused by pressure from within.

bulk *n.* A large mass; anything that has great size, volume, or units; materials or substances measured by volume rather than number. **bulky** *adj.*, **bulkiness** *n.*

bull *n.* The adult male in cattle and other large mammals; one confident that the value of stocks or other marketable commodities will rise in the future.

bul·let *n.* A projectile fired from a gun.

bul·le·tin *n.* A broadcast statement of public interest, containing new and important information; a public notice.

bul·le·tin board *n.* A board, often of cork or other soft material, on which messages and temporary notices are posted.

bul·ly *n.* A person who is mean or cruel to weaker people; one who intimidates by oppression or threat of violence.

bum·ble·bee *n.* A large hairy bee, solitary in habit and habitat.

bump *v.* To collide with, knock, or strike something; to take advantage of one's rank or seniority to replace someone of lower rank or privilege. *n.* A swelling or lump on a person's body; an area risen up from a relatively flat surface. **bumpy** *adj.*

bump·er *n.* A device on vehicles that absorbs shock and prevents damage.

bun *n.* Any of a variety of plain or sweet small breads; tightly rolled hair that resembles a bun.

bunch *n.* A cluster or group of like items. *v.* To gather into an informal group.

bun·dle *n.* Anything wrapped or held together. **bundler** *n.*

bun·dle up *v.* To dress warmly, using many layers of clothing.

bun·ga·low *n.* A small one-story cottage with a pitched roof, usually rural or rustic.

bun·gle *v.* To act awkwardly or clumsily; to damage a project or activity by inexpert or careless handling. **bungler** *n.*

bunk *n.* A narrow bed that is built in; one of a tier of berths on a ship.

bun·ny *n.* Child's name for a rabbit.

bu·oy *n.* A floating object to mark a channel or danger; any nautical marker or channel divider.

buoy·an·cy *n.* The tendency of an object or body to remain afloat in liquid or to rise in gas or air.

bur•den *n.* The physical cargo or materials carried by a person or beast; something hard to bear; a duty or responsibility taken on unwillingly but patiently. **burden** *v.*, **burdensome** *adj.*

burg•er *n. slang* A hamburger; ground meat shaped into a patty and served on a bun with condiments and relishes.

bur•glar *n.* One who steals personal items from another person's home without detection. **burglarize** *v.*, **burglary** *n.*

bur•lap *n.* A coarse cloth woven from hemp or jute.

bur•lesque *n.* Theatrical entertainment of a low nature, with comedy, mocking imitations, and dance performances.

bur•ly *adj.* Very heavy and strong; stocky.

burn *v.* To be destroyed by fire; to consume fuel and give off heat. *n.* An injury produced by fire, heat, or steam; the firing of a rocket engine in space. **burnable** *adj.*

burn•er *n.* The part of a fuel-burning device where the fire is contained.

burnt *adj.* Affected by burning; charred or damaged by fire.

bur•ro *n.* A small donkey.

burst *adj.* To explode or experience a sudden outbreak; to very suddenly become visible or audible. *n.* A sudden explosion or outburst.

bur•y *v.* To hide by covering with earth; to inter a body at a funeral service; to place in an inconspicuous position.

bus *n.* A large passenger vehicle; a small hand truck; a conductor for collecting electric currents. **buses, busses** *pl.*

bus•boy *n.* A waiter's assistant; one who removes dirty dishes and resets a table.

bush *n.* A low plant with branches near the ground; a dense tuft or growth; land covered intensely with undergrowth.

bush•el *n.* A unit of dry measurement which equals four pecks or 2,150.42 cubic inches; a basket container that holds a bushel.

bush•y *adj.* Overgrown with a dense growth of bushes; hirsute.

busi•ness *n.* A person's professional dealings or occupation; an industrial or commercial establishment; concerns or activities occupying a period of time.

bus•ing *n.* The practice of transporting children by bus to a school outside their area, to establish racial balance.

bust *n.* A sculpture that resembles the upper part of a human body; the breasts of a woman. *v.* To break or burst; to become short of money.

bus•y *adj.* Full of activity; engaged in some form of work; occupied with another task; already in use. *v.* To occupy one's self. **busily** *adv.*, **busyness** *n.*

but *conj.* On the contrary to; other than; if not; except for the fact; on the other hand.

butch•er *n.* One who slaughters animals and dresses them for food.

but•ter *n.* A yellow fatty substance churned from milk, used as a spread or cooking oil.

but•ter•fly *n.* A narrow-bodied flying insect with four broad, colorful wings, emerging from the cocoon of the caterpillar; a person occupied with the pursuit of pleasure; a swimming stroke.

but•ter•scotch *n.* A candy made from brown sugar and melted butter.

but•ton *n.* A small disk that interlocks with a buttonhole to close a piece of garment; a badge bearing a stamped design or slogan; an immature mushroom. **buttoned** *adj.*

but•ton•hole *n.* The slit through which a button is inserted.

buy *v.* To purchase in exchange for money; to acquire possession of something. *n.* Anything bought, especially a bargain.

buy•er *v.* A person who buys from a store or an individual; a person employed to make wholesale purchases for a company.

buzz *v.* To make a low vibrating humming sound, as a bee.

buz•zard *n.* A broad-winged vulture from the same family as the hawk.

buzz•er *n.* An electrical signaling device

that makes a buzzing sound.

by *prep.* Up to and beyond; to go past; not later than; next to; according to; beside or near; according to; in relation to; as a product or creation of.

bye-bye *interj.* Farewell; goodbye.

by·law *n.* A rule or law governing internal affairs of a group or organization.

by·pass *n.* A road that goes around an obstructed area; a detour; a secondary route; a freeway that avoids the congestion of the urban business district.

byte *n.* In computer science, a string of binary digits operated on as a unit.

C

C, c The third letter of the English alphabet; the Roman numeral for 100.

cab·i·net *n.* A unit for displaying and storing dishes and other objects; a selected group of people appointed by the head of state to officially advise and to take charge of government departments.

ca·ble *n.* A heavy rope made from fiber or steel; a bound group of insulated conductors.

ca·ble tel·e·vi·sion *n.* A private television system which picks up signals from stations and transmits them by cable.

ca·boose *n.* The last car of a train, containing the eating and sleeping quarters for the crew.

cack·le *v.* To laugh with the characteristic shrill noise a hen makes after laying an egg; to talk or laugh with a similar sound. **cackler** *n.*

cac·tus *n.* A leafless plant with a thick, prickly surface, growing primarily in hot and dry regions. **cacti** or **cactuses** *pl.*

cad·die *n.* A person employed by a golfer to assist by carrying clubs and advising the player during the game of golf.

ca·dence *n.* A rhythmic movement or flow; the keeping of time by a marching or musical group.

ca·det *n.* A student in training at a naval or military academy. **cadetship** *n.*

caf·e·te·ri·a *n.* A restaurant where a patron chooses food and then carries it on a tray to the table.

caf·feine *n.* A stimulant found in coffee, tea, and dark colas.

cage *n.* A box-like structure enclosed with bars or grating for the confinement of animals; any enclosure used for confinement. *v.* To capture or restrain in an enclosure.

ca·jole *v.* To wheedle or coax; to convince by gentle emotional argument.

cake *n.* A sweet, baked dessert food made from flour, eggs, and shortening. *v.* To coat or cover over with a layer. **caked** *adj.*

ca·lam·i·ty *n.* Misfortune or great distress; a disaster. **calamitous** *adj.*, **calamitously** *adv.*

cal·ci·um *n.* The alkaline element found in teeth and bones; the element symbolized by Ca.

cal·cu·late *v.* To figure by a mathematical process, to evaluate; to estimate. **calculable** *adj.*

cal·cu·lat·ed *adj.* Worked out beforehand with careful estimation.

cal·cu·lat·ing *adj.* Shrewdly considering one's self-interest; acting from a thought-out design.

cal·cu·la·tor *n.* A machine with a keyboard for automatic mathematical operation.

cal·cu·lus *n.* The mathematics of integral and differential equations; a stone in the gallbladder or kidneys.

cal·dron *n.* A large boiler or kettle; a cauldron.

cal·en·dar *n.* A system for showing time divisions by years, months, weeks, and days; the twelve months in a year; a printed sheet or book divided into days, weeks, and months.

calf *n.* The young offspring of the domestic cow; the young of large animals as the whale and elephant. **calves** *pl.*

cal·i·ber *n.* The inner diameter of a tube or gun; the quality or worth of something.

call *v.* To speak out to someone; to shout;

to name or designate; to telephone.

call•ing *n.* The occupation or profession of a person; one's chosen life work; a natural tendency toward a talent or skill.

cal•lous *adj.* Having calluses; without emotional feelings; hardened or insensitive.

calm *adj.* Absent of motion; having little or no wind, storms, or rough water; eventempered; judicious.

cal•o•rie *n.* A measurement of the amount of heat or energy produced by food. **caloric** *adj.*

cam *n.* A curved wheel used to produce a reciprocating motion; an off-center portion of a rotating shaft which converts circular to vertical motion.

came *v.* Past tense of *come*.

cam•el *n.* A large ruminant mammal used in desert regions as transportation and as a beast of burden, having either one (dromedary) or two (bactrian) humps on its back.

cam•er•a *n.* An apparatus for taking photographs in a lightproof enclosure with an aperture and shuttered lens through which the image is focused and recorded on photosensitive film.

cam•ou•flage *v.* To disguise by creating the effect of being part of the natural surroundings. *n.* Material or process that disguises.

camp *n.* A temporary lodging or makeshift shelter; a military bivouac; an outdoororiented recreational area accommodating groups, especially youth, in organized activities.

cam•paign *n.* An organized operation designed to bring about a particular political, commercial, military, or social goal; a long-range project of the will.

camp•er *n.* A person who camps in makeshift shelters for recreation; a vehicle equipped for casual travel and camping.

camp•fire *n.* An outdoor fire used for cooking and heat while camping, making use of fuel such as twigs and branches.

camp•ground *n.* A specially prepared area for camping; a campsite.

cam•pus *n.* The buildings and grounds of a college, school, or university.

can *v.* To be able to; to know how to do something; to be physically or mentally able; to have the ability to do something; to preserve fruit or vegetables by sealing in an airtight container; to release from employment suddenly. *n.* An airtight container.

ca•nal *n.* A man-made water channel for irrigating land; a waterway built through land, connecting two bodies of navigable water.

ca•nar•y *n.* A green or yellow songbird popular as a caged pet; a wild finch, brown in winter, turning yellow in spring.

can•cel *v.* To invalidate or annul; to cross out; to neutralize; to abort or stop a procedure or program; in mathematics, to remove a common factor from the numerator and the denominator of a fraction. **cancellation** *n.*

can•cer *n.* A malignant tumor that invades healthy tissue and spreads to other areas; the disease marked by such tumors. **cancerous** *adj.*

can•di•date *n.* A person who aspires to or is nominated or qualified for a membership, award, or office; one of a group of possible choices.

can•dy *n.* A confection made from sugar and flavored in a variety of ways. *v.* To preserve, cook, coat, or saturate with syrup or sugar. **candied** *adj.*

cane *n.* A pithy or hollow, flexible, jointed stem of bamboo or rattan split for basketry or wickerwork; a walking stick or other aid to mobility; a crutch for one hand; the stalk of the sugar plant.

ca•nine *adj.* Relating to or resembling a dog; of the dog family.

canned *adj.* Preserved and sealed under pressure; artificial; recorded in advance; *slang* Fired or relieved of employment.

can•ner•y *n.* A company that processes

canned meat, vegetables, and other foods.

can•ni•bal *n.* Any animal who survives by eating one of its own kind; a person who survives by eating the flesh of human beings; member of certain primitive tribes whose rituals include the token consumption of human flesh.

can•non *n.* A heavy war weapon made of metal and mounted on wheels or a base for discharging projectiles.

ca•noe *n.* A lightweight, slender boat with pointed ends which moves by paddling. **canoe** *v.*, **canoeist** *n.*

can•o•py *n.* A cloth covering used as ornamental protection over a bed or other structure; the supporting surface of a parachute.

can't *contr.* Contraction of *cannot.*

can•ta•loupe *n.* A sweet-tasting, orange-colored muskmelon.

can•teen *n.* A small metal container for carrying water or other drinking liquids; a place where refreshments are sold or served.

can•vas *n.* A heavy fabric used in making tents and sails for boats; a piece of such material, or any surface, used for oil paintings.

can•yon *n.* A deep and narrow gorge with steep sides.

cap *n.* A covering for the head, usually brimless and made of a soft material; the top of any container; the final or finishing touch to something; a small explosive charge enclosed in paper and detonated by compression; a small portion; a capsule. **capped** *adj.*

ca•pa•ble *adj.* Having the ability to perform in an efficient way; qualified; able. **capability** *n.*, **capably** *adv.*

ca•pac•i•ty *n.* The ability to contain, receive, or absorb; the aptitude or ability to do something; the maximum production or output.

cap•i•tal *n.* The town or city designated as the seat of government for a nation or state; material wealth in the form of money or property used to produce more wealth; funds contributed to a business by the stockholders or owners; net worth of a company or business; an uppercase letter.

cap•i•tal•ism *n.* The economic system in which the means of distribution and production are privately owned and operated for private profit. **capitalist** *n.*, **capitalistic** *adj.*

cap•puc•ci•no *n.* A hot drink of espresso coffee mixed with hot milk and cinnamon.

cap•size *v.* To overturn in a boat or ship.

cap•sule *n.* A small gelatinous case for a dose of oral medicine; a close vehicle housing vital material in a rocket launch; a summary or abstract in a brief form. **capsular** *adj.*

cap•tain *n.* The chief leader of a group; the commander or master of a ship; the commissioned naval officer ranking below a commodore or rear admiral.

cap•tion *n.* A subtitle; a description of an illustration or picture.

cap•ti•vate *v.* To hold in captivity by attention or emotional influence; to hold the attention, fascinate, or charm a person or group of people.

cap•tive *n.* A person being held as a prisoner. *adj.* Held as a captive; captivated.

cap•ture *v.* To take something or someone by force; to hold after flight. **capturer** *n.*

car *n.* An automobile; an enclosed vehicle, as a railroad car.

car•a•mel *n.* A chewy substance primarily composed of sugar, butter, and milk.

car•at *n.* The unit of weight for gems that equals 200 milligrams.

car•a•van *n.* A group of people traveling together; a recreational vehicle or trailer for itinerant living.

car•bo•hy•drate *n.* A group of compounds, including starches, celluloses, and sugars that contain carbon, hydrogen, and oxygen; one of the essential food groups.

car•bon *n.* A nonmetallic element that occurs as a powdery noncrystalline solid; the element symbolized by C; the single essential element in carbon-based life forms; the required common substance in organic chemistry.

car•bon•ate v. To add or charge with carbon dioxide gas, as in a beverage.

car•bu•re•tor n. The device in gasoline engines that mixes vapor, fuel, and air for efficient combustion.

car•cass n. The dead body of an animal; something that no longer has life.

card n. A small piece of pasteboard or very stiff paper, used in a wide variety of ways, as a greeting card, a business card, a postcard, and the like; one of a deck of playing cards; a comic person.

card cat•a•log n. An alphabetical catalog of books, composed of individual cards for each book, found in libraries.

car•di•nal adj. Of prime importance; principal; of a number, simple and used for counting.

care n. A feeling of concern, anxiety, or worry; guardianship or custody; attendance on one's needs or desires, especially of the ill. v. To show interest or regard; to concern oneself; to have an emotional reaction toward; [with for] to tend or minister to; to have affection for.

ca•reen v. To lurch or twist from one side to another while moving rapidly; to turn a boat's hull up, for cleaning or repair.

ca•reer n. The profession or occupation a person takes in life; a professional or lifelong compensation-earning activity.

care•free adj. Free from all cares, worries, and concerns; unworried or unburdened.

care•ful adj. Exercising care; cautious; watchful; acting with great attention to detail and subtlety; safe or conscious of preventing damage or injury.

ca•ress v. To show affection or admiration by gentle touching or stroking; to pet; to touch in a romantic manner. **caress** n.

car•go n. Freight; the goods carried on a ship, plane, or other vehicle.

car•na•tion n. A fragrant perennial flower in a variety of colors, often used as a decoration in a man's lapel.

car•ni•val n. A traveling amusement show

with side shows, rides such as a ferris wheel, and merry-go-rounds; any kind of a happy celebration.

car•ni•vore n. A flesh-eating animal. **carnivorous** adj.

car•ol n. A song to celebrate joy or praise, especially Christmas. **caroler** n., **carol** v.

ca•rou•sel n. A merry-go-round; a child's ride consisting of a menagerie of life-sized carved animals moving around an axis. **carrousel** var.

carp v. To find unreasonable fault with something or someone; to complain unduly. n. A freshwater fish that contains many small bones but can be eaten with caution; a goldfish.

car•pen•ter n. A person who builds and repairs wooden structures. **carpentry** n.

car•pet n. A thick woven or felt floor covering that insulates and protects the floors. **carpeting** n.

car•rot n. An orange root vegetable.

car•ry v. To transport from one place to another; to bear the burden, weight, or responsibility of; to keep or have available for sale; to move a digit to the next decimal place in addition or multiplication; to travel over a long distance, as sound.

cart n. A two-wheeled vehicle for moving heavy goods; a small lightweight vehicle that can be moved around by hand.

car•ton n. A container made from cardboard or corrugated material, of various sizes, for transport and storage.

car•toon n. A caricature depicting a humorous situation; animated pictures produced by photographing a series of action drawings; a humorous, illustrated story in one or several panels; a comic strip. **cartoonist** n.

car•tridge n. A case made of metal, pasteboard, or other material, that contains a charge of powder; an inexpensive reel for audio or video tape operation.

cart•wheel n. A sideways handspring with the arms over the head and the legs spread like the spokes of a wheel.

carve v. To slice meat or poultry; to cut

into something; to create by shaping material, as sculpture.

cas•cade *n.* A waterfall that flows over steep rocks.

case *n.* A particular occurrence or instance; an injury or disease; a box or housing to carry things in, as a briefcase; in the law, a suit of action brought against a person.

cash•ier *n.* An employee who handles cash as part of the job description; an officer in a bank in charge of receiving or distributing money.

cash•mere *n.* The wool from the Kashmir goat; the yarn from this wool.

cas•ket *n.* A coffin; a small chest or box.

cast *v.* To hurl or throw with force; to direct or turn; to shed; to give a certain part or role; to deposit or give a vote on something; to make or throw, as with a fishing line. *n.* A dressing made from plaster of paris used on a broken bone.

cast•a•way *n.* One who is shipwrecked or discarded.

cast•ing *n.* The act of one who casts; the assignment of roles in a dramatic work.

cas•tle *n.* A fort or fortified dwelling for nobility; any large house or place of refuge; a stronghold.

cast-off *adj.* Discarded; thrown away. *n.* A thing discarded.

ca•su•al *adj.* Informal; occurring by chance; relaxed. **casually** *adv.*, **casualness** *n.*

ca•su•al•ty *n.* One who is injured or killed in an accident; a soldier who is killed, wounded, taken prisoner by the enemy, or missing in action.

cat *n.* A small domesticated animal of the feline family, a pet; any animal in the cat family, such as the lion, lynx, or tiger.

cat•a•log *n.* A publication containing a list of names, objects, and the like; a book of items for sale; a list of offerings, as in a college.

cat•a•lyst *n.* Any substance that alters or decreases the time of a chemical reaction without altering its own chemical composition.

ca•tas•tro•phe *n.* A terrible and sudden disaster; a cataclysm. **catastrophic** *adj.*

catch *v.* To take; to grasp from flight; to seize or capture; to reach in time; to intercept; to become entangled or fastened.

catch•er *n.* A person who catches a ball, specifically the receiver of a pitched ball.

cat•e•go•ry *n.* A general group to which something belongs; a taxonomical branch of related entries.

ca•ter *v.* To provide a food service; to bring directly to a location; to attend to diligently; to indulge. **caterer** *n.*

cat•er•pil•lar *n.* The very fuzzy, worm-like, brightly-colored spiny larva of a moth or butterfly, often destructive of foliage, and encased in a cocoon during metamorphosis.

ca•the•dral *n.* A large and important church, containing the seat of a bishop.

CAT scan *n.* Computerized axial tomography; a cross-sectional picture produced by a scanner, used to x-ray the body.

cat•tle *pl. n.* Farm animals, especially bovines, raised for meat and dairy products.

Cau•ca•sian *n.* An inhabitant of Caucasus. *adj.* Relating to a major ethnic division of the human race; of or relating to the race of peoples originating in the Caucasus Mountains.

cause *v.* To produce a result, consequence, or effect. *n.* A goal, principle; a reason; motive; a project of the will. **causer** *n.*

cau•tion *n.* A warning advising careful planning or procedure. **cau•tious** *adj.*, **caution** *v.*

cav•al•ry *n.* Army troops trained to fight on horseback or in armored vehicles.

cave *n.* An underground tomb or chamber with an opening at the ground surface; any underground space.

ca•vern *n.* A very large underground cave. **cavernous** *adj.*

cav•i•ar *n.* The eggs of large fish, eaten as an appetizer.

cav•i•ty *n.* A decayed place in a tooth; a hollow or hole; any indentation or crevice.

CD *abbr.* Compact disk.

cease *v.* To come to an end or put an end to; to stop; to halt.

cease·fire *n.* An action or agreement to stop fighting, usually the first step in a truce or temporary halt in aggression.

ceil·ing *n.* The overhead covering of a room; the maximum limit to something.

cel·e·brate *v.* To observe with ceremonies, rejoicing, or festivity; to enjoy the achievement of. **celebration** *n.*

cel·eb·ri·ty *n.* A famous, notorious, or well-known person; the condition of being widely recognized.

ce·les·tial *adj.* Heavenly; spiritual; pertaining to astronomy.

cell *n.* A prison; a small room; the smallest unit of any organism capable of independent function, composed of a small mass of cytoplasm, usually enclosing a central nucleus, and surrounded by a membrane or a rigid cell wall; the part of a battery that generates the electricity.

cel·lar *n.* An underground area, beneath a building, used for storage; a basement room.

cel·lo *n.* A violoncello; a bass instrument of the violin family, held on the floor and played by bowing or plucking. **cellist** *n.*

cel·lu·lar *adj.* Consisting of or pertaining to cells.

ce·ment *n.* A construction material made up of powdered, calcined rock and clay materials which, when added with water, set up as a hard, solid mass.

cem·e·ter·y *n.* A place for burying the dead; a graveyard.

cen·sor *n.* A person who examines documents, films, or printed materials to determine what might be objectionable and remove it before distribution. **censorship** *n.*

cen·sure *n.* An expression of criticism and/or disapproval; a public admonishment by a group to one of its members.

cen·sus *n.* An official count of the population; usually at regular intervals; any survey of opinion or attitude.

cent *n.* One; one hundredth of a dollar; a penny.

cen·ter *n.* The place of equal distance from all sides; the point in a circle equidistant from all points on the circumferential arc of the circle; the heart.

cen·ti·pede *n.* A flat arthropod with numerous (literally, a hundred) body segments and legs.

cen·tral *adj.* In, near, or at the center; of primary importance. **centralize** *v.*

cen·tu·ry *n.* A period consisting of 100 years.

ce·ram·ic *adj.* Of or relating to a brittle material made by firing a nonmetallic mineral, such as clay.

ce·ram·ics *n.* The art of making a ceramic piece.

ce·re·al *n.* An edible grain eaten as a breakfast food; any grain product or crop.

cer·e·mo·ny *n.* A ritual or formal act performed in a certain manner; a public procedure acknowledging or finalizing an official act.

cer·tain *adj.* Very sure; without any doubt; inevitable; not mentioned but assumed; lacking the possibility of alteration. **certainly** *adv.*

cer·tif·i·cate *n.* A document stating the `truth or accuracy of something; a document that certifies fulfillment of duties or requirements, as of a course of study.

chain *n.* A connection of several links; anything that confines or restrains; a combination of linked metal loops, hooks, or other closed forms arranged in a string, giving flexibility without sacrificing strength; any series of events or cause-and-effect occurrences.

chair *n.* A seat with four legs and a back, intended for one person; a seat of office; the person who runs a committee.

chair lift *n.* A chair suspended from cables used to carry people and snow equipment up or down the ski slopes.

chair·per·son *n.* A person of either gender presiding over a committee, board, or other meeting.

chair•wo•man *n.* A female person presiding over a committee, board, or other meeting.

chalk *n.* A soft mineral made from fossil seashells, used for marking on a surface, such as a slate board. **chalky** *adj.*

chalk•board *n.* A blackboard made from slate, for writing with chalk.

chal•lenge *n.* A demand for a contest; a protest; a difficult endeavor that tests one's abilities. *v.* To call into question; to invite to combat or competition. **challenger** *n.*

cham•ber *n.* A bedroom in a large home; a judge's office; a meeting hall for a legislative body; the compartment of a gun that holds a cartridge about to be fired.

cham•pagne *n.* A white sparkling wine.

cham•pi•on *n.* The holder of first place in a contest; one who defends another person. *v.* To extol or encourage, as a cause. **championship** *n.*

chance *n.* The random existence of something happening; a gamble or a risk; a possibility.

chan•de•lier *n.* A light fixture with many branches for lights suspended from the ceiling.

change *v.* To become or make different; to alter; to mutate; to use to take the place of another; to put on a different wardrobe; to reduce a bill into smaller bills or coins. *n.* Coins; money given back when the payment exceeds the bill. **changeable** *adj.*

chan•nel *n.* The deepest part of a stream, river, or harbor; the course that anything moves through or past; a groove. *pl.* The line of communication, bureaucracy, or instruction.

chant *n.* A melody in which all words are sung on the same note. *v.* To celebrate with a song. **chanter** *n.*

cha•os *n.* Total disorder; the absence of purpose or design; the state of the universe before creation. **chaotic** *adj.*

chap *v.* To dry and split open from the cold and wind; to chafe. *n. slang* A fellow; a man. **chapped** *adj.*

chap•el *n.* A place to worship, usually contained in a church; a small place of meditation or devotion.

chap•er•one *n.* An older person who supervises younger people in social or travel settings.

chap•lain *n.* A member of the clergy who conducts religious services for a group.

chap•ter *n.* One of a major division of a book; a branch of a fraternity, religious order, or society.

char•ac•ter *n.* A quality or trait that distinguishes an individual or group; a person portrayed in a play; a distinctive quality or trait; nobility, integrity, or ethical stability.

cha•rades *pl. n.* A game in which the syllables of words are acted out by players.

char•coal *n.* A carbonaceous material resulting from the imperfect combustion of organic matter, such as wood; material used to draw pictures.

charge *v.* To give responsibility; to ask a price; to accuse; to give power to; to replenish, as a battery; to contain an electrical potential; to record a debt owed; to defer payment for a purchase until receipt of a bill. *n.* Management; custody; supervision; an expense or price; an electrical potential.

char•i•ot *n.* An ancient horse-drawn vehicle used to fight battles; a fine or elaborately decorated horse-drawn vehicle. **charioteer** *n.*

char•i•ty *n.* Money or help given to aid the needy; an organization, fund, or institution whose purpose is to aid those in need; the state of loving generosity.

charm *n.* The ability to delight or please; an inherent power bordering on magic; a small ornament with a special meaning, usually worn on a bracelet or around the neck.

chart *n.* A map, graph, or table that gives information in a form easy to read; a nautical register of depths, distances, aids to navigation, and other details of navigable waters. *v.* To generate, draw, or create a chart; to mark one's anticipated passage on a chart; to plan a voyage or effort.

char·ter *n.* An official document that grants certain privileges and rights; the commission, bylaws, and principles of an organization. *v.* To lease or hire a vehicle, especially a boat or aircraft.

chase *v.* To follow quickly; to pursue; to run after.

chat *v.* To converse in a friendly manner; to carry on a dialogue without purpose.

chauf·feur *n.* A person hired to drive an automobile for another person.

cheap *adj.* Inexpensive; low in cost; of poor quality.

cheat *v.* To deprive of by deceit; to break the rules; to violate one's own promise.

check *v.* To control or restrain; to examine for correctness or condition; to review for accuracy. *n.* The act of verifying, comparing, or testing; a bill one receives at a restaurant; a written order on one's bank to pay money from funds on deposit; a move in chess which threatens the immediate capture of the king.

check·book *n.* A book containing blank checks for a checking account.

check·er·board *n.* A game board used to play various games, especially checkers; a pattern arranged like a checkerboard.

check·ers *pl. n.* A board game played by two people on a red-and-black checkered board, in which pieces are moved, jumped, and captured; the pieces of the game.

check·mate *n.* The move in chess which places the opponent's king in a position from which escape is impossible.

check·up *n.* A complete physical wellness examination.

ched·dar *n.* A firm, smooth cheese ranging in flavor from mild to sharp.

cheek *n.* The fleshy part of the face just below the eye and above and to the side of the mouth.

cheer *v.* To give courage to; to instill with courage or hope; to make glad or happy; to shout with encouragement or applause. *n.* Good spirits; happiness.

cheer·ful *adj.* Having or being in good spirits; merry; happy; outwardly positive.

cheer·lead·er *n.* Someone who leads cheers at a sporting event; one who encourages the effort of another.

cheese *n.* A food made from the curd of milk, seasoned and aged.

cheese·cake *n.* A cake made from cream cheese, cottage cheese, eggs, and sugar.

chef *n.* A cook who manages a kitchen or supervises a restaurant's cuisine.

chem·i·cal *adj.* Of or related to chemistry; in the nature of molecular and atomic interaction.

chem·ist *n.* A person trained in the science of chemistry; a pharmacist.

chem·is·try *n.* The scientific study of the composition, structure, and properties of substances and their reactions on the molecular level.

cher·ish *v.* To treat with love; to hold dear; to respond with deep emotion and a sense of ownership or belonging.

cher·ry *n.* A fruit tree bearing a small, round, deep, or purplish red fruit with a small, hard stone; the fruit of that tree.

chess *n.* A game played on a chessboard by two people, each with sixteen pieces of various properties, in which one tries to put the opponent's king in checkmate.

chess·board *n.* A board with sixty-four squares used to play chess or checkers.

chest *n.* The part of the upper body enclosed by the thorax; the ribs; a box for storage, usually having a hinged lid.

chew *v.* To crush or grind with the teeth; to masticate. *n.* The act of chewing.

chick·en *n.* A domestic fowl; the edible meat of a chicken.

chief *n.* The person of highest rank. *adj.* Main, major, most important. **chiefly** *adv.*

chief·tain *n.* The head of a group or tribe.

child *n.* A young person of either sex; an adolescent; a person between infancy and youth. **childish** *adj.*, **children** *pl.*

child a·buse *n.* Sexual or physical maltreatment of a child by a guardian, parent, or other adult.

child·birth *n.* The act of giving birth.

child•hood *n.* The period of being a child.

chil•i *n.* A hot pepper; a sauce made with meat and chili or chili powder; a nonmeat dish of beans, tomatoes, chili powder, onions, and other ingredients.

chill *v.* To be cold, often with shivering; to reduce to a lower temperature. *n.* A feeling of cold. **chilly** *adj.*

chime *n.* A group or set of bells tuned to a scale. *v.* To announce on the hour, by sounding a chime.

chim•ney *n.* A flue for smoke to escape, as from a fireplace.

chim•pan•zee *n.* An anthropoid ape with large ears and dark brown hair, smaller and more intelligent than the gorilla.

chin *n.* The lower part of the face. *v.* To lift oneself up while grasping an overhead bar until the chin is level with the bar.

chip *n.* A small piece that has been broken or cut from another source; a disk used as money in gambling; in computers, an integrated circuit engraved on a silicone substrate.

chip•munk *n.* A burrowing striped rodent of the squirrel family.

chis•el *n.* A tool with a sharp edge used to shape and cut metal, wood, or stone.

chiv•al•ry *n.* The brave and courteous qualities of an ideal knight; any gentlemanly or courteous behavior, especially if protective or attentive of a woman.

chlo•ro•phyll *n.* The green pigment found in deciduous vegetation and plant organisms, necessary to photosynthesis but absent in fall foliage.

choc•o•late *n.* A preparation of ground and roasted cacao nuts, usually sweetened; a candy or beverage made from chocolate.

choice *n.* The act of selection; the opportunity, right, or power to choose; freedom of action; the act of selecting among alternatives. **choose** *v.*

choir *n.* An organized group of singers, usually performing religious or celebratory works in a church.

choose *v.* To select or pick out; to prefer; to make a choice; to decide among alternatives. **chosen, choosy** *adj.*

chop *v.* To cut by making a sharp downward stroke; to cut into small pieces.

cho•ral *adj.* Pertaining to, written for, or sung by a choir or chorus. **chorally** *adv.*

chore *n.* A daily task; any task that becomes burdensome over time.

cho•rus *n.* A group of people who sing together; repeated verses of a song; the singers and dancers in ancient dramas representing the citizens or other collective body.

cho•sen *adj.* Selected or preferred above all; participle of *choose*.

chron•i•cle *n.* A record of events written in the order in which they occurred; a history, especially of a sovereign, dynasty, or significant period of time.

chub•by *adj.* Plump; rounded; full-faced.

chum *n.* A close friend or pal.

church *n.* A building for religious worship, especially a Christian ceremony; a congregation of public Christian worship.

churn *n.* The container in which cream or milk is beaten vigorously to make butter. *v.* To agitate in a churn in order to make butter; to agitate violently.

chute *n.* An inclined passage on or through which water, coal, or other bulk material may travel to a destination by gravity.

ci•der *n.* The juice from apples, fermented or unfermented.

ci•gar *n.* Rolled tobacco leaves used for smoking.

cig•a•rette *n.* A small amount of tobacco rolled in thin paper for smoking, usually sold in packs of twenty.

cin•e•ma *n.* A motion picture; a motion picture theater; the art or business of making a motion picture.

cin•na•mon *n.* The aromatic inner bark of a tropical Asian tree, used as a spice, reddish brown in color.

cir•cle *n.* A process that ends at its starting point; a group of people having a common interest or activity; the definition of all points on a plane equidistant from a

circuit

center point.

cir·cuit *n.* The closed path through which an electric current flows; any prearranged order of passage or distribution; an area of common activity, as theater.

cir·cu·lar *adj.* Moving in a circle or round-like fashion; relating to something in a circle; of a design or direction similar to a circle.

cir·cu·late *v.* To pass from place to place or person to person; to distribute in a wide area; to follow a circuit; to mingle among a group. **circulation** *n.*

cir·cum·fer·ence *n.* The perimeter or boundary of a circle; the arc described by all points equidistant from the center of a circle; the outer boundaries of any area.

cir·cum·stance *n.* A physical event or series of events; a fact or condition to be considered when making a decision.

cir·cus *n.* Entertainment traveling from venue to venue, often under temporary facilities, featuring clowns, acrobats, trained animals, and other acts.

cit·i·zen *n.* A resident of a town or city, especially one entitled to representation or a vote; a native or naturalized person entitled to protection from a government. **citizenship** *n.*

cit·rus *n.* Any of a variety of trees bearing fruit with thick skins, as limes, oranges, lemons, and grapefruits.

cit·y *n.* An urban self-governed permanently located community of residences and businesses, larger than a town but smaller than a metropolis.

civ·ic *adj.* Relating to or of a citizen, city, or citizenship.

civ·il *adj.* Relating to citizens; reasonable and fair in dealings with others.

ci·vil·i·ty *n.* The condition of shared reasonable exchange of freedoms and responsibilities; mutual respect for individuality of choice along with unity of communal values.

civ·i·li·za·tion *n.* A high level of social, cultural, and political development; the human condition after the establishment of laws, history, and generational adhesion.

civ·i·lize *v.* To bring out of a state of savagery into one of education and refinement.

civ·il rights *pl. n.* Rights guaranteed to citizens, specifically the equal rights afforded to all races, creeds, genders, and countries of origin; the rights provided by the 13th and 14th amendments of the United States Constitution.

claim *v.* To ask for one's due; to take into possession as one's own; to hold to be true; to state that something is true.

clam *n.* Any of various marine and fresh-water bivalve mollusks.

clamp *n.* A device for holding or fastening together, especially temporarily.

clan *n.* A large group of people related to one another by a common ancestor; a community into whose membership one must be related by blood or marriage to enter.

clap *v.* To applaud; to strike the hands together with an explosive sound.

clar·i·fy *v.* To become or make clearer; to explain, enlighten, simplify, or restate. **clarification** *n.*

clar·i·net *n.* A woodwind instrument with a single reed.

clar·i·ty *n.* The state or quality of being clear; purity of vision or sound.

clash *v.* To bring or strike together; to collide; to conflict. *n.* A conflict or combat, usually sudden and short-lived.

clasp *n.* A hook to hold parts of objects together; a grasp or grip of the hands. **clasp** *v.*

class *n.* A group or set of units separated from others by specific traits; a group of students who study the same subject in the same room; students who graduate at the same time; quality of behavior; one's inherited social level or position.

clas·sic *adj.* Belonging in a certain category of excellence; having a lasting artistic worth.

clas·si·cal *adj.* Relating to the style of the

ancient Roman or Greek classics; standard and authoritative; not new.

clas•si•fy *v.* To arrange or assign items, people, and the like into the same class or category; to organize by traits or properties. **classification** *n.*

clat•ter *v.* To make or to cause a rattling sound.

clause *n.* A group of words which are part of a simple compound, or complex sentence, containing a subject and predicate; a section, paragraph, or partition in a document treating a specific element of an agreement or contract.

claw *n.* A sharp, curved nail on the foot of an animal; the pincer of certain crustaceans, such as the crab or lobster.

clay *n.* A fine-grained, pliable earth that hardens when fired, used to make pottery, bricks, and tiles.

clean *adj.* Free from impurities, dirt, or contamination; neat in habits.

cleanse *v.* To make pure or clean.

clear *adj.* Free from precipitation and clouds; able to hear, see, or think easily; free from doubt or confusion; free from a burden, obligation, or guilt. *v.* To free one's name or reputation from accusations; to make clear. **clearly** *adv.*, **clearness, clarity** *n.*

clear•ance *n.* The distance that one object clears another by; a permission to proceed.

cleat *n.* A metal projection that provides support, grips, or prevents slipping.

cler•gy *n.* The group of men and women ordained as religious leaders and servants of God.

cler•i•cal *adj.* Trained to handle office duties; relating to office maintenance, record-keeping, and similar tasks.

clerk *n.* A worker in an office who keeps accounts, records, and correspondence up to date; a person who works in the sales department of a store.

clev•er *adj.* Mentally quick; showing dexterity and skill.

cli•ent *n.* A person who secures the professional services of another; in computers, a

program serviced by another program.

cliff *n.* A high, steep edge or face of a rock.

cli•mate *n.* The weather conditions of a certain region generalized or averaged over a period of years; the prevailing atmosphere. **climatic** *adj.*

cli•max *n.* The point of greatest intensity and fullest suspense; the culmination; the dramatic structural peak of a work.

climb *v.* To move to a higher or lower location; to advance in rank or status.

clinch *v.* To secure; to fasten; to settle definitely.

cling *v.* To hold fast to; to grasp or stick; to hold on and resist emotional separation.

clin•ic *n.* A medical establishment connected with a hospital; a center that offers instruction or counseling.

clip *v.* To cut off; to curtail; to cut short. *n.* Something that grips, holds, or clasps articles together; a fast pace or cadence.

cloak *n.* A loose outer garment that conceals or covers.

clock *n.* An instrument that measures time. *v.* To time with a clock, stopwatch, or other timepiece.

clod *n.* A large piece or lump of earth; a stupid, ignorant person.

clone *n.* An identical reproduction grown from a single cell of the original; an exact duplicate or match.

close *adj.* Near, as in time, space, or relationship; nearly even, as in competition; fitting tightly. *v.* To shut; to seal; to complete. *n.* The end or final action of a story, musical composition, or other action.

closed *adj.* Not open; lidded, protected; not available for business; private, secretive, or uncommunicative.

clo•ser *n.* A sales person who finalizes transactions.

clos•et *n.* A small cabinet, compartment, or room for storage. *v.* To meet with in private.

cloth *n.* A knitted, woven, or matted piece of fabric, used to cover a table; the professional clothing of the clergy. **cloths** *pl.*

clothe *v.* To provide clothes; to cover with

clothes; to wrap.

cloud *n.* A visible body of water or ice particles floating in the atmosphere; something that obscures.

clout *n.* A heavy blow with the hand.

clo•ver *n.* A plant with a dense flower and trifoliate leaves, frequented by bees.

clown *n.* A professional comedian who entertains by jokes, tricks, and jest; a circus comedian who dresses in outlandish costumes and heavy makeup. **clownish** *adj.*

club *n.* A heavy wooden stick, used as a weapon; a group of people who have organized themselves with or for a common purpose.

clump *n.* A very thick cluster or group; a dull, heavy sound. *v.* To plant or place in a clump.

clum•sy *adj.* Lacking coordination, grace, or dexterity; not tactful or skillful.

clus•ter *n.* A bunch; a bouquet; a group or gathering, especially spontaneous.

clutch *v.* To seize or attempt to seize and hold tightly. *n.* A tight grasp; a device for connecting and disconnecting the engine and the drive shaft in the automobile or other mechanism.

clut•ter *n.* A confused mass of disorder; a mess; any unorganized collection of miscellaneous items.

coach *n.* A closed carriage; a bus or large passenger vehicle; a trainer or director of athletics, drama, or other skill.

coal *n.* A mineral composed of fossilized organic matter, mainly carbon, widely used as a natural fuel; an ember or burning carbon substance in a fireplace or stove.

coarse *adj.* Lacking in refinement; of inferior or low quality; having large particles.

coast *v.* To move without propelling oneself; to use the force of gravity alone; to slide or glide along. *n.* The land bordering the sea.

coat *n.* An outer garment with sleeves, worn over other clothing; a layer that covers a surface. **coat** *v.*, **coating** *n.*

coax *v.* To persuade by tact, gentleness, or flattery.

co•bra *n.* A venomous snake from Asia or Africa whose neck, when excited, dilates into a broad hood.

cob•web *n.* The fine thread from a spider spun into a web and used to catch prey.

cock *n.* The adult male in the domestic fowl family; the rooster; the hammer of a firearm and the readiness for firing. *v.* To raise in preparation for hitting; to ready a firearm for firing.

cock•pit *n.* The compartment of an airplane containing the pilot, crew, and operating controls and instruments.

cock•roach *n.* A flat-bodied, fast running, chiefly nocturnal, hard-shelled insect.

co•coa *n.* The powder from the roasted husked seed kernels of the cacao plant.

co•coon *n.* The protective fiber or silk pupal case spun by insect larvae.

cod *n.* A large fish of the North Atlantic, important as food.

code *n.* A system of set rules; a set of secret words, numbers, or letters used as a means of communication; in computers, the method of representing information or data by using a set sequence of characters, symbols, or words. **encode, decode** *v.*

cof•fee *n.* A beverage prepared from ground beans of the coffee tree.

cof•fin *n.* A box in which a corpse is buried.

coil *n.* A series of connecting rings; part of an electrical system delivering power to a mechanism. *v.* To wind in spirals; to retract into a striking position.

coin *n.* A flat, rounded piece of metal used as money. *v.* To invent or make a new phrase or word.

co•in•cide *v.* To happen at the same time; to agree exactly; to be congruent in all temporal respects.

co•in•ci•dence *n.* Two events happening at the same time by accident but appearing to have some connection.

cold *adj.* Having a low temperature; feeling uncomfortable; without sufficient warmth; lacking in affection or desire; frigid; without preparation or rehearsal.

n. An infection of the upper respiratory tract resulting in coughing, sneezing, and other symptoms.

cold-blood•ed *adj.* Done without feeling; having a body temperature that varies according to the temperature of the surroundings.

cold boot *n.* In computers, the start-up of operations performed when power is turned on for the first time each day.

cold cuts *pl. n.* A selection of freshly sliced cold meats.

col•lapse *v.* To fall; to give way; to fold and assume a smaller size; to lose all or part of the air in a lung.

col•lar *n.* The upper part of a garment that encircles the neck, often folded over.

col•lect *v.* To gather or assemble; to gather donations or payments. **collectible**, **collection** *n.*

col•lege *n.* An institution of higher education which grants a bachelor's degree; one division of a university.

col•lide *v.* To come together with a direct impact; to clash; to come into conflict.

col•o•ny *n.* A group of emigrants living in a new land away from, but under the control of, the parent country; a group of insects, as ants.

col•or *n.* The aspect of things apart from the shape, size, and solidity; a hue or tint caused by the different degrees of light reflected or emitted by them.

colt *n.* A very young male horse.

col•umn *n.* A decorative or supporting pillar used in construction; a vertical division of typed or printed lines on paper; a regular news or magazine feature, usually by one person.

comb *n.* A toothed instrument made from a material such as plastic used for smoothing and arranging hair or other fibers; the fleshy crest on the head of a fowl. *v.* To search diligently by careful examination.

com•bat *v.* To fight against; to oppose; to contend. *n.* A struggle; a fight or contest especially with armed conflict, as a battle.

com•bi•na•tion *n.* The process of combining or the state of being combined; a series of numbers or letters needed to open certain locks.

com•bine *v.* To unite; to merge. *n.* A farm machine that harvests by cutting, threshing, and cleaning the grain.

com•bus•ti•ble *adj.* Having the capability of burning.

com•bus•tion *n.* A chemical change occurring rapidly and producing heat and light; a burning.

come *v.* To arrive; to approach; to reach a certain position, state, or result; to appear; to come into view.

com•e•dy *n.* A humorous, entertaining performance with a happy ending; a real-life comical situation. **comedian** *n.*

com•et *n.* A celestial body that moves in an orbit around the sun, consisting of a solid head surrounded by a bright cloud with a long, vaporous conical section called a tail, but actually a stream of particles driven away from the sun.

com•fort *v.* To console in time of grief or fear; to make someone feel better; to help.

com•fort•a•ble *adj.* In a state of comfort; financially secure. **comfortably** *adv.*

com•fort•er *n.* A heavy blanket or quilt; someone who comforts.

com•ic *adj.* Characteristic of comedy; lighthearted or laughable; not serious. *n.* A comedian.

com•ma *n.* The punctuation mark used to indicate separation of ideas or a series in a sentence, or to clarify meaning for the reader.

com•mand *v.* To rule; to give orders; to dominate; to act in charge of a force. *n.* In computers, the instruction that specifies an operation to be performed.

com•ment *n.* A statement of criticism, analysis, or observation. **comment** *v.*

com•mer•cial *adj.* Of or relating to a product; supported by advertising; business-like in nature. *n.* An advertisement on radio or television.

com•mit•tee *n.* A group of persons appointed or elected to perform a particular task or function.

com·mon *adj.* Having to do with, belonging to, or used by an entire community or public; usual; ordinary; of the expected variety; vulgar; unrefined.

com·mon de·nom·i·na·tor *n.* A number that can be evenly divided by all the denominators of a set of fractions.

com·mon frac·tion *n.* A fraction with whole numbers in the denominator and numerator.

com·mu·ni·cate *v.* To make known; to cause others to partake or share something; to talk or commune with.

com·mu·ni·ca·tion *n.* The act of transmitting ideas through writing or speech; the means to transmit messages between person or places. *pl.* The profession, specialty, or commercial field of communicating.

com·mun·ion *n.* The mutual sharing of feelings and thoughts; a religious fellowship among members of a church.

com·mu·nism *n.* A system of government in which goods and production are commonly owned.

com·mu·ni·ty *n.* A group of people living in the same area and under the same government; a class or group having common interests and likes.

com·pact *adj.* Packed together or solidly united; firmly and closely united.

com·pan·ion *n.* An associate; a close friend or fellow traveller; a partner in life activities; a person employed to accompany or assist another. **companionship** *n.*

com·pa·ny *n.* The gathering of persons for a social purpose; a number of persons associated for a common purpose, as in business; a business or corporation created and maintained for profit of its owners.

com·pare *v.* To speak of or represent as similar or equal to; to note the similarities or likenesses of. **comparison** *n.*

com·pass *n.* An instrument used to determine geographic direction by magnetic attraction or other means; a device shaped like a V used for drawing circles.

com·pas·sion *n.* Deep, sincere, and long-standing sympathy for someone suffering or distressed in some way; an empathetic relationship.

com·pete *v.* To vie or contend with others; to engage in a contest or competition.

com·pe·tent *adj.* Having sufficient ability; capable; possessing the necessary skills.

com·pe·ti·tion *n.* The act of rivalry or competing; a trial of skill or ability; a contest among teams or individuals.

com·plaint *n.* An expression of pain, dissatisfaction, or resentment; a cause or reason for complaining; a legal registered grievance to be settled by a court of law.

com·plete *adj.* Having all the necessary parts; whole; concluded. *v.* To finish; to make whole; to come to the conclusion of. **completion** *n.*

com·plex *adj.* Consisting of various intricate parts; not simple; containing more than one clause.

com·pli·cate *v.* To make or become involved or complex; to introduce a variation.

com·pli·ment *n.* An expression of praise or admiration; a statement of satisfaction or approval. **complimentary** *adj.*

com·pose *v.* To make up from elements or parts; to produce or create a song; to arrange, as to typeset. **composer** *n.*

com·posed *adj.* Calm; in control of one's emotion or reaction; centered or balanced.

com·pos·ite *adj.* Made up from separate elements or parts; combined or compounded.

com·po·si·tion *n.* The act of putting together artistic, musical, or literary work; a short essay written for school.

com·pro·mise *n.* The process of settling or the settlement of differences between opposing sides, with each side making concessions.

com·put·er *n.* A person who computes; a high-speed electronic machine for performing logical calculations, processes, storage, and retrieval of programmed information.

com·put·er lan·guage *n.* The various codes and information used to give data and instructions to computers.

com·rade *n.* An associate, friend, or companion who shares one's interest or occupation. **comradeship** *n.*

con·ceal *v.* To keep from disclosure, sight, or knowledge; to hide.

con·cen·trate *v.* To give intense thought to; to draw to a common point; to intensify by removing certain elements; to become compact.

con·cen·tra·tion *n.* The state of being concentrated or the act of concentrating; the process or act of giving complete attention to a problem or task; total absorption in a mental or physical activity.

con·cept *n.* A generalized idea formed from particular instances; an abstraction; an opinion. **conceptual** *adj.*

con·cern *n.* Something to consider; sincere interest; something that affects one's business or affairs; an important element in one's attention. *v.* To be interested in; to be involved with. **concerned** *adj.*

con·cert *n.* A musical performance for a group of people; agreement in purpose, action, or feeling.

con·cise *adj.* Short and to the point; brief.

con·clude *v.* To close or bring to an end; to bring about an agreement; to arrive at a decision; to resolve. **conclusion** *n.*

con·crete *adj.* Pertaining to a specific instance or thing; naming a specific class of things; real and measurable; actual; not abstract. *n.* A construction material made from sand, gravel, and cement.

con·demn *v.* To find to be wrong; to show the guilt; to announce judgment upon; to officially declare unfit for use; to rule as damned.

con·dense *v.* To make more concentrated or compact; to change something from a liquid state to a solid state or from a gaseous to a liquid state; to abstract, summarize, or edit for essentials.

con·di·tion *n.* The mode or state of existence of a thing or person; a circumstance found to be necessary to the occurrence of another; a provision in a contract or will that leaves room for modification or changes at a future date; a medical determination of wellness or illness.

con·di·tion *v.* To train or manipulate in preparation for strenuous activity; to soften to a more malleable state, as leather.

con·duct *v.* To lead and direct a performance of a band or orchestra; to guide or show the way; to lead; to transmit heat, electricity, or sound. *n.* Behavior.

cone *n.* A solid body tapered evenly to a point from a base that is circular; a cone-shaped wafer used for holding ice cream.

con·fer·ence *n.* A formal meeting for discussion; a league of churches, schools, or athletic teams.

con·fess *v.* To disclose or admit to a crime, fault, sin, or guilt; to tell a priest or God of one's sins. **confession** *n.*

con·fi·dence *n.* A feeling of self-assurance; trust in the success of an endeavor; a feeling of trust in a person; reliance.

con·flict *n.* A battle; clash; a disagreement of ideas, or interests.

con·front *v.* To put or stand face to face with defiance; to physically, mentally, or verbally address opposition or impediment directly.

con·fuse *v.* To mislead or bewilder; to jumble or mix up. **confusion** *n.*

con·grat·u·late *v.* To acknowledge an achievement with praise; to join others in praise or acknowledgment.

con·grat·u·la·tions *pl. n.* The expression of or the act of congratulating.

con·nect *v.* To join; to unite; to associate, as to relate.

con·nec·tion *n.* An association of one person or thing to another; a link, or bond.

con·quer *v.* To subdue; to win; to overcome by physical or mental force; to replace a government by physical usurpation of power.

con·science *n.* The ability to recognize right and wrong regarding one's own behavior; the internal sense of self-assessment.

con·scious *adj.* Aware of one's own existence and environment; aware of facts or objects; in a state of mental alertness; not comatose.

con·sent *v.* To agree; to allow; to give approval.

con·se·quence *n.* The natural result from a preceding condition or action; the effect.

con·serve *v.* To save something from decay, loss, or depletion; to maintain; to preserve fruits with sugar; to use a perishable or depletable commodity with thrift and care. *n.* A mixture of several fruits cooked together with sugar and sometimes raisins or nuts.

con·si·der *v.* To think about with some care; to examine mentally; to believe or hold as an opinion; to deliberate.

con·sid·er·a·ble *adj.* Large or substantial in amount or extent; important; worthy of consideration.

con·sid·er·a·tion *n.* The taking into account of circumstance before forming an opinion; care and thought; a kind or thoughtful treatment or feeling.

con·sid·er·ing *prep.* In regard to; taking into account.

con·sist *v.* To be made up of.

con·stant *adj.* Faithful; unchanging; steady in action, purpose, and affection; permanently present. *n.* A quantity whose presence or value remains the same throughout an activity. **constancy** *n.*

con·sti·tu·tion *n.* The fundamental laws that govern a nation; structure or composition; health of state or wellness.

con·struct *n.* To create, make, or build.

con·struc·tion *n.* The act of constructing or building something; the product of building with materials; an organized and ordered arrangement of ideas or arguments.

con·struc·tive *adj.* Useful; helpful; building, advancing, or improving; resulting in a positive conclusion; not destructive.

con·sult *v.* To seek advice or information from; to compare views; to use as reference. **consultant, consultation** *n.*

con·sume *v.* To ingest; to eat or drink; to destroy completely; to absorb.

con·sum·er *n.* A person who buys services or goods.

con·tact *n.* The place, spot, or junction where two or more surfaces or objects touch; the connection between two electric conductors. *pl.* Contact lenses; connections in a network of influential persons or offices.

con·tact lens *n.* A thin lens of plastic or glass with an optical prescription, worn directly on the cornea of the eye.

con·tain *v.* To include or enclose; to restrain or hold back.

con·tent *adj.* Satisfied; calm and happy; in agreement with prevailing conditions.

con·tents *pl. n.* Something contained within; the subject matter of a book or document; the proportion of a specified part.

con·test *n.* A competition; strife; conflict; any activity in which participants can earn or win a prize. *v.* To challenge. **contestant** *n.*

con·ti·nent *n.* One of the seven large land masses of the earth: Africa, Asia, Australia, Europe, North America, South America, and Antarctica.

con·tin·ue *v.* To maintain without interruption a course or condition; to resume; to postpone or adjourn.

con·tract *v.* To pull in; to become smaller.

con·tract *n.* A formal agreement among two or more parties to perform the duties as stated.

con·tra·dict *v.* To say against; to express the opposite side or idea; to be inconsistent.

con·trar·y *adj.* Unfavorable; incompatible with another.

con·trast *v.* To note the differences between two or more people or things.

con·trib·ute *v.* To give something to someone; to submit for publication; to offer without pay or compensation.

con·tri·bu·tion n.

con·trol v. To have the authority or ability to regulate, direct, or dominate a situation; to enclose inside rules or parameters; to regulate, steer, or limit.

con·tro·ver·sy n. A dispute, especially of ideas or ideologies, in which both sides are polarized; a debate; a quarrel. **controversial** adj.

con·ven·ience n. The quality of being suitable; something easy to use or made simple to operate.

con·ver·sa·tion n. An informal talk, generally void of argument.

con·vict v. To prove someone guilty; to find for the prosecution in a criminal trial. n. A prisoner.

con·vic·tion n. The act of being convicted; a strong belief.

con·vince v. To cause to believe without doubt; to change another's opinion or point of view.

cook v. To apply heat to food before eating; to prepare food for a meal. n. A person who prepares food.

cook·book n. A book containing directions for preparing and cooking food; a book of recipes.

cook·ie n. A sweet, flat cake; a biscuit; in computers, a customized web site feature sent to a browser.

cool adj. Without warmth; indifferent or unenthusiastic; neither cold nor lukewarm.

co·op·er·ate v. To work together toward a common cause. **cooperation** n.

cop·per n. A metallic element that is a good conductor of electricity and heat, reddish-brown in color.

cop·y v. To reproduce an original; to make a duplicate of; to emulate or imitate. n. A single printed text.

cor·al n. The stony skeleton of a small sea creature, forming large islands under and just above the surface of tropical seas, often used for jewelry.

core n. The innermost or central part of something; the inedible center of a fruit that contains the seeds.

cork n. The elastic bark of the oak tree used for bottle stoppers and craft projects.

corn n. An American-cultivated cereal plant bearing seeds on a large ear or cob; any grain crop; the seed of this plant.

cor·ner n. The point formed when two surfaces or lines meet and form an angle; the location where two streets meet. v. To enclose in a corner; to hold; to gain control of.

cor·ner·stone n. A stone that forms part of the corner of a building's foundation.

cor·po·ra·tion n. A group of merchants united in a trade guild; any group or persons that act as one; an organization limiting its responsibilities to its own assets and not those of the members.

cor·rect v. To make free from fault or mistakes; to change toward rightness; to adjust toward a true course. **correction, correctness** n., **correctly** adv.

cor·re·spond v. To communicate by letter or written words; to be harmonious, equal or similar.

cor·ri·dor n. A long hallway.

cos·met·ic n. A preparation designed to beautify, especially the face.

cos·mo·naut n. A Soviet astronaut.

cost n. The amount paid or charged for a purchase.

cost·ly adj. Expensive; taking a large expenditure of energy or effort; damaging in its results.

cos·tume n. A suit, dress, or set of clothes characteristic of a particular season or occasion; clothes worn by a person playing a part or dressing up in disguise.

cot n. A small, often collapsible bed.

cot·tage n. A small house; a rural dwelling.

cot·ton n. A plant or shrub cultivated for the fiber surrounding its seeds; a fabric created by the weaving of cotton fibers; yarn spun from cotton fibers.

cot·ton can·dy n. Spun sugar, served on a paper cone.

cough v. To suddenly expel air from the

lungs with an explosive noise. *n.* The harsh sound from clearing one's throat or lungs.

could *v.* Past tense of *can.*

count *v.* To name or number so as to find the total number of units involved; to name numbers in order; to take account of in a tally or reckoning; to rely or depend on; to have significance.

coun•ter *n.* A level surface over which transactions are conducted, on which food is served, or on which articles are displayed. *v.* To move or act in a contrary, or opposing direction or wrong way; to balance with an opposing action.

coun•try *n.* A given area or region; the land of one's birth, residence, or citizenship; a state, nation, or its territory.

coun•try mu•sic *n.* Music derived from the folk style of the southern United States, or from the culture of the pioneer, cowboy, and adventurer.

coun•ty *n.* A territorial division for local government within a state.

cou•ple *v.* To join two together; to pair. *n.* A pair.

cou•pon *n.* A statement of interest due, to be removed from a bearer bond and presented for payment when it is payable; a form surrendered to obtain a product, service, or discount.

cour•age *n.* Mental or moral strength to face danger with fear; bravery over an extended period.

course *n.* The act of moving in a path from one point to another; the path over which something moves; a period of time; a series or sequence; a series of studies.

court *n.* The residence of a sovereign or similar dignitary; an assembly for the transaction of judicial business; a place where trials are conducted; an area marked off for game playing.

cour•te•ous *adj.* Marked by respect for and consideration of others; graciously thoughtful and considerate; cognizant of and following the practices of unspoken social etiquette. **courtesy** *n.*

court•house *n.* A building for holding courts of law.

cous•in *n.* A child of one's uncle or aunt; any person whose parent was a sibling to one's own parent; a member of a culturally similar race or nationality; a relative.

cov•er *v.* To place something on or over; to lie over; to spread over; to guard from attack; to hide or conceal; to act as a stand-in during another's absence. *n.* Any object used to protect or cover.

cow *n.* The mature female of cattle or of any bovine; the female of any species when the adult male is referred to as a bull.

cow•ard *n.* One who shows great fear or timidity. **cowardice** *n.*

co•zy *adj.* Comfortable and warm; snug.

crack *v.* To make a loud explosive sound; to break, snap, or split apart; to break open without completely separating; to lose control under pressure (often used with *up*). *n.* A fissure or opening in a long, deep shape; a sharp, witty remark; a weakness caused by decay or age.

cra•dle *n.* A small bed for infants, usually on rockers or rollers; a framework of support, such as that for a telephone receiver.

craft *n.* A special skill or ability; a trade that requires dexterity or artistic skill; an aircraft, boat, or ship.

crash *v.* To break violently or noisily; to damage in landing, usually a vehicle; to collapse suddenly, usually a business; to cause to make a loud noise. *n.* A collision; in computers, the unplanned termination of a computer operation or program; the failure of a computer to respond.

crate *n.* A container, usually made of wooden slats, for protection during shipping or storage.

cra•ter *n.* A bowl-shaped depression at the mouth of a volcano; a depression formed by a meteorite; a hole made by an explosion.

crawl *v.* To move slowly by dragging the body along the ground in a prone position; to move on hands and knees.

cray•on *n.* A stick of white or colored wax, covered with paper and ending in a point, used for writing or drawing.

craze *v.* To make insane or as if insane; to become insane; to develop a fine mesh of narrow cracks. *n.* Something that lasts for a short period of time; a fad.

cra•zy *adj.* Insane; impractical; unusually fond; without sense.

creak *n.* A squeaking or grating noise.

cream *n.* The yellowish, fatty part of milk, containing a great amount of butterfat; something having the consistency of cream; the best part; a pale yellow-white color. **creaminess** *n.*, **creamy** *adj.*

crease *n.* A line or mark made by folding and pressing a pliable substance; a slim space between two guarded areas.

cre•ate *v.* To bring something into existence; to give rise to; to make.

cre•a•tion *n.* The act of creating; something created; the universe.

cre•a•tive *adj.* Marked by the ability to create; inventive; imaginative; artistic. **creativity** *n.*

cre•a•tor *n.* One who creates or has created. *cap.* The Creator; God.

crea•ture *n.* Something created; a living being; a member of the animal kingdom.

cred•it *n.* An amount at a person's disposal in a bank; one's ability to borrow or to buy in advance of payment; recognition by name for a contribution.

creed *n.* A belief; a saying or maxim from which one builds one's behavior; a brief authoritative statement of religious belief.

creek *n.* A narrow stream or brook, navigable only by small craft.

creep *v.* To advance at a slow pace; to go timidly or cautiously; to move on one's knees; to crawl.

cres•cent *n.* The shape of the moon in its first and fourth quarters, defined with a convex and a concave edge; a curved portion of a sphere.

crest *n.* A tuft or comb on the head of a bird or animal; the top line of a mountain or hill; a helmet or crown.

crev•ice *n.* A narrow crack; a long space between hard surfaces.

crew *n.* A group of people who work together in the operation or completion of a project; the whole company belonging to an aircraft or ship.

crime *n.* The commission of an act forbidden by law.

cri•sis *n.* An unstable or uncertain time or state of affairs, the outcome of which will have a major impact; the turning point for better or worse in a disease or fever. **crises** *pl.*

crisp *adj.* Easily broken; brittle; brisk or cold; sharp; clear. *v.* To make or become crisp.

crit•i•cal *adj.* Very important, as a decision; serious, or at the point of most tension.

crit•i•cism *n.* The act of close analysis and examination; discussion of the details of a work or product; severe or negative observation.

crit•i•cize *v.* To be a critic; to find fault with; to judge critically; to blame.

crop *n.* A plant which is grown and harvested for use or for sale.

cro•quet *n.* An outdoor game played by driving wooden balls through hoops by means of long-handled mallets.

cross *n.* A structure consisting of an upright post and a crossbar; a method of execution used especially by the Romans; a symbol of the Christian religion. *v.* To go over; to intersect; in biology, to interbreed a plant or an animal with one of a different kind. *adj.* Discourteous, or short of patience.

crouch *v.* To bend at the knees and lower the body close to the ground.

crowd *n.* A large group of people gathered together. *v.* To assemble in large numbers; to press close; to fill so that elements are touching or pressed together.

crown *n.* A circular ornament or head covering made of precious metal and jewels, worn as the headdress of a sovereign; the highest point; top-most part of the skull.

crude *adj.* Unrefined; lacking refinement

or tact; haphazardly made. *n.* Unrefined petroleum; crude oil. **crudity** *n.*

cruel *adj.* Inflicting suffering; causing pain; intentionally destructive without regard to feelings. **cruelty** *n.*

cruise *v.* To drive or sail about for pleasure; to move about the streets at leisure; to travel at a speed that provides maximum efficiency. *n.* A trip, usually by boat, taken for pleasure at a leisurely pace.

crumb *n.* A small fragment of material, particularly bread or other baked material.

crum•ble *v.* To break into small pieces; to flake off; to lose structural integrity.

crunch *v.* To chew with a crackling noise; to run, walk, or move with a crushing noise; to summarize or condense toward a conclusion or final amount.

crush *v.* To squeeze or force by pressure so as to damage or injure; to reduce to particles by pounding or grinding; to put down or suppress.

crust *n.* The hardened exterior or surface of bread; a hard or brittle surface layer; the outer layer of the earth; the shell of a pie, normally made of pastry. *v.* To cover or become covered with crust; to cake over.

cry *v.* To shed tears; to call out loudly; to utter a characteristic call or sound; to proclaim publicly.

crys•tal *n.* Quartz that is transparent or nearly transparent; a body formed by the solidification of a chemical element; a clear, high-quality glass. **crystalline** *adj.*

cube *n.* A regular solid with six equal squares, having all its angles right angles; a number expressed in the third power; a number multiplied by the square of itself.

cud•dle *v.* To caress fondly and hold close; to snuggle; to hug. **cuddly** *adj.*

cue *n.* A signal given to a technician or operator calling for a specific response; a line or action on stage signalling an actor to perform.

cul•ti•vate *v.* To improve land for planting by fertilizing and plowing; to improve by study; to nourish or improve, as in friendship; to encourage.

cul•ture *n.* The act of developing intellectual ability with education; the cumulative habits, beliefs, and shared experiences of a social, political, or hereditary group; a form of civilization, particularly the beliefs, arts, and customs; in biology, the growth of living material in a prepared nutrient media.

cun•ning *adj.* Crafty; sly; carefully and cleverly planned or thought out.

cup *n.* A small, open container with a handle, used for drinking; a measure of capacity that equals 1/2 pint, 8 ounces, or 16 tablespoons.

curb *n.* Something that restrains or controls; the raised border along the edge of a street. *v.* To restrain or restrict.

cure *n.* Recovery from a sickness; a medical treatment; the process of preserving food with the use of salt, smoke, or aging.

cur•few *n.* An order for people to clear the streets at a certain hour; the hour at which an adolescent has been told to be home.

cu•ri•ous *adj.* Questioning; inquisitive; eager for information; strangely inconsistent in fact or sense.

curl *v.* To twist into curves; to shape like a coil; to play the sport of curling. *n.* A ringlet of hair.

cur•rent *adj.* Belonging or occurring in the present time; in use or valid now; most recent. *n.* Water or air with a steady flow in a definite direction; the flow of electrical power.

cur•sor *n.* In computers, the flashing square, underline, or other indicator on the screen that shows where the next character will be deleted or inserted.

cur•tain *n.* A piece of material that covers a window and can be either drawn to the sides or raised; the drape in front of a proscenium stage concealing the set.

cush•ion *n.* A pillow with a soft filling. *v.* To absorb the shock or effect.

cus•to•di•an *n.* One who has the custody or care of something or someone; one who maintains, cleans, replenishes, and repairs a building; a caretaker; a janitor.

cus•to•dy *n.* The act of guarding; the care and protection of a minor; any ownership or possession.

cus•tom *n.* An accepted practice of a community or people; the usual manner of doing something; habitual way.

cus•to•mer *n.* One who purchases from a buyer; a person with whom a merchant or business person must deal, usually on a regular basis.

cut *v.* To penetrate with a sharp edge, as with a knife; to omit or leave out; to separate from a larger group; to reap or harvest crops in the fields. *n.* A laceration that penetrates the skin; any reduction or separation; a share of the profits.

cute *adj.* Attractive in a delightful way; pretty; mildly pleasing.

cy•ber•space *n.* Theoretical and metaphorical universe of interconnected computers.

cy•cle *n.* A recurring time in which an event occurs repeatedly; a bicycle or motorcycle.

cy•clist *n.* A person who rides a cycle.

cyl•in•der *n.* A long, round body that is either hollow or solid; a barrel or tube shape; a geometric design whose top and bottom are circles. **cylindrical** *adj.*

D

D, d The fourth letter of the English alphabet; the Roman numeral for 500.

dab *v.* To touch quickly with light, short strokes.

dab•ble *v.* To play in a liquid with the hands. **dabbler** *n.*

daf•fo•dil *n.* A bulb plant with solitary yellow flowers.

daft *adj.* Crazy; foolish.

dag•ger *n.* A short pointed hand weapon.

dai•ly *adj.* Happening every day. *n.* A newspaper published every day.

dain•ty *adj.* Delicately beautiful.

dair•y *n.* A place where milk is made and bottled for sale.

dai•sy *n.* Flowers with yellow disks and white rays.

dale *n.* A small valley.

dal•ly *v.* To waste time; to dawdle.

Dal•ma•tian *n.* A large white dog with black spots

dam *n.* A barrier across a river that makes a lake or gives power; an animal mother.

dam•age *n.* An injury to person or property.

damn *v.* To express anger; to swear or curse at.

damp *adj.* Between dry and wet.

dance *v.* To move the body to music.

dan•de•li•on *n.* A common yellow wildflower found on lawns.

dan•druff *n.* Scaly dry skin on the scalp and in the hair.

dan•dy *n.* A fashionable man who dresses well. *adj.* Excellent, very fine.

dan•ger *n.* Something unsafe, causing injury or loss. **dangerous** *adj.*

dan•gle *v.* To hang loosely and swing to and fro.

dank *adj.* Uncomfortably damp; wet and cold.

dap•per *adj.* Stylishly dressed.

dap•pled *adj.* Spotted in color.

dare *v.* To be brave or bold; to challenge a person to show courage.

dark *adj.* Dim; having little or no light. **darken** *v.*

dar•ling *n.* A favorite person; someone very dear.

darn *v.* To mend a hole with stitches in cloth.

dart *n.* A small pointed arrow either shot or thrown.

dash *v.* To move quickly; to rush; to break.

da•ta *pl. n.* The numbers or facts of a study or survey.

da•ta bank *n.* The place where a computer stores information.

date *n.* The day, month, and year; a social appointment.

da•tum *n.* A single piece of information.

daub *v.* To coat or smear with something gooey.

daugh•ter *n.* The female child of a man or woman.

daw•dle *n.* To waste; to take more time than is needed.

dawn *n.* The beginning of a new day; a sunrise.

day *n.* The time between dawn and nightfall; one rotation of the earth upon its axis; twenty-four hours.

day•care *n.* A service giving daytime safekeeping for children.

daze *v.* To stun with a heavy blow or shock.

dead *adj.* Without life; not living.

dead•end *n.* A street having no outlet; the end of a path.

dead•line *n.* A time limit for something to be done.

dead•ly *adj.* Very dangerous; likely to cause death.

deaf *adj.* Totally or partially unable to hear.

deal *v.* To pass out playing cards; to be in business.

dean *n.* The academic head of a college or university.

dear *adj.* Loved; greatly cherished.

death *n.* The end of life; the stopping of all vital functions.

de•bate *v.* To discuss or argue opposite points reasonably.

de•bris *n.* Waste; garbage on the ground or in water.

debt *n.* The money or promise someone owes to someone else.

de•but *n.* A first public appearance of someone or something.

dec•ade *n.* A period of ten years.

de•caf•fein•at•ed *adj.* Having the caffeine removed.

dec•a•gon *n.* A polygon with ten sides and ten angles.

dec•a•gram *n.* A measure of weight equal to 10 grams.

de•cal *n.* A design or picture transferred onto a surface.

de•cant•er *n.* A decorative stoppered bottle for serving wine or other liquids.

de•cay *v.* To rot; to fall apart slowly.

de•ceased *adj.* Dead; not living.

de•ceive *v.* To mislead or trick by falsehood.

De•cem•ber *n..* The twelfth month of the year, having 31 days.

de•cent *adj.* Satisfactory; kind; generous.

de•ci•bel *n.* A measurement of sound.

de•cide *v.* To settle; to make up one's mind. **decision** *n.*

de•cid•u•ous *adj.* Shedding leaves in the fall.

dec•i•mal *n.* A proper fraction based on the number 10 and indicated by the use of a decimal point.

de•c•i•mal point *n.* A period placed to the left of a decimal fraction.

de•ci•pher *v.* To decode; to figure out.

deck *n.* A set of playing cards; the outside floor of a boat.

de•clare *v.* To make known or clear; to state officially. **declaration** *n.*

de•cline *v.* To reject or refuse something politely.

de•code *v.* To turn a coded message into plain language.

de•cor *n.* The decoration of a room, office, or home.

dec•o•rate *v.* To make fancy or pleasing; to add beautiful things.

dec•o•ra•tion *n.* The art of decorating; something that makes a place more pleasing; an emblem, badge, or medal.

de•coy *n.* A make-believe animal used to lure real animals; anything misleading or distracting.

de•crease *v.* To grow less or smaller.

ded•i•cate *v.* To set apart for special use or purpose; to promise to do something. **dedication** *n.*

deed *n.* Something done; a task or act; proof of ownership of property.

deep *adj.* Going far below a surface; low in voice or sound.

deep•freeze *n.* A food freezer for storing frozen foods.

deer *n.* A hoofed mammal with antlers, living in the forests and farmlands. **deer** *pl.*

de•feat *v.* To win a victory; to beat someone in a contest.

de·fend *v.* To protect against attack; to explain a choice. **defense** *n.*

de·fend·ant *n.* The person charged with a crime

de·frost *v.* To thaw out; to remove ice or frost.

de·fy *v.* To resist boldly and openly; to challenge someone; to dare.

de·gree *n.* A unit of cold or heat on a thermometer; a stage or step toward a goal; an academic title for passing all the courses of a special study.

de·lay *v.* To put off until a later time; to make something late.

de·lib·er·ate *adj.* Done on purpose; thought out and careful.

del·i·ca·cy *n.* A special tasty or dainty food.

del·i·cate *adj.* Pleasing in color, taste, or aroma; made finely and carefully; fragile.

del·i·cious *adj.* Extremely pleasant to the taste. *n.* A variety of red, sweet apples.

de·light *n.* A great joy or pleasure. *v.* To give or take great pleasure. **delightful** *adj.*

de·liv·er *v.* To take to another place; to hand over; to assist in the birth of an offspring. **delivery** *n.*

dell *n.* A small secluded valley.

del·uge *n.* A great flood. *v.* To flood with water; to cover over.

de·luxe *adj.* The best quality; filled with luxury.

de·mand *v.* To ask for in a firm tone; to claim as due.

de·mer·it *n.* A fault; a mark against the school record for bad conduct.

de·moc·ra·cy *n.* A form of government by the people or through their elected representatives; rule by the majority. **democrat** *n.*

dem·on·strate *v.* To show how something works; to prove by reasoning or evidence.

den *n.* A wild animal's shelter; a small study room in a home.

de·ni·al *n.* A refusal to grant a request; the act of saying accusations are not true.

den·im *n.* A strong woven cotton used for blue jeans.

de·nom·i·na·tor *n.* The bottom half of a fraction, showing the number of equal parts into which the unit is divided.

dense *adj.* Compact; thick. **density** *n.*

dent *n.* A small hollow fault on a surface, caused by bumping or pressing.

den·tal *adj.* Having to do with the teeth.

den·tist *n.* A person who inspects, cleans, and repairs teeth. **dentistry** *n.*

de·ny *v.* To declare as untrue; to withhold; to refuse to grant.

de·ox·y·ri·bo·nu·cle·ic ac·id *n.* A main message-carrying ingredient of genes, known as DNA.

de·part *v.* To leave; to go away; to start on a trip.

de·part·ment *n.* The division or part of a company, college, or store.

de·part·ment store *n.* A large retail store selling many types of merchandise.

de·pend *v.* To rely on; to trust with responsibilities.

de·pend·a·ble *adj.* Trustworthy; able to be depended upon.

de·pend·ent *n.* A person who depends on another person for financial support.

de·port *v.* To banish or expel someone from a country.

de·port·ment *n.* The way one behaves or acts.

de·pos·it *v.* To put, place, or set something down; to put money in a bank. *n.* A layer or formation of natural substance in the ground.

de·pot *n.* A railroad or bus station.

de·pressed *adj.* Dejected; sad; low in spirits.

de·pres·sion *n.* The state of being or the act of depressing; a dent or hollow in a surface.

depth *n.* The state of being deep; the measurement of distance downward; seriousness or complexity.

dep·u·ty *n.* A person authorized to act for another, especially a police officer helping a sheriff.

de·rail *v.* To run off the rails; to cause a

train to run off the rails.

der•by *n.* An annual horse race open to all; an old-fashioned stiff hat with a round crown.

de•scend *v.* To move from a higher to a lower level; to go down. **descent** *n.*

de•scribe *v.* To tell how something looks or feels; to explain in written or spoken words. **description** *n.*, **descriptive** *adj.*

de•sert *v.* To abandon or leave; to be absent without leave (AWOL) in the armed forces.

des•ert *n.* A dry, barren region of land without adequate water supply.

de•served *adj.* Merited; earned. **deserving** *adj.*

de•sign *v.* To invent or create in the mind; to draw and sketch an idea or outline.

de•sir•a•ble *adj.* Pleasing, attractive, or valuable.

de•sire *v.* To long for; to wish; to crave; to request.

desk *n.* A table with drawers and a top for writing.

de•spair *v.* To lose or give up hope. *n.* A sense of hopelessness.

de•spite *prep.* Nevertheless; in spite of; even though.

des•sert *n.* A serving of sweet foods at the end of a meal.

des•ti•na•tion *n.* The point or place where someone or something is going; the purpose or end for which something is created or intended.

des•ti•ny *n.* The fate or final outcome of an act or person; a course of events whose end is already determined.

de•stroy *v.* To ruin; to tear down; to demolish. **destruction** *n.*, **destructive** *adj.*

de•tail *n.* A small part or item looked at separately and carefully.

de•tec•tive *n.* A person who investigates crimes and discovers evidence.

de•ten•tion *n.* A punishment by holding or stopping; a time of temporary custody while the court decides guilt or innocence.

de•ter•mine *v.* To settle or decide by the facts; to figure out.

de•ter•mined *adj.* Showing or having a fixed purpose; firm and resolute.

de•tour *n.* A road used temporarily instead of a main road; a sidetrack from the goal.

deuce *n.* Two; a playing card with two spots; in tennis, an even score.

de•vel•op *v.* To bring out or expand; to make fancier; to turn exposed film into pictures.

de•vice *n.* Something made and used for a special purpose; a gadget.

dev•il *n.* The spirit of evil, the ruler of Hell; Satan.

dev•il's ad•vo•cate *n.* One who argues a side of a debate just for the sake of argument.

de•vote *v.* To apply time completely to some activity; to concentrate time or energy. **devoted** *adj.*

de•vo•tion *n.* A strong attachment or affection to a person or cause; zeal.

de•vour *v.* To destroy or waste; to eat up greedily; to engulf.

dew *n.* Early morning moisture from the atmosphere in minute drops on cool surfaces.

di•ag•o•nal *adj.* Joining two opposite corners of a polygon *n.* A diagonal or slanting plane or line.

di•a•gram *n.* A sketch or drawing that outlines a plan or process. **diagrammatic, diagrammatical** *adj.*

di•al *n.* Any circular plate or face with measuring marks; the face of a clock, watch, or sundial; a control for selecting a radio or television station. *v.* To make a phone call with a dial telephone.

di•a•logue *n.* A conversation among several persons; a passage of talking in a literary work; the lines said in a play.

di•am•e•ter *n.* A straight line passing through the center of a circle or sphere and stopping at the circumference.

dia•mond *n.* A very hard colorless or white crystalline of carbon used as a gem; something in the shape of a diamond.

dia•mond•back *n.* A large venomous U.S.

rattlesnake.

di•a•per *n.* A folded piece of absorbent material placed between a baby's legs and fastened at the waist.

di•a•ry *n.* A daily record; a journal or day-book, especially one containing one's personal experiences.

dice *pl. n.* Two or more small cubes of wood, bone, or ivory marked with dots.

dic•tion•ar•y *n.* A reference book containing alphabetically arranged words together with their definitions and usages.

did *v.* Past tense of *do*.

die *v.* To expire; to stop living; to cease to exist; to stop working.

di•et *n.* The selection of food and drink one eats regularly.

dif•fer *v.* To disagree; to be different from.

dif•fer•ence *n.* The amount by which a number is less or greater than another.

dif•fer•ent *adj.* Not the same; separate; other; out of the ordinary.

dif•fi•cult *adj.* Hard to do; hard to please.

dif•fi•cul•ty *n.* A hardship or obstruction; something not easy.

dig *v.* To make a hole in the ground; to break up or remove earth with a shovel; to investigate.

dig•it *n.* A toe or finger; the Arabic numerals 0 through 9.

dig•i•tal *adj.* Pertaining to or like the fingers or digits; expressed in digits, especially for computer use.

dig•ni•fied *adj.* Showing dignity; noble.

dig•ni•ty *n.* The quality or state of being excellent, poised, or reserved; nobility.

dike *n.* An embankment of earth to hold and control flood waters; a levee.

dim *adj.* Dull; lacking sharp perception; faint; poorly lit.

dime *n.* A U.S. coin worth one tenth of a dollar.

di•men•sion *n.* A measurement, as length, thickness, or breadth.

dim•mer *n.* A device used to soften or turn down the intensity of an electric light.

dim•ple *n.* A slight depression in the surface of the skin.

din *n.* A loud, confused, harsh noise.

dine *v.* To eat, especially dinner.

din•ner *n.* The chief meal of the day.

di•no•saur *n.* Any extinct reptile from prehistoric times, some of which were the largest animals in existence.

dip *v.* To put down into a liquid for a moment.

dip•per *n.* A long-handled cup container for ladling liquids.

di•rect *v.* To command or order; to supervise or instruct the performance of a job. **director** *n.*

di•rec•tion *n.* An instruction, order or command; the path or line along which something points.

dirt *n.* Soil or earth; broken ore or rock; washed-down earth.

dirt•y *adj.* Not clean; grimy; indecent; obscene.

dis•a•ble *v.* To make powerless; to stop from working.

dis•ad•van•tage *n.* An unfavorable condition; a handicap.

dis•a•gree *v.* To vary in opinion; to differ; to argue.

dis•a•gree•a•ble *adj.* Offensive or unpleasant.

dis•ap•pear *v.* To vanish; to drop from sight.

dis•ap•point *v.* To fail to satisfy; to let down.

dis•as•ter *n.* A catastrophe or great ruin.

dis•count *n.* A special price lower than the normal one; a deduction or bargain.

dis•cour•age *v.* To take enthusiasm away; to advise against.

dis•cov•er *v.* To make known or visible; to find for the first time.

dis•cuss *v.* To hold a conversation; to talk; to exchange ideas about. **discussion** *n.*

dis•ease *n.* An illness; a sickness, often spread from one person to another; a group of symptoms with its own name.

dis•grace *n.* Loss of grace, favor, or respect. *v.* To bring shame to; to humiliate.

dis•guise *v.* To change appearance to

hide; to conceal the actual existence or character of. *n.* Clothes or make-up that hides the identity.

dis•gust *v.* To cause ill feeling or even sickness; to repel from ugliness.

dish *n.* A vessel for serving food; one part of a multi-course meal; any flat curved object shaped like a plate.

dis•hon•est *adj.* Lacking honesty; coming from falseness.

dish•wash•er *n.* A person or a machine for washing dishes.

disk *n.* A thin, flat, circular object; a round, flat plate coated with a magnetic substance for storing data.

dis•like *v.* To regard with disapproval; to feel badly toward.

dis•loy•al *adj.* Not loyal; untrue to obligations or duty.

dis•mal *adj.* Gloomy; depressing; low in merit.

dis•miss *v.* To allow to leave; to take off the list; to remove from position.

dis•o•bey *v.* To refuse or fail to follow commands; to be disobedient.

dis•or•der *n.* Lack of good order; messiness; chaos; an ailment.

dis•play *v.* To show or put on exhibit; to give a demonstration of; to show off. *n.* The part of a computer or other device that shows data visually on a screen.

dis•sat•is•fy *v.* To fail to satisfy; to disappoint.

dis•sect *v.* To cut into pieces for examination; to expose; to analyze in detail. **dis•section** *n.*

dis•solve *v.* To pass into solution; to absorb solid particles into a liquid; to lose structure.

dis•tance *n.* Separation in time or space; the measure between two points; a large amount of space between. **distant** *adj.*

dis•till *v.* To condense by boiling or other means; to give off in drops. **distillery** *n.*

dis•tinct *adj.* Separate from all others; clearly seen; different.

dis•tin•guish *v.* To recognize as being different; to make important the differences between two things.

dis•tin•guished *adj.* Set apart; honored; worthy of praise.

dis•tort *v.* To twist or bend out of shape; to warp the true meaning of.

dis•tress *v.* To cause suffering of mind or body; to upset or make tense. *n.* Pain or suffering; severe physical or mental strain.

dis•trib•ute *v.* To divide among many; to deliver or give out to many.

dis•trict *n.* A section of a territory; a distinctive area.

dis•turb *v.* To destroy the balance or rest; to unsettle; to bother.

ditch *n.* A trench in the earth; an excavation for pipes or lines. *v.* To discard.

dit•to *n.* An exact copy; the same as stated before.

dive *v.* To plunge into water headfirst; to plunge downward at a sharp angle. **diver** *n.*

di•vide *v.* To separate into halves or portions and give out in shares; to cause to be apart; to do mathematical division on a number. **division** *n.*

di•vine *adj.* Of or pertaining to God.

di•vi•sor *n.* The number by which a dividend is to be divided.

di•vorce *n.* The legal breaking up of a marriage; the complete separation of things.

diz•zy *adj.* Whirling until balance is lost; confused; giddy.

do *v.* To bring to pass; to bring about; to perform or execute; to put forth; to exert; to bring to an end.

dock *n.* A pier or parking place for ships or boats; a loading area for trucks or trains.

dock•yard *n.* A shipyard; a place where ships are repaired or built.

doc•tor *n.* A person who practices medicine, such as a physician, surgeon, dentist, or veterinarian; a person holding the highest degree offered by a university.

doc•trine *n.* A body of principles; a statement of beliefs.

doc•u•ment *n.* An official paper or written record.

dodge *v.* To avoid by moving suddenly; to

shift suddenly.

do•do *n.* An extinct flightless bird.

doe *n.* A mature female deer, hare, or kangaroo.

dog *n.* A domesticated member of the wolf family; a canine.

dog pad•dle *n.* A beginner's swimming stroke.

doll *n.* A child's toy having a human form.

dol•lar *n.* A unit of money in the U.S. and elsewhere; one hundred cents.

dol•ly *n.* A child's word for a doll

dol•phin *n.* Any of various intelligent marine animals with the snout in the shape of a beak.

do•main *n.* In computers, electronic messages sent to specific network addresses.

dome *n.* A roof resembling a hemisphere.

do•mes•tic *adj.* Relating to the home, household, or family life.

dom•i•nant *adj.* Having the most control or influence; strongest.

dom•i•nate *v.* To rule or control; to stand above.

dom•i•no *n.* A small rectangular block of wood or plastic with the face marked with dots. **dominoes** *pl.* A game containing 28 of such pieces.

done *adj.* Completely finished or through; cooked adequately.

don•key *n.* The domesticated beast of burden.

do•nor *n.* One who gives or contributes.

doo•dle *v.* To scribble, design, or sketch aimlessly.

doom *n.* To condemn to a severe penalty or death.

door *n.* A swinging or sliding panel, by which an entry is closed and opened; a means of entrance or exit.

dose *n.* The measured amount of a substance.

dot *n.* A small round spot; a period used in punctuation.

dou•ble *adj.* Twice as much; composed of two like parts; designed for two.

doubt *v.* To be uncertain about something; to distrust.

dough *n.* A soft mixture of flour, liquids, and other ingredients baked to make bread, pastry, and other foods.

dough•nut or **do•nut** *n.* A small cake with a hole in the middle, made of rich, light, deep-fried dough.

dove *n.* Any of numerous pigeons; a gentle, innocent person.

dow•el *n.* A round wooden pin which fits tightly into a hole to fasten together the two pieces.

down *adv.* Toward a lower position or condition; the direction that is opposite of up.

doz•en *n.* Twelve of a kind; a set of twelve things.

drab *adj.* Light, dull brown or olive brown color; commonplace or dull.

draft *n.* A current of air; a sketch or plan of something to be made.

drag *v.* To pull along or haul by force; to move with painful or undue slowness; to bring by force.

drag•on *n.* A mythical, giant, serpentlike, winged, fire-breathing monster.

drain *v.* To draw off liquid gradually; to use up; to exhaust.

drake *n.* A male duck.

dra•ma *n.* An imitation of an action without narrator, acted on the stage or composed in a story.

drank *v.* Past tense of *drink.*

drape *v.* To cover or adorn with something; to arrange or hang in loose folds. *n.* A heavy cloth curtain for windows.

draw *v.* To move toward a direction; to lead; to sketch.

draw•bridge *n.* A bridge that can be raised or lowered to allow ships and boats to pass.

draw•er *n.* One that draws pictures; a sliding box or receptacle in furniture.

draw•ing *n.* The art of representing something or someone by means of lines.

dread *v.* To fear greatly; to imagine with alarm or worry. **dreadful** *adj.*

dream *n.* Thoughts, images, or emotions occurring during sleep; something that is strongly desired; something that fully satisfies a desire.

drea•ry *adj.* Bleak and gloomy; dull.

drench *v.* To wet thoroughly.

dress *n.* An outer garment for women and girls. *v.* To put clothes on.

drew *v.* Past tense of *draw*.

drib•ble *v.* To drip; to slobber or drool; to bounce a ball repeatedly.

drift *v.* To be carried along by currents of air or water; to move aimlessly; to float. *n.* A hill or dune of blown snow or sand.

drill *n.* A tool used in boring holes; the act of training soldiers in marching and the use of weapons. *v.* To make a hole by boring with a hard sharp point.

drink *v.* To take liquid into the mouth and swallow.

drip *v.* To fall in drops. *n.* Liquid which falls in drops; the sound made by falling drops.

drive *v.* To push, or press onward; to operate a vehicle; to supply a moving force.

drive-in *n.* A place of business where customers stay in their vehicles to be served.

driz•zle *n.* A fine, quiet, gentle rain.

drom•e•dar•y *n.* A one-humped camel.

drool *v.* To dribble from the mouth.

droop *v.* To hang or bend downward; to lose stiffness.

drop *n.* A tiny, pear-shaped or rounded mass of liquid; a small quantity of a substance; the smallest unit of liquid measure. *v.* To fall or let go of an object in air.

drove *n.* A herd being driven in a body; a crowd. *v.* Past tense of *drive*.

drown *v.* To kill or die by suffocating in a liquid; to cause not to be heard by making a loud noise.

drows•y *adj.* Sleepy.

drug *n.* A substance used to treat a disease or illness; a narcotic.

drum *n.* A musical instrument made of a hollow frame with a cover stretched across one or both ends, played by beating or pounding.

drunk *adj.* Intoxicated with alcohol.

drunk•ard *adj.* A person who is intoxicated by liquor.

dry *adj.* Free from moisture or liquid; having little or no rain.

dry•ad *n.* A wood nymph.

du•al *adj.* Made up or composed of two parts; having a double purpose.

duck *n.* Any of various swimming birds with short necks and legs. *v.* To lower the head and body quickly; to plunge quickly under water.

due *adj.* Owed; payable; owed or owing as a right.

du•et *n.* A musical piece for two performers or musical instruments.

dull *adj.* Not sharp; stupid; lacking in intelligence or understanding; boring or not exciting.

dumb *adj.* Unable to speak; temporarily speechless.

dum•my *n.* A human shaped imitation or copy, used as a substitute.

dump•ling *n.* A small mass of dough cooked in soup or stew; sweetened dough wrapped around fruit and baked.

dunce *n.* A slow-witted person; a person not prepared for lessons.

dune *n.* A ridge or hill of sand blown or drifted by the wind.

dun•ga•rees *pl. n.* Trousers made of sturdy, coarse, cotton fabric.

dun•geon *n.* A dark, confining, underground prison chamber.

dunk *v.* To dip a piece of food into liquid before eating; to submerge someone in a playful fashion.

du•o *n.* An instrument duet; two people in close association.

du•pli•cate *adj.* Identical with another; existing in or consisting of two corresponding parts; a copy.

du•ra•ble *adj.* Able to continue for a prolonged period of time without damage; physically strong; able to last.

dur•ing *prep.* While; throughout the time of; within the time of.

dusk *n.* The earliest part of the evening, just before darkness.

dust *n.* Fine, dry particles of matter. *v.* To remove fine particles from a surface with a cloth.

du•ty *n.* Something a person must or ought to do; an obligation.

dwarf *n.* A human, plant, or animal of a much smaller than normal size.

dwell *v.* To live, as an inhabitant.

dwell•ing *n.* A house or building where one lives.

dy•na•mite *n.* An explosive composed of nitroglycerin and other materials, usually packaged in stick form. *v.* To blow up with dynamite.

E

E, e The fifth letter of the English alphabet; in music, the third tone in the natural scale of C.

each *adj.* Every one of two or more considered separately. *adv.* Apiece.

ea•ger *adj.* Enthusiastic or anxious; having a great desire or wanting something.

ea•gle *n.* A large bird of prey having a powerful bill, broad strong wings, and soaring flight.

ear *n.* The hearing organ in vertebrates, located on either side of the head; the ability to hear keenly.

earl *n.* A British title for a nobleman ranking above a viscount and below a marquis. **earldom** *n.*

ear•ly *adj.* Occurring near the beginning of a period of time; before the usual or expected time; occurring in the near future.

ear•ly bird *n.* An early riser; a person who arrives early.

earn *v.* To receive payment in return for work done or services rendered; to gain as a result of one's efforts.

ear•nest *adj.* Serious; sincere; without trickery or guile;

earn•ings *pl. n.* Something earned, such as a salary.

earth *n.* The third planet from the sun and the planet on which there is life; the outer layer of the world; ground; soil; dirt.

ease *n.* A state of being comfortable; relaxation; freedom from pain, discomfort, or care.

ea•sel *n.* A frame used by artists to support a canvas or picture.

east *n.* The direction opposite of west; the direction in which the sun rises.

eas•y *adj.* Done with little difficulty; free from worry or pain; simple.

eas•y•go•ing *adj.* Taking life easy; without worry, concern, or haste.

eat *v.* To chew and swallow food; to take a meal.

eaves *pl. n.* The overhanging edge of a roof.

ebb *n.* The return of the tide towards the sea; a time of decline. *v.* To recede, as the tide does; to fall or flow back; to weaken.

ebb tide *n.* The tide while at ebb; a period of decline.

eb•o•ny *n.* The dark, hard, colored wood from the center of the ebony tree of Asia and Africa. *adj.* Resembling ebony; black.

ech•o *n.* Repetition of a sound by reflecting sound waves from a surface; the sound produced by reflection; a repetition. *v.* To repeat or be repeated by; to imitate. **echoes** *pl.*

ec•lec•tic *adj.* Having components from many different sources or styles.

e•clipse *n.* A total or partial blocking of one celestial body by another. *v.* To fall into obscurity or decline; to cause an eclipse of.

e•col•o•gy *n.* The branch of science concerned with how organisms relate to their environments. **ecologist** *n.*

ec•o•nom•i•cal *adj.* Not wasteful; frugal; operating with little waste.

ec•o•nom•ics *n.* The science relating to the development, production, and management of material wealth, and which treats production, distribution, and consumption of commodities.

e•con•o•mize *v.* To manage thriftily; to use sparingly.

e•con•o•my *n.* Careful management of

money, materials, and resources; a reduction in expenses.

ec•ru *n.* A light yellowish brown, as the color of unbleached linen.

ec•sta•sy *n.* The state of intense joy or delight. **ecstatic** *adj.*, **ecstatically** *adv.*

ec•ze•ma *n.* A noncontagious inflammatory skin condition, marked by itching and scaly patches. **eczematous** *adj.*

ed•dy *n.* A current, as of water, running against the direction of the main current, especially in a circular motion.

edge *n.* The thin, sharp, cutting side of a blade; keenness; sharpness.

ed•i•ble *adj.* Safe or fit to eat.

e•dict *n.* A public decree; an order or command officially proclaimed.

ed•i•fy *v.* To benefit and enlighten, morally or spiritually. **edification** *n.*

ed•it *v.* To prepare and correct for publication; to put together for an edition; to delete or change. **editor** *n.*

e•di•tion *n.* The form in which a book is published; the total number of copies printed at one time.

ed•i•to•ri•al *n.* An article in a newspaper or magazine which expresses the opinion of a publisher or editor.

ed•u•cate *v.* To supply with training or schooling; to supervise the mental or moral growth of. **educator** *n.*

eel *n.* A snake-like marine or freshwater fish without scales or pelvic fins.

ee•rie or **ee•ry** *adj.* Suggesting the unexplainable or strange; spooky. **eerily** *adv.*, **eeriness** *n.*

ef•face *v.* To remove or rub out; to make unnoticeable

ef•fect *n.* Something produced by a cause; the power to produce a desired result.

ef•fec•tive *adj.* Producing an expected effect or proper result.

ef•fi•cient *adj.* Adequate in performance with a minimum of waste or effort.

ef•fi•gy *n.* A life-size sculpture or painting representing a crude image or dummy, especially of a disliked person.

ef•fort *n.* Voluntary exertion of physical or mental energy; a normally earnest attempt or achievement.

egg *n.* The hard-shelled reproductive cell of female animals, especially one produced by a chicken, used as food.

egg•head *n.* An intellectual; highbrow.

egg•nog *n.* A drink of beaten eggs, sugar, and milk, often mixed with alcohol.

egg•roll *n.* A thin egg-dough fried casing filled with minced vegetables and sometimes meat or seafood.

e•go *n.* The self-thinking, feeling, and acting distinct from the external world; the consciousness of self.

e•go•cen•tric *adj.* Self-centered; thinking, observing, and regarding oneself as the object of all experiences.

e•go•ma•ni•a *n.* Self-obsession. **egomaniac** *n.*, **egomaniacal** *adj.*

e•gret *n.* Any of several species of white wading birds having long plumes.

eight *n.* The cardinal number which follows seven.

ei•ther *pron.* One or the other. *adj.* One or the other of two. *adv.* Likewise; also. *conj.* Used before the first of two or more alternatives linked by *or.*

e•ject *v.* To throw out; to expel.

e•lab•o•rate *adj.* Planned or carried out with great detail; very complex; intricate. *v.* To give more detail.

e•lapse *v.* To slip or glide away; to pass in time.

e•las•tic *adj.* Flexible; capable of easy adjustment. **elasticity** *n.*

e•late *v.* To fill with joy; to become exuberant; to make proud of.

el•bow *n.* The outer joint of the arm between the upper arm and forearm; a sharp turn, as in a river or road, which resembles an elbow.

el•bow•room *n.* Ample room to move about; enough space for comfort.

eld•er *adj.* Older. *n.* One who is older than others; a person of great influence; an official of the church; a shrub bearing reddish fruit.

e•lect *v.* To choose or select by vote, as for

an office; to make a choice.

e•lec•tric *adj.* Relating to electricity.

e•lec•tri•cian *n.* A person who installs or maintains electric equipment.

e•lec•tric•i•ty *n.* An interchange of charged particles on the atomic level; a force that causes bodies to attract or repel each other, responsible for a natural phenomena as lightning; electric current as a power source; emotional excitement.

e•lec•tro•cute *v.* To kill or execute by the use of electric current.

e•lec•trode *n.* A conductor by which an electric current enters or leaves.

e•lec•tro•mag•net *n.* A magnet consisting of a soft iron core magnetized by electric current passing through a wire which is coiled around the core.

e•lec•tron *n.* A subatomic particle with a negative electric charge found outside of an atom's nucleus.

e•lec•tro•stat•ic *adj.* Pertaining to static electric charges.

el•e•gance *n.* Refinement in appearance, movement, or manners.

el•e•gy *n.* A poem expressing sorrow for one who is dead.

el•e•ment *n.* A basic part of a construction; a substance not separable into less complex substances by chemical means. *pl.* The conditions of the weather; natural forces.

el•e•men•ta•ry *adj.* Fundamental, essential; referring to elementary school.

el•e•phant *n.* A large mammal with thick grey hide, a long flexible trunk, and curved tusks.

el•e•vate *v.* To lift up or raise; to promote to a higher rank.

e•lev•en *n.* A cardinal number with a sum equal to ten plus one.

elf *n.* An imaginary being with magical powers, often mischievous; a small, mischievous child. **elves** *pl.*, **elfish** *adj.*

e•lic•it *v.* To bring or draw out; to evoke.

e•lim•i•nate *v.* To get rid of, remove; to omit.

e•lite *n.* The most skilled members of a group; a small, powerful group.

elk *n.* The largest deer of Europe and Asia.

ell *n.* An extension of a building at right angles to the main structure.

el•lipse *n.* A closed curve, somewhat oval in shape, with two focal points. **elliptic**, **elliptical** *adj.*

elm *n.* Any of various valuable timber and shade trees with arching branches.

e•lope *v.* To run away, especially in order to get married, usually without parental permission. **elopement** *n.*

el•o•quent *adj.* Having the power to speak fluently and persuasively; vividly expressive.

else *adj.* Different; other; more; additional. *adv.* In addition; besides.

else•where *adv.* To or in another place.

e•lude *v.* To evade or avoid; to escape understanding.

e-mail or **e•mail** *n.* In computers, electronic messages sent to specific network addresses.

e•man•ci•pate *v.* To liberate; to set free from bondage.

em•balm *v.* To treat with preservatives in order to protect from decay.

em•bank•ment *n.* A support or defense made of a bank of earth or stone.

em•bar•go *n.* A prohibition or restraint on trade, as a government order forbidding the entry or departure of merchant vessels.

em•bark *v.* To board a ship; to set out on a venture.

em•bar•rass *v.* To cause to feel self-conscious; to make one feel confusion or inadequacy.

em•bas•sy *n.* The headquarters of an ambassador; the center of representation of a government on foreign soil.

em•bel•lish *v.* To adorn or make beautiful with ornamentation; to decorate; to add to the details of.

em•ber *n.* A small piece of glowing coal or wood, as in a dying fire. *pl.* The smoldering ashes or remains of a fire.

em•bez•zle *v.* To take money or other items fraudulently and secretly.

em·blem *n.* A symbol of something; a distinctive design.

em·bo·dy *v.* To give a bodily form to; to personify. **embodiment** *n.*

em·boss *v.* To shape or decorate in relief; to represent in relief.

em·brace *v.* To clasp or hold in the arms; to hug; to surround.

em·broi·der *v.* To decorate with ornamental needlework; to add fictitious details to.

em·broil *v.* To involve in contention or violent actions; to throw into confusion.

em·bry·o *n.* An organism in its early developmental stage, before it has a distinctive form. **embryonic** *adj.*

em·er·ald *n.* A bright-green, transparent gemstone variety of beryl.

e·merge *v.* To rise into view; to come into existence.

e·mer·gen·cy *n.* A sudden and unexpected situation requiring prompt action.

em·i·grate *v.* To move from one country or region to settle elsewhere. **emigrant** *n.*

em·i·nent *adj.* High in esteem, rank, or office.

em·i·nent do·main *n.* The claim of a government's right to take or control property for public use.

em·is·sar·y *n.* A person sent out on a mission; an ambassador.

e·mit *v.* To send forth; to throw or give out.

e·mote *v.* To show emotion, as in acting; to express one's feelings.

e·mot·i·con *n.* In computers, a combination of keyboard symbols representing caricatures of human emotions such as happiness, skepticism, and surprise.

e·mo·tion *n.* A strong surge of feeling; any of the feelings of fear, sorrow, joy, hate, or love.

em·pa·thy *n.* Identification with and understanding the feelings of another person. **empathetic, empathic** *adj.*

em·per·or *n.* The ruler of an empire made of many countries.

em·pha·sis *n.* Special attention, significance or importance attached to anything. **emphatic** *adj.*

em·pire *n.* Several territories or nations governed by a single supreme authority, the emperor.

em·ploy *v.* To engage the service or use of; to hire; to use.

em·ploy·ee or **em·ploy·e** *n.* A person who works for another in return for salary or wages.

em·po·ri·um *n.* A large store carrying general merchandise; a department store.

em·pow·er *v.* To authorize; to give power to; to license.

em·press *n.* A woman who rules an empire; an emperor's wife or widow.

emp·ty *adj.* Containing nothing; vacant; lacking substance. **emptiness** *n.*

e·mu *n.* A swift-running flightless Australian bird related to the ostrich.

em·u·late *v.* To strive to equal by imitating; to admire and follow as a role model.

en·a·ble *v.* To give the power or ability to; to supply with adequate power, knowledge, or opportunity.

en·act *v.* To make into law; to carry out a plan.

e·nam·el *n.* A decorative or protective coating on a surface, as of pottery; a paint that dries to a hard, glossy surface; the hard outermost covering of a tooth.

en·chain *v.* To put in chains; to enslave.

en·chant *v.* To put under a spell; to bewitch; to charm; to delight greatly.

en·cir·cle *v.* To form a circle around; to move around.

en·close *v.* To surround on all sides; to put in the same envelope or package with something else. **enclosure** *n.*

en·core *n.* An audience's demand for a repeat performance; a performance in response to an encore. *v.* To call for an encore.

en·coun·ter *n.* A meeting or conflict. *v.* To come upon unexpectedly; to confront in a hostile situation.

en·cour·age *v.* To inspire with courage or

hope. **encouragingly** *adv.*

en•croach *v.* To intrude upon the rights or possessions of another; to step over onto another's property

en•crust *v.* To cover with a crust; to crust. **encrustation** *n.*

en•cryp•tion *n.* In computers, the process of encoding electronic information for privacy and security during transfer.

en•cum•ber *v.* To hinder or burden with difficulties or obligations. **encumbrance** *n.*

en•cy•clo•pe•di•a *n.* A comprehensive work with articles covering a broad range of subjects. **encyclopedic** *adj.*

end *n.* A part lying at a boundary; the terminal point.

en•dan•ger *v.* To expose or put into danger or imperil.

en•dan•gered *adj.* Threatened with extinction; in danger.

en•dear *v.* To make beloved or dear. **endearment** *n.*

en•deav•or *n.* A valiant try; a sincere attempt to attain or do something.

en•dorse *v.* To support or recommend; to sign the back of a check.

en•dure *v.* To undergo; to put up with; to bear.

end•wise *adv.* On end; lengthwise.

en•e•my *n.* One who seeks to inflict injury on another; a foe; a hostile force or power.

en•er•gy *n.* Power for working or acting; vigor; strength; vitality.

en•fold *v.* To enclose; to wrap in layers; to embrace.

en•force *v.* To carry out the rules; to demand obedience.

en•gage *v.* To employ or hire; to hook together parts of a machine; to pledge oneself to marry.

en•gine *n.* A machine that converts energy into mechanical motion; a mechanical instrument; a locomotive.

Eng•lish *adj.* Relating to England, its people, language, and customs. *n.* The language of Great Britain, the United States, and many other countries.

en•grave *v.* To carve or etch into a surface, such as stone, metal, or wood for printing; to print from plates made by such a process. **engraving** *n.*

en•hance *v.* To make greater; to raise to a higher degree.

e•nig•ma *n.* Something that baffles; anything puzzling; a riddle.

en•joy *v.* To feel joy or find pleasure in something.

en•large *v.* To make larger; to speak or write in greater detail.

en•light•en *v.* To give broadening or revealing knowledge; to give spiritual guidance or light to.

en•list *v.* To secure the help or active aid of; to sign up for the armed forces.

en•liv•en *v.* To make livelier or more or vigorous.

e•nor•mous *adj.* Very great in size or degree; huge. **enormously** *adv.*, **enormousness, enormity** *n.*

e•nough *adj.* Adequate to satisfy demands or needs. *adv.* To a satisfactory degree.

en•rage *v.* To put or throw into a rage; to make very angry.

en•rap•ture *v.* To enter into a state of rapture; to delight.

en•rich *v.* To make rich or richer; to make more productive.

en•roll or **en•rol** *v.* To sign up for; to enter one's name on a roll or register.

en•sem•ble *n.* A group of parts in harmony; a coordinated outfit of clothing; a group performing music together.

en•shrine *v.* To place in a shrine; to hold sacred.

en•slave *v.* To make a slave of; to put in bondage.

en•snare *v.* To catch; to trap in a snare.

en•sue *v.* To follow as a consequence; to occur afterwards.

en•sure *v.* To make certain of; to guarantee.

en•tan•gle *v.* To tangle; to make more complex.

en•ter *v.* To go or come into; to penetrate; to begin.

enterprise

en·ter·prise *n.* A large or risky undertaking; a business organization; boldness and energy in practical affairs.

en·ter·tain *v.* To receive as a guest; to amuse; to consider as a possibility. **entertainer, entertainment** *n.*

en·thrall *v.* To fascinate; to captivate.

en·throne *v.* To place on a throne; to crown as leader.

en·thu·si·asm *n.* Intense feeling for a cause; eagerness.

en·tice *v.* To attract by arousing desire; to coax or convince.

en·tire *adj.* Having no part left out; whole; complete.

en·ti·tle *v.* To give a name to; to furnish with a right.

en·ti·tle·ment *n.* The right by birth and equality; one's automatic consideration and due.

en·ti·ty *n.* The fact of real existence; something that exists alone.

en·to·mol·o·gy *n.* The study of insects.

en·trance *n.* The act of entering; the means or place of entry; the first appearance of an actor in a play.

en·trance *v.* To fascinate; to put in a trance. **entrancing** *adj.*

en·trap *v.* To catch in a trap. **entrapment** *n.*

en·treat *v.* To make an earnest request; to beg for favor or permission.

en·trust *v.* To transfer to another for care; to share with.

en·try *n.* An opening or place for entering; an item entered in a book list.

e·nu·mer·ate *v.* To count off one by one; to number

e·nun·ci·ate *v.* To pronounce with clarity; to announce; proclaim.

en·ve·lope *n.* Something that covers or encloses; a paper case, especially for a letter, having a flap for sealing.

en·vi·a·ble *adj.* Highly desirable; able to be envied.

en·vi·ron·ment *n.* Surroundings; the combination of external conditions affecting the development and existence of an individual group or organism.

en·vi·ron·men·tal·ist *n.* A person who seeks to preserve the natural environment.

en·voy *n.* A messenger or agent; an ambassador.

en·vy *n.* A feeling of discontent or resentment for someone else's possessions or advantages.

e·on *n.* An indefinite but very long period of time.

ep·ic *n.* A long narrative poem or story celebrating the adventures and achievements of a hero.

ep·i·dem·ic *adj.* Breaking out suddenly and affecting many individuals at the same time. *n.* A fast-moving contagious disease.

ep·i·sode *n.* A section of a novel or drama complete in itself; an occurrence; an incident.

ep·och *n.* A point in time marking the beginning of a new era.

ep·ox·y *n.* A durable, corrosion-resistant resin used especially in surface glues and coatings.

e·qual *adj.* Of the same measurement, quantity, or value as another; having the same privileges or rights.

e·qual·ize *v.* To become or make equal or uniform. **equalization, equalizer** *n.*

e·quate *v.* To consider or make equal.

e·qua·tion *n.* The act or process of being equal; a mathematical statement expressing the equality of two quantities.

e·qua·tor *n.* The great imaginary circle around the earth. **equatorial** *adj.*

e·ques·tri·an *n.* A person who rides or performs on a horse. **equestrienne** *fem. n.*

e·qui·an·gu·lar *adj.* Having all angles equal.

e·qui·dis·tant *adj.* Having equal distances.

e·qui·lat·er·al *adj.* Having all sides equal.

e·qui·lib·ri·um *n.* The state of balance between two opposing forces or influences.

e·quine *adj.* Pertaining to or like a horse.

e•qui•nox *n.* Either of the two times a year when the sun crosses the celestial equator and the days and nights are equal in time. **equinoctial** *adj.*

e•quip *v.* To furnish or fit with whatever is needed for any undertaking or purpose.

e•quip•ment *n.* The materials used for a special purpose; gear; tools.

eq•ui•ty Fairness or impartiality; the value of property beyond a mortgage or liability.

e•quiv•a•lent *adj.* Being equal or virtually equal, as in effect or meaning. **equivalence**, **equivalency**, **equivalent** *n.*

er•a *n.* An extended period of time or point in the past used as the basis of a chronology.

e•rase *v.* To remove something written; to wipe out. **erasure** *n.*

e•rect *adj.* In a vertical position; standing up straight. *v.* To construct; build.

er•mine *n.* A weasel whose fur changes from brown to white depending on the season.

e•rode *v.* To wear away gradually by constant friction; to corrode; to eat away. **erosion** *n.*

err *v.* To make a mistake; to sin.

er•rand *n.* A short trip to carry a message or to perform a specific task, usually for someone else.

er•rat•ic *adj.* Lacking a fixed course; irregular; inconsistent.

er•ro•ne•ous *adj.* Containing an error.

er•ror *n.* Something said, believed, or done incorrectly; a mistake; the state of being wrong or mistaken.

e•rupt *v.* To burst forth violently and suddenly; to explode with steam or lava, as a volcano or geyser.

es•ca•late *v.* To intensify, increase, or raise in energy.

es•ca•la•tor *n.* A moving stairway with steps attached to an endless belt.

es•ca•pade *n.* An adventure, especially a dangerous or illegal one.

es•cape *v.* To break free from capture or restraint; to enjoy temporary freedom from unpleasant realities.

es•cap•ism *n.* An escape from unpleasant realities through daydreams or other mental diversions.

es•cort *n.* A person or persons accompanying another to give protection or guidance.

es•say *n.* A short composition on a single topic, expressing the author's viewpoint on a subject; an effort or attempt.

es•sence *n.* The real nature; the central true element.

es•sen•tial *adj.* Necessary; indispensable; containing of, or being an essence.

es•tab•lish *v.* To make permanent, stable, or secure; to install; to prove.

es•tab•lish•ment *n.* A place of business or residence; those who occupy positions of influence and status in a society.

es•tate *n.* An unusually large or extensive piece of land containing a large house.

es•teem *v.* To regard with respect. *n.* High regard; admiration.

es•ti•mate *v.* To form or give an approximate opinion or calculation. *n.* A preliminary opinion or statement of the approximate cost for certain work.

es•tu•ar•y *n.* The wide mouth of a river where the current meets the sea and is influenced by tides.

etch *v.* To engrave or cut into the surface by the action of acid; to sketch or outline by scratching lines with a pointed instrument. **etching** *n.*

e•ter•nal *adj.* Existing without beginning or end; unending; meant to last indefinitely. **eternity** *n.*

eth•ics *pl. n.* The system of moral values; the principle of right or good conduct. **ethical** *adj.*

eth•nic *adj.* Relating to or of a national, cultural, or racial group. **ethnicity** *n.*

et•i•quette *n.* The prescribed rules, forms and practices for behavior in polite society; manners.

eu•tha•na•sia *n.* The act or practice of putting to death painlessly a person suffering from an incurable disease; mercy killing.

e•vac•u•ate *v.* To leave a threatened area or building.

e•val•u•ate *v.* To examine carefully; to determine the value of; to appraise.

e•vap•o•rate *v.* To convert into vapor; to remove the liquid or moisture from fruit, milk, or other products.

eve *n.* The evening before a special day or holiday; the period immediately preceding some event; evening.

e•ven *adj.* Having a flat, smooth, and level surface; having no irregularities; smooth; equal in strength or number.

e•ven•hand•ed *adj.* Fair; impartial.

eve•ning *n* The time between sunset and bedtime.

eve•ning star *n.* The brightest planet visible in the west just after sunset, especially Venus.

e•vent *n.* A significant occurrence; something that takes place; a scheduled activity.

e•ven•tu•al *adj.* Happening or expected to happen in due course of time. **eventually** *adv.*

ev•er *adv.* At any time; on any occasion; by any possible chance or conceivable way.

ev•er•last•ing *adj.* Lasting or existing forever; eternal.

eve•ry *adj.* Without exceptions; the utmost; all possible.

eve•ry•bo•dy *pron.* Every person.

eve•ry•day *adj.* Happening every day; daily; suitable for ordinary days.

eve•ry•one *pron.* Everybody; every person.

eve•ry•place *adv.* Everywhere.

eve•ry•thing *pron.* All things; whatever exists; whatever is needed, relevant, or important.

eve•ry•where *adv.* In, at, or to every place; in all places.

e•vict *v.* To put out or expel a tenant by legal process.

ev•i•dence *n.* Signs or facts on which a conclusion can be based.

ev•i•dent *adj.* Easily understood or seen; obvious.

e•vil *adj.* Morally bad or wrong; causing injury or any other undesirable result.

ev•o•lu•tion *n.* The gradual process of development or change; a theory that all forms of life originated by descent from earlier forms.

ewe *n.* A female sheep.

ex•act *adj.* Perfectly complete and clear in every detail; accurate in every detail with something taken as a model; similar. *v.* To force unjustly for the payment of something; to insist upon as strict right or obligation.

ex•act•ly *adv.* Precisely; entirely accurately.

ex•ag•ger•ate *v.* To represent something as being greater than it really is; to make greater in intensity or size than would be normal or expected.

ex•am *n.* An examination; a test of skill or knowledge; the act of examining or the state of being examined; medical testing and scrutiny.

ex•am•ine *v.* To observe or inspect; to test by questions or exercises, as to fitness or qualification. **examination** *n.*

ex•am•ple *n.* A representative as a sample; one worthy of imitation; a problem or exercise in arithmetic to show a rule or practice.

ex•ca•vate *v.* To dig a hole or cavity; to dig, scoop, or hollow out.

ex•ceed *v.* To surpass in quality or quantity; to go beyond the limit.

ex•cel *v.* To surpass or to do better than others.

ex•cel•lence *n.* The state or quality of being superior or outstanding; the highest grade; a superior trait or quality. **excellent** *adj.*

ex•cept *prep.* With the omission or exclusion of; aside from; not including.

ex•cep•tion *n.* Something excluded from; an example not conforming to the general class.

ex•cep•tion•al *adj.* Being an exception to the rule; well above average; outstanding.

ex•cerpt *n.* A passage from a book, speech, or other work.

ex•cess *n.* The condition of going beyond what is necessary, usual, or proper; overindulgence, as in drink or food. **excessive** *adj.*

ex•change *v.* To give in return for something else; to trade; to return as unsatisfactory and get a replacement; to barter.

ex•cite *v.* To stir up strong feeling, action, or emotion. **excitable** *adj.*

ex•claim *v.* To cry out abruptly; to utter suddenly, as from emotion.

ex•cla•ma•tion *n.* An abrupt or sudden forceful utterance.

ex•cla•ma•tion point *n.* A punctuation mark used after an interjection or exclamation.

ex•clude *v.* To keep out; to omit from consideration.

ex•clu•sive *adj.* Intended for the sole use and purpose of a single individual or group. **exclusivity, exclusiveness** *n.*

ex•cru•ci•at•ing *adj.* Intensely painful; agonizing.

ex•cur•sion *n.* A short trip, usually made for pleasure; a trip available at a special reduced fare.

ex•cuse *v.* To ask forgiveness or pardon for oneself; to grant pardon or forgiveness. *n.* A reason or explanation.

ex•e•cute *v.* To carry out; to put into effect; to validate. **execution** *n.*

ex•ec•u•tive *n.* A manager or administrator in an organization; the branch of the government responsible for activating or putting laws into effect.

ex•em•pla•ry *adj.* Serving as a model; worthy of imitation; commendable as an example.

ex•empt *adj.* Free from an obligation or duty to which others are subject.

ex•er•cise *n.* A drill or repeated activity to gain skill, such as practice on the piano.

ex•ert *v.* To put into action; to put oneself through a strenuous effort.

ex•hale *v.* To breathe out; the opposite of inhale; to breathe forth or give off, as air, vapor, or aroma.

ex•haust *v.* To make extremely tired; to drain oneself of resources or strength. *n.* The escape or discharge of waste gases from a machine or factory. **exhaustible** *adj.*, **exhaustion** *n.*

ex•hib•it *v.* To display, as to put up for public view; to bring documents or evidence into a court of law. *n.* An exhibition or display of objects.

ex•ile *n.* The separation by necessity or choice from one's native country or home; banishment; one who has left or been driven from his or her country.

ex•ist *v.* To have actual being or reality; to live.

ex•is•tence *n.* The state of existing, living, or occurring; the manner of existing.

ex•is•ten•tial•ism *n.* A philosophy that stressed the active role of the will rather than of reason in facing problems posed by a hostile universe. **existentialist** *n.*

ex•it *n.* A way or passage out; the act of going away or out; the departure from a stage.

ex•ot•ic *adj.* Belonging by nature or origin to another part of the world; foreign; strangely different and fascinating.

ex•pand *v.* To increase the scope, range, volume, or size; to open up or spread out. **expansion** *n.*

ex•panse *n.* A wide, open space.

ex•pect *v.* To look forward to something as probable or certain; to look for as proper, right, or necessary.

ex•pec•ta•tion *n.* The state or act of expecting; something that is expected and looked forward to.

ex•pe•di•tion *n.* A journey of some length for a definite purpose.

ex•pel *v.* To drive or force out, as to dismiss from a school. **expulsion** *n.*

ex•pense *n.* The outlay or cost; the amount of money required to buy or do something.

ex•pen•sive *adj.* Costing a lot of money; high-priced.

ex•pe•ri•ence *n.* The actual participation in something; the direct contact with; the knowledge or skill acquired from actual participation. **experienced** *adj.*

ex·per·i·ment *n.* The act or test performed to demonstrate or illustrate a truth. **experimentation** *n.*

ex·pert *n.* A person having great knowledge, experience, or skill in a certain field. *adj.* Skilled as the result of training or experience.

ex·pi·ra·tion *n.* The emission of breath; the act of breathing out; the time when something is no longer allowed or alive.

ex·pire *v.* To come to an end; to breathe out, as from the mouth; to exhale.

ex·plain *v.* To make understandable; to clarify; to give reasons for.

ex·plode *v.* To burst or blow up violently with a loud noise; to increase rapidly without control.

ex·ploit *n.* A notable or difficult deed or act. *v.* To use to the best advantage of; to make use of in a selfish or unethical way.

ex·plore *v.* To examine and investigate in a systematic way; to travel through unfamiliar territory. **exploration** *n.*, **exploratory** *adj.*

ex·plo·sion *n.* A sudden, violent release of energy; the sudden, violent outbreak of personal feelings. **explosive** *adj.*

ex·port *v.* To carry or send merchandise or raw materials to other countries for resale or trade. *n.* A commodity exported.

ex·pose *v.* To lay open, as to criticism or ridicule; to lay bare and uncovered.

ex·po·si·tion *n.* A statement of intent or meaning; a detailed presentation of subject matter; a commentary or interpretation; a large public exhibition.

ex·po·sure *n.* The act or state of being exposed; an indication of which way something faces; the act of exposing a sensitive plate or film; the time required for the film or plate to be exposed.

ex·press *v.* To formulate in words; to verbalize; to state; to communicate through some medium other than words or signs; to release outward without regard to effect.

ex·pres·sion *n.* Communication of opinion, thought, or feeling; the outward indication of a condition, feeling, or quality; a particular phrase or word from a certain region of the country.

ex·pres·sion·ism *n.* An early twentieth century movement in the fine arts that emphasizes subjective expression of the artist's inner experiences rather than realistic representation.

ex·pul·sion *n.* The act of expelling or the state of being expelled.

ex·qui·site *adj.* Delicately or intricately beautiful in design or craftsmanship; highly sensitive.

ex·tend *v.* To stretch or open to full length; to make longer, broader, or wider.

ex·ten·sion *n.* The act or state of being extended; something protruding past its normal point.

ex·te·ri·or *adj.* Pertaining to or of the outside; the external layer.

ex·ter·mi·nate *v.* To annihilate; to destroy completely; to cause to cease to exist.

ex·ter·nal *adj.* For or on the outside; acting from the outside.

ex·tinct *adj.* Inactive; no longer existing; extinguished.

ex·tin·guish *v.* To put an end to; to put out, as a fire; to make extinct.

ex·tra *adj.* Over and above what is normal, required, or expected.

ex·tract *v.* To pull or draw out by force; to obtain in spite of resistance; to obtain from a substance as by pressure or distillation.

ex·tra·cur·ric·u·lar *adj.* Pertaining to activities not directly a part of the curriculum of a school or college.

ex·tra·or·di·nar·y *adj.* Outstanding; unusual; beyond what is usual or common; remarkable.

ex·tra·ter·res·tri·al *adj.* Occurring, or originating outside the earth or its atmosphere.

ex·trav·a·gant *adj.* Overly lavish in expenditure; wasteful; exceeding reasonable limits; immoderate; unrestrained.

ex•trav•a•gan•za *n.* A lavish, spectacular, showy entertainment.

ex•treme *adj.* Greatly exceeding; going far beyond the bounds of moderation; exceeding what is considered moderate, usual, or reasonable.

ex•trem•ist *n.* A person who advocates or resorts to extreme measures or holds extreme views.

ex•u•ber•ant *adj.* Full of high spirits, vitality, vigor, and joy.

eye *n.* An organ of sight consisting of the cornea, iris, pupil, retina, and lens; a look; gaze; the ability to judge, perceive, or discriminate.

eye•ball *n.* The ball of the eye, enclosed by the socket and eyelids and connected at the rear to the optic nerve.

eye•glass *n.* A corrective lens used to assist vision. *pl.* A pair of corrective lenses set in a frame.

eye•lin•er *n.* Makeup used to highlight the outline of the eyes.

eye•sight *n.* The faculty or power of sight; the range of vision.

F

F, f The sixth letter of the English alphabet; in music, the fourth tone in the scale of C major; a failing grade.

fa•ble *n.* A brief, fictitious story embodying a moral and using persons, animals, or inanimate objects as characters. **fabulist**, **fabler** *n.*, **fabled** *adj.*

fab•ric *n.* A cloth produced by knitting, weaving, or spinning fibers.

fab•u•lous *adj.* Past the limits of belief; incredible. **fabulously** *adv.*

face *n.* The front surface of the head from ear to ear and from forehead to chin; the principal, front, finished, or working surface of anything. *v.* To confront with awareness.

fac•et *n.* One of the flat, polished surfaces cut upon a gemstone; the small, smooth surface on a bone or tooth; a phase, aspect, or side of a person or subject. **faceted**, **facetted** *adj.*

fa•cial *adj.* Near, of, or for the face; a massage or other cosmetic treatment for the face.

fa•cil•i•ty *n.* Ease in performance, moving, or doing something; something that makes an operation or action easier.

fac•ing *n.* The lining or covering sewn to a garment.

fact *n.* Something that actually occurred or exists; something that has real and demonstrable existence; actuality.

fac•tor *n.* One of the elements or causes that contribute to produce the result; in mathematics, one of two or more quantities that when multiplied together give or yield a given product

fac•to•ry *n.* An establishment where goods are manufactured; an industrial plant.

fac•tu•al *adj.* Containing or consisting of facts, literal and exact. **factually** *adv.*

fac•ul•ty *n.* A natural ability or power; the complete teaching staff of a school or any other educational institution.

fad *n.* A temporary fashion adopted with wide enthusiasm.

fade *v.* To lose brightness, brilliance, or loudness gradually; to vanish slowly; to disappear gradually.

fail *v.* To be totally ineffective, unsuccessful; to go bankrupt; to receive an academic grade below the acceptable standards.

fail•ing *n.* A minor fault; a defect.

fail•ure *n.* The fact or state of failing; a breaking down in health, action, strength, or efficiency; in school, a failing grade.

faint *adj.* Having a little strength or vigor; feeble; lacking brightness or clarity; dim. *n.* A sudden, temporary loss of consciousness; a swoon. **faintly** *adv.*, **faintness** *n.*

faint•heart•ed *adj.* Lacking courage or conviction; cowardly; timid.

fair *adj.* Visually light in coloring; pleasing to the eye; beautiful; impartial; not stormy; without precipitation.

fair-weath•er *adj.* Friendly only during

good times.

fair•y *n.* A tiny imaginary being, capable of working good or ill.

fair•y•land *n.* Any delightful, enchanting place; the land of the fairies.

fair•y tale *n.* An incredible or fictitious tale of fanciful creatures; a tale about fairies.

faith *n.* A belief in the value, truth, or trustworthiness of someone or something; belief and trust in God; a system of religious beliefs.

faith•ful *adj.* True and trustworthy in the performance of duty, promises or obligations.

faith•less *adj.* Not being true to one's obligations or duties; lacking a religious faith; unworthy of belief or trust.

fake *adj.* Having a false or misleading appearance; not genuine.

fall *v.* To drop down from a higher place or position due to the removal of support or loss of hold or attachment; to collapse; to become less in rank or importance. *n.* The act of falling; a moral lapse or loss of innocence; autumn.

fal•la•cy *n.* A deception; an error in logic.

false *adj.* Contrary to truth or fact; incorrect. **falsity** *n.*

false•hood *n.* The act of lying; an intentional untruth.

fal•set•to *n.* An artificially high singing voice, usually male.

fal•si•fy *v.* To give an untruthful account of; to misrepresent

fal•ter *v.* To be uncertain or hesitant in action or voice; to waver.

fame *n.* Public esteem; a good reputation.

fa•mil•iar *adj.* Being well acquainted with; common; having good and complete knowledge of something. **familiarity** *n.*

fa•mil•iar•ize *v.* To make oneself or someone familiar with something.

fam•i•ly *n.* Parents and their children; a group of people connected by blood or marriage and sharing common ancestry.

fam•i•ly name *n.* A last name shared by family members.

fam•i•ly tree *n.* A genealogical diagram showing family descent.

fam•ine *n.* A widespread scarcity of food; severe hunger; starvation.

fam•ish *v.* To starve or cause to starve. **famished** *adj.*

fa•mous *adj.* Well known; renowned.

fan *n.* A device for putting air into motion, especially a flat, lightweight, collapsible, wedge-like shape; a machine that rotates thin, rigid vanes; an enthusiastic devotee of a sport, celebrity, or diversion.

fa•nat•ic *n.* One moved by a frenzy of enthusiasm or zeal. **fanatically** *adv.*, **fanaticism** *n.*

fan•ci•ful *adj.* Existing or produced only in the fancy; indulging in fancies.

fan•cy *n.* Imagination of a fantastic or whimsical nature; a notion or idea not based on evidence or fact; a whim or caprice.

fang *n.* A long, pointed tooth or tusk an animal uses to seize or tear at its prey; a snake's hollow tooth.

fan•tas•tic *adj.* Existing only in fantasy; unreal; wildly fanciful or exaggerated; impulsive or capricious; coming from the imagination or fancy; superb.

fan•ta•sy *n.* A creative imagination; a creation of the fancy; an unreal or odd mental image.

FAQ *abbr.* Frequently asked questions; in computers, a list of informational answers to queries from network browsers to specific web sites.

far *adv.* From, to, or at a considerable distance; very remote in time, quality, or degree.

far•a•way *adj.* Very distant; remote; absent-minded; dreamy.

fare *v.* To be in a specific state; to turn out. *v.* A fee paid for hired transportation; food or a variety of foods.

fare•well *n.* Good-bye; a departure. *adj.* Closing; parting.

far-fetched *adj.* Neither natural nor obvious; highly improbable.

farm *n.* Land cultivated for agricultural

production or to breed and raise domestic animals.

farm•house *n.* The homestead on a farm.

farm•land *n.* Land that is suitable for agricultural production.

farm•yard *n.* The area surrounded by farm buildings and enclosed for confining stock.

far-sight•ed *adj.* Able to see things at a distance more clearly than things nearby; wise.

far•ther *adv.* To or at a more distant point.

fas•ci•nate *v.* To attract irresistibly, as by beauty or other qualities.

fas•cism *n.* A one-party system of government marked by a centralized dictatorship, social and economic controls, and strong nationalism.

fash•ion *n.* The mode or manner of dress, living, and style that prevails in society; good form or style; current style.

fast *adj.* Swift; rapid; performed quickly; constant; steadfast. *v.* To give up food, especially for a religious reason.

fast•en *v.* To join something else; to connect; to securely fix.

fat *adj.* Having superfluous flesh or fat; obese; plump; containing much fat or oil. *n.* Any of a large class of yellowish to white, greasy liquids or solid substances widely distributed in animal and plant tissues. **fat•ten** *v.*

fat•al *adj.* Causing death; deadly; bringing ruin or disaster; destructive; decisively important; fateful.

fa•tal•i•ty *n.* A death caused by a disaster or accident.

fate *n.* The force or power held to predetermine events; fortune; inevitability. **fateful** *adj.*

fa•ther *n.* The male parent; any male forefather; ancestor; a male who establishes or founds something; a priest.

fa•ther-in-law *n.* The father of one's spouse.

fa•tigue *n.* The condition of extreme tiredness or weariness from prolonged physical or mental exertion.

fat•ty *adj.* Greasy; oily; having an excess of fat.

fau•cet *n.* A fixture with an adjustable valve to draw liquids from a pipe or cask.

fault *n.* An impairment or defect; a weakness; a minor offense or mistake; a break in the earth's crust allowing adjoining surfaces to shift in a direction parallel to the crack.

fau•na *n.* Animals living within a given area or environment. **faunal** *adj.*

fa•vor *n.* A helpful or considerate act; the attitude of friendliness or approval. *v.* To benefit; to give advantage; to prefer or like one more than another.

fa•vor•a•ble *adj.* Beneficial; advantageous; building up hope or confidence.

fa•vor•ite *n.* Anything regarded with special favor or preferred above all others.

fawn *n.* A young deer less than a year old; a light yellowish-brown color.

fear *n.* The agitated feeling caused by the anticipation or the realization of danger; an uneasy feeling that something may happen contrary to one's hopes. **fearfulness** *n.*, **fearful** *adj.*, **fearfully** *adv.*

fear•less *adj.* Without fear; brave; courageous.

fea•si•ble *adj.* Able to be put into effect or accomplished; practical. **feasibility** *n.*, **feasibly** *adv.*

feast *n.* A delicious meal; a banquet.

feat *n.* A notable act or difficult physical achievement.

feath•er *n.* One of the light, hollow-shafted structures that form the covering of birds.

fea•ture *n.* The appearance or shape of the face; the main presentation at a movie theater; a special article in a magazine or newspaper.

Feb•ru•ar•y *n.* The second month of the year, having 28 days or, in a leap year, 29 days.

fed *v.* Past tense of *feed*.

fed•er•al *adj.* Relating to an agreement between two or more states or groups retaining certain controlling powers while being united under a central authority.

fee *n.* A fixed charge or payment for something; a charge for professional services.

fee·ble *adj.* Very weak; lacking in strength; ineffective.

feed *v.* To supply with food; to provide as food; to consume food; to keep supplied.

feel *v.* To examine, explore, or perceive through the sense of touch; to perceive as a physical sensation; to believe.

feet *n.* The plural of *foot.*

fe·lic·i·ty *n.* Happiness; bliss; a natural and suitable juxtaposition of conditions.

fe·line *adj.* Of or relating to cats, including wild and domestic cats.

fell *v.* Past tense of *fall;* to strike or cause to fall down, as a tree.

fel·low *n.* A boy or man; an associate, comrade; one of a pair.

fel·low·ship *n.* A friendly relationship; the condition or fact of having common interests, ideals, or experiences.

fel·o·ny *n. pl.* **-ies** A serious crime, such as rape, murder, or burglary, punishable by a severe sentence. **felon** *n.,* **felonious** *adj.*

felt *v.* Past tense of *feel. n.* An unwoven fabric made from pressed animal fibers, as wool or fur.

fe·male *n.* The sex that produces ova or bears young; a plant with a pistil but no stamen, capable of being fertilized and producing fruit. *adj.* Of or relating to the sex that produces ova or bears young.

fem·i·nine *adj.* Pertaining to or of the female gender; female.

fem·i·nism *n.* The movement of advocating the granting of the same social, political, and economic rights to women as the ones granted to men. **feminist** *n.,* **feministic** *adj.*

fence *n.* A structure made from rails, stakes, or strung wire functioning as a boundary or barrier.

fenc·ing *n.* The sport of using a foil or saber; the material used to make fences; fences collectively.

fe·ro·cious *adj.* Extremely savage, fierce, or bloodthirsty. **ferocity** *n.*

fer·ry *n.* A boat or other craft used to transport people and vehicles across a body of water; a ferryboat.

fer·tile *adj.* Having the ability to reproduce; rich in material required to maintain plant growth. **fertility, fertileness** *n.*

fer·til·ize *v.* To make fertile; to cause to be productive or fruitful.

fes·ti·val *n.* A particular holiday or celebration or a regularly occurring occasion.

fes·tive *adj.* Relating to or suitable for a feast or other celebration. **festively** *adv.,* **festiveness, festivities** *n.*

fetch *v.* To go after and return with; to draw forth.

fe·tus *n.* The individual unborn organism carried within the womb from the time major features appear. **fetal** *adj.*

feud *n.* A bitter quarrel between two families, usually lasting a long period of time.

feu·dal·ism *n.* The political, social, and economic system of the Medieval period offering labor in exchange for protection from marauding hordes. **feudalist** *n.,* **feudalistic** *adj.*

fe·ver *n.* Abnormally high body temperature and rapid pulse; a craze; a heightened emotion or activity.

few *adj.* Small in number; not many; several. *n.* A select or limited group.

fib *n.* A trivial lie. **fib** *v.,* **fibber** *n.*

fi·ber *n.* A fine, long, continuous piece of natural or synthetic material made from a filament of asbestos, spun glass, textile, or fabric; internal strength; character. **fibrous** *adj.*

fick·le *adj.* Inconstant in purpose or feeling; changeable.

fic·tion *n.* Something created or imaginary; a literary work produced by the imagination and not based on fact. **fictional** *adj.*

fic·ti·tious *adj.* Nonexistent; not genuine; false; not real.

fid·dle *n.* A violin. *v.* To play the violin; to fidget or make nervous or restless movements.

fi·del·i·ty *n.* Faithfulness or loyalty to

obligations, vows, or duties; a sound system's ability to deliver pure rich sound without distortion.

fidg•et To move nervously or restlessly.

field *n.* A piece of land with few or no trees; a cultivated piece of land devoted to the growing of crops; an area in which a natural resource such as oil is found; an airport; the complete extent of knowledge in a given area; in sports, the playing area.

fierce *adj.* Savage, violent, or frightening.

fier•y *adj.* Containing or composed of fire; brightly glowing; blazing; hot and inflamed.

fig *n.* A tree or shrub bearing a sweet, pear-shaped, edible fruit.

fight *v.* To struggle against in combat; to quarrel; to argue; to make one's way by struggling.

fight•er *n.* A person who fights; a fast, highly maneuverable airplane used in combat.

fig•ure *n.* A symbol or character that represents a number; anything other than a letter; the visible form of something; the human form or body. *v.* To represent; to depict; to compute.

fig•ure eight *n.* A skating maneuver shaped like an 8; anything shaped like the number 8.

file *n.* A device for storing papers in proper order; a collection of papers so arranged; a hard, steel instrument with ridged cutting surfaces, used to smooth or polish. *v.* To march as a soldier; to make an application as for a job.

fill *v.* To put into or hold as much of something as can be contained; to supply fully.

fill•er *n.* Something added to increase weight or bulk or to take up space; a material used to fill cracks, pores, or holes.

fill•ing *n.* That which fills something, especially the substance put into a prepared cavity in a tooth.

fill•ing sta•tion *n.* A retail business where vehicles are serviced with gasoline, oil, water, and air for tires.

film *n.* A thin covering, layer, or membrane; a photosensitive strip or sheet of flexible cellulose material used to make photographic negatives or transparencies; an entertainment on film; a movie.

fil•ter *n.* A cloth, paper, or charcoal device that separates matter from liquid. *v.* To strain or use a filter. **filterability** *n.*

filth *n.* Anything dirty or foul; something considered offensive.

filth•y *adj.* Highly unpleasant; morally foul; obscene.

fin *n.* A thin membranous extension of the body of a fish or other aquatic animal, used for swimming and balancing.

fi•nal *adj.* Coming to the end; last or terminal. **finality** *n.*, **finally** *adv.*

fi•na•le *n.* The last part, as the final scene in a play or the last part of a musical composition.

fi•nal•ist *n.* A contestant taking part in the final round of a contest.

fi•nals *pl. n.* Something decisively final, as the last of a series of athletic contests; the final academic examination.

fi•nance *n.* The science of monetary affairs. *pl.* Monetary resources; funds. *v.* To supply the capital or funds for something; to sell or provide on a credit basis. **financial** *adj.*, **financially** *adv.*

find *v.* To discover unexpectedly; to achieve, attain, or ascertain; to determine; to recover or regain. **finding** *n.*

find•er *n.* A person who finds; the device on a camera that indicates what will be in the picture.

fine *adj.* Superior in skill or quality; very enjoyable and pleasant; light and delicate in workmanship, texture, or structure.

fine arts *pl. n.* The arts of painting, sculpture, architecture, literature, music, dance, and drama.

fin•ger *n.* One of the digits of the hand, usually excluding the thumb.

fin•ger•nail *n.* The transparent covering on the dorsal surface of each fingertip.

fin•ger•print *n.* An inked impression of the pattern formed by the ridges of the skin on the tips of each finger and thumb.

fin•ger•tip *n.* The extreme end of a finger.

fin·ick·y *adj.* Hard to please; choosy.

fin·ish *v.* To bring to or reach an end; to conclude; to give a glossy polish. *n.* The surface texture or gloss of a flat structure.

fi·nite *adj.* Having bounds or limits; of or relating to a number which can be determined, counted, or measured.

fir *n.* An evergreen tree with flat needles and erect cones.

fire *n.* The chemical reaction of burning, which releases heat and light; combustion; rapid oxidation. *v.* To bake in a kiln; to discharge a firearm or explosive; to let a person go from a job; to dismiss.

fire a·larm *n.* A safety device to signal the outbreak of a fire.

fire·arm *n.* A small weapon used for firing a missile.

fire·crack·er *n.* A small paper cylinder charged with an explosive to make noise.

fire en·gine *n.* A large motor vehicle equipped to carry firefighters and their equipment to a fire.

fire es·cape *n.* A structure, often metal, used as an emergency exit from a building.

fire ex·tin·guish·er *n.* A portable apparatus for fire extinguishing chemicals, ejected through a short nozzle and hose.

fire fight·er *n.* A person who fights fires.

fire·fly *n.* A beetle that flies at night, having an abdominal organ that gives off a flashing light.

fire·place *n.* An open recess in which a fire is built, especially the base of a chimney that opens into a room.

fire-wall *n.* In computers, a security system using software to prevent unauthorized entry to files or information.

fire·works *pl. n.* Explosives used to generate colored lights, smoke, and noise for entertainment or celebrations.

firm *adj.* Relatively solid, compact, or unyielding to pressure or touch; strong and sure. *n.* A partnership of two or more persons for conducting a business.

first *adj.* Preceding all others in the order of numbering; taking place or acting prior to all others; earliest.

first aid *n.* The emergency care given to a person before full treatment and medical care can be obtained.

first per·son *n.* A category for verbs or pronouns indicating the speaker or writer of a sentence in which they are used.

fish *n.* A cold-blooded, vertebrated aquatic animal with fins, gills, and usually scales. *v.* To try to catch fish.

fish·er·man *n.* Any person who fishes commercially or for sport and relaxation; a commercial fishing boat; an angler.

fis·sion *n.* The process or act of splitting into parts; the exploding of the nucleus of an atom and the release of large quantities of energy. **fissionable** *adj.*

fis·sure *n.* A narrow opening, crack, or cleft in a rock.

fist *n.* The hand closed lightly with the fingers bent into the palm.

fit *v.* To be the proper size and shape; to come together well; to be in good physical condition. *adj.* Adapted or adequate for a particular circumstance or purpose.

fit·ting *adj.* Suitable or proper. *n.* The act of trying on clothes for alteration; a piece of equipment or an appliance used in an adjustment.

fix *v.* To make stationary, firm, or stable; to direct or hold steadily; to repair; to prepare, as a meal. *n.* A position of embarrassment or difficulty; the position of a ship under way.

fix·ture *n.* Anything installed as a part of structure or building.

fizz *n.* A hissing or bubbling sound; effervescence; tiny gas bubbles.

flag *n.* A piece of cloth, usually oblong, bearing colors and designs to designate a nation, state, city, or organization.

flair *n.* An aptitude or talent for something; a dashing style.

flake *n.* A small, flat, thin piece split or peeled off from a surface.

flame *n.* A mass of burning vapor or gas rising from a fire, often having a bright color and forming a tongue-shaped area of light.

fla·min·go *n.* A large, long-necked, tropical wading bird, having very long legs, and pink or red plumage.

flam·ma·ble *adj.* Capable of catching fire and burning rapidly.

flare *v.* To blaze up with a bright light; to break out suddenly or violently; to open or spread outward. *n.* An incendiary device for signalling for help.

flash *v.* To burst forth suddenly into a brilliant fire or light; to occur or appear briefly or suddenly. *n.* A short and important news break or transmission. **flashed**, **flashing** *v.*

flash card *n.* A card printed with numbers or words and displayed as a learning drill.

flash·y *adj.* Showing brilliance for a moment; tastelessly showy; gaudy.

flask *n.* A small laboratory container of glass.

flat *adj.* Extending horizontally with no curvature or tilt; stretched out level; below the correct pitch.

flat·ten *v.* To make flat; to knock down.

flat·ter *v.* To praise without sincerity; to gratify the vanity of. **flattery** *n.*

flau·tist *n.* A flutist; a person who plays the flute.

fla·vor *n.* A distinctive taste of something; a distinctive, characteristic quality.

fla·vor·ing *n.* A substance, as an extract, used to increase the flavor.

flaw *n.* A defect or blemish, often hidden, that may cause failure under stress; a weakness in character.

flaw·less *adj.* Without flaws or defects.

flax *n.* A plant with blue flowers, with seeds that yield oil, and slender stems from which a fine textile fiber is derived.

flea *n.* A small, wingless, blood-sucking, parasitic jumping insect.

flea mar·ket *n.* A place where antiques and used items are bought and sold.

fleck *n.* A tiny spot or streak.

fledg·ling or **fledge·ling** *n.* A young bird with newly acquired feathers; a beginner.

flee *v.* To run away from; to move swiftly away.

fleece *n.* A coat of wool covering a sheep. *v.* To shear the fleece from; to swindle; to cover with fleece.

fleet *n.* A number of warships operating together under the same command; a number of vehicles, as taxicabs or fishing boats, operated under one command. *adj.* Moving rapidly or nimbly.

flesh *n.* Soft tissue on the body of a human or animal, especially skeletal muscle.

flex·i·ble *adj.* Capable of being bent or flexed; pliable.

flick·er *v.* To burn or shine unsteadily, as a candle. *n.* A North American woodpecker having a brownish back and a spotted breast.

fli·er or **fly·er** *n.* An aviator; a daring or risky venture; a printed handbill.

flight *n.* The act or manner of flying; a scheduled airline trip; a group of stairs leading from one floor to another; an instance of fleeing.

flight at·ten·dant *n.* A person employed to assist passengers on an aircraft; a steward or stewardess.

flim·sy *adj.* Lacking in physical strength or substance; thin and weak.

flinch *v.* To wince or pull back, as from pain; to draw away.

fling *v.* To throw or toss violently.

flint *n.* A hard quartz that produces a spark when struck by steel.

flip *v.* To turn or throw over suddenly with a jerk.

flip-flop *n.* The sound or motion of something flapping loosely; a backward somersault; a sudden reversal of direction or point of view.

flip·per *n.* A broad flat limb, as of a seal, adapted for swimming; a paddle-like rubber shoe used by swimmers.

flip side *n.* The reverse or opposite side.

flirt *v.* To make teasing romantic or sexual overtures; to act so as to attract attention.

float *n.* Something that floats on the surface of or in a liquid; a device used to buoy the baited end of a fishing line.

flock *n.* A group of animals of all the same

flood

kind, especially birds or sheep, living, feeding, or kept together.

flood *n*. An overflow of water onto land that is normally dry; an overwhelming quantity.

flood·gate *n*. A valve for controlling the flow or depth of a large body of water.

flood·light *n*. An electric lamp that gives off a broad and intensely bright light.

floor *n*. The level base of a room; the lower inside surface of a structure; a ground surface. *v*. To overwhelm, to knock out.

flop *v*. To fall down clumsily; to move about in a clumsy way.

flop·py disk *n*. In computer science, a flexible plastic disk coated with magnetic material, used to record and store data.

flo·ra *n*. Plants growing in a specific region or season.

flo·ral *adj*. Of or pertaining to flowers.

flo·res·cence *n*. A state or process of blossoming.

flo·rist *n*. One who grows or sells real or artificial flowers.

floss *n*. A loosely-twisted embroidery thread; a soft, silky fiber, such as the tassel on corn; dental floss. *v*. To clean between the teeth with dental floss.

flo·ta·tion *n*. The act or state of floating.

flot·sam *n*. Any goods remaining afloat after a ship has sunk.

flour *n*. A soft, fine, powder-like substance obtained by grinding the meal of grain, especially wheat.

flour·ish *v*. To thrive; to fare well; to prosper and succeed.

flow *v*. To move freely, as a fluid; to circulate, as blood; to proceed or move steadily and easily; to rise.

flow chart *n*. A chart or diagram showing the sequence and progress of a series of operations on a specific project.

flow·er *n*. A cluster of petals, bright in color, near or at the tip of a seed-bearing plant.

flu *n*. Influenza.

flu·ent *adj*. Having an understanding of a language use; flowing smoothly and naturally. **fluency** *n*., **fluently** *adv*.

fluff *n*. A ball, tuft, or light cluster of loosely gathered fibers of cotton or wool.

flu·id *n*. A substance, as water or gas, capable of flowing. *adj*. Changing readily, as a liquid.

flunk *v*. To fail in, as an examination or course.

flur·ry *n*. A sudden gust of wind; a brief, light fall of snow or rain.

flush *v*. To flow or rush out suddenly and abundantly; to become red in the face; to blush; to glow with a reddish color; to wash out with a brief, rapid gush of water.

flute *n*. A high-pitched musical woodwind instrument with finger holes and keys.

flut·ist *n*. A flute player; a flautist.

flut·ter *v*. To flap or wave rapidly and irregularly; to fly as with a light, rapid beating of the wings.

fly *v*. To move through the air on wings or wing-like parts; to travel by air; to float or cause to float in the air. *n*. Any of numerous winged insects, including the housefly and the tsetse; a fishing lure that resembles an insect.

foal *n*. The young animal, as a horse, especially one under a year old. *v*. To give birth to a foal.

foam *n*. A mass of bubbles produced on the surface of a liquid by agitation; a froth; a firm, spongy material used especially for insulation and upholstery.

fo·cus *n*. A point at which rays converge or from which they appear to diverge; a center of activity or interest. *v*. To produce a sharp, clear image of; to adjust a lens in order to produce a clean image; to direct; to come together at a point of focus. **focuses, foci** *pl*., **focal** *adj*., **focally** *adv*.

fod·der *n*. A coarse feed for livestock.

foe *n*. An enemy in war; an opponent or adversary.

fog *n*. A vapor mass of condensed water which lies close to the ground; a state of mental confusion or bewilderment. *v*. To obscure or cover with.

fog·horn *n*. A horn sounded in fog.

foil *v.* To prevent from being successful; to thwart. *n.* A very thin, flexible sheet of metal; a fencing sword.

fold *v.* To double or lay one part over another; to bring from an opened to a closed position; to put together and intertwine; to envelop or wrap.

fo•li•age *n.* The leaves of growing plants and trees.

fo•li•o *n.* A large sheet of paper folded once in a middle.

folk *n.* An ethnic group of people forming a nation or tribe.

fol•li•cle *n.* A small anatomical cavity or sac.

fol•low *v.* To proceed or come after; to pursue; to follow the course of; to obey.

fol•ly *n.* Lack of good judgment; an instance of foolishness.

fond *adj.* Affectionate; liking; cherished with great affection.

fon•dle *v.* To stroke, handle, or caress affectionately.

font *n.* A source of nourishment; a holy water receptacle in a church; printing type of the same size and face.

food *n.* A substance to be eaten, used to sustain life and growth in the body of an organism; nourishment.

fool *n.* One lacking good sense or judgment. *v.* To trick or mislead someone.

foot *n.* The lower extremity of the vertebrate leg upon which one stands; a unit of measurement equal to 12 inches. **feet** *pl.*

foot•ball *n.* A team game whose object is to get the ball over a goal line or between goalposts by running, passing or kicking; the oval ball used in the game of football.

foot•hill *n.* A low hill near the foot of a mountain or a higher hill.

foot•note *n.* A note of reference or comment below the text on a printed page; a commentary.

for *prep.* Used to indicate the extent of something; used to indicate the number or amount of; considering the usual characteristics of; on behalf of someone; to be in favor of. *conj.* Because; in as much as;

with the purpose of.

for•age *n.* Food for cattle or other domestic animals. *v.* To make a raid so as to find supplies; to plunder or rummage through.

for•bid *v.* To command someone not to do something; to prohibit by law; to prevent.

for•bade *v.* Past tense of *forbid*.

for•bid•ding *adj.* Very difficult; disagreeable.

force *n.* Energy or power; strength; a group organized for a certain purpose. *v.* To compel or make happen by force.

for•ceps *n.* A pair of tongs used for manipulating, grasping or extracting, especially in surgery. **forceps** *pl.*

ford *n.* A shallow place in a body of water that can be crossed without a boat. *v.* To wade across a body of water.

fore•cast *v.* To predict, as weather; to calculate in advance.

fore•fa•ther *n.* An ancestor.

fore•fin•ger *n.* The finger next to the thumb.

fore•go *v.* To go before; to precede in time.

fore•gone *adj.* Already finished or gone; established in advance.

fore•ground *n.* The part of a picture represented as nearest to the viewer.

fore•head *n.* The part of the face from the eyebrows to the hair.

for•eign *adj.* Situated outside one's native country; belonging to a country or region other than one's own.

for•eign•er *n.* A person from a different place or country; an alien.

fore•man *n.* A person of either gender who oversees a group of people; the spokesperson for a jury. **forewoman** *n.*

fore•most *adj.* First in rank, position, time, or order.

fo•ren•sic med•i•cine *n.* A science dealing with the application of medicine in legal problems.

fore•run•ner *n.* One sent before to give notice of the approach of others; a harbinger.

fore•see *v.* To know or see beforehand.

foreshadow

fore·shad·ow *v.* To represent or warn of beforehand.

for·est *n.* A large tract of land covered with trees.

fore·taste *n.* A sample or indication beforehand.

fore·tell *v.* To tell about in advance; to predict.

fore·thought *n.* Prior thought or planning; a plan for the future.

for·ev·er *adv.* For eternity; without end.

fore·ward *n.* An introductory statement before the text of a book.

for·feit *n.* Something taken away as punishment; a penalty; something placed in escrow and redeemed on payment of a fine.

forge *n.* A furnace where metals are heated and wrought; a smithy. *v.* To form by heating and hammering; to give shape to; to imitate falsely.

for·get *v.* To lose the memory of; to fail to remember.

for·give *v.* To pardon; to cease to feel resentment against.

for·go *v.* To give up or refrain from; to do without.

fork *n.* A tool consisting of a handle at one end of which are two or more prongs; a division of something into two or more parts that continue, as a river or road. **forked** *adj.*

fork lift *n.* A self-propelled industrial vehicle with a pronged platform for hoisting and transporting heavy objects.

for·lorn *adj.* Abandoned or left in distress; hopeless.

form *n.* The shape or contour of something; a body of a living being; the basic nature of or particular state of something; a document with blank spaces to fill out with information.

for·mal *adj.* Of or pertaining to the outward aspect of something; based on accepted conventions.

for·mat *n.* A general style of a publication; the general form or layout of a publication. *v.* In computers, to produce data in a specified form.

for·ma·tion *n.* The act or state of being formed; the manner in which something is formed.

for·mer *adj.* Previous; preceding in place.

for·mer·ly *adv.* Previously.

form-fit·ting *adj.* Following closely to the contours of the body.

form let·ter *n.* A standardized format of an impersonal letter sent to a large number of people.

for·mu·la *n.* A prescribed method of words or rules for use in a certain ceremony or procedure; a nutritious food for an infant in liquid form; a combination used to express an algebraic or symbolic form; a symbolic representation of the composition of a chemical compound. **formulas**, **formulae** *pl.*, **formulaic** *adj.*

fort *n.* A fortified structure for defense against invasion.

forte *n.* An activity one does with excellence; a person's strong point.

forth *adv.* Out into plain sight; forward in order, place, or time.

for·ti·fy *v.* To make more secure; to provide physical strength or courage to; to strengthen.

for·ti·tude *n.* Strength of mind in adversity, pain, or peril.

for·tress *n.* A fort; a fortified place.

for·tu·nate *adj.* Brought about by good fortune; having good fortune.

for·tune *n.* A force that determines events and issues favorably and unfavorably; success that results from luck; wealth.

for·tune-tell·er *n.* A person who claims to predict the future.

fo·rum *n.* A public marketplace in an ancient Roman city; any place or opportunity for group discussion or expression.

for·ward *adv.* At, near, or toward a place or time in advance; overstepping the usual bounds.

fos·sil *n.* The remains of an animal or plant of a past geologic age preserved in the rocks of the earth's surface.

fos·ter *v.* To give parental care to; to

nurture; to encourage.

foul *adj.* Revolting to the senses; spoiled or rotten; unfavorable. *v.* To physically contact or entangle; to become foul or dirty.

found *v.* To establish; to set up; to establish the basis or lay the foundation of.

foun·da·tion *n.* The basis on which anything is founded; an institution supported by an endowment.

foun·dry *n.* A place where metal is cast.

fount *n.* A fountain; an abundant source.

foun·tain *n.* A natural spring coming from the earth; an artificially created spray of water.

four·score *adj.* Being four times twenty; eighty.

fowl *n.* A bird used as food or hunted as game.

fox *n.* A wild mammal having a pointed snout, upright ears, and a long bushy tail.

frac·tion *n.* A small part; in mathematics, an indicated quantity less than a whole number that is expressed as a decimal.

frac·ture *n.* The act of breaking; the state of being broken; something broken or cracked, as a bone.

frag·ile *adj.* Easily damaged or broken; frail; tenuous; flimsy.

frag·ment *n.* A part detached or broken; part unfinished or incomplete. *v.* To break into fragments.

fra·grant *adj.* Having an agreeable, especially sweet odor. **fragrance** *n.*

frail *adj.* Delicate; weak; easily damaged.

frame *v.* To put into a frame, as a picture; to build; to design.

fran·chise *n.* A privilege or right granted to a person or group by a government.

frank *adj.* Sincere and straightforward; open and honest.

frank·furt·er *n.* A smoked sausage.

fran·tic *adj.* Emotionally out of control with worry or fear. **frantically,** *adv.*

fra·ter·nal *adj.* Relating to brothers; of a fraternity.

fraud *n.* A deliberate and willful deception for unlawful gain. **fraudulent** *adj.*

freak *n.* A capricious event; a whimsical quality or disposition.

freck·le *n.* One of the small brownish spots on the skin, usually due to pigmentation, and increased by the sun.

free *adj.* Not imprisoned; not under obligation; able to choose. *v.* To give freedom to; to unlock or disentangle; to give away.

free·dom *n.* The condition or state of being free; political independence.

free trade *n.* Unrestricted international exchange between nations or states.

free·way *n.* A highway with more than two lanes; a superhighway.

free will *n.* The ability to choose freely; the belief that a human being's choices can be made freely, without external constraint.

freeze *v.* To become ice or a similar solid through loss of heat; to preserve by cooling at an extremely low temperature.

freeze-dry *v.* To preserve by drying in a frozen state under a high vacuum.

freez·er *n.* An insulated cabinet for freezing and storing perishable foods.

freight *n.* A service of transporting commodities by air, land or water; the price paid for such transportation; a train that transports goods only.

freight·er *n.* A ship used for transporting cargo.

fren·zy *n.* A state of extreme excitement or agitation; temporary insanity.

fre·quent *adj.* Happening often or time after time. *v.* To go to a place repeatedly.

fres·co *n.* A painting on moist plaster with water-based paint.

fresh *adj.* Newly made, gathered, or obtained; not spoiled, musty, or stale; new.

fresh·man *n.* A student in the first year of studies in a high school, university, or college; a beginner.

fret *v.* To be anxious or irritated; a ridge of metal fixed across the finger-board of a stringed instrument, as a guitar.

fri·ar *n.* A member of a religious order, usually reclusive.

fric·tion *n.* The rubbing of one surface or object against another.

friend *n.* Someone personally well known

and liked; a supporter of a cause or group.

fright *n.* Sudden violent alarm or fear; a feeling of alarm.

fright•en *v.* To fill with fear; to force by arousing fear.

frig•id *adj.* Very cold; lacking warmth of feeling or emotional warmth.

frill *n.* A decorative ruffled or gathered border.

fringe *n.* An edging that consists of hanging threads, cords, or loops.

frisk *v.* To skip or leap about playfully; to search for a concealed weapon by running the hands over the clothing quickly.

friv•o•lous *adj.* Trivial; insignificant; lacking importance.

frog *n.* Any of various small, smooth-skinned, web-footed, largely aquatic, tailless, leaping amphibians.

frol•ic *n.* Merriness; a playful, carefree occasion.

from *prep.* Starting at a particular time or place; used to indicate a specific place.

front *n.* The forward surface of an object or body; the area or position located before or ahead.

fron•tier *n.* A part of an international border or the area adjacent to it; an unexplored area of knowledge or thought.

fron•tis•piece *n.* An illustration preceding the title page of a book or periodical.

frost *n.* A feathery covering of minute ice crystals on a cold surface; the act or process of freezing.

frost•bite *n.* The local destruction of bodily tissue due to exposure to freezing temperatures, often resulting in gangrene.

frost•ing *n.* Icing; a mixture of egg whites, sugar, and butter.

froth *n.* A mass of bubbles on or in a liquid, resulting from agitation or fermentation; a salivary foam.

frown *v.* To contract the brow as in displeasure or concentration.

fro•zen *adj.* Covered with or made into ice; extremely cold, as a climate; immobilized or made rigid, as by fear.

fru•gal *adj.* Economical; thrifty.

fruit *n.* The ripened, mature, seed-bearing part of a flowering plant, especially the edible, fleshy kind, as an apple or plum.

frus•trate *v.* To thwart; to prevent; to keep from attaining a goal or fulfilling a desire.

fry *v.* To cook in hot fat or oil, especially over direct heat. *n.* A dish of any fried food.

fudge *n.* A soft, cooked candy containing sugar, butter, and a flavoring, as chocolate. *v.* To falsify or fit together in a clumsy way; to evade.

fuel *n.* A combustible matter consumed to generate energy, especially a material such as wood, coal, or oil burned to generate heat.

fu•gi•tive *adj.* Fleeing or having fled, as from arrest or pursuit. *n.* One who has fled from a place.

ful•crum *n.* The point on which a lever turns. **fulcrums, fulcra** *pl.*

ful•fill or **ful•fil** *v.* To convert into actuality; to complete; to carry out; to satisfy. **fulfillment** *n.*

fum•ble *v.* To handle idly; to blunder; to mishandle.

fumes *pl. n.* An irritating smoke, gas, or vapor.

fu•mi•gate *v.* To spray or apply airborne insecticides to exterminate vermin or insects.

func•tion *n.* The purpose of a thing or process; the reason something is used or made; a specific occupation, duty, or role; an official ceremony.

fund *n.* A source of supply; a sum of money reserved for a specific purpose.

fun•da•men•tal *adj.* Basic or essential; of major significance; most important.

fu•ner•al *n.* The service performed in conjunction with the burial or cremation of a dead person; an interment.

fun•gus *n.* Any of numerous spore-bearing plants which have no chlorophyll, such as yeasts, molds, mildews, and mushrooms. **fungous, fungal** *adj.*

fun•nel *n.* A cone-shaped utensil having a tube for channeling a substance into a container.

fu·ri·ous *adj.* Extremely angry; marked by rage or activity.

furl *v.* To roll up and secure to something, as a pole or mast; to curl or fold.

fur·lough *n.* Permission granted to be absent from duty, especially to members of the armed forces.

fur·nace *n.* A large enclosure designed to produce intense heat.

fur·nish *v.* To outfit or equip, as with fittings or furniture.

fur·ni·ture *n.* Movable articles, such as chairs and tables, used in a home, office, or other interior.

fu·ror *n.* Violent anger; rage; great excitement; commotion.

fur·row *n.* A long, narrow trench in the ground, made by a plow or other tool.

fu·ry *n.* Uncontrolled anger; turbulence; in mythology, an angry or spiteful woman.

fu·sil·lage *n.* The central section of an airplane, containing the wings and tail assembly.

fu·tile *adj.* Ineffectual; of no avail.

fuzz *n.* A mass of fine, loose particles, fibers, or hairs.

G

G, g The seventh letter of the English alphabet; in music, the fifth tone in the scale of C major.

gad *v.* To wander about restlessly with little or no purpose.

gadg·et *n.* A small device or tool used in performing odd tasks.

gag *n.* An obstacle to or any restraint of free speech; a practical joke or hoax.

gag·gle *n.* A flock of geese; a group; a cluster.

gai·e·ty *n.* The state of being happy; cheerfulness; fun.

gai·ly *adv.* In a cheerful manner.

gain *v.* To acquire possession of something; to succeed in winning a victory; to develop an increase of; to put on weight.

gain·ful *adj.* Producing profits; lucrative. **gainfully** *adv.*

gait *n.* A way or manner of moving on foot; one of the foot movements in which a horse steps or runs.

ga·la *n.* A festive celebration.

gal·ax·y *n.* Any of the very large systems of stars, nebulae, or other celestial bodies that constitute the universe; a brilliant, distinguished group or assembly.

gale *n.* A very powerful wind.

gal·lant *adj.* Dashing in appearance or dress; chivalrously attentive to women; courteous.

gal·lant·ry *n.* Nobility and bravery; a gallant act.

gal·ler·y *n.* A long, narrow passageway; a place for showing artwork.

gal·ley *n.* A long medieval ship propelled by sails and oars.

gal·lon *n.* A liquid measurement used in the U.S., equal to 4 quarts.

gal·lop *n.* A horse's gait faster than a canter and characterized by regular leaps during which all four feet are off the ground at once.

gal·lows *n.* A framework of two or more upright beams and a crossbeam, used for execution by hanging.

ga·lore *adj.* In great numbers; abundant.

gam·bit *n.* In chess, an opening in which a piece is sacrificed for a favorable position; a carefully planned maneuver.

gam·ble *v.* To take a chance on an uncertain outcome as a contest or a weekly lottery number. *n.* Any risky venture.

game *n.* A contest governed by specific rules; a way of entertaining oneself; amusement; animals or birds hunted for sport or food.

gam·ma ray *n.* Electromagnetic radiation that has energy greater than several hundred thousand electron volts.

gan·der *n.* A male goose; a quick glance; a look or peek.

gang *n.* A group of persons organized to work or socialize regularly; a group of adolescent hoodlums or criminals.

gan•gling *adj.* Tall and thin; lanky.

gang•plank *n.* A temporary board or ramp used to board or leave a ship.

gang•ster *n.* A member of a criminal gang.

gap *n.* An opening or wide crack, as in a wall; a cleft; a deep notch or ravine in a mountain ridge, offering passage.

gape *v.* To open the mouth wide, as in yawning; to stare in amazement with the mouth wide open.

ga•rage *n.* A building or structure to store or repair motor vehicles.

gar•bage *n.* Food wastes, consisting of unwanted or unusable pieces of meat, vegetables, and other food products; trash.

gar•ble *v.* To mix up or confuse; to change or distort the meaning of.

gar•den *n.* A place for growing flowers, vegetables, or fruit; a piece of ground commonly used as a public resort. *v.* To work in or make into a garden.

gar•gle *v.* To force air from the lungs through a liquid held in the back of the mouth and throat.

gar•land *n.* A wreath, chain, or rope of flowers or leaves.

gar•lic *n.* A plant related to the onion with a compound bulb which contains a strong odor and flavor, used as a seasoning.

gar•ment *n.* An article of clothing.

gar•net *n.* A dark-red silicate mineral used as a gemstone or abrasive.

gar•ret *n.* A room in an attic with a steep roof.

gas *n.* A form of matter capable of expanding to fill a container and taking on the shape of the container; a combustible mixture used as fuel; gasoline.

gash *n.* A long, deep cut.

gas mask *n.* A protective respirator for the face, containing a chemical air filter to protect against poisonous gases.

gas•o•line *n.* A colorless, highly flammable mixture of liquid hydrocarbons made from crude petroleum and used as a fuel.

gasp *v.* To inhale suddenly and sharply, as from fear or surprise; to make labored or violent attempts to breathe.

gate *n.* A movable opening in a wall or fence, commonly swinging on hinges, that closes or opens.

gath•er *v.* To bring or come together into one place or group; to harvest or pick; to accumulate slowly.

gaud•y *adj.* Too highly decorated to be in good taste.

gauge *n.* A standard measurement, dimension, or capacity; an instrument used for measuring, testing, or registering. *v.* To measure or estimate.

gaunt *adj.* Thin and bony; haggard.

gauze *n.* A loosely woven, transparent material used for surgical bandages; any thin, open-mesh material, a mist.

gav•el *n.* A mallet used by a presiding officer to call for order or attention.

gawk *v.* To gape; to stare stupidly.

gay *adj.* Merry; happy and carefree.

gaze *v.* To look intently at something in admiration or wonder; to stare.

ga•zelle *n.* A small antelope, having curved horns and large eyes.

gear *n.* A toothed wheel which interacts with another toothed part to transmit motion; equipment for a special task.

gel•a•tin *n.* An almost tasteless, odorless, dried protein derived from boiled animal tissues, used in making foods, drugs, and photographic film.

gem *n.* A cut and polished precious or semiprecious stone.

gen•der *n.* Any of two or more categories for pronouns, as feminine, masculine, and neuter; the quality of being of the male or female sex.

gene *n.* A functional unit on a chromosome, responsible for the transmission of hereditary characteristics.

gen•er•al *adj.* Including or affecting the whole or every member of a group or class; common to or typical of most.

gen•er•al•ize *v.* To draw a general conclusion from particular facts, experiences, or observations.

gen•er•al store *n.* A retail store selling a

large variety of merchandise but not subdivided into departments.

gen·er·ate *v.* To cause to be; to produce; to bring into existence, especially by a chemical or physical process. **generative** *adj.*

gen·er·a·tion *n.* A group of individuals born at about the same time; the average time interval between the birth of parents and that of their offspring. **generational** *adj.*

gen·er·a·tor *n.* A machine that changes mechanical energy into electrical energy.

gen·er·ous *adj.* Sharing freely; abundant. **generosity** *n.*, **generously** *adv.*

ge·net·ic *adj.* Of or pertaining to the origin or development of something; of or relating to genetics.

ge·net·ic code *n.* The biochemical basis of heredity that specifies the amino acid sequence in the synthesis of proteins and on which heredity is based.

gen·ius *n.* Exceptional intellectual ability or creative power; a strong, natural talent.

gen·tle *adj.* Not harsh, severe, rough, or loud; easily handled or managed; docile; not sudden or steep.

gen·tle·man *n.* A man of noble birth and social position; a courteous or polite man.

gen·tle·wo·man *n.* A woman of noble birth and social position; a well-bred or polite woman.

gen·u·ine *adj.* Real; authentic; not counterfeit; sincere. **genuinely** *adv.*, **genuineness** *n.*

ge·og·ra·phy *n.* The science of the earth's natural climate, resources, and population. **geographer** *n.*

ge·ol·o·gy *n.* The science of the history, origin, and structure of the earth. **geologist** *n.*

ge·om·e·try *n.* The branch of mathematics that deals with the measurement, properties, and relationship of lines, angles, points, surfaces and solids.

ge·ra·ni·um *n.* A plant having rounded leaves and clusters of pink, red, or white flowers.

ger·bil *n.* An animal of the rodent family having long hind legs and a long tail.

germ *n.* A small cell or organic structure from which a new organism may develop; a microorganism which causes disease.

Ger·man shep·herd *n.* A large breed of dog, often trained to help the police and the blind.

ger·und *n.* *gram.* A verb form used as a noun.

ges·ture *n.* A bodily motion, especially with the hands in speaking, to emphasize some idea or emotion.

get *v.* To come into possession of, as by receiving, winning, earning, or buying.

gey·ser *n.* A natural hot spring that intermittently ejects hot water and steam.

ghast·ly *adj.* Horrible; terrifying; very unpleasant or bad; ghost-like in appearance; deathly pale.

ghost *n.* The spirit of a dead person believed to appear to or haunt living persons; a spirit; a ghostwriter.

gi·ant *n.* A legendary man-like being of supernatural size and strength; one of great power, importance, or size.

gib·ber·ish *n.* Meaningless speech.

gib·bon *n.* A slender, long-armed ape.

gid·dy *adj.* Affected by a reeling or whirling sensation; dizzy; frivolous and silly.

GIF *abbr.* Graphic Interchange Format; in computers, a system for compressing visual material otherwise too large for easy electronic transfer.

gift *n.* Something given from one person to another; a natural aptitude; a talent.

gift·ed *adj.* The state of having a special talent or ability.

gi·gan·tic *adj.* Of tremendous or extraordinary size; huge.

gig·gle *v.* To laugh in high-pitched, repeated, short sounds.

gill *n.* The organ, as of fishes and various other aquatic invertebrates, used for taking oxygen from water.

gilt *adj.* Covered with or of the color of gold. *n.* A thin layer of gold or a gold-colored substance applied to a surface.

gim·mick n. A tricky feature obscured or misrepresented; a tricky device, especially when used dishonestly or secretly.

gin n. An aromatic, clear, alcoholic liquor distilled from grain and flavored with juniper berries; a machine used to separate seeds from cotton fibers.

gin·ger n. A tropical Asian plant that has a pungent aromatic root, used in medicine and cooking.

gin·ger·bread n. A dark, ginger and molasses flavored cake or cookie.

gin·ger·snap n. A brittle, molasses and ginger cookie.

gi·raffe n. The tallest mammal, having an extremely long neck and very long legs.

gir·dle n. A cord or belt worn around the waist; a supporting undergarment worn by women to give support and to shape.

girl n. A female child or infant; a very young, unmarried woman.

girl·friend n. A female friend; a regular female companion of a boy or man.

give v. To make a present of; to bestow; to accord or yield to another; to put into the possession of another.

give·a·way n. Something given free as a premium; something that betrays, generally unintentionally.

giv·en adj. Bestowed; presented; specified or assumed.

gi·ven name n. The name bestowed or given at birth or baptism.

gla·cial adj. Relating to glaciers; extremely cold.

gla·cier n. A large mass of compacted snow that moves slowly until it either breaks off to form icebergs or melts when it reaches warmer climates.

glad adj. Displaying or experiencing; a state of being happy; being willing to help.

glad·den v. To make glad.

glade n. A clearing in a forest or woods.

glam·or·ize v. To make glamorous; to portray or treat in a romantic way.

glam·our n. Alluring fascination or charm. **glamourous** adj.

glance v. To take a brief or quick look at something; to give a light, brief touch; to brush against.

gland n. Any of various body organs which excrete or secrete substances. **glandular** adj.

glare v. To stare fiercely or angrily; to shine intensely; to dazzle. n. An uncomfortably harsh or bright light.

glass n. A hard, amorphous, brittle, usually transparent material which hardens from the molten state; a mirror, tumbler, windowpane, lens, or other material made of glass.

glass blow·ing n. The art or process of shaping objects from molten glass by blowing air into them.

glass·es pl. n. A pair of eyeglasses used as an aid to vision; glassware.

glaze n. A thin, smooth coating as on ceramics. v. To become covered with a thin glassy coating of ice; to coat or cover with a glaze; to fit with glass.

gleam n. A momentary ray or beam of light. v. To shine or emit light softly; to appear briefly.

glee n. Joy; merriment. **gleeful** adj.

glee club n. A singing group organized to sing short pieces of choral music.

glen n. A small, secluded valley.

glib adj. Spoken easily and fluently; superficial. **glibly** adv., **glibness** n.

glide v. To pass or move smoothly with little or no effort; to fly without motor power.

glid·er n. One that glides; a swing gliding in a metal frame; an aircraft without an engine, constructed to soar on air currents.

glim·mer n. A faint suggestion; an indication; a dim unsteady light.

glimpse n. A momentary look; a brief view.

glis·ten v. To shine softly as reflected by light.

glitch n. A minor mishap or malfunction.

glit·ter n. A brilliant sparkle; small bits of light-reflecting material used for decoration. *v.* To sparkle with brilliance. **glittery** *adj.*

gloat *v.* To express, feel, or observe with malicious pleasure or self-satisfaction.

glob·al *adj.* Spherical; involving the whole world. **globalize** *v.*

globe *n.* A spherical object; anything perfectly rounded; the earth.

globe-trot·ter *n.* One who travels all over the world.

gloom *n.* Partial or total darkness; depression of the mind or spirits.

glo·ri·fy *v.* To worship and give glory to; to give high praise. **glorification** *n.*

glo·ri·ous *adj.* Magnificent; resplendent; full of glory.

glo·ry *n.* Distinguished praise or honor; exalted reputation; adoration and praise offered in worship.

gloss *n.* The sheen or luster of a polished surface; a deceptively or superficially attractive appearance.

glos·sa·ry *n.* A list of terms and their meanings.

gloss·y *adj.* Having a bright sheen; lustrous; superficially attractive.

glove *n.* A covering for the hand with a separate section for each finger; an oversized protective covering for the hand.

glow *v.* To give off heat or light, especially without a flame; to have a bright, warm, ruddy color.

glow·worm *n.* A luminous larva or grub-like female of an insect which displays phosphorescent light; the firefly.

glue *n.* Any of various adhesives used to stick and hold items together.

glum *adj.* Moody and silent.

glut·ton *n.* Someone who eats immoderately. **gluttony** *n.*

gnat *n.* A small, winged insect, specially one that bites or stings.

gnaw *v.* To chew or eat with persistence.

gnu *n.* South African antelope with an ox-like head, curved horns, a long tail, and a mane.

go *v.* To proceed or pass along; to leave; to move away from; to follow a certain course of action; to function.

goal *n.* A purpose; the terminal point of a race or journey.

goal·keep·er *n.* The player responsible for defending the goal in hockey, soccer, and other games.

goat *n.* A horned, cud-chewing mammal related to the sheep.

goat·ee *n.* A short, pointed beard on a man's chin.

goat·skin *n.* The skin of a goat, often used for leather.

gob·ble *v.* To eat and swallow food greedily; to take greedily.

gob·bler *n.* A male turkey.

gob·let *n.* A drinking glass, typically with a base and stem.

god *n.* Someone considered to be extremely important or valuable; an image, symbol, or statue of such a being.

God *n.* The Supreme Being; the ruler of life and the universe.

god·child *n.* A child for whom an adult serves as sponsor at baptism and other rites.

god·dess *n.* A female of exceptional charm, beauty, or grace.

god·fa·ther *n.* A man who sponsors a child at his or her baptism or other such ceremony.

god·moth·er *n.* A woman who sponsors a child at his or her baptism or other such ceremony.

god·par·ent *n.* A godfather or godmother.

god·send *n.* Something received unexpectedly and needed or wanted.

god·son *n.* A male godchild.

go-get·ter *n.* An enterprising, aggressive person.

gog·gles *pl. n.* Spectacles or eyeglasses to protect the eyes against dust, wind, sparks, and other debris.

go·ing *n.* The act of moving, leaving, or departing; the condition of roads or ground that affects walking, riding, and other movement.

gold *n.* A soft, yellow, metallic element highly ductile and resistant to oxidation;

used especially in coins and jewelry.

gold•en *adj.* Made of or containing gold; bright yellow in color; rich; lustrous; marked by prosperity.

gold•en an•ni•ver•sa•ry *n.* The fiftieth anniversary.

gold•en rule *n.* The principle of treating others as one wants to be treated.

gold•fish *n.* A reddish or brass-colored freshwater fish, cultivated as an aquarium fish; a carp.

gold mine *n.* A mine which produces gold ore; any source of great riches or profit.

golf *n.* A game played outdoors with a hard ball and various clubs, on a grassy course with nine or eighteen holes.

gon•do•la *n.* A long, narrow, flat-bottomed boat propelled by a single oar and used on the canals of Venice.

gone *adj.* Past; bygone; dead; beyond hope; participle of *go.*

good *adj.* Having desirable or favorable qualities or characteristics; morally excellent; virtuous; well-behaved.

good-by or **good-bye** *interj.* Used to express farewell. *n.* A farewell; a parting word; an expression of farewell.

good-heart•ed *adj.* Having a kind and generous disposition. **good-hearted-ness** *n.*

good-hu•mored *adj.* Having a cheerful temper or mood; amiable.

good-look•ing *adj.* Handsome; having a pleasing appearance.

good-na•tured *adj.* Having an easygoing and pleasant disposition.

good•ness *n.* The state or quality of being good.

good•will *n.* A desire for the well-being of others; the pleasant feeling or relationship between a business and its customers.

goose *n.* A large water bird related to swans and ducks. **geese** *pl.*

go•pher *n.* A burrowing North American rodent with large cheek pouches.

gorge *n.* A deep, narrow ravine; deep or violent disgust.

gor•geous *adj.* Beautiful; dazzling; extremely attractive.

go•ril•la *n.* A large African jungle ape, having a massive, stocky body, long arms, and tusk-like canine teeth.

gos•ling *n.* A young goose.

gos•pel or **Gos•pel** *n.* The teachings of Christ and the apostles; any information accepted as unquestionably true; any of the first four books of the New Testament.

gos•pel mus•ic *n.* American religious music based on simple folk melodies blended with rhythmic and melodic elements of spirituals and jazz.

gos•sip *n.* Idle, often malicious talk; a person who spreads sensational or intimate facts.

gou•lash *n.* A stew made from beef or veal and vegetables seasoned chiefly with paprika.

gourd *n.* A vine fruit related to the pumpkin, squash, and cucumber and bearing inedible fruit with a hard rind.

gour•met *n.* Someone who appreciates and understands fine food and drink.

gov•ern *v.* To guide, rule, or control by right or authority; to control or guide the action of something. **governable** *adj.*, **governance** *n.*

gov•ern•ess *n.* A woman employed in a private household to train and instruct children.

gov•ern•ment *n.* The authoritative administration of public policy and affairs of a nation, state, or city; the system or policy by which a political unit is governed.

gov•er•nor *n.* Someone who governs, as the elected chief executive of any state in the United States.

gown *n.* A woman's dress, especially for a formal affair; any long, loose-fitting garment; a robe worn by certain officials.

grab *v.* To snatch or take suddenly; to take possession of by force.

grace *n.* Seemingly effortless beauty and charm of movement, proportion, or form; a charming quality or characteristic.

gra•cious *adj.* Marked by having or

showing kindness and courtesy; full of compassion; merciful.

grade *n.* A step or degree in a process or series; a group or category; a level of progress in school, usually constituting a year's work.

grade school *n.* Elementary school, which will usually teach from kindergarten to grade six or eight.

grad·u·al *adj.* Moving or changing slowly by degrees; not steep or abrupt. **gradually** *adv.*

grad·u·ate *v.* To receive or be granted an academic diploma or degree upon completion of a course of study. **graduation** *n.*

graf·fi·to *n.* An inscription or drawing made on a public wall, subway train, rock, or any other surface. **graffiti** *pl.*

gra·ham *n.* Whole wheat flour.

grain *n.* A small, hard seed or kernel of cereal, wheat, or oats; the seeds or fruits of such plants as a group; a very small amount; the direction of growth in a fibrous substance such as wood.

gram *n.* A metric unit of mass and weight equal to 1/1000 kilogram and nearly equal to one cubic centimeter of water at its maximum density.

gram·mar *n.* The study and description of the classes of words, their relations to each other, and their arrangement into sentences.

gram·mar school *n.* An elementary school.

grand *adj.* To be large in size, extent, or scope; magnificent; of high rank or great importance.

grand·child *n.* The child of one's son or daughter.

grand·dad *n.* The father of one's mother or father.

grand·daugh·ter *n.* The daughter of one's son or daughter.

gran·deur *n.* The quality or condition of being grand; splendor.

grand·fa·ther *n.* The father of one's father or mother; an ancestor.

grand·fa·ther clock *n.* A pendulum clock enclosed in a tall narrow cabinet.

grand·moth·er *n.* The mother of one's father or mother; a female ancestor.

grand·par·ent *n.* A parent of one's mother or father.

grand pi·an·o *n.* A piano with the strings arranged horizontally in a curved, wooden case.

grand·son *n.* A son of one's son or daughter.

grand·stand *n.* A raised stand of seats, usually roofed, for spectators at a racetrack or sports event.

gran·ite *n.* A hard, coarse-grained igneous rock composed chiefly of quartz and mica, used for building material and in sculpture.

grant *v.* To allow; to consent to; to admit something as being the truth. *n.* An award of money for a study or experiment.

grape *n.* Any of numerous woody vines bearing clusters of smooth-skinned, juicy, edible berries.

grape·fruit *n.* A tropical, large, round citrus fruit with a pale yellow rind and tart, juicy pulp.

grape·vine *n.* A climbing vine that produces grapes; a secret or informal means of transmitting information or rumor from person to person.

graph *n.* A visual diagram representing the relationship between sets of things.

graph·ic or **graph·i·cal** *adj.* Describing in full detail; of or pertaining to drawings or blueprints, as in architecture.

grasp *v.* To seize and grip firmly; to comprehend; to understand.

grasp·ing *adj.* Urgently desiring material possessions; greedy.

grass *n.* Any of numerous plants having narrow leaves and jointed stems; the ground on which grass is growing.

grass·hop·per *n.* Any of several jumping insects with long powerful hind legs.

grate *v.* To reduce, shred or pulverize by rubbing against a rough or sharp surface; to make or cause to make a harsh sound.

n. A framework or bars placed over a window or other opening; an iron frame to hold burning fuel in a fireplace or furnace.

grate·ful *adj.* Thankful or appreciative for benefits or kindnesses; expressing gratitude.

grat·i·fy *v.* To give pleasure or satisfaction to; to fulfill the desires of; to indulge. **gratification** *n.*

grat·ing *n.* A grate.

grat·i·tude *n.* Appreciation and gratefulness; thankfulness.

grave *n.* A burial place for a dead body, usually an excavation in the earth. *adj.* Very serious or important in nature; filled with danger; critical.

grav·el *n.* Loose rock fragments often with sand.

grave·stone *n.* A stone that marks a grave; a tombstone.

grave·yard *n.* An area set aside as a burial place; a cemetery.

grav·i·ty *n.* The gravitational force manifested by the tendency of material bodies to fall toward the center of the earth.

gra·vy *n.* The juices exuded by cooking meat; a sauce made by seasoning and thickening these juices.

gray or **grey** *adj.* A neutral color between black and white; gloomy; dismal; characteristic of old age.

graze *v.* To feed upon growing grasses or herbage; to put livestock to feed on grass or pasturage; to brush against lightly in passing.

grease *n.* Melted or soft animal fat; any thick fatty or oily substance; lubrication.

great *adj.* Very large in size or volume; prolonged in duration or extent; more than ordinary.

greed *n.* Selfish desire for more than one needs or deserves.

greed·y *adj.* Excessively eager to acquire or gain something.

green *adj.* Of the color between yellow and blue in the spectrum; not fully matured or developed; lacking in skill or experience.

green·house *n.* An enclosed structure equipped with heat and moisture designed for the cultivation of plants.

greet *v.* To address someone in a friendly way; to welcome.

greet·ing *n.* A word of salutation.

grew *v.* Past tense of *grow.*

grey·hound *n.* One of a breed of slender, swift-running dogs with long legs.

grid *n.* An arrangement of regularly spaced bars; the system of intersecting parallel lines that divide maps, charts, and aerial photographs, used as a reference for locating points.

grid·dle *n.* A flat pan used for cooking.

grief *n.* Deep sadness or mental distress caused by a loss or bereavement.

griev·ance *n.* A real or imagined wrong regarded as cause for complaint or resentment; a complaint of unfair treatment.

grieve *v.* To cause or feel grief or sorrow. **grievous** *adj.*

grill *n.* A cooking utensil made from parallel metal bars; a grating with open metalwork used as a decorative screen or room divider.

grim *adj.* Stern or forbidding in appearance or character.

grime *n.* Dirt, especially soot clinging to or coating a surface. **griminess** *n.*, **grimy** *adj.*

grin *v.* To smile broadly.

grind *v.* To reduce to fine particles; to sharpen, polish, or shape by friction.

grip *n.* A firm hold; a grasp; the ability to seize or maintain a hold; a suitcase. *v.* To grasp and keep a firm hold on.

gripe *v.* To anger; to annoy; to complain.

groan *v.* To utter a deep, prolonged sound of pain or disapproval.

gro·cer *n.* A storekeeper who deals in foodstuffs and various household supplies. **grocery** *n.*

gro·cer·ies *pl. n.* The merchandise sold in a grocery.

grog·gy *adj.* Dazed, weak, or not fully conscious.

groom *n.* A male person hired to tend horses; a stableman; a bridegroom. *v.* To make neat in appearance.

groove *n.* A long, narrow channel or indentation; a fixed, settled habit or routine; a rut. **groove** *v.*

grope *v.* The act of feeling about, as in the dark; to look for uncertainly or blindly.

gross *adj.* Relating to the total amount received; excessively large or fat; lacking refinement or delicacy; coarse; vulgar. *n.* An amount that equals 12 dozen or 144 items.

gro·tesque *adj.* Distorted or incongruous in appearance or style; bizarre; outlandish.

grot·to *n.* A cave or cave-like structure; a natural place of meditation or prayer.

grouch *n.* A habitually irritable or complaining person.

ground *n.* The surface of the earth; soil, sand, and other natural material at or near the earth's surface.

ground *v.* Past tense of *grind*; to prohibit flight; to run a boat onto the bottom.

grounds *n.* The land that surrounds a building; the basis for an argument, action or belief; the sediment at the bottom of a liquid, such as coffee or tea.

group *n.* A collection or assemblage of people, objects, or things having something in common.

grove *n.* A small group of trees, lacking undergrowth.

grow *v.* To increase in size, develop, and reach maturity; to expand; to increase.

growl *v.* To utter a deep, guttural, threatening sound.

grown·up *n.* A mature adult.

growth *n.* The act or process of growing; a gradual increase in size or amount.

gru·el *n.* A thin liquid made by boiling meal in water or milk.

gru·el·ing or **gru·el·ling** *adj.* Extremely tiring; exhausting.

grue·some *adj.* Causing horror or fright.

gruff *adj.* Surly or ill-tempered; deep-voiced; rough.

grum·ble *v.* To complain in low, throaty sounds; to growl.

grump·y *adj.* Irritable and moody; sour of temperament.

grunt *n.* The deep, guttural sound of a hog.

guar·an·tee *v.* To promise or assure the durability or quality of a product.

guar·an·ty *n.* A pledge or promise to be responsible for the debt, duty, or contract of another person in case of default; something that guarantees.

guard *v.* To watch over or shield from danger or harm; to keep watch.

guard·i·an *n.* One legally assigned responsibility for the care of the person and property of an infant, minor or other person.

guard·rail *n.* The protective rail, as on a highway or any area that poses danger.

guess *v.* To make a judgment or form an opinion on uncertain or incomplete knowledge; to suppose; to believe.

guest *n.* A person who is the recipient of hospitality from another; a customer who pays for lodging.

guide *n.* One who leads or directs another, as in a course of action; a person employed to conduct others on trips through museums and sightseeing tours. **guid·ance** *n.* Advice or direction toward a goal.

guide·book *n.* A handbook containing directions and other information for tourists and visitors.

guide·line *n.* Any suggestion, statement, or outline of policy or procedure.

guilt *n.* The condition or fact of having committed a crime or wrongdoing.

guilt·less *adj.* A state or condition of being without guilt; innocent.

guilt·y *adj.* Deserving of blame for an offense that has been committed; convicted of some offense.

gui·tar *n.* A musical instrument with six strings, played by plucking or strumming.

gulf *n.* A large area of ocean or sea partially enclosed by land; a wide, impassable difference.

gull *n.* A long-winged, web-footed sea bird, usually white and gray, with a hooked upper mandible.

gulp *v.* To swallow rapidly or in large

amounts; to gasp or choke.

gum *n.* A sticky, viscous substance exuded from various trees and plants, soluble in water and hardening on exposure to air; chewing gum.

gum•drop *n.* A small, round, firm piece of jelly-like, sugar-coated candy.

gun *n.* A weapon made of metal from which a projectile is thrown by the force of an explosion; a portable firearm.

gun•pow•der *n.* An explosive powder used in blasting, fireworks, and guns.

gun•shot *n.* A shot fired from a gun.

gun•smith *n.* A person who makes or repairs guns.

gush•er *n.* An oil well with a plentiful natural flow of oil; a person who gushes.

gust *n.* A sudden, violent rush of wind or air; a sudden outburst, as of emotion.

gut *n.* The alimentary canal or part of it.

gut•ter *n.* A channel or ditch at the side of a street for carrying off water; a trough for carrying off rain water from the roof.

gym *n.* A gymnasium.

gym•na•si•um *n.* A room or building equipped for indoor sports.

gym•nas•tics *pl. n.* Physical exercises requiring strength and flexibility, especially those performed with special apparatus in a gymnasium.

H

H, h The eighth letter of the English alphabet.

hab•it *n.* Involuntary pattern of behavior acquired by frequent repetition; manner of conducting oneself; an addiction.

hab•it•able *adj.* Suitable for habitation.

hab•i•tat *n.* The region in which an animal or plant lives or grows; the place of residence of a person or group.

hab•it•form•ing *adj.* Producing physiological addiction.

ha•bit•u•al *adj.* Practicing by or acting according to habit; resorted to on a regular basis; regular. **habitually** *adv.*

hack *v.* To cut with repeated irregular blows; to enter a computer memory without permission. *n.* A tool used for hacking; a rough, dry cough; a taxi driver.

hack•er *n.* In computers, an electronics expert capable of improvising creative solutions; especially, intruders who use such expertise to enter unauthorized files.

hadn't *contr.* Had not.

hag *n.* A woman who will not be wooed; a witch. **haggish** *adj.*

hag•gard *adj.* Worn-out, exhausted; gaunt, as from hunger or fatigue. **haggardly** *adv.*, **haggardness** *n.*

hag•gle *v.* To argue or bargain on price or terms.

hai•ku *n.* An unrhymed Japanese verse form with three short lines of five, seven, and five syllables.

hail *n.* Precipitation of small, hard lumps of ice and snow; a hailstone; an exclamation, greeting, acclamation. *v.* To call loudly in greeting or welcome; to shout with enthusiasm.

hail•stone *n.* A type of hard pellet made of frozen snow and ice.

hair *n.* One of the pigmented filaments that grow from the skin of most mammals; a covering of such structures, as on the human head and on the skin; a slender margin. **hairy** *adj.*

hair•brush *n.* An instrument used for grooming the hair.

hair•cloth *n.* A wiry, stiff fabric of horsehair.

hale *adj.* Healthy and robust; free from defect.

half *n.* One of two equal divisible parts; part of a thing approximately equal to the remainder; one of a pair.

hall•mark *n.* An official mark placed on gold and silver products to attest to their purity.

hal•low *v.* To sanctify; to make holy; to honor.

Hal•low•een *n.* October 31, the eve of All Saints' Day, celebrated particularly by children.

hal·lu·ci·na·tion *n.* An illusion of seeing something nonexistent; a delusion. **hallucinate** *v.*

ha·lo *n.* A ring of colored light surrounding the head; an aura.

hal·ter *n.* A rope or strap for leading or tying an animal; a woman's upper garment tied behind the neck and across the back.

halve *v.* To divide into two equal parts; to lessen by half.

ham *n.* The meat of a hog's thigh; the back of the knee or thigh; an amateur or showy actor or performer.

ham·let *n.* A small rural village or town.

ham·mer *n.* A hand tool with a heavy head used to drive or strike forcefully, especially nails.

ham·mock *n.* A hanging bed or couch of fabric or heavy netting, suspended from supports at each end.

ham·per *v.* To interfere with movement or progress of. *n.* A ventilated, covered, receptacle used to store dirty laundry.

ham·ster *n.* Any of various rodents with large cheek pouches and a short tail.

ham·string *n.* Either of two tendons located at the back of the human knee; the large tendon at the back of the hock of four-footed animals.

hand *n.* The part of the arm below the wrist, consisting of the palm, four fingers, and a thumb; a set of cards dealt to a player in a card game.

hand·book *n.* A small guide or reference book giving information or instructions.

hand·cuff *v.* To put handcuffs on; to make ineffective. *pl.* A pair of circular metal shackles chained together that can be fastened around the wrists.

hand·gun *n.* A gun that can be held and fired with one hand.

hand·i·cap *n.* Any disadvantage that makes achievement unusually difficult; a contest in which odds are equalized; an obstacle. *v.* To give a handicap to.

hand·i·craft or **hand·craft** *n.* Skill and expertise in working with the hands; an occupation requiring manual dexterity.

hand·ker·chief *n.* A small piece of cloth used for wiping the face or nose; a kerchief or scarf.

han·dle *v.* To touch, pick up, or hold with the hands; to represent.

hand·made *adj.* Made by hand or by a hand process.

hand·out *n.* Free food, clothing, or cash given to the needy; a folder distributed free of charge; a flyer.

hand·shake *n.* The act of clasping hands by two people, as in greeting, agreement, or parting.

hand·some *adj.* Very good-looking or attractive.

hand·spring *n.* An acrobatic feat in which the body flips entirely backward or forward, while the feet pass quickly in an arc over the head.

hand·stand *n.* The feat of supporting the body on the hands with feet balanced in the air.

hand·writ·ing *n.* Writing performed with the hand, especially cursive, the type of writing of a person.

hand·y *adj.* Easy to use or reach; helpful or useful. **handily** *adv.*

hand·y·man *n.* A person who does odd jobs and repairs.

hang *v.* To be attached from above and unsupported from below; to fasten or be suspended so as to swing freely.

hang·ar *n.* A building for housing aircraft.

hang·er *n.* A device from which something may be hung or on which something hangs.

hang glid·er *n.* A device shaped like a kite from which a person hangs suspended in a harness while gliding through the air.

hang·nail *n.* The small piece of skin that hangs loose from the side or root of a fingernail.

hap·haz·ard *adj.* Occurring by accident; happening by chance or at random; hit-or-miss.

hap·less *adj.* Unfortunate; unlucky. **haplessly** *adv.*

hap·pen *v.* To occur or come to pass; to

take place; to discover by chance; to turn up or appear by chance. **happening** *n.*

hap•py *adj.* Enjoying contentment and well-being; glad, joyous, satisfied or pleased. **happily** *adv.*, **happiness** *n.*

hap•py-go-luck•y *adj.* Carefree and unconcerned.

ha•rangue *n.* A long, extravagant, speech; a lecture.

ha•rass *v.* To disturb or annoy constantly; to torment persistently. **harassment**, **harasser** *n.*

har•bor *n.* A place of refuge or shelter; a bay or cove; an anchorage for ships. *v.* To provide shelter.

hard *adj.* Difficult to perform, endure, or comprehend; solid in texture or substance; resistant to cutting or penetration.

hard-boiled *adj.* Boiled or cooked in the shell to a hard or solid state.

hard co•py *n.* In computer science, the printed information from a computer.

hard disk *n.* In computer science, magnetic storage consisting of a rigid disk of aluminum coated with a magnetic recording substance, contained within a removable cartridge or mounted in the hard disk of a microcomputer.

hard•en *v.* To make or become hard or harder; to make or become physically or mentally tough.

hard hat *n.* A protective head covering made of rigid material, worn by construction workers.

hard•ly *adj.* Very little; almost certainly not. *adv.* Forcefully; painfully; barely.

hard-nosed *adj.* Stubborn; hard-headed; unyielding.

hard rock *n.* Rock music featuring amplified sound and modulations.

hard sell *n.* A sales method involving aggressive, high-pressure selling and closing techniques.

hard•ship *n.* A painful, difficult condition.

hard•tack *n.* A hard, cracker-like biscuit made from flour and water.

hard•top *n.* A car with a permanent top designed to resemble a convertible.

hard•ware *n.* Manufactured machine parts, such as tools and utensils; the mechanical components of a computer installation.

har•dy *adj.* Bold and robust; able to survive very unfavorable conditions as extreme cold; daring. **-iness** *n.*, **-ily** *adv.*

hare *n.* Various mammals related to the rabbits but having longer ears and legs.

hare-brained *adj.* Foolish or silly.

har•em *n.* The women living in a Muslim residence; the living quarters of a harem.

hark *v.* To listen closely.

har•le•quin *n.* A jester; a clown. *adj.* Patterned with vividly colored diamond shapes.

harm *n.* Emotional or physical damage or injury. *v.* To cause damage or injury to. **harmful** *adj.* **harmless** *adj.*

har•mon•ic *adj.* Relating to musical harmony; in harmony; concordant. **harmonically** *adv.*

har•mon•i•ca *n.* A small, rectangular musical instrument having a series of tuned metal reeds that vibrate with the player's breath.

har•mo•ny *n.* Complete agreement, as of feeling or opinion; an agreeable combination of components; pleasing sounds; a combination of musical tones into chords.

har•ness *n.* The working gear of a horse or other draft animal.

harp *n.* A musical instrument having a triangular upright frame with strings plucked with the fingers. **harpist** *n.*

har•poon *n.* A barbed spear used in hunting whales and fish.

harsh *adj.* Disagreeable; extremely severe.

har•vest *n.* The process or act of gathering a crop; the season or time for gathering crops. *v.* To reap; to obtain as if by gathering. **harvester** *n.*

hash *n.* A fried or baked mixture of chopped meat and potatoes. *v.* To chop up into small pieces.

haste *n.* Speed; swiftness of motion or action; excessive eagerness to act.

has•ten *v.* To act or move with speed.

hast•y *adj.* Rapid; swift; made or done with excessive speed.

hat *n.* A covering for the head with a crown and brim.

hat•box *n.* A container or box used for storing or carrying hats.

hatch *n.* A small opening or door, as in a ship's deck. *v.* To bring forth, as young from an egg; to devise.

hatch•back *n.* An automobile with a sloped roof in the back that opens upward.

hatch•et *n.* A small ax with a short handle.

hate *v.* To feel hostility or animosity toward; to dislike intensely.

ha•tred *n.* A deep-seated animosity.

haugh•ty *adj.* Arrogantly proud; disdainful. **haughtiness** *n.*

haul *v.* To pull or draw with force; to move or transport, as in a truck or cart. *n.* The distance over which someone travels or something is transported; an amount collected at one time.

haunch *n.* The hip; the buttock and upper thigh of an animal; the loin and leg of a four-footed animal.

haunt *v.* To appear to or visit as a ghost or spirit; to linger in the mind. **haunting** *adj.*

have *n.* To hold or own, as a possession or as property; to possess.

hav•oc *n.* Mass confusion; widespread destruction; devastation.

hawk *n.* Any of several predatory birds, with a short, hooked bill and strong claws for seizing small prey; one who advocates a war-like foreign policy.

hay *n.* Alfalfa or grass that has been cut and dried for animal food.

hay fe•ver *n.* An acute allergy to certain airborne pollens, marked by severe irritation of the upper respiratory tract and the eyes.

hay•loft *n.* An upper loft in a barn or stable used to store hay.

hay•stack *n.* A pile of hay stored outdoors.

haz•ard *n.* A risk; chance; an accident; a danger or source of danger.

haze *n.* A fog-like suspension of dust, smoke, and vapor in the air; a confused or vague state of mind. *v.* To harass as part of an initiation ceremony.

haz•y *adj.* Lacking clarity; vague; seen through a haze.

head *n.* The upper part of a human or animal body, containing the brain, the principal nerve centers, the eyes, ears, nose and mouth.

head•ache *n.* A pain or ache in the head.

head•band *n.* A band of cloth worn around the head.

head•board *n.* A frame or panel that stands at the head of a bed.

head cold *n.* A common cold or viral infection that centers primarily in the nasal passages.

head•first *adv.* With the head in a forward position; headlong.

head•ing *n.* A title or caption that acts as a front or upper part of anything; the direction or course of a ship or aircraft.

head•line *n.* A title, caption, or summarizing words of a newspaper story or article printed in large type. *v.* To serve as the star performer. **headliner** *n.*

head•quar•ters *pl. n.* The official location from which a leader directs a complex activity; the home offices of a corporation.

head•set *n.* A pair of headphones.

head•y *adj.* Tending to intoxicate; affecting the senses.

heal *v.* To restore to good health; to mend. **healable** *adj.*

health *n.* The overall sound condition or function of a living organism at a particular time; freedom from disease or defect. **healthful** *adj.*, **healthfully** *adv.*, **healthfulness** *n.*

health•y *adj.* In a state of or having good health; characteristic of a sound condition.

heap *n.* A haphazard assortment of things; a large number or quantity; a pile. *v.* To throw or pile into a heap.

hear *v.* To perceive by the ear; to listen with careful attention; to be informed of; to listen to officially or formally.

hear•ing *n.* One of the five senses; the

range by which sound can be heard; an opportunity to be heard.

hear·ing aid *n.* An electronic device used to amplify the hearing of partially deaf persons.

hear·say *n.* Information heard from another; common talk; rumor.

hearse *n.* A vehicle for conveying a dead body to the place of burial.

heart *n.* The hollow, primary muscular organ of vertebrates which circulates blood throughout the body; the emotional center, such as in love, hate, consideration, or compassion; the most essential part of something.

heart·ache *n.* Emotional grief; sorrow.

heart at·tack *n.* An acute malfunction or interrupted heart function.

heart·beat *n.* A pulsation of the heart, consisting of one contraction and one relaxation.

heart·break *n.* Great sorrow; deep grief. **heartbreaking** *adj.*

heart·burn *n.* A sensation of burning in the stomach and esophagus, usually caused by excess acid in the stomach.

heart·en *v.* To give courage to; to strengthen the heart.

heart·felt *adj.* Deeply felt; sincere.

heart·land *n.* A strategically important central region, or one regarded as vital to a nation's character.

heart·less *adj.* Having no sympathy; lacking compassion. **heartlessness** *n.*, **heartlessly** *adv.*

heart·y *adj.* Marked by exuberant warmth; full of vigor; nourishing; substantial.

heat *n.* A quality of being hot or warm; a degree of warmth; depth of feeling.

hea·then *n.* A person or nation that does not recognize the God of Christianity, Judaism, or Islam.

heave *v.* To raise or lift, especially forcibly; to hurl or throw.

heav·en *n.* The sky; the region above and around the earth; the abode of God, the angels, and the blessed souls of the dead; a state or place of blissful happiness.

heav·y *adj.* Of great weight; very thick or dense; forceful; powerful; rough and violent, as stormy weather.

heav·y-du·ty *adj.* Designed for hard use; sturdy and durable.

heck·le *v.* To badger or annoy.

hec·tic *adj.* Intensely active, rushed, or excited; confusingly complex.

hedge *n.* A boundary or fence formed of shrubs or low-growing trees.

hedge·hog *n.* A small nocturnal mammal with dense spines on the back for defense.

heed *v.* To pay attention; to take notice of something.

heel *n.* The rounded back part of the human foot under and behind the ankle; the part of a shoe supporting or covering the heel; a lower or bottom part; the crusty ends of a loaf of bread.

heft·y *adj.* Bulky; heavy; sizable.

heif·er *n.* A young cow that has not yet produced a calf.

height *n.* The quality of being high; the highest or most advanced point; the distance from the base of something.

height·en *v.* To increase or become high in quality or degree.

Heim·lich ma·neu·ver *n.* An emergency maneuver used to dislodge food from a choking person's throat; the closed fist is placed below the rib cage and pressed inward to force air from the lungs upward.

heir *n.* A person who inherits another's property or title.

heir·ess *n.* A female heir, especially to a large fortune.

heir·loom *n.* A family possession handed down from generation to generation.

hel·i·cop·ter *n.* An aircraft propelled by rotors which can take off vertically.

hel·i·port *n.* A designed area where helicopters land and take off.

hell or **Hell** *n.* The abode of the dead souls condemned to eternal punishment; a place of evil, torment, or destruction.

helm *n.* A wheel or steering apparatus for a ship.

hel·met *n.* A protective covering for the

head made of metal, leather, or plastic.

helms·man *n.* One who guides a ship.

help *v.* To assist or aid. *n.* Assistance; relief; one who assists; one hired to help.

help·ing *n.* A single serving of food.

help·less *adj.* Without help; powerless; lacking strength.

hem *n.* A finished edge of fabric folded under and stitched.

hem·i·sphere *n.* A half sphere divided by a plane passing through its center; either symmetrical half of an approximately spherical shape; the northern or southern half of the earth.

hemp *n.* An Asian herb whose tough fiber is used in the manufacture of rope.

hen *n.* A mature female bird, especially an adult female domestic fowl.

her·ald *n.* A person who announces important news; an official whose duty is to announce royal proclamations.

her·ald·ry *n.* The art or science of tracing genealogies and devising and granting coats of arms.

herb *n.* A soft-stemmed plant without woody tissue that usually withers and dies each year; an often pleasant-smelling plant. **herbal** *adj.*

herb·al·ist *n.* One who gathers, grows, and deals in herbs.

herd *n.* A number of cattle or other animals of the same kind, kept or staying together as a group.

here·af·ter *adv.* From now on; at some future time. *n.* Existence after death.

here·by *adv.* By means or by virtue of this.

he·red·i·tar·y *adj.* Passing or transmitted from an ancestor to a legal heir; transmitted or transmissible by genetic inheritance.

he·red·i·ty *n.* The genetic transmission of physical traits from parents to offspring.

her·i·tage *n.* Property inherited; something handed down from past generations.

her·mit *n.* A person who lives in seclusion, often for religious reasons. **hermitage** *n.*

he·ro *n.* A figure in mythology and legend renowned for exceptional courage and fortitude. **heroes** *pl.*

her·o·ine *n.* A woman of heroic character; the principal female character in a story or play.

her·o·ism *n.* Heroic behavior.

her·on *n.* A wading bird with a long slender bill and long legs and neck.

hes·i·tant *adj.* Given to hesitating; lacking decisiveness. **hesitancy** *n.*

hes·i·tate *v.* To pause or to be slow before acting, speaking, or deciding; to be uncertain.

hew *v.* To make or shape with an axe; to adhere strictly; to conform.

hex·a·gon *n.* A polygon having six sides and six angles.

hi·ber·nate *v.* To pass the winter in an inactive, dormant, sleep-like state. **hibernation** *n.*

hic·cup or **hic·cough** *n.* An involuntary contraction of the diaphragm that occurs on inhalation and spasmodically closes the glottis, producing a short, sharp sound.

hick·o·ry *n.* A North American tree with a smooth or shaggy bark, hard edible nuts, and heavy, tough wood.

hide *v.* To put, or keep out of sight; to keep secret; to obscure from sight. *n.* The skin of an animal.

hid·e·ous *adj.* Physically repulsive; extremely ugly.

hi·er·ar·chy *n.* An authoritative body or group of things or persons arranged in successive order; a ranked series of persons or things.

high *adj.* Extending upward; located at a distance above the ground; more than normal in degree or amount.

high·brow *n.* One who claims superior knowledge or culture.

high·land *n.* Land elevated as a plateau; a hilly or mountainous region.

high·light *n.* A significant event or detail of special importance. *v.* To give emphasis to; to provide with highlights.

high-rise *n.* An extremely tall residential building; a skyscraper.

high·road *n.* A main road; a direct or

honorable method or course.

high school *n.* A secondary school of grades nine through twelve or grades ten through twelve.

high seas *pl. n.* The open waters of an ocean or sea beyond the territorial jurisdiction of any one nation.

high tide *n.* The highest level reached by the incoming tide each day.

high•way *n.* A main or principal road or thoroughfare of some length connecting towns and cities.

hi•jack *v.* To seize illegally or steal while in transit; to commandeer a vehicle, especially an airplane in flight. **hijacker** *n.*

hike *v.* To walk for a lengthy amount of time, usually through rugged terrain or woods.

hi•lar•i•ous *adj.* Boisterously happy or cheerful. **hilarity** *n.*

hill *n.* A rounded, elevation of the earth's surface, smaller than a mountain; a pile or heap.

hill•side *n.* The side or slope of a hill.

hill•top *n.* The summit or top of a hill.

him *pron.* The objective case of the pronoun *he.*

him•self *pron.* That identical male one; a form of the third person, singular masculine pronoun.

hinge *n.* A jointed device which allows a part, as a door or gate, to swing or turn on another frame.

hint *n.* An indirect indication or suggestion. *v.* To make something known by a hint.

hip *n.* The part of the human body that projects outward below the waist and thigh; the hip joint.

hip *n.* The bright, red seed case of a rose; a rosehip.

hip•po•pot•a•mus *n.* A large, aquatic mammal, native to Africa, having short legs, a massive, thick-skinned hairless body, and a broad wide-mouthed muzzle.

hire *v.* To obtain the service of another for pay. **hirer** *n.*

his *adj.* The possessive case of the pronoun *he.*

hiss *n.* A sound resembling a prolonged, sibilant sound, as that of *sss. v.* To remit such a sound as an expression of disapproval. **hisser** *n.*

his•to•ri•an *n.* A person who specializes in the writing or study of history.

his•tor•ic *adj.* Significant or famous in history; historical.

hi•stor•i•cal *adj.* Relating to or taking place in history; serving as a source of knowledge of the past; historic. **historically** *adv.,* **historicalness, historicity** *n.*

his•to•ry *n.* Past events, especially those involving human affairs; an account or record of past events written in chronological order.

hit *v.* To give a blow to; to strike with force; to come forcibly in contact with; to collide with.

hitch *v.* To fasten or tie temporarily with a hoot or knot. *n.* A device for attaching a trailer to a vehicle; a delay or difficulty.

hitch•hike *v.* To travel by signaling and obtaining rides from a passing driver. **hitchhiker** *n.*

hive *n.* A natural or man-made structure serving as a habitation for honeybees; a beehive.

hoard *n.* The accumulation of something stored away for safekeeping or future use. *v.* To amass and hide or store valuables, money. **hoarder** *n.*

hoarse *adj.* Having a husky, gruff, or croaking voice.

hoar•y *adj.* Ancient; aged; frosty; gray or white with age.

hoax *n.* A trick or deception. *v.* To deceive by a hoax. **hoaxer** *n.*

hob•ble *v.* To limp or walk with a limp; to progress irregularly or clumsily; to fetter a horse or other animal.

hob•by *n.* An activity or interest undertaken for pleasure during one's leisure time.

ho•bo *n.* A vagrant who travels aimlessly about; a vagabond; a tramp. **hoboes, hobos** *pl.*

hock•ey *n.* A game played on ice between two teams of skaters whose object is to drive a puck into the opponent's goal using curved wooden sticks.

hoe *n.* A tool with a long handle and flat blade used for weeding, cultivating, and loosening the soil.

hog *n.* A pig, especially one weighing more than 120 pounds and raised for the market.

hoist *v.* To haul or raise up. *n.* A machine used for raising large objects.

hold *v.* To take and keep as in one's hand; to grasp; to possess; to put or keep in a particular place, position, or relationship.

hold•ing *n.* Property, such as land, money, or stocks.

hole *n.* A cavity or opening in a solid mass or body.

hol•i•day *n.* A day set aside by law to commemorate a special person or event; a day free from work; any day of rest.

ho•li•ness *n.* The state of being holy.

hol•low *adj.* Having a cavity or space within; concaved or sunken; not genuine; empty; meaningless.

hol•ly *n.* A tree or shrub with glossy spiny leaves and bright-red berries.

ho•ly *adj.* Regarded with or characterized by divine power; sacred.

hom•age *n.* Great respect or honor, especially when expressed publicly.

home *n.* The place where one resides; a place of origin; one's birthplace or residence during the formative years.

home•com•ing *n.* A return to one's home; a yearly celebration during which graduates return to their old schools.

home•sick *adj.* Longing or yearning for home and family. **homesickness** *n.*

home•work *n.* Work done at home, especially school assignments.

home•y or **hom•y** *adj.* Suggesting the coziness, intimacy, and comforts of home.

hom•i•cide *n.* The killing of one person by another; a person killed by another.

hom•ing pi•geon *n.* A pigeon trained to find its way home from great distances.

ho•mog•e•nize *v.* To process with milk by breaking up fat globules and dispersing them uniformly.

hom•o•nym *n.* A word that has the same sound and often the same spelling as another, but a different meaning and origin.

hom•o•phone *n.* One of two or more words that have the same sound but different spelling, origin, and meaning.

hon•est *adj.* Truthful; not lying, cheating, or stealing; having or giving full worth or value. **honestly** *adv.*, **honesty** *n.*

hon•ey *n.* A sweet, sticky substance made by bees from the nectar gathered from flowers; sweetness; dear; darling.

hon•ey•bee *n.* Any of various bees living in colonies and producing honey.

hon•ey•comb *n.* A structure of hexagonal cells made by bees for the storage of honey, pollen, or their eggs.

hon•ey•moon *n.* A trip taken by a newly married couple.

honk *n.* The harsh, loud sound made by a goose; the sound made by an automobile horn.

hon•or *n.* High regard or respect; personal integrity; reputation.

hon•or•a•ble *adj.* Worthy of honor.

hon•or•ar•y *adj.* Relating to an office or title bestowed as an honor, without the customary powers, duties, or salaries.

hood *n.* A covering for the head and neck, often attached to a garment; the metal hinged cover of an automobile engine.

hood•lum *n.* A young, tough, wild, or destructive fellow.

hoof *n.* The horny covering of the foot in various mammals, as horses, cattle, and oxen. **hooves** *pl.*, **hoofed** *adj.*

hook *n.* A curved or bent piece of metal used to catch, drag, suspend, or fasten something.

hoop *n.* A circular band of metal or wood used to hold staves of a cask or barrel together; in basketball, the basket.

hoot *n.* The loud sound or cry of an owl.

hop *n.* A perennial herb with lobed leaves

and green flowers, used in brewing beer; an informal dance; a quick trip on a planc. *v.* To move with light springing motions.

hope *v.* To want or wish for something with a feeling of confident expectation.

hope•ful *adj.* Manifesting or full of hope. *n.* A young person who shows signs of succeeding.

hope•less *adj.* Totally without hope; despairing; having no grounds for hope.

ho•ri•zon *n.* The line along which the earth and sky seem to meet.

hor•i•zon•tal *adj.* Parallel to the horizon.

horn *n.* A hard, bone-like, permanent projection on the heads of certain hoofed animals, as cattle, sheep, or deer; the two antlers of a deer which are shed annually.

hor•net *n.* Any of various wasps capable of inflicting a severe sting.

hor•o•scope *n.* A chart or diagram of the relative positions of the planets and signs of the zodiac at a certain time.

hor•ri•ble *adj.* Shocking; inducing or producing horror.

hor•rid *adj.* Horrible; terrible; frightening.

hor•ri•fy *v.* To cause a feeling of horror; to dismay or shock.

hor•ror *n.* The painful, strong emotion caused by extreme dread, fear, or repugnance.

horse *n.* A large, strong, hoofed quadruped mammal with a long mane and tail, used for riding and for pulling heavy objects.

horse•man *n.* A person who rides horseback; an equestrian; one who breeds or raises horses. **horsemanship** *n.*

horse•pow•er *n.* A unit of power equal to 746 watts and nearly equivalent to the gravitational unit of 550 foot-pounds per second.

horse•shoe *n.* A protective U-shaped shoe for a horse, consisting of a narrow plate of iron shaped to fit the rim of a horse's hoof. *pl.* A game pitching horseshoes at a post target.

hose *n.* A sock; a stocking; a flexible tube for carrying fluids or gases under pressure. *v.* To wash; to water; to squirt with a hose.

ho•sier•y *n.* Stockings or socks.

hos•pice *n.* A lodging for travelers or the needy; a home taking care of terminally ill patients.

hos•pi•ta•ble *adj.* Treating guests with warmth and generosity; receptive.

hos•pi•tal *n.* An institution where the injured or sick receive medical, surgical, and emergency care.

hos•pi•tal•i•ty *n.* Hospitable treatment, disposition, or reception.

hos•pi•tal•ize *v.* To place or admit in a hospital as a patient for care or treatment.

host *n.* One who receives or entertains guests; one who provides a room or building for an event or function.

hos•tage *n.* A person held as security that promises will be kept or terms met by a third party.

host•ess *n.* A woman who entertains socially; a woman who greets patrons at a restaurant and escorts them to their tables.

hos•tile *adj.* Of or relating to an enemy; antagonistic. **hostility** *n.*

hot *adj.* Having heat that exceeds normal body temperature; electrically charged.

ho•tel *n.* A business that provides lodging, meals, entertainment, and other services.

hot•head•ed *adj.* Having a fiery temper.

hot•house *n.* A heated greenhouse.

hound *n.* Any of several kinds of long-eared dogs with deep voices which follow their prey by scent.

hour *n.* A measure of time equal to 60 minutes; one 24th of the day; the time of day or night.

hour•ly *adj.* Something that happens or is done every hour.

house *n.* A building that serves as living quarters for one or more families; home; a shelter or refuge.

how *adv.* In what manner or way; to what effect; in what condition or state.

how•ev•er *adv.* In whatever way. *conj.* Nevertheless.

howl *v.* To utter a loud, sustained, plaintive sound, as a wolf.

hub *n.* The center of a wheel; the center of activity.

hub•cap *n.* The removable metal cap that covers the end of an axle, as on the wheel of a motor vehicle.

hud•dle *n.* To crowd together; in football, a brief meeting of teammates to prepare for the next play.

hue *n.* A gradation of color running from red through yellow, green and blue to violet; a particular color; a shade.

huff *n.* A fit of resentment or of ill temper. *v.* To exhale or breathe heavily, as from extreme exertion.

hug *v.* To embrace; to hold fast; to keep, cling, or stay close to.

huge *adj.* Of great quantity, size, or extent.

hu•la *n.* A Hawaiian dance characterized by beautiful rhythmic movement of the hips and gestures with the hands.

hulk *n.* A heavy, bulky ship; the body of an old ship no longer fit for service.

hulk•ing *adj.* Unwieldy or awkward.

hull *n.* The outer cover of a fruit or seed; the framework of a boat.

hum *v.* To make a continuous low-pitched sound; to be busily active; to sing with the lips closed.

hu•man *adj.* Of, relating to, or typical of man; having or manifesting human form or attributes. **humanity** *n.*

hu•mane *adj.* To be marked by compassion, sympathy, or consideration for other people or animals. **humanely** *adv.*, **humaneness** *n.*

hu•man•i•tar•i•an *n.* A person who is concerned for human welfare, especially through philanthropy. **humanitarian** *adj.*, **humanitarianism** *n.*

hu•man•i•ty *n.* The quality or state of being human; humankind.

hum•ble *adj.* Marked by meekness or modesty; unpretentious; lowly. *v.* To make humble. **humility** *n.*

hu•mid *adj.* Containing or characterized by a large amount of moisture; damp.

hu•mid•i•ty *n.* A moderate amount of wetness in the air; dampness.

hu•mil•i•ate *v.* To reduce one's dignity or pride to a lower position; to shame.

hum•ming•bird *n.* A very small bird with narrow wings, a slender bill, and a very long tongue.

hu•mor *n.* Something with the ability to be comical or amusing.

hump *n.* The rounded lump or protuberance, as on the back of a camel.

hunch *n.* A strong, intuitive feeling about a future event or result.

hun•dred *n.* The cardinal number equal to 10 x 10. **hundred** *adj.*

hun•ger *n.* A strong need or desire for food. **hungrily** *adv.*, **hungry** *adj.*

hunt *v.* To search or look for food; to pursue with the intent of capture; to look in an attempt to find.

hur•dle *n.* A portable barrier used to jump over in a race; an obstacle one must overcome. *v.* To leap over.

hurl *v.* To throw with great force.

hur•rah *interj.* Used to express approval, pleasure, or exultation.

hur•ri•cane *n.* A tropical cyclone with winds exceeding 74 miles per hour, usually accompanied by rain, thunder, and lightning.

hur•ry *v.* To move or cause to move with haste. **hurriedly** *adv.*

hurt *v.* To experience or inflict with physical pain; to cause physical or emotional harm to; to damage. **hurtful** *adj.*

hus•band *n.* A man who is married.

hush *v.* To make or become quiet; to calm; to keep secret.

husk *n.* The dry or membranous outer cover of certain vegetables, fruits, and seeds.

husk•y *adj.* Having a dry cough or grating sound; burly or robust.

husk•y *n.* A heavy-coated working dog of the arctic region.

hus•tle *v.* To urge or move hurriedly along; to work busily and quickly.

hut *n.* An often small and temporary dwelling made of simple construction; a shack.

hydrant

hy•drant *n.* A pipe with a valve and spout which supplies water from a main source.

hy•drau•lic *adj.* Operated, moved, or effected by the means of water, hardening or setting under water.

hy•drau•lics *pl. n.* The scientific study that deals with practical applications of liquids in motion.

hy•dro•gen *n.* A colorless, normally odorless, highly flammable gas that is the simplest and lightest of the elements.

hy•dro•gen bomb *n.* An extremely destructive bomb with an explosive power obtained from the rapid release of atomic energy.

hy•e•na *n.* Any of several strong carnivorous scavenger mammals of Africa and Asia, with coarse hair and powerful jaws.

hy•giene *n.* The science of the establishment and maintenance of good health and the prevention of disease. **hygienic** *adj.*, **-ically** *adv.*

hy•per•link *n.* In computers, a specialized text allowing one network site to contact another; a web page feature allowing such transfer.

hy•per•text *n.* In computers, a selectable part of a text, usually highlighted, allowing immediate linking to related areas of inquiry.

hy•phen *n.* A punctuation mark used to show connection between two or more words. **hyphenate** *v.*, **hyphenation** *n.*

hyp•no•sis *n.* A state that resembles sleep but is brought on or induced by another person whose subconscious suggestions are accepted by the subject.

hyp•not•ic *adj.* Inducing sleep. *n.* An agent, such as a drug, which induces sleep

I

I, i The ninth letter of the English alphabet; the Roman numeral for one.

I *pron.* The person speaking or writing. *n.* The self; the ego.

ice *n.* Solidly frozen water; a dessert of flavored and sweetened crushed ice.

ice•berg *n.* A thick mass of floating ice separated from a glacier.

ice•boat *n.* A vehicle with runners and usually a sail, used for sailing over ice; an icebreaker. **iceboating, iceboater** *n.*

ice•box *n.* A structure designed for holding ice in which food and other perishables are stored.

ice cap *n.* An extreme perennial covering of ice and snow that covers a large area.

ice cream *n.* A smooth mixture of milk, cream, flavoring, sweeteners, and other ingredients, beaten and frozen.

ice-cream cone *n.* A crisp and edible cone for the purpose of holding ice cream.

ice field *n.* Pieces of glaciers that have joined and frozen together causing a sheet of ice so large that one cannot see its end.

ice floe *n.* A mass of sea ice that floats free upon the water.

ice pack *n.* A large mass of floating, compacted ice; a folded bag filled with ice and applied to sore parts of the body.

ice skate *n.* A shoe or boot with a runner fixed to it for skating on ice.

ice storm *n.* A storm with frozen rain.

ice wa•ter *n.* Water cooled by ice.

i•ci•cle *n.* A hanging spike of ice formed by dripping water that freezes.

ic•ing *n.* A sweet preparation for coating cakes and cookies.

i•cy *adj.* Covered with or consisting of ice; extremely cold; freezing; characterized by coldness.

i•de•a *n.* Something existing in the mind; conception or thought; an opinion; a plan of action.

i•de•al *n.* A concept or imagined state of perfection; highly desirable; perfect; an ultimate objective; an honorable principle or motive. *adj.* Conforming to absolute excellence.

i•de•al•ism *n.* The practice or tendency of seeing things in ideal form; pursuit of an ideal; a philosophical system believing that reality consists of ideas or perceptions. **idealist** *n.*, **idealistic** *adj.*

i·de·al·ize *v.* To regard or represent as ideal. **idealization** *n.*

i·de·al·ly *adv.* In respect to an ideal; theoretically.

i·den·ti·cal *adj.* Being the same; exactly equal or much alike; designating a twin or twins developed from the same ovum. **identically** *adv.,* **-ness** *n.*

i·den·ti·fi·a·ble *adj.* Having the capability of being identified or recognized.

i·den·ti·fy *v.* To recognize the identity of; to establish as the same or similar; to equate; to associate oneself closely with an individual or group. **identifiable** *adj.,* **identification** *n.*

i·den·ti·ty *n.* The condition or state of being a specific person or thing and recognizable as such.

i·de·ol·o·gy *n.* A body of ideas that influence a person, group, culture, or political party.

id·i·om *n.* A form of expression having a meaning not readily understood from the meaning of its component words; the dialect of people or a region; a kind of language or vocabulary.

i·dle *adj.* Doing nothing; inactive; moving lazily; unemployed or inactive.

i·dol *n.* A symbol or representation of a god or deity that is worshipped; a person or thing adored. **idolatry** *n.*

i·dol·ize *v.* To admire with excessive admiration or devotion; to worship as an idol.

if *conj.* On the condition that; allowing that; supposing or granting that.

ig·loo *n.* A dome-shaped Eskimo dwelling or hut often made of blocks of snow.

ig·nite *v.* To start or set a fire; to render luminous by heat.

ig·ni·tion *n.* An act or action of igniting; a process or means for igniting the fuel mixture in an engine.

ig·no·rant *adj.* Lacking education or knowledge; not aware; lacking comprehension. **ignorance** *n.*

ig·nore *v.* To pay no attention to; to reject; to disregard; refuse to consider, recognize or notice.

ill *adj.* Not healthy; sick; destructive in effect; harmful.

I'll *contr.* I will; I shall.

ill-bred *adj.* Ill-mannered; impolite; rude.

il·le·gal *adj.* Contrary to law or official rules.

il·leg·i·ble *adj.* Not readable; not legible.

ill-hu·mored *adj.* Irritable; cross.

il·lit·er·ate *adj.* Unable to read and write; uneducated; having or showing a lack of knowledge of fundamentals on a particular subject.

ill-man·nered *adj.* Lacking or showing a lack of good manners; rude.

ill-na·tured *adj.* Disagreeable or unpleasant disposition.

ill·ness *n.* Sickness; a state of being in poor health; the unhealthy condition of one's body or mind.

il·log·i·cal *adj.* Contrary to the principles of logic; not logical.

ill-tem·pered *adj.* Having or showing a cross temper or disposition.

il·lu·mi·nate *v.* To give light; to make clear; to provide with understanding; to decorate with pictures or designs.

il·lu·sion *n.* A misleading perception of reality; an overly optimistic idea or belief; misconception; the act of deceiving.

il·lus·trate *v.* To explain or clarify, especially by the use of examples; to clarify by serving as an example; to provide a publication with explanatory features. **illustrator** *n.*

il·lus·tra·tion *n.* The act of illustrating; an example or comparison used to illustrate.

il·lus·tri·ous *adj.* Greatly celebrated; renowned; brilliantly outstanding because of actions or achievements.

I'm *contr.* I am.

im·age *n.* A representation of the form and features of someone or something; an optically formed representation of an object made by a mirror or lens; a mental picture of something imaginary.

im·ag·in·a·ble *adj.* Capable of being imagined. **imaginably** *adv.*

im·ag·i·nar·y *adj.* Existing only in the

imagination

imagination.

im•ag•i•na•tion *n.* The power of forming mental images of unreal or absent objects; such power used creatively; resourcefulness.

im•ag•ine *v.* To form a mental picture or idea of; to suppose; to guess.

im•i•tate *v.* To copy the actions or appearance of another; to adopt the style of; to duplicate; to appear like. **imitator** *n.*

im•i•ta•tion *n.* An act of imitating; something copied from an original.

im•i•ta•tive *adj.* To be marked by imitation.

im•mac•u•late *adj.* Free from sin, stain, or fault; impeccably clean.

im•ma•te•ri•al *adj.* Lacking material body or form; of no importance or relevance.

im•ma•ture *adj.* Not fully grown; undeveloped; suggesting a lack of maturity.

im•meas•ur•a•ble *adj.* Not capable of being measured.

im•me•di•a•cy *n.* The quality of being immediate; directness; something of urgent importance.

im•me•di•ate *adj.* Acting or happening without an intervening object, agent, or cause; directly perceived; occurring at once.

im•me•di•ate•ly *adv.* In direct relationship or connection.

im•mense *adj.* Exceptionally large. **immensely** *adv.*, **immenseness** *n.*

im•men•si•ty *n.* The state of something being immense or very large in size.

im•merse *v.* To put into a liquid; to baptize by submerging in water; to engross; to absorb. **immersible** *adj.*, **immersion** *n.*

im•mersed *adj.* To be growing completely underwater such as a plant.

im•mers•i•ble *adj.* Having the capability of being totally underwater without damaging any working parts.

im•mer•sion *n.* The act or state of being totally immersed.

im•mi•grant *n.* One who leaves his country to settle in another and who takes up permanent residence in the new country.

im•mi•grate *v.* To leave one country and settle in another; to bring in as immigrants. **immigration** *n.*, **immigrational** *adj.*

im•mi•nent *adj.* About to happen or take place. **imminentness, imminence** *n.*, **imminently** *adv.*

im•mo•bile *adj.* Not moving or incapable of motion. **immobility** *n.*

im•mo•bi•lize *v.* To render motionless, preventing movement. **immobilization, immobilizer** *n.*

im•mod•er•ate *adj.* Exceeding normal bounds.

im•mod•est *adj.* Lacking modesty; indecent; boastful.

im•mor•al *adj.* Not moral; confliction with moral principles.

im•mo•ral•i•ty *n.* Lack of morality; an immoral act or practice.

im•mor•tal *adj.* Exempt from death; lasting forever, as in fame. *n.* A person of lasting fame.

im•mor•tal•ize *v.* To make something immortal.

im•mov•a•ble *adj.* Not capable of moving or being moved.

im•mune *adj.* Not affected or responsive; resistant, or protected as to a disease.

im•mu•ni•ty *n.* The state at which something is immune.

im•mu•nize *v.* To make immune.

im•mu•nol•o•gy *n.* The study of immunity to diseases.

imp *n.* A mischievous child.

im•pact *n.* A collision; the impetus or force produced by a collision; an initial, usually strong effect. *v.* To pack firmly together; to strike or affect forcefully.

im•pair *v.* To diminish in strength, value, quantity, or quality.

im•part *v.* To grant; to bestow; to convey; to make known; to communicate.

im•par•tial *adj.* Not partial; unbiased.

im•pass•a•ble *adj.* Impossible to travel over or across.

im•passe *n.* A road or passage having no exit; a difficult situation with no apparent way out; a deadlock.

im•pas•sioned *adj.* To be filled with passion.

im•pas•sive *adj.* Unemotional; showing no emotion; expressionless.

im•pa•tience *n.* The quality of being impatient.

im•pa•tient *adj.* Unwilling to wait or tolerate delay; expressing or caused by irritation at having to wait; restlessly eager; intolerant. **impatiently** *adv.*

im•peach *v.* To charge with misconduct in public office before a proper court of justice; to make an accusation against. **impeachable** *adj.*, **impeachment** *n.*

im•pec•ca•ble *adj.* Having no flaws; perfect; not capable of sin.

im•pede *v.* To obstruct or slow down the progress of.

im•ped•i•ment *n.* One that stands in the way; something that impedes, especially an organic speech defect.

im•pel *v.* To spur to action; to provoke; to drive forward; to propel.

im•pen•e•tra•bil•i•ty *n.* The inability of two parts of anything to occupy the same space at exactly the same time.

im•pen•e•tra•ble *adj.* Not capable of being penetrated; not capable of being seen through or understood; unfathomable.

im•per•a•tive *adj.* Expressing a command or request; empowered to command or control; compulsory.

im•per•cep•ti•ble *adj.* Not perceptible by the mind or senses; extremely small.

im•per•fect *adj.* Not perfect; of or being a verb tense which shows an uncompleted or continuous action or condition.

im•per•fec•tion *n.* The quality or condition or being imperfect; a defect.

im•pe•ri•al *adj.* Of or relating to an empire or emperor; designating a nation or government having dependent colonies; majestic; regal.

im•pe•ri•al•ism *n.* The national policy or practice of acquiring foreign territories or establishing dominance over other nations.

im•per•il *v.* To put in peril; endanger.

im•per•ish•a•ble *adj.* Not perishable; permanently enduring.

im•per•me•a•ble *adj.* Not permeable; incapable of penetration. *adv.*

im•per•mis•si•ble *adj.* Not allowed.

im•per•son•al *adj.* Having no personal reference or connection; showing no emotion or personality.

im•per•son•ate *v.* To assume the character or manner of.

im•per•ti•nent *adj.* Overly bold or disrespectful; not pertinent; irrelevant.

im•pet•u•ous *adj.* Marked by sudden action or emotion; impulsive.

im•pe•tus *n.* A driving force; an incitement; a stimulus; momentum.

im•plant *v.* To set in firmly; to fix in the mind; to insert surgically.

im•plau•si•ble *adj.* Difficult to believe; unlikely.

im•ple•ment *n.* A utensil or tool. *v.* To put into effect; to carry out; to furnish with implements. **implementation** *n.*

im•pli•cate *v.* To involve, especially in illegal activity; to imply. **implication** *n.*

im•plic•it *adj.* Contained in the nature of someone or something but not readily apparent; understood but not directly expressed; complete; absolute.

im•plore *v.* To appeal urgently to.

im•ply *v.* To involve by logical necessity; to express indirectly; to suggest.

im•po•lite *adj.* Rude; without courtesy.

im•port *v.* To bring in goods from a foreign country for trade or sale; to mean; to signify; to be significant. *n.* Something imported; meaning; significance.

im•por•tant *adj.* Likely to determine or influence events; significant; having fame or authority.

im•pose *v.* To enact or apply as compulsory; to obtrude or force oneself or a burden on another; to take unfair advantage.

im•pos•si•ble *adj.* Not capable of existing or happening; unlikely to take place or be done; unacceptable; difficult to tolerate or

impostor

deal with. **impossibility** *n.*, **impossibly** *adv.*

im·pos·tor or **im·pos·ter** *n.* One who assumes a false identity or title.

im·po·tent *adj.* Without strength or vigor; having no power; ineffectual.

im·pov·er·ished *adj.* Poor; in a state of poverty.

im·prac·ti·cal *adj.* Unwise to put into effect; unable to deal with practical or financial matters efficiently.

im·press *v.* To apply or produce with pressure; to stamp or mark with or as if with pressure; to fix firmly in the mind; to affect strongly and usually favorably.

im·pres·sion *n.* A mark or design made on a surface by pressure; an effect or feeling retained in the mind as a result of experience; an indistinct notion or recollection; a satiric or humorous imitation; the copies of a publication printed at one time.

im·pres·sion·ism *n.* A style of late nineteenth century painting in which the immediate appearance of scenes is depicted with unmixed primary colors applied in small strokes to simulate reflected light. **impressionist** *n.*, **impressionistic** *adj.*

im·pres·sive *adj.* Making a strong impression; striking.

im·print *v.* To make or impress a mark or design on a surface; to make or stamp a mark on; to fix firmly in the mind. *n.* A mark or design made by imprinting; a lasting influence or effect; a publisher's name, often with the date and place of publication, printed at the bottom of a title page.

im·prob·a·ble *adj.* Not likely to occur or be true.

im·promp·tu *adj.* Devised or performed without prior planning or preparation.

im·prop·er *adj.* Unsuitable; indecorous; incorrect.

im·prove *v.* To make or become better; to increase something's productivity or value.

im·prove·ment *n.* The act or process of improving or the condition of being improved; a change that improves.

im·pro·vise *v.* To make up, compose, or perform without preparation; to make from available materials.

im·pru·dent *adj.* Not prudent; unwise.

im·pu·dent *adj.* Marked by rude boldness or disrespect.

im·pulse *n.* A driving force or the motion produced by it; a sudden spontaneous urge; a motivating force; a general tendency.

im·pul·sive *adj.* Acting on impulse rather than thought; resulting from impulse; uncalculated.

im·pure *adj.* Not pure; unclean; unchaste or obscene; mixed with another substance; adulterated; deriving from more than one source or style.

in·a·bil·i·ty *n.* A lack of sufficient power or capacity.

in·ac·ces·si·ble *adj.* Not accessible.

in·ac·cu·ra·cy *n.* The state of being inaccurate.

in·ac·tion *n.* The lack of activity or lack of action.

in·ac·ti·vate *v.* To make something or someone inactive.

in·ac·tive *adj.* Not active or inclined to be active; out of current use or service.

in·ad·e·quate *adj.* Not adequate.

in·ad·vis·a·ble *adj.* Being not advisable.

in·al·ien·a·ble *adj.* Not capable of being given up or transferred.

in·an·i·mate *adj.* Not having the qualities of life; not animated.

in·ap·pro·pri·ate *adj.* Being not appropriate; out of place in a setting; out of proportion.

in·ar·tic·u·late *adj.* Not uttering or forming intelligible words or syllables; unable to speak; speechless; unable to speak clearly or effectively; unexpressed.

in·as·much as *conj.* Because of the fact that; since.

in·at·ten·tive *adj.* Not paying attention.

in·au·gu·ral *adj.* Of or for an inauguration.

in·au·gu·rate *v.* To put into office with a

formal ceremony; to begin officially. **inau-gurator, inauguration** n.

in be•tween adv. or prep. Between.

in•cal•cu•la•ble adj. Not calculable; indeterminate; unpredictable; very large.

in•can•des•cent adj. Giving off visible light when heated; shining brightly; ardently intense. **incandescence** n.

in•ca•pa•ble adj. Lacking the ability for doing or performing.

in•ca•pac•i•ty n. Inadequate ability or strength; a defect; in law, a disqualification.

in•car•cer•ate v. To place in jail.

in•car•nate v. To give actual form to.

in•car•na•tion n. The act of incarnating or state of being incarnated; one regarded as personifying a given abstract quality or idea; the embodiment.

in•cen•di•ar•y adj. Causing or capable of causing fires; of or relating to arson; tending to inflame; inflammatory.

in•cense v. To make angry. n. A substance, as gum or wood, burned to produce a pleasant smell; the smoke or odor produced.

in•cen•tive n. Something inciting one to action or effort; a stimulus.

inch n. A unit of measurement equal to one twelfth of a foot. v. To move slowly.

in•ci•dent n. An event; an event that disrupts normal procedure or causes a crisis.

in•ci•den•tal adj. Occurring or likely to occur at the same time or as a result; minor; subordinate. n. A minor attendant occurrence or condition.

in•cin•er•ate v. To burn up.

in•cin•er•a•tor n. One that incinerates; a furnace for burning waste.

in•ci•sor n. A cutting tool at the front of the mouth.

in•cite v. To provoke to action. **incitement** n.

in•cli•na•tion n. An attitude; a disposition; a tendency to act or think in a certain way; a preference; a bow or tilt; a slope.

in•cline v. To deviate or cause to deviate from the horizontal or vertical; to slant; to dispose or be disposed; to bow or nod. n. An inclined surface.

in•clude v. To have as a part or member; to contain; to put into a group or total. **inclusion** n.

in•cog•ni•to adv. or adj. With one's identity hidden.

in•co•her•ent adj. Lacking order; connection, or harmony; unable to think or speak clearly or consecutively.

in•come n. Money or its equivalent received in return for work or as profit from investments.

in•com•ing adj. Coming in or soon to come in.

in•com•pa•ra•ble adj. Incapable of being compared; without rival.

in•com•pat•i•ble adj. Not suited for combination or association; inconsistent.

in•com•pe•tent adj. Not competent; not capable of performance. **incompetence, incompetency** n.

in•com•plete adj. Not complete; lacking completeness.

in•com•pre•hen•si•ble adj. Being unable to understand; opaque to reason.

in•con•ceiv•a•ble adj. Impossible to understand.

in•con•clu•sive adj. Having no definite result.

in•con•gru•ous adj. Not corresponding; disagreeing; made up of diverse or discordant elements; unsuited to the surrounding or setting. **incongruity** n.

in•con•sid•er•ate adj. Not considerate; thoughtless.

in•con•sis•tent adj. Lacking firmness, harmony, or compatibility; incoherent in thought or actions.

in•con•sol•a•ble adj. Not capable of being consoled.

in•con•spic•u•ous adj. Not readily seen or noticed.

in•con•stant adj. Likely to change; unpredictable; faithless; fickle. **inconstancy** n., **inconstantly** adv.

in•con•ven•ience n. The quality or state of being inconvenient; something

inconvenient

inconvenient. *v.* To cause inconvenience to; to bother.

in·con·ven·ient *adj.* Not convenient; awkward or out of the way.

in·cor·po·rate *v.* To combine into a unified whole; to unite; to form or cause to form a legal corporation; to give a physical form to; to embody.

in·crease *v.* To make or become greater or larger; to have offspring; to reproduce. *n.* The act of increasing; the amount or rate of increasing.

in·cred·i·ble *adj.* Too unlikely to be believed; unbelievable; astonishing.

in·cum·bent *adj.* Lying or resting on something else; imposed as an obligation; obligatory; currently in office. *n.* A person currently in office. **incumbency** *n.*

in·cur·able *adj.* Unable to be cured.

in·debt·ed *adj.* Obligated to another, as for money or a favor; beholden. **indebtedness** *n.*

in·de·cent *adj.* Morally offensive or contrary to good taste. **indecency** *n.*, **indecently** *adv.*

in·de·ci·sion *n.* Inability to make up one's mind; irresolution.

in·de·ci·sive *adj.* Without a clear-cut result; marked by indecision. **indecisively** *adv.*, **indecisiveness** *n.*

in·deed *adv.* Most certainly; without doubt; in reality; in fact. *interj.* Used to express surprise; irony, or disbelief.

in·de·fen·si·ble *adj.* Incapable of being justified; not able to protect against a physical fight.

in·def·i·nite *adj.* Not decided or specified; vague; unclear; lacking fixed limits. **indefinitely** *adv.*

in·del·i·ble *adj.* Not able to be erased or washed away; permanent.

in·del·i·cate *adj.* Lacking sensitivity; tactless. **indelicacy** *n.*, **indelicately** *adv.*

in·dent *v.* To set in from the margin; to notch the edge of; to serrate; to make a dent or depression in; to impress; to stamp. *n.* An indentation.

in·den·ta·tion *n.* The act of indenting or the state of being indented; an angular cut in an edge; a recess in a surface.

in·de·pend·ence *n.* The quality or state of being independent.

in·de·pend·ent *adj.* Politically self-governing; free from the control of others; not committed to a political party or faction; not relying on others; especially for financial support; providing or having enough income to enable one to live without working. *n.* One who is independent, especially a candidate or voter not committed to a political party.

in-depth *adj.* Thorough; detailed.

in·de·scrib·a·ble *adj.* Surpassing description; incapable of being described.

in·de·struc·ti·ble *adj.* Unable to be destroyed.

in·dex *n.* A list for aiding reference, especially an alphabetized listing in a printed work which gives the pages on which various names, places, and subjects are mentioned. *v.* To provide with or enter in an index; to indicate; to adjust through. **indexer** *n.*, **indexes, indices** *pl.*

in·di·cate *v.* To point out; to show; to serve as a sign or symptom; to signify; to suggest the advisability of; to call for. **indication, indicator** *n.*

in·dif·fer·ent *adj.* Having no marked feeling or preference; impartial; neither good nor bad. **indifference** *n.*

in·di·ges·tion *n.* Difficulty or discomfort in digesting food.

in·dig·nant *adj.* Marked by or filled with indignation. **indignantly** *adv.*

in·dig·na·tion *n.* Anger aroused by injustice, unworthiness, or unfairness.

in·dig·ni·ty *n.* Humiliating treatment; something that offends one's pride.

in·di·rect *adj.* Not taking a direct course; not straight to the point.

in·dis·tin·guish·a·ble *adj.* Unable to determine in shape or structure; not clearly recognizable; lacking identity.

in·di·vid·u·al *adj.* Of, for, or relating to a single human being. **individually** *adv.*

in·di·vis·i·ble *adj.* Not able to be divided.

in·dulge *v.* To give in to the desires of, especially to excess; to yield to; to allow oneself a special pleasure.

in·dus·tri·al *adj.* Of, relating to, or used in industry.

in·dus·tri·ous *adj.* Working steadily and hard; diligent.

in·dus·try *n.* The commercial production and sale of goods and services; a branch of manufacture and trade; industrial management; diligence.

in·ef·fi·cient *adj.* Wasteful of time, energy, or materials.

in·e·qual·i·ty *n.* The condition or an instance of being unequal; social or economic disparity; lack of regularity.

in·ert *adj.* Not able to move or act; slow to move or act; sluggish; displaying no chemical activity.

in·er·tia *n.* The tendency of a body to remain at rest or to stay in motion unless acted upon by an external force; resistance to motion or change. **inertial** *adj.*, **inertially** *adv.*

in·ev·i·ta·ble *adj.* Not able to be avoided.

in·fal·li·ble *adj.* Not capable of making mistakes; not capable of failing; never wrong. **infallibility** *n.*, **infallibly** *adv.*

in·fan·cy *n.* The condition or time of being an infant; an early stage of existence; in law, minority.

in·fant *n.* A child in the first period of life; a very young child; in law, a minor.

in·fat·u·ate *v.* To arouse an extravagant or foolish love in. **infatuated** *adj.*, **infatuation** *n.*

in·fect *v.* To contaminate with disease-causing microorganisms; to transmit a disease to; to affect as if by contagion.

in·fec·tion *n.* Invasion of a bodily part by disease-causing microorganisms; the condition resulting from such an invasion; an infectious disease.

in·fer *v.* To conclude by reasoning; to deduce; to have as a logical consequence; to lead to as a result or conclusion. **inference** *n.*

in·fe·ri·or *adj.* Located under or below; low or lower in order, rank, or quality. **inferiority** *n.*

in·fer·nal *adj.* Of, like, or relating to hell; damnable; abominable.

in·fer·no *n.* A place or condition suggestive of hell.

in·fest *v.* To spread in or over so as to be harmful or offensive. **infestation** *n.*

in·fi·nite *adj.* Without boundaries; limitless; immeasurably great or large; in mathematics, greater in value than any specified number, however large. **infinity** *n.*

in·flame *v.* To set on fire; to arouse to strong or excessive feeling; to intensify; to produce, affect or be affected by inflammation.

in·flam·ma·ble *adj.* Tending to catch fire easily; easily excited.

in·flam·ma·tion *n.* Localized redness, swelling, heat, and pain in response to an injury or infection.

in·flate *v.* To fill and expand with a gas; to increase unsoundly; to puff up; to raise prices abnormally. **inflatable** *adj.*

in·fla·tion *n.* The act or process of inflating; a period during which there is an increase in the monetary supply, causing a continuous rise in the price of goods.

in·flex·i·ble *adj.* Not flexible; rigid; not subject to change; unalterable. **inflexibility** *n.*, **inflexibly** *adv.*

in·flict *v.* To cause to be suffered; to impose.

in·flu·ence *n.* The power to produce effects, especially indirectly or through an intermediary; the condition of being affected; one exercising indirect power to sway or affect. *v.* To exert influence over; to modify. **influential** *adj.*

in·flu·en·za *n.* An acute, infectious viral disease marked by respiratory inflammation, fever, muscular pain, and often intestinal discomfort; the flu.

in·for·ma·tive *adj.* Providing information; instructive.

in·fringe *v.* To break a law; to violate; to encroach; to trespass. **infringement** *n.*

in·fu·ri·ate *v.* To make very angry or

furious; to enrage.

in·gen·ious *adj.* Showing great ingenuity; to have inventive ability; clever. **ingeniously** *adv.*, **ingeniousness, ingenuity** *n.*

in·gen·u·ous *adj.* Frank and straightforward; lacking sophistication; innocent and guileless.

in·gre·di·ent *n.* An element that enters into the composition of a mixture; a part of anything.

in·hab·it *v.* To reside in; to occupy as a home.

in·hab·i·tant *n.* A person who resides permanently.

in·hale *v.* To breathe or draw into the lungs, as air or tobacco smoke; the opposite of exhale. **inhalation** *n.*

in·hal·er *n.* One that inhales; a respirator.

in·her·it *v.* To receive something, as property, money, or other valuables, by legal succession or will. In biology, to receive traits or qualities from one's ancestors or parents.

in·her·i·tance *n.* The act of inheriting; that which is inherited or to be inherited by legal transmission to a heir.

in·hu·mane *adj.* Lacking compassion or pity; cruel. **inhumanely** *adv.*

in·hu·man·i·ty *n.* The lack of compassion or pity; an inhumane or cruel act.

in·i·tial *adj.* Of or pertaining to the beginning. *n.* The first letter of a name or word. *v.* To mark or sign with initials. **initially** *adv.*

in·ject *v.* To force a drug or fluid into the body through a blood vessel or the skin with a hypodermic syringe; to throw in or introduce a comment abruptly.

in·jure *v.* To cause physical harm, damage, or pain.

in·ju·ry *n.* Damage or harm inflicted or suffered.

in·jus·tice *n.* The violation of another person's rights; an unjust act; a wrong.

ink *n.* Any of variously colored liquids or paste, used for writing, drawing, and printing. **inky** *adj.*

ink·well *n.* A small container or reservoir for holding ink.

in·laid *adj.* Ornamental with wood, ivory, or other materials embedded flush with the surface.

in·land *adj.* Pertaining to or located in the interior of a country.

in·law *n.* A relative by marriage.

in·let *n.* A bay or stream that leads into land; a passage between nearby islands.

in·mate *n.* A person who dwells in a building with another; one confined in a prison, asylum, or hospital.

inn *n.* A place of lodging where a traveler may obtain meals and/or lodging.

in·ner *adj.* Situated or occurring farther inside; relating to or of the mind or spirit.

in·ner ear *n.* The part of the ear which includes the semicircular canals, vestibule, and cochlea.

inn·keep·er *n.* The proprietor or manager of an inn.

in·no·cent *adj.* Free from sin, evil, or moral wrong; pure; legally free from blame or guilt; not maliciously intended; lacking in experience or knowledge; naïve. **innocence** *n.*

in·oc·u·late *v.* To introduce a mild form of a disease or virus to a person or animal in order to produce immunity.

in·or·gan·ic *adj.* Not having or involving living organisms, their remains, or products.

in·put *n.* The amount of energy delivered to a machine; in computer science, information that is put into a data processing system.

in·quire *v.* To ask a question; to make an investigation.

in·quir·y *n.* The act of seeking or inquiring; a request or question for information; a very close examination; an investigation or examination of facts or evidence.

in·sane *adj.* Afflicted with a serious mental disorder impairing a person's ability to function; the characteristic of a person who is not sane. **insanity** *n.*

in·sect *n.* Any of a numerous cosmopolitan class of small to minute winged invertebrate animals with three pairs of legs, a segmented body, and usually two pairs of wings.

in•se•cure *adj.* Troubled by anxiety and apprehension; threatened; not securely guarded; unsafe; liable to break, fail, or collapse. **insecurely** *adv.*, **insecurity** *n.*

in•sep•a•ra•ble *adj.* Incapable of being separated or parted.

in•sert *v.* To put in place; to set. *n.* In printing, something inserted or to be inserted. **insertion** *n.*

in•side *n.* The part, surface, or space that lies within.

in•sides *n.* The internal parts or organs.

in•sight *n.* Perception into the true or hidden nature of things. **insightful** *adj.*, **insightfully** *adv.*

in•sig•ni•a *n.* A badge or emblem used to mark membership, honor, or office.

in•sin•cere *adj.* Not sincere; hypocritical. **insincerely** *adv.*, **insincerity** *n.*

in•sist *v.* To demand firmly; to dwell on something repeatedly for emphasis. **insistent** *adj.*, **insistently** *adv.*

in•spect *v.* To examine or look at very carefully for flaws; to examine or review officially. **inspection**, **inspector** *n.*

in•spi•ra•tion *n.* The stimulation within the mind of some idea, feeling, or impulse which leads to creative action; a divine or holy presence which inspires; the act of inhaling air.

in•spire *v.* To exert or guide by a divine influence; to arouse and create high emotion; to exalt; to inhale; breathe in.

in•stall or **in•stal** *v.* To put in position for service; to place into an office or position; to settle. **installation**, **installer** *n.*

in•stall•ment or **in•stal•ment** *n.* One of several payments due in specified amounts at specified intervals.

in•stance *n.* An illustrative case or example; a step in proceedings.

in•stant *n.* A very short time; a moment; a certain or specific point in time. *adj.* Instantaneously; immediate; urgent.

in•stan•ta•ne•ous *adj.* Happening with no delay; instantly; completed in a moment. **instantaneously** *adv.*

in•stant•ly *adv.* Immediately; at once.

in•stead *adv.* In lieu of that just mentioned.

in•stinct *n.* The complex and normal tendency or response of a given species to act in ways essential to its existence, development, and survival. **instinctive**, **instinctual** *adj.*

in•sti•tute *v.* To establish or set up; to find; to initiate; to set in operation; to start. *n.* An organization set up to promote or further a cause; an institution for educating.

in•sti•tu•tion *n.* The principle custom that forms part of a society or civilization; an organization which performs a particular job or function, such as research, charity, or education; a place of confinement such as a prison or mental hospital.

in•struct *v.* To impart skill or knowledge; to teach; to give orders or direction. **instructive** *adj.*

in•struc•tion *n.* The act of teaching or instructing; important knowledge; a lesson; an order or direction.

in•struc•tor *n.* One who instructs; a teacher; a low-rank college teacher, not having tenure.

in•stru•ment *n.* A mechanical tool or implement; a device used to produce music; a person who is controlled by another; a dupe; in law, a formal legal document, deed, or contract.

in•suf•fi•cient *adj.* Not enough.

in•su•late *v.* To isolate; to wrap or surround with nonconducting material in order to prevent the passage of heat, electricity, or sound into or out of; to protect with wrapping or insulation.

in•sult *v.* To speak or to treat with insolence or contempt; to abuse verbally. *n.* An act or remark that offends someone. **insulting** *adj.*, **insultingly** *adv.*

in•sur•ance *n.* Protection against risk, loss, or ruin; the coverage an insurer guarantees to pay in the event of death, loss, or medical bills; a contract guaranteeing such protection on future specified losses in return for annual payments; any safeguard against risk or harm. **insurability** *n.*, **insurable** *adj.*

in•sure *v.* To guarantee against loss of life, property, or other types of losses; to make certain; to ensure; to buy or issue insurance. **insurability** *n.*, **insurable** *adj.*

in•sured *n.* A person protected by an insurance policy.

in•sur•er *n.* The person or company which insures someone against loss or damage.

in•tact *adj.* Remaining whole and not damaged in any way. **intactness** *n.*

in•take *n.* The act of taking in or absorbing; the amount or quantity taken in.

in•tan•gi•ble *adj.* Incapable of being touched; vague or indefinite to the mind. **intangibility, intangibleness** *n.*, **intangibly** *adv.*

in•te•ger *n.* Any of the numbers 1, 2, 3, etc., including all the positive whole numbers and all the negative numbers and zero; a whole entity.

in•te•gral *adj.* Being an essential and indispensable part of a whole; made up, from, or formed of parts that constitute a unity.

in•te•grate *v.* To make into a whole by joining parts together; to unify; to be open to people of all races or ethnic groups. **integration** *n.*

in•teg•ri•ty *n.* Uprightness of character; honesty; the condition, quality, or state of being complete or undivided.

in•tel•li•gence *n.* The capacity to perceive and comprehend meaning; information; news; the gathering of secret information, as by military or police authorities.

in•tel•li•gent *adj.* Having or showing intelligence.

in•tend *v.* To have a plan or purpose in mind; to design for a particular use.

in•tense *adj.* Extreme in strength, effect, or degree; expressing strong emotion, concentration, or strain; profound.

intensely *adv.*, **intenseness** *n.*

in•ten•si•fy *v.* To become or make more intense or acute. **intensification** *n.*

in•ten•si•ty *n.* The quality of being intense or acute; a great effect, concentration, or force.

in•ten•sive *adj.* Forceful and concentrated; marked by a full and complete application of all resources. **intensively** *adv.*

in•ten•sive care *n.* The hospital care provided for a gravely ill patient in specially designed rooms with monitoring devices and life-support systems.

in•tent *n.* A purpose, goal, aim, or design. **intently** *adv.*, **intentness, intention** *n.*

in•ten•tion•al *adj.* To be deliberately intended or done. **intentionality** *n.*, **intentionally** *adv.*

in•ter•act *v.* To act on each other or with each other. **interactive** *adj.*

in•ter•cept *v.* To interrupt the course of; to seize or stop. **interception** *n.*

in•ter•change *v.* To put each in the place of another; to give and receive in return. *n.* The intersection of a highway which allows traffic to enter or turn off without obstructing other traffic.

in•ter•change•a•ble *adj.* To be capable of being interchanged with something.

in•ter•de•pen•dence *n.* A mutual dependence. **interdependency** *n.*

in•ter•de•pen•dent *adj.* To be mutually dependent.

in•ter•dis•ci•plin•ar•y *adj.* To be involving or containing two or more artistic, academic, or scientific disciplines.

in•ter•est *n.* Curiosity or concern about something; that which is to one's benefit; legal or financial right, claim or share, as in a business; a charge for a loan of money, usually a percent of the amount borrowed.

in•ter•est•ed *adj.* Having or displaying curiosity; having a right to share in something. **interestedly** *adv.*

in•ter•est group *n.* A group of people who have a common identifying interest.

in•ter•est•ing *adj.* Stimulating interest, attention, or curiosity.

in·ter·face *n.* A surface forming a common boundary between adjacent areas; in computer science, the software or hardware connecting one device or system to another. **interface** *v.*

in·ter·fere *v.* To come between; to get in the way; to be an obstacle or obstruction. **interferer** *n.*

in·ter·fer·ence *n.* The process of interfering in something.

in·ter·ga·lac·tic *adj.* To be occurring between galaxies.

in·ter·im *n.* A time between events or periods. *adj.* Temporary.

in·te·ri·or *adj.* Of, or contained in the inside; inner; away from coast or border; inland; private; not exposed to view.

in·ter·jec·tion *n.* A word used to express excitement or emotion, as an exclamation; a casual insertion into a conversation.

in·ter·li·brar·y *adj.* To be taking place between two or more libraries.

in·ter·lock *v.* To join closely.

in·ter·lude *n.* A period of time that occurs in and divides some longer process; light entertainment between the acts of a show, play, or other more serious entertainment.

in·ter·me·di·ar·y *n.* A mediator. *adj.* Coming between; intermediate.

in·ter·mi·na·ble *adj.* Seeming to have no end; without cessation.

in·ter·mis·sion *n.* A temporary interval of time between events or activities; the pause in the middle of a performance.

in·ter·mit·tent *adj.* Ceasing from time to time; coming at intervals.

in·tern *n.* A medical school graduate undergoing supervised practical training in a hospital.

in·ter·nal *adj.* Of or pertaining to the inside; pertaining to the domestic affairs of a country; intended to be consumed by the body from the inside. **internally** *adv.*, **internality** *n.*

in·ter·nal-com·bus·tion en·gine *n.* An engine in which fuel is burned inside the engine.

in·ter·na·tion·al *adj.* Relating to more than one nation; global in scope.

in·ter·na·tion·al·ism *n.* The policy of cooperation among nations where politics and economics are concerned. **internationalist** *n.*, **internationalize** *v.*

in·ter·net *n.* In computers, any interconnecting series of electronic networks. The Internet: a widely used networking interface, connecting several very large information servers.

in·ter·per·son·al *adj.* To be relating or to pertaining to relations between people.

in·ter·plan·e·tar·y *adj.* To be happening or operating between the planets.

in·ter·pret *v.* To convey the meaning of something by explaining or restating; to present the meaning of something, as in a picture; to take words spoken or written in one language and put them into another language. **interpretation** *n.*

in·ter·pret·er *n.* A person who will interpret things, such as languages, for others.

in·ter·ra·cial *adj.* Between, among, or affecting different races.

in·ter·re·lat·ed *adj.* Having a mutual relation with someone or something. **interrelatedly** *adv.*, **interrelatedness** *n.*

in·ter·ro·gate *v.* To question formally. **interrogation, interrogator** *n.*

in·ter·rog·a·tive *adj.* Asking or having the nature of a question. *n.* A word used to ask a question.

in·ter·rupt *v.* To break the continuity of something; to intervene abruptly while someone else is speaking or performing.

in·ter·sect *v.* To divide by cutting through or across; to form an intersection; to cross.

in·ter·sec·tion *n.* A place of crossing; a place where streets or roads cross; in mathematics, the point common to two or more geometric elements.

in·ter·state *adj.* Between, involving, or among two or more states.

in·ter·twine *v.* To unite by twisting together. **intertwinement** *n.*

in·ter·ur·ban *adj.* Between or among connecting urban areas.

in•ter•val *n.* The time coming between two points or objects; a period of time between events or moments.

in•ter•vene *v.* To interfere or take a decisive role so as to modify or settle something; to interfere with force in a conflict. **intervention** *n.*

in•ter•view *n.* A conversation conducted by a reporter to elicit information; a conversation led by an employer who is trying to decide whether to hire someone. **interview** *v.*, **interviewer** *n.*

in•ter•weave *v.* To weave things together; to intertwine.

in•tes•tine *n.* The section of the alimentary canal from the stomach to the rectum.

in•ti•mate *adj.* Characterized by close friendship or association. **intimacy** *n.*

in•tim•i•date *v.* To make timid or fearful; to frighten; to discourage or suppress by threats or by violence. **intimidation**, **intimidator** *n.*

in•to *prep.* Inside of; to a form or condition of; to a time in the midst of.

in•tol•er•a•ble *adj.* Unbearable.

in•tol•er•ant *adj.* Not able to endure; not tolerant of the rights or beliefs of others. **intolerance** *n.*

in•tone *v.* To utter or recite in a monotone; to chant.

in•tra•ca•cy *n.* The state of something being intricate.

in•tra•ga•lac•tic *adj.* Occurring within a single galaxy.

in•tra•mu•ral *adj.* Taking place within a school, college, or institution; the competition which is limited to a school community. **intramurally** *adv.*

in•tran•si•gent *adj.* Refusing to moderate a position; uncompromising. **intransigency, intransigent** *n.*

in•tra•state *adj.* To be occurring or happening within a state.

in•tra•ve•nous *adj.* To be occurring within a vein. **intravenously** *adv.*

in•trep•id *adj.* Courageous; unshaken by fever; bold. **intrepidly** *adv.*, **intrepidity, intrepidness** *n.*

in•tri•cate *adj.* Having many perplexingly entangled parts or elements; complex; difficult to understand. **intricately** *adv.*

in•trigue *v.* To arouse the curiosity or interest; to fascinate; to plot; to conspire; to engage in intrigues. *n.* A secret or illicit love affair; a secret plot or plan.

in•trigu•ing *adj.* Engaging the interest of something or of someone to a marked degree.

in•tro•duce *v.* To present a person face to face to another; to make acquainted; to bring into use or practice for the first time; to bring to the attention of. **introductory** *adj.*

in•tro•duc•tion *n.* A passage of a book that will introduce the story or the content of a book; something which introduces.

in•tro•vert *n.* A person who directs his interest to himself and not to friends or social activities. **introversion** *n.*, **introverted** *adj.*

in•trude *v.* To thrust or push oneself in; to come in without being asked or wanted. **intruder** *n.*

in•tru•sion *n.* The act of intruding; an invasion of another's space or attention. **intrusive** *adj.*, **intrusiveness** *n.*

in•tu•i•tion *n.* The direct knowledge or awareness of something without conscious attention or reasoning; knowledge that is acquired in this way. **intuitive** *adj.*, **intuitively** *adv.*

in•un•date *v.* To overwhelm with abundance or excess, as with work. **inundation** *n.*, **inundatory** *adj.*

in•vade *v.* To enter by force with the intent to conquer or to pillage; to penetrate and to overrun harmfully; to violate; to encroach upon. **invader** *n.*

in•va•lid *n.* A chronically sick, bedridden, or disabled person. **invalid** *adj.*

in•val•id *adj.* Disabled by injury or disease; not valid; unsound. **unvalidity** *n.*, **invalidly** *adv.*

in•val•u•a•ble *adj.* Priceless; of great value; to be of great help or use.

in•var•i•a•ble *adj.* Constant and not changing. **invariably** *adv.*

in·va·sion *n.* The act of invading; an entrance made with the intent of overrunning or occupying.

in·vent *v.* To desire or create by original effort or design. **inventor** *n.*

in·ven·tion *n.* The act or process of inventing; a new process, method, or device conceived from study and testing.

in·ven·to·ry *n.* A list of items with descriptions and quantities of each; the process of making such a list.

in·ver·te·brate *adj.* Lacking a backbone or spinal column. **invertebrate** *n.*

in·vest *v.* To use money for the purchase of stocks or property in order to obtain profit or interest; to place in office formally; to install; to make an investment. **investor** *n.*

in·ves·ti·gate *v.* To search or inquire into; to examine carefully. **investigation**, **investigator** *n.*

in·vest·ment *n.* The act of investing money or capital to gain interest or income; property acquired and kept for future benefit.

in·vis·i·ble *adj.* Not capable of being seen; not visible; not open to view; hidden. **invisibility** *n.*, **invisibly** *adv.*

in·vi·ta·tion *n.* The act of inviting; the means or words that request someone's presence or participation.

in·vite *v.* To request the presence or participation of; to make a formal or polite request for; to provoke; to entice; to issue an invitation.

in·vit·ing *adj.* Tempting; attractive. **invitingly** *adv.*

in·voice *n.* An itemized list of merchandise shipped or services rendered, including prices, shipping instructions, and other costs; a bill.

in·vol·un·tar·y *adj.* Not done by choice or willingly.

in·volve *v.* To include as a part; to make a participant of; to absorb; to engross. **involvement** *n.*

in·volved *adj.* To be complex in an extreme manner.

in·vul·ner·a·ble *adj.* To be immune to attack; impregnable; not able to be physically injured or wounded. **invulnerability** *n.*, **invulnerably** *adv.*

in·ward *adj.* To be situated toward the inside, the center, or the interior; of or existing in the mind or thoughts. **inwardness** *n.*, **inwardly** *adv.*

i·o·dine *n.* A grayish-black, corrosive, poisonous element, symbolized by I; a solution made up of iodine, alcohol, and sodium iodide or potassium iodide which is used as an antiseptic.

i·rate *adj.* To be raging; to be angry. **irately** *adv.*, **irateness** *n.*

i·ris *n.* The pigmented part of the eye which regulates the size of the pupil by contracting and expanding around it; in botany, a plant with narrow sword-shaped leaves and large, handsome flowers, as the gladiolus and crocus.

I·rish set·ter *n.* A type of bird dog that has a chestnut-brown or reddish coat.

irk *v.* To annoy or to weary someone.

irk·some *adj.* Tending to irk someone or something. **irksomeness** *n.*

i·ron *n.* A type of heavy malleable ductile magnetic metallic element that is silver-white and will rust easily in moist air.

i·ron·ic *adj.* To be marked by or characterized by irony.

i·ron·ing *n.* The process or action of pressing or smoothing with a heated iron; clothes that have been ironed or are to be ironed.

i·ro·ny *n.* A literary device for conveying meaning by saying the direct opposite of what is really meant.

ir·ra·tion·al *adj.* Unable to reason; contrary to reason; absurd; in mathematics, a number which is not expressible as an integer or a quotient of integers. **irrationality** *n.*

ir·reg·u·lar *adj.* Not according to the general rule or practice; not straight, uniform, or orderly; uneven. *n.* One who is irregular. **irregularity** *n.*, **irregularly** *adv.*

ir·rel·e·vant *adj.* Not pertinent or related to the subject matter.

ir·re·place·a·ble *adj.* Unable to be replaced; precious; unique.

ir·re·sist·i·ble *adj.* Completely fascinating; impossible to resist.

ir·re·spon·si·ble *adj.* Lacking in responsibility; not accountable. **irresponsibility** *n.,* **irresponsibly** *adv.*

ir·re·vers·i·ble *adj.* Impossible to reverse.

ir·ri·gate *v.* To water land or crops artificially, as by means of ditches or sprinklers; to refresh with water. **irrigation** *n.*

ir·ri·ta·ble *adj.* Easily annoyed; ill-tempered.

ir·ri·tate *v.* To annoy or bother; to provoke; to be sore, chafed, or inflamed. **irritator, irritation** *n.*

is *v.* Third person, singular, present tense of the verb *to be.*

is·land *n.* A piece of land smaller than a continent, completely surrounded by water.

is·n't *contr.* Is not.

i·so·late *v.* To set apart from the others; to put by itself; to place or be placed in quarantine. **isolation, isolator** *n.*

is·sue *n.* The act of giving out; something that is given out or published; a matter of importance to solve. *v.* To come forth; to flow out; to emerge; to distribute or give out, as supplies. **issuable** *adj.,* **issuer** *n.*

it *pron.* Used as a substitute for a specific noun or name when referring to places, things, or animals of unspecified sex; used to refer to the general state of something.

i·tal·ic *adj.* A style of printing type in which the letters slant to the right. **italicize** *v.*

itch *n.* A skin irritation which causes a desire to scratch; a contagious skin disease accompanied by a desire to scratch; a restless desire or craving. **itch** *v.,* **itchiness** *n.,* **itchy** *adj.*

i·tem *n.* A separately-noted unit or article included in a category or series; a short article, as in a magazine or newspaper.

i·tem·ize *v.* To specify by item; to list.

itemizer, itemization *n.*

its *adj.* The possessive case of the pronoun *it.*

it's *contr.* It is; it has.

i·vo·ry *n.* A hard, smooth, yellowish-white material which forms the tusks of elephants, walruses, and other animals; any substance similar to ivory. *pl.* The keys on a piano; teeth.

i·vy *n.* A climbing plant having glossy evergreen leaves.

J

J, j The tenth letter of the English alphabet.

jab *v.* To poke or thrust sharply with short blows; a rapid punch.

jab·ber *v.* To speak quickly or without making sense.

jack *n.* The playing card that ranks just below a queen and bears a representation of a knave; any of various tools or devises used for raising heavy objects.

jack·al *n.* An African or Asian dog-like, carnivorous mammal.

jack·ass *n.* A male donkey or ass; a stupid person or one who acts in a stupid fashion.

jack·et *n.* A short coat worn by men and women; a protective cover for a book.

jack·knife *n.* A large pocketknife; a dive executed by doubling the body forward with the knees unbent and the hands touching the ankles and then straightening before entering the water.

jack·pot *n.* Any post, prize, or pool in which the amount won is cumulative.

jacks *n.* A game played with a set of six-pronged metal pieces and a small ball.

jade *n.* A hard, translucent, green gemstone; an old, worn-out unmanageable horse.

jag·ged *adj.* Having jags or sharp notches; serrated. **jaggedness** *n.*

jag·uar *n.* A large, spotted feline mammal of tropical America with a tawny coat and black spots.

jail *n.* A place of confinement for incarceration.

jail·bird *n.* A prisoner or ex-prisoner.

jail·er *n.* The officer in charge of a jail and its prisoners.

ja·lop·y *n.* *slang* An old, rundown automobile.

jam *v.* To force or wedge into a tight position; to apply the brakes of a car suddenly; to be locked in a position; to block; to crush.

jam *n.* A preserve or whole fruit boiled with sugar.

jan·i·tor *n.* A person who cleans and cares for a building.

jar *n.* A deep, cylindrical vessel with a wide mouth; a harsh sound. *v.* To strike against or bump into; to affect one's feelings unpleasantly.

jaunt *n.* A short journey for pleasure.

jaun·ty *adj.* Having a buoyantly carefree and self-confident air or manner about oneself. **jauntily** *adv.*, **jauntiness** *n.*

jaw *n.* Either of two bony structures forming the framework of the mouth and holding the teeth.

jay·walk *v.* To cross a street carelessly, violating traffic regulations. **jaywalker** *n.*

jazz *n.* A kind of music which has a strong rhythmic structure with frequent syncopation and often involving ensemble and solo improvisation.

jeal·ous *adj.* Suspicious or fearful of being replaced by a rival; resentful or bitter in rivalry; demanding exclusive love. **jealousness, jealousy** *n.*

jean *n.* A strong, twilled cotton cloth. *pl.* Pants made of denim.

jel·ly *n.* Any food preparation made with pectin or gelatin and having a somewhat elastic consistency; a food made of boiled and sweetened fruit juice and used as a filter or spread.

jel·ly·bean *n.* A small candy having a hard colored coating over a gelatinous center.

jel·ly·fish *n.* Any of a number of free-swimming marine animals of jellylike substance, often having bell or umbrella-shaped bodies with trailing tentacles.

jeop·ard·ize *v.* To put in jeopardy; to expose to loss or danger.

jeop·ard·y *n.* Exposure to loss or danger.

jerk *v.* To give a sharp twist or pull to. *n.* A sudden movement, as a tug or twist; an involuntary contraction of a muscle resulting from a reflex action.

jer·sey *n.* A soft ribbed fabric of wool, cotton, or other material; a knitted sweater, jacket, or shirt; fawn-colored, small dairy cattle which yield milk rich in butter fat.

jest *n.* An action or remark intended to provoke laughter; a joke; a playful mood. **jester** *n.*

Je·sus *n.* The founder of Christianity, son of Mary and regarded in the Christian faith as Christ the son of God, the Messiah; also referred to as Jesus Christ or Jesus of Nazareth.

jet *n.* A sudden spurt or gush of liquid or gas emitted through a narrow opening; a jet airplane; a hard, black mineral which takes a high polish and is used in jewelry; a deep glossy black.

jet stream *n.* A high-velocity wind near the troposphere, generally moving from west to east, often at speeds over 250 mph.

Jew *n.* A descendant of the ancient Hebrew people; a person believing in Judaism. **Jewess** *n.*

jew·el *n.* A precious stone used for personal adornment; a person or thing of very rare excellence or value. *v.* To furnish with jewels. **jewelry** *n.*

jew·eler or **jew·el·ler** *n.* A person who makes or deals in jewelry.

jif·fy *n.* A very short time; in a hurry.

jig·saw *n.* A saw having a slim blade set vertically, used for cutting curved and irregular lines.

jig·saw puz·zle *n.* A puzzle consisting of many irregularly shaped pieces which fit together and form a picture.

jilt *v.* To discard a romantic interest.

jin·gle *v.* To make a light clinking or ringing sound. *n.* A short, catchy song or poem, as one used for advertising.

jinx *n.* A person or thing thought to bring

bad luck; a period of bad luck.

jit•ter•bug *n.* A lively dance or one who performs this dance.

jit•ters *n.* Nervousness; uneasiness caused by external forces.

job *n.* Anything that is done; work that is done for a set fee; the project worked on; a position of employment.

job•name *n.* In computers, a code assigned to a specific job instruction in a computer program, for the operator's use.

jock•ey *n.* A person who rides a horse as a professional in a race; one who works with a specific object or device.

jog *n.* A slight movement or a slight shake; the slow steady trot of a horse, especially when exercising or participating in a sport; a projecting or retreating part in a surface or line. *v.* To shift direction abruptly; to exercise by running at a slow but steady pace.

join *v.* To bring or put together so as to form a unit; to become a member of an organization; to participate.

join•er *n.* A person whose occupation is to build articles by joining pieces of wood; a cabinetmaker; a carpenter.

joint *n.* The place where two or more things or parts are joined; a point where bones are connected.

joke *n.* Something said or done to cause laughter, such as a brief story with a punch line; something not taken seriously. *v.* To tell or play jokes.

jok•er *n.* A person who jokes; a playing card, used in certain card games as a wild card; an unsuspected or unapparent fact which nullifies a seeming advantage.

jol•ly *adj.* Full of good humor; merry.

jolt *v.* To knock or shake about. *n.* A sudden bump or jar, as from a blow.

jos•tle *v.* To make one's way through a crowd by pushing or shoving. **jostler** *n.*

jot *v.* To make a brief note of something. *n.* A tiny bit.

jour•nal *n.* A diary or personal daily record of observations and experiences; in bookkeeping, a book in which daily financial transactions are recorded.

jour•nal•ism *n.* The occupation, collection, writing, editing, and publishing of newspapers and other periodicals. **journalist** *n.*, **journalistic** *adj.*

jour•ney *n.* A trip from one place to another over a long distance; the distance that is traveled. *v.* To make a trip; to travel a long distance.

jo•vi•al *adj.* Good-natured; good-humored; jolly. **joviality** *n.*

joy *n.* A strong feeling of great happiness; delight; a state or source of contentment or satisfaction; anything which makes one delighted or happy. **joyfully** *adv.*, **joyfulness** *n.*

joy•ous *adj.* Joyful; causing or feeling joy. **joyously** *adv.*, **joyousness** *n.*

ju•bi•lant *adj.* Exultantly joyful or triumphant; expressing joy. **jubilation** *n.*, **jubilantly** *adv.*

ju•bi•lee *n.* A special anniversary of an event; any time of rejoicing.

Ju•da•ism *n.* The religious practices or beliefs of the Jews; a religion based on the belief in one God.

judge *n.* A public officer who passes judgment in a court. *v.* To decide authoritatively after deliberation.

judg•ment *n.* The ability to make a wise decision or to form an opinion; the act of judging. In law, the sentence or determination of a court. **judgmental** *adj.*

ju•di•cial *adj.* Pertaining to the administering of justice, to courts of law, or to judges; enforced or decreed by a court of law. **judicially** *adv.*

ju•di•cious *adj.* Having, showing, or exercising good sound judgment. **judiciously** *adv.*, **judiciousness** *n.*

jug *n.* A small pitcher or similar vessel for holding liquids.

jug•gle *v.* To keep several objects continuously moving from the hand into the air. **juggler** *n.*

juice *n.* The liquid part of a vegetable, fruit, or animal.

juic•y *adj.* Full of; abounding with juice;

full of interest; richly rewarding, especially financially. **juiciness** *n.*

juke box *n.* A large, automatic, coin-operated record player.

jum•ble *v.* To mix in a confused mass; to throw together without order; to confuse or mix something up in the mind.

jump *v.* To spring from the ground, floor, or other surface into the air by using a muscular effort of the legs and feet; to move in astonishment; to leap over; to increase greatly, as prices.

jump•er *n.* One who or that which jumps; a sleeveless dress, usually worn over a blouse.

jump•y *adj.* Nervous; jittery.

junc•tion *n.* The place where lines or routes meet, as roads or railways; the process of joining or the act of joining.

jun•gle *n.* A densely covered land with tropical vegetation, usually inhabited by wild animals.

jun•ior *adj.* Younger in years or rank; used to distinguish a son from a father of the same first name; the younger of two. *n.* The third year of high school or college.

junk *n.* Discarded material, as glass, scrap iron, paper, or rags; a flat-bottomed Chinese ship with battened sails; rubbish.

jun•ket *n.* A party, banquet, or trip; a trip taken by a public official with all expenses paid for by public funds; a custard-like dessert of flavored milk set with rennet. **junket** *v.*, **junketeer** *n.*

junk food *n.* Food containing very little nutritional value in proportion to the number of calories.

ju•ris•dic•tion *n.* The lawful right or power to interpret and apply the law; the territory within which power is exercised. **jurisdictional** *adj.*

ju•ror *n.* A person who serves on a jury.

ju•ry *n.* A group of persons summoned to serve on a judicial tribunal to give a verdict according to evidence presented.

just *adj.* Fair and impartial in acting or judging; morally right; merited; deserved; based on sound reason. *adv.* To the exact point; precisely; exactly right. **justly** *adv.*, **justness** *n.*

jus•tice *n.* The principle of moral or ideal rightness; conformity to the law; the abstract principle by which right and wrong are defined; a judge.

jus•ti•fy *v.* To be just, right, or valid; to declare guiltless; to adjust or space lines to the proper length.

jut *v.* To extend beyond the main portion; to project.

ju•ve•nile *adj.* Young, youthful; not yet an adult. *n.* A young person; an actor who plays youthful roles; a child's book.

ju•ve•nile court *n.* A court which deals only with cases involving dependent, neglected, and delinquent children.

ju•ve•nile de•lin•quent *n.* A person who is guilty of violations of the law, but is too young to be punished as an adult criminal; a young person whose behavior is out of control.

K

K, k The eleventh letter of the English alphabet; symbol for *kilo*, one thousand; in computers, a unit of capacity equal to 1024 bytes.

ka•bu•ki *n.* A traditional Japanese drama in which dances and songs are performed in a stylized fashion.

kale *n.* A green cabbage having crinkled leaves which do not form a tight head.

ka•lie•do•scope *n.* A tubular instrument rotated to make successive symmetrical designs by using mirrors reflecting the changing patterns made by pieces of loose colored glass.

kan•ga•roo *n.* Any of various herbivorous marsupials of Australia, with short forelegs and large hind limbs, capable of jumping, and a large tail.

kar•at *n.* A unit of measure for the fineness of gold; a measure of weight for precious gems.

ka•ra•te *n.* The Japanese art of self-defense.

kar·ma *n.* The over-all effect of one's behavior, held in Hinduism and Buddhism to determine one's destiny in a future existence. **karmic** *adj.*

ka·ty·did *n.* Any of various green insects related to grasshoppers and crickets.

kay·ak *n.* A watertight Eskimo boat with a light frame and covered with sealskin.

kay·o *n.* To knock out (K.O.) an opponent, in boxing.

ka·zoo *n.* A toy musical instrument with a paper membrane which vibrates when a player hums into the tube.

keel *n.* The central main stem of a ship or aircraft which runs lengthwise along the center line from bow to stern.

keel·boat *n.* A boat used on rivers; shallow boat used for freight.

keen *adj.* Having a sharp edge or point; acutely painful or harsh; intellectually acute; strong; intense.

keep *v.* To have and hold; to not let go; to maintain, as business records; to know a secret and not divulge it; to protect and defend.

keep·er *n.* One who keeps, guards, or maintains something; a person who respects or observes a requirement.

keep·ing *n.* Charge or possession; conformity or harmony; maintenance or support.

keep·sake *n.* A memento or souvenir; a token or remembrance of friendship.

keg *n.* A small barrel usually having the capacity of five to ten gallons; the unit of measure for nails which equals 100 pounds.

kelp *n.* Any of a variety of large brown seaweed.

ken·nel *n.* A shelter for or a place where dogs or cats are bred, boarded, or trained.

ke·no *n.* A game of chance resembling bingo; a lottery game.

ker·chief *n.* A piece of cloth usually worn around the neck or on the head; scarf. **kerchiefed** *adj.*

ker·nel *n.* A grain or seed, as of corn, enclosed in a hard husk; the inner sub-stance of a nut; the central, most important part; a device for holding something in place, as a latch, or clasp.

ker·o·sene or **ker·o·sine** *n.* An oil distilled from petroleum or coal.

ketch·up *n.* A thick, smooth sauce made from tomatoes; catsup.

ket·tle *n.* A large metal pot for stewing or boiling.

ket·tle·drum *n.* A musical instrument with a parchment head tuned by adjusting the tension.

key *n.* An object used to open a lock; button or lever used on a keyboard of a typewriter or piano; the crucial or main element. **keyed** *adj.*

key·board *n.* A bank of keys, as on a piano, typewriter, or computer terminal.

key·hole *n.* Lock; area that a key is inserted into.

key·note *n.* The first and harmonically fundamental tone of a scale; main principle or theme.

key·stone *n.* The wedge-shaped stone at the center of an arch that locks its parts together; an essential part.

key·stroke *n.* A stroke of a key.

kha·ki *n.* A yellowish brown or olive-drab color; a sturdy cloth, khaki in color. *pl.* Trousers or a uniform of khaki cloth.

kick *v.* To strike something with force by the foot.

kick·back *n.* A secret payment to a person who can influence a source of income; repercussion; a strong reaction.

kick·off *n.* The play that begins a game of soccer or football.

kick·stand *n.* The swiveling bar for holding a two-wheeled vehicle upright.

kid *n.* A young goat; leather made from the skin of a young goat. *slang* A child; youngster. *v.* To mock or tease playfully, to deceive for fun; to fool.

kid·nap *v.* To seize and hold a person unlawfully, often for ransom. **kidnapper** *n.*

kid·ney *n.* Either of two organs situated in the abdominal cavity of vertebrates whose function is to keep proper water balance in the body and to excrete wastes in the form of urine.

kid•ney bean *n.* A bean whose edible seeds are in the shape of a kidney.

kill *v.* To put to death; nullify; cancel; to slaughter for food; to deprive of life.

kill•ing *n.* The act of a person who kills; a slaying.

kill•joy *n.* One who spoils the enjoyment of others.

kiln *n.* An oven or furnace for hardening or drying a substance, especially one for firing ceramics or pottery.

ki•lo *n.* A kilogram.

kil•o•gram *n.* A measurement of weight in the metric system equal to slightly more than one third of a pound.

kil•o•li•ter *n.* Metric measurement equal to one thousand liters.

kil•o•me•ter *n.* Metric measurement equal to one thousand meters.

kil•o•volt *n.* One thousand volts.

kil•o•watt *n.* A unit of power equal to one thousand watts.

kil•o•watt hour *n.* A unit of electric power consumption of one thousand watts throughout one hour.

kilt *n.* A knee-length wool skirt with deep pleats, usually of tartan, worn especially by men in the Scottish Highlands.

kin *n.* One's relatives by blood; relatives collectively.

kind *n.* A characteristic; a variety.

kind *adj.* Of a friendly, or good-natured disposition; coming from a good-natured readiness to please others. **kindness** *n.*

kin•der•gar•ten *n.* A school or class for young children from the ages of four to six. **kindergartner** *n.*

kind•heart•ed *adj.* Having much generosity and kindness.

kin•dle *v.* To ignite; to catch fire; to stir up; to excite, as feelings.

kind•less *adj.* Mean, cruel, unkind, unfriendly.

kin•dling *n.* Easily ignited material such as sticks and wood chips, used to start a fire.

kind•ly *adv.* Pleasantly, in a natural way; with a good disposition, or character; benevolently. **kindliness** *n.*

kind•ness *n.* An act of good will; state or quality of being kind.

kin•dred *n.* A person's relatives by blood. *adj.* Having a like nature; similar.

ki•net•ic *adj.* Relating to, or produced by, motion.

king *n.* One who rules over a country; a male monarch; a playing card with a picture of a king; the main piece in the games of chess and checkers.

king•dom *n.* The area or the country ruled by a king or queen.

king•ly *adj.* Pertaining to or belonging to a king or kings; monarchical; splendid.

kink *n.* A tight twist or knot-like curl; a sharp painful muscle cramp. **kinky** *adj.*

kiss *v.* To touch two lips together in greeting between two people. **kissable** *adj.*

kit *n.* A collection of tools, supplies, or items for a special purpose.

kitch•en *n.* A room in a house or building used to prepare and cook food.

kitch•en•ette *n.* A small area that functions as a kitchen.

kitch•en•ware *n.* Dishes, pots, pans, and other utensils used in a kitchen.

kite *n.* A light-weight framework of wood and paper designed to fly in a steady breeze at the end of a string.

kith or **kin** *n.* Acquaintances or family.

kit•ten *n.* A young cat.

kit•ty *n.* A small collection or accumulation of objects or money; a young cat or kitten.

klep•to•ma•ni•a *n.* Obsessive desire to steal or impulse to steal, especially without economic motive.

klutz *n.* A clumsy person. **klutzy** *adj.*

knack *n.* A natural talent; aptitude.

knack•wurst or **knock•wurst** *n.* A thick or short, heavily seasoned sausage.

knap•sack *n.* A supply or equipment bag, as of canvas or nylon, worn strapped across the shoulders.

knave *n.* A tricky or dishonest person.

knead *v.* To work dough into a uniform

mass by folding over; to shape by or as if by kneading.

knee *n.* The hinged joint in the leg connecting the calf with the thigh.

knee•cap *n.* Patella; bone covering the joint of the knee.

knee-deep *adj.* So deep that it reaches one's knees.

kneel *v.* To go down upon one's knees. **kneeler** *n.*

knell *v.* To sound a bell, especially when rung for a funeral; to toll. *n.* An act or instance of knelling; a signal of disaster.

knick•knack *n.* A trinket; trifling article.

knife *n.* An instrument used to cut an item.

knife edge *n.* A very sharp edge; the edge of a knife.

knife switch *n.* A switch used to close a circuit.

knight *n.* A medieval soldier serving a monarch; a chess piece bearing the shape of a horse's head. **knighthood** *n.*, **knightly** *adj.*

knit *v.* To form by intertwining thread or yarn, by interlocking loops of a single yarn by means of needles; to fasten securely; to draw together.

knit•ting nee•dle *n.* A long, slender, pointed rod for knitting.

knob *n.* A rounded protuberance; a lump; a rounded mountain; a rounded handle. **knobbed** *adj.*, **knobby** *adj.*

knock *v.* To hit or strike with a hard blow; to criticize; to collide.

knock•er *n.* A metal ring for knocking on a door.

knock•knee *n.* A condition in which one or both knees turn inward and knock or rub together while walking. **knock-kneed** *adj.*

knoll *n.* A small round hill; a mound.

knot *n.* An interwinding of string or rope; a fastening made by typing together lengths of material, as string; a unifying bond, especially of marriage; a hard node on a tree from which a branch grows; a nautical unit of speed, also called a nautical mile, which equals approximately 1.15 statute miles per hour.

knot•hole *n.* A hole in lumber left by the falling out of a knot.

know *v.* To perceive directly as fact or truth; to believe to be true; to be certain of; to be familiar with or have experience.

know•how *n.* Craft or expertise in something.

know•ing *adj.* Astute, knowledgeable; possessing secret knowledge. **knowingly** *adv.*

know•ledge *n.* Facts, information; the state of knowing. **knowledgeable** *adj.*

knuck•le *n.* The hinge or joint of the finger where it joins the hand or fist.

knuck•le•bone *n.* The bone of the finger which forms the knuckle.

ko•a•la *n.* An Australian marsupial with large hairy ears and gray fur, which feeds on eucalyptus leaves.

L

L, l The twelfth letter of the English alphabet; the Roman numeral for fifty.

la•bel *n.* Something that identifies or describes. *v.* To attach a label to.

lab•y•rinth *n.* A system of winding, intricate passages; a maze.

lace *n.* A delicate open-work fabric of silk, cotton, or linen made by hand or on a machine. *v.* To fasten or tie together; to interlace or intertwine. **lacy** *adj.*

lac•er•ate *v.* To open with a jagged tear; to wound the flesh by tearing. **laceration** *n.*

lack *n.* The deficiency or complete absence of something. *v.* To have little of something or to be completely without.

lack•lus•ter *adj.* Lacking sheen; dull.

lac•quer *n.* A transparent varnish which is dissolved in a volatile solution and dries to give surfaces a glossy finish.

lad *n.* A boy or young man.

lad•der *n.* An implement used for climbing up or down in order to reach another place or area.

lad•en *adj.* Heavily burdened; oppressed; weighed down; loaded.

lad•ing *n.* Cargo; freight.

la•dle *n.* A cup-shaped vessel with a deep bowl and a long handle, used for dipping or conveying liquids.

la•dy *n.* A woman showing refinement, cultivation, and often high social position; an address or term of reference for any woman.

la•dy•like *adj.* Having the characteristics of a lady; delicate; gentle.

lag *v.* To stray or fall behind; to move slowly; to weaken gradually.

la•goon *n.* A body of shallow water separated from the ocean by a coral reef or sandbars.

laid *v.* Past tense of *lay*.

lain *v.* Past tense of *lie*.

lake *n.* A large inland body of either salt or fresh water.

lamb *n.* A young sheep; the meat of a lamb used as food; a gentle person.

lame *adj.* Disabled or crippled, especially in the legs or feet so as to impair free movement.

la•ment *v.* To express sorrow; to mourn. *n.* An expression of regret or sorrow.

lam•i•nate *v.* To form or press into thin sheets; to form layers by the action of pressure and heat. **lamination** *n.*, **laminated** *adj.*

lamp *n.* A device for generating heat or light.

lam•poon *n.* A satirical, humorous, attack in verse or prose, especially one that ridicules a group, person, or institution.

lance *n.* A spear-like implement used as a weapon by mounted knights or soldiers.

land *n.* The solid, exposed surface of the earth as distinguished from the waters. *v.* To arrive at a destination from water.

land•fill *n.* A system of trash and garbage disposal in which the waste is buried in low-lying land to build up the ground surface; a section built up by landfill.

land grant *n.* A grant of land made by a government, especially for railroads, roads, or agricultural colleges.

land•ing *n.* The act of coming, going, or placing ashore from any kind of vessel or craft; the act of descending and settling on the ground in an airplane.

land•locked *adj.* Almost or completely surrounded by land.

land•lord *n.* A person who owns property and rents or leases to another.

land•mark *n.* A fixed object that serves as a boundary marker.

land•scape *n.* A view or vista of natural scenery as seen from a single point. *v.* To decorate outside with flowers, shrubbery, and lawns.

lane *n.* A small or narrow path between walls, fences, or hedges.

lan•guage *n.* The words, sounds, pronunciation and method of combining words used and understood by people.

lank *adj.* Slender; lean.

lan•tern *n.* A portable light having transparent or translucent sides.

la•pel *n.* The front part of a garment, especially a coat, that is turned back, usually a continuation of the collar.

lapse *n.* A temporary deviation or fall to a less desirable state.

lar•ce•ny *n.* The unlawful taking of another person's property.

large *adj.* Greater than usual or average in amount or size.

lark *n.* A bird having a melodious ability to sing; a merry or carefree adventure.

lar•va *n.* The immature, wingless, often worm-like form of a newly hatched insect; the early form of an animal that differs greatly from the adult, such as the tadpole. **larval** *adj.*, **larvae** *pl.*

la•ser *n.* A device which utilizes the natural oscillations of molecules or atoms between energy levels for generating coherent electromagnetic radiation in the visible, ultraviolet, or infrared parts of the spectrum.

lash *v.* To strike or move violently or suddenly; to attack verbally; to whip. *n.* An eyelash.

lass *n.* A young girl or woman.

last *adj.* Following all the rest; of or relating to the final stages, as of life; worst; lowest in rank. *adv.* After all others in sequence or chronology. *v.* To continue; to endure.

latch *n.* A device used to secure a gate or door, consisting of a bar that usually fits into a notch.

late *adj.* Coming, staying, happening after the proper or usual time; having recently died.

lath·er *n.* A foam formed by detergent or soap and water.

lat·i·tude *n.* The angular distance of the earth's surface north or south of the equator, measured in degrees along a meridian; freedom to act and to choose.

lat·ter *adj.* Being the second of two persons or two things.

lat·tice *n.* A structure made of strips of wood, metal, or other materials, interlaced or crossed, framing regularly spaced openings.

laugh *v.* To express amusement, satisfaction, or joy with a smile and inarticulate sounds. **laughable** *adj.*, **laughter** *n.*

launch *v.* To push or move a vessel into the water for the first time; to set a rocket or missile into flight. *n.* A large boat carried by a ship.

laun·der *v.* To wash clothes or other materials in soap and water.

laun·dro·mat *n.* A place to wash and dry clothes in coin operated machines.

laun·dry *n.* A business where laundering is done professionally; clothes or other articles to be or that have been laundered.

la·va *n.* Molten rock which erupts or flows from an active volcano; the rock formed after lava has cooled and hardened.

lav·a·to·ry *n.* A room with permanently installed washing and toilet facilities.

law *n.* A rule of conduct or action, recognized by custom or decreed by formal enactment, considered binding on the members of a nation, community, or group; a system or body of such rules.

lawn *n.* A stretch of ground covered with grass mowed regularly.

law·suit *n.* A case or proceeding brought before a court of law for settlement.

law·yer *n.* A person trained in the legal profession who acts for and advises clients or pleads in court.

lax *adj.* Lacking disciplinary control; lacking rigidity or firmness.

lay *v.* To cause to lie; to place on a surface; past tense of *lie*.

lay·er *n.* A single thickness, coating, or covering that lies over or under another. **layered** *adj.*

la·zy *adj.* Unwilling to work; moving slowly; sluggish. **lazily** *adv.*

la·zy·bones *n.* A lazy person.

lead *v.* To go ahead so as to show the way; to control the affairs or action of.

leaf *n.* A flat outgrowth from a plant structure or tree, usually green in color and functioning as the principal area of photosynthesis; a page in a book. **leafy** *adj.*

leaf·let *n.* A part or a segment of a compound leaf; a small printed handbill or circular, often folded.

league *n.* An association of persons, organizations, or states for common interest; an association of athletic competition.

leak *n.* An opening, as a flaw or small crack, permitting an escape or entrance of light or fluid. **leakage** *n.*

lean *v.* To rest or incline the weight of the body for support; to rest or incline anything against a large object or wall; to rely or depend on; to have a tendency or preference for. *adj.* Having little or no fat; thin. **leanly** *adv.*, **leanness** *n.*

lean·ing *n.* An inclination; a predisposition.

leap *v.* To rise or project oneself by a sudden thrust from the ground with a spring of the legs; to spring; to jump.

leap year *n.* A year containing 366 days, occurring every fourth year, with the extra day added to make 29 days in February.

learn·ing *n.* The process of acquiring knowledge, understanding, or mastery of a study or experience. **learner** *n.*, **learn-able** *adj.*, **learn** *v.*

lease *n.* A contract for the temporary use or occupation of property or premises in exchange for payment of rent.

leash *n.* A strong cord or rope for restraining a dog or other animal.

leath·er *n.* An animal skin or hide with the hair removed, prepared for use by tanning.

leave *v.* To go or depart from; to permit to remain behind or in a specified place or condition; to forsake; to abandon; to bequeath, as in a will.

lec·ture *n.* A speech on a specific subject, delivered to an audience for information or instruction. *v.* To give a speech or lecture; to criticize or reprimand.

led *v.* Past tense of *lead*.

ledge *n.* A narrow, shelf-like projection forming a shelf.

ledg·er *n.* A book in which sums of money received and paid out are recorded.

left *adj.* Pertaining to or being on the side of the body that faces north when the subject is facing east.

leg *n.* A limb or appendage serving as a means of support and movement in animals and man.

leg·a·cy *n.* Personal property, money, and other valuables bequeathed by will; anything handed down from an ancestor, predecessor, or earlier era.

le·gal *adj.* Of, pertaining to, or concerned with the law or lawyers; something based on or authorized by law.

leg·end *n.* An unverifiable story handed down from the past; a body of such stories, as those connected with a culture or people. **legendary** *adj.*

leg·i·ble *adj.* Capable of being read or deciphered. **legibility** *n.*, **legibly** *adv.*

leg·is·la·tion *n.* The act or procedures of passing laws; lawmaking; an enacted law. **legislate** *v.*, **legislative** *adj.*

leg·is·la·ture *n.* A body of persons officially constituted and empowered to make and change laws.

lei·sure *n.* A time of freedom from work or duty.

lem·on *n.* An oval citrus fruit grown on a tree, having juicy, acid pulp and a yellow rind that yields an essential oil used as a flavoring and as a perfuming agent.

lem·on·ade *n.* A drink made from water, lemon juice, and sugar.

lend *v.* To allow the temporary use or possession of something with the understanding that it is to be returned; to offer oneself as to a specific purpose. **lender** *n.*

length *n.* The linear extent of something from end to end, usually the longest dimension of a thing as distinguished from its thickness and width. **lengthy** *adj.*, **lengthen** *v.*

le·ni·ent *adj.* Gentle, forgiving, and mild; merciful; undemanding; tolerant. **leniency, lenience** *n.*

lens *n.* In optics, the curved piece of glass or other transparent substance used to refract light rays so that they converge or diverge to form an image; the transparent structure in the eye, situated behind the iris, which serves to focus an image on the retina.

lent *v.* Past tense of *lend*.

leo·pard *n.* A large member of the cat family of Africa and Asia, having a tawny coat with dark brown or black spots grouped in rounded clusters, also called a panther.

le·o·tard *n.* A close-fitting garment worn by dancers and acrobats.

lep·er *n.* One who suffers from leprosy.

lep·re·chaun *n.* A mischief-making elf of Irish folklore, supposed to own hidden treasure.

less *adj.* Smaller; of smaller or lower importance or degree. *prep.* With the subtraction of; minus.

les·son *n.* An instance from which something is to be or has been learned; an assignment to be learned or studied.

let *v.* To give permission; to allow.

le·thal *adj.* Pertaining to or being able to cause death.

let's *contr.* Let us.

let·ter *n.* A standard character or sign used in writing or printing to represent an alphabetical unit or speech sound; a written or printed means of communication sent to another person.

let·tuce *n.* A plant having crisp, edible leaves used specially in salads.

lev·el *n.* A relative position, rank, or height on a scale; a standard position from which other heights and depths are measured. *adj.* Balanced in height; even. *v.* To make or become flat or level.

lev·er *n.* A handle that projects and is used to operate or adjust a mechanism.

lev·er·age *n.* The use of a lever; the mechanical advantage gained by using a lever; power to act effectively.

li·a·bil·i·ty *n.* The condition or state of being liable; that which is owed to another. **liable** *adj.*

li·ar *n.* A person who tells falsehoods.

lib·er·al *adj.* Characterized by generosity or lavishness in giving; abundant; ample. **liberalism, liberality** *n.,* **liberally** *adv.*

lib·er·ate *v.* To set free, as from bondage, oppression, or foreign control. **liberation** *n.*

lib·er·ty *n.* The state of being free from oppression, tyranny, confinement, or slavery; freedom.

li·brar·y *n.* A collection of books, pamphlets, magazines, and reference books kept for reading, reference, or borrowing; a commercial establishment, usually in connection with a city or school, which rents books. **librarian** *n.*

lice *n.* Plural of *louse*.

li·cense *n.* An official document that gives permission to engage in a specified activity or to perform a specified act. **license** *v.,* **licenser** *n.*

lick *v.* To pass the tongue over or along the surface of.

lic·o·rice *n.* A perennial herb of Europe, the dried root of which is used to flavor medicines and candy.

lid *n.* A hinged or removable cover for a container; an eyelid. **lidded, lidless** *adj.*

lie *v.* To be in or take a horizontal recumbent position; to recline. *n.* A false or untrue statement.

life *n.* The form of existence that distinguishes living organisms from dead organisms or inanimate matter in the ability to carry on metabolism, respond to stimuli, reproduce, and grow.

life·time *n.* The period between one's birth and death.

life·work *n.* The main work of a person's lifetime.

lift *v.* To raise from a lower to a higher position; to elevate; to take from. *n.* The act or process of lifting; force or power available for lifting; an elevation of spirits; a device or machine designed to pick up, raise, or carry something.

light *n.* Electromagnetic radiation that can be seen by the naked eye; brightness; a source of light; spiritual illumination; enlightenment. *adj.* Having light; bright; of less force, quantity, intensity, or weight than normal.

light·er *n.* A device used to light a pipe, cigar or cigarette; a barge used to load and unload a cargo ship.

light·ning *n.* The flash of light produced by a high-tension natural electric discharge into the atmosphere. *adj.* Moving with or as if with the suddenness of lightning.

light-year or **light year** *n.* A measure equal to the distance light travels in one year, approximately 5,878 trillion miles.

like·ness *n.* Resemblance; a copy.

like·wise *adv.* In a similar way.

li·ma bean *n.* Any of several varieties of tropical American plants having flat pods with light green edible seeds.

limb *n.* A large bough of a tree; an animal's appendage used for movement or grasping; an arm or leg.

lim·ber *adj.* Bending easily; pliable; moving easily; agile. *v.* To make or become limber.

lime *n.* A tropical citrus tree with evergreen

leaves, fragrant white flowers, and edible green fruit; calcium oxide.

lime·light *n.* A focus of public attention; the center of attention.

lim·er·ick *n.* A humorous verse of five lines.

lime·stone *n.* A form of sedimentary rock composed mainly of calcium carbonate, used in building and in making lime and cement.

lim·it *n.* A boundary; a maximum or a minimum number or amount; a restriction on frequency or amount. *v.* To restrict; to establish boundaries. **limitation** *n.*

lim·ou·sine *n.* A luxurious large vehicle; a small bus used to carry passengers to airports and hotels.

limp *v.* To walk lamely.

lin·e·age *n.* A direct line of descent from an ancestor.

lin·e·ar *adj.* Of, pertaining to, or resembling a line; long and narrow.

lin·en *n.* Thread, yarn, or fabric made of flax; household articles, such as sheets and pillow cases, made of linen or a similar fabric.

lin·ger *v.* To be slow in parting or reluctant to leave; to be slow in acting; to procrastinate. **lingeringly** *adv.*

lin·ing *n.* A material which is used to cover an inside surface.

link *n.* One of the rings forming a chain; something in the form of a link; a tie or bond. *v.* To connect by or as if by a link or links. **linkage** *n.*

li·no·le·um *n.* A floor covering consisting of a surface of hardened linseed oil and a filler, as wood or powdered cork, on a canvas or burlap backing.

li·on *n.* A large carnivorous mammal of the cat family, found in Africa and India, having a short, tawny coat and a long, heavy mane in the male. **lioness** *n.*

liq·uid *adj.* Being in the physical state between gas and solid at room temperature. *n.* A substance that takes on the form of the vessel containing it; a beverage or drink.

liq·uor *n.* A distilled alcoholic beverage; a liquid substance, as a watery solution of a drug.

list *n.* A series of numbers or words; a tilt to one side. **list** *v.*

list·less *adj.* Lacking energy.

list·serv *n.* In computers, a mailing list capable of sending information to sites linked by common interests.

lit·er·al *adj.* Conforming to the exact meaning of a word; concerned primarily with facts; without embellishment or exaggeration. **literally** *adv.*

lit·er·ar·y *adj.* Pertaining to literature; appropriate to or used in literature; of or relating to the knowledge of literature.

lit·er·a·ture *n.* Printed material; written words of lasting excellence.

lit·ter *n.* A stretcher used to carry a sick or injured person; material used as bedding for animals; the offspring at one birth of a multiparous animal; an accumulation of waste material. **litter** *v.*, **litterer** *n.*

lit·tle *adj.* Small

Lit·tle Dip·per *n.* Ursa Minor.

live·ly *adj.* Vigorous, active. **liveliness** *n.*

live·stock *n.* Farm animals raised for human use.

liz·ard *n.* One of various reptiles, usually with an elongated scaly body, four legs, and a tapering tail.

load *n.* A mass or weight that is lifted or supported; anything as cargo, put in a ship, aircraft, or vehicle for conveyance; something that is a heavy responsibility; a burden.

loaf *n.* A food, especially bread, shaped into a mass. *v.* To spend time in idleness. **loafer** *n.*

loan *n.* Money lent with interest to be repaid; something borrowed for temporary use. *v.* To lend.

loathe *v.* To dislike intensely. **loathing** *n.*, **loathsome** *adj.*

lob *v.* To hit or throw in a high arc.

lob·by *n.* An entranceway, as in a hotel or theatre; a group of private persons trying to influence legislators. **lobbyist** *n.*

lobe

lobe *n.* A curved or rounded projection or division, as the fleshy lower part of the ear.

lob•ster *n.* Any of several large, edible marine crustaceans with five pairs of legs, the first pair being large and claw-like.

lo•cal *adj.* Pertaining to, being in, or serving a particular area or place. **locally** *adv.*

lo•cale *n.* A locality where a particular event takes place; the setting or scene.

lo•cal•i•ty *n.* A specific neighborhood, place, or district.

lo•cate *v.* To determine the place, position, or boundaries of; to look for and find. **location** *n.*

lock *n.* A device used to secure or fasten; a part of a waterway closed off with gates to allow the raising or lowering of boats by changing the level of the water; a strand or curl of hair. **lock** *v.*

lock•et *n.* A small, ornamental case for a keepsake, often a picture, worn as a pendant on a necklace.

lock•smith *n.* A person who makes or repairs locks.

lo•co•mo•tive *n.* A self-propelled vehicle, generally steam, electric, or diesel-powered, used for moving railroad cars.

lo•cust *n.* Any of numerous grasshoppers which often travel in swarms and damage vegetation; any of various hardwood leguminous trees, such as carob, black locust, or honey locust.

lodge *n.* A house, such as a cabin, used as a temporary or seasonal dwelling or shelter; an inn. **lodger** *n.*

loft *n.* One of the upper, generally unpartitioned floors of an industrial or commercial building, such as a warehouse; an attic; a gallery in a church or hall.

log•ic *n.* The science of dealing with the principles of reasoning, especially of the method and validity of deductive reasoning. **logical** *adj.*, **logically** *adv.*

loi•ter *v.* To stay for no apparent reason; to dawdle or delay.

lone *adj.* Single; isolated; sole.

lone•ly *adj.* Being without companions; dejected from being alone. **loneliness** *n.*

lon•er *n.* A person who avoids the company of others.

lone•some *adj.* Dejected because of the lack of companionship.

lon•gi•tude *n.* The angular distance east and west of the prime meridian at Greenwich, England, measured in degrees. **longitudi•nal** *adj.*

look *v.* To examine with the eyes; to see; to glance, gaze, or stare at. *n.* The act of looking; the physical appearance of something or someone; a glance.

look•out *n.* A person positioned to keep watch or look for something or someone.

loom *v.* To come into view as a image; to seem to be threatening. *n.* A machine used for interweaving thread or yarn to produce cloth.

loop *n.* A circular length of line folded over and joined at the ends; a loop-shaped pattern, figure, or path. *v.* To form into a loop; to join, fasten, or encircle with a loop.

loose *adj.* Not tightly fastened; not confined or fitting; free.

loot *n.* Goods; usually of significant value, taken in time of war; goods that have been stolen. *v.* To plunder; to steal. **looter** *n.*

lop *v.* To remove branches from; to trim.

lope *v.* To run with a steady gait. **lope** *n.*

lop•sid•ed *adj.* Larger or heavier on one side than on the other; tilting to one side.

lore *n.* Traditional fact; knowledge gained through education or experience.

lose *v.* To mislay; to fail to keep; to be beaten in a competition.

loss *n.* The suffering or damage caused by losing; someone or something that is lost.

lost *adj.* Unable to find one's way; out of a familiar place.

lot *n.* Fate; fortune; a parcel of land having boundaries; a plot.

lo•tion *n.* A liquid medicine for external use on the hands and body.

lot•ter•y *n.* A contest in which winners are selected by a random drawing among paying participants.

loud *adj.* Marked by intense sound and

high volume. **loudly** *adv.*, **loudness** *n.*

lounge *v.* To move or act in a lazy, relaxed manner. *n.* A room, as in a hotel or theatre, where people may wait; a couch.

love *n.* Intense affection for another arising out of kinship or personal ties; a strong feeling of attraction resulting from sexual desire; enthusiasm or fondness.

love•ly *adj.* Beautiful. **loveliness** *n.*

low *adj.* Not high; being below or under normal height, rank, or level; depressed.

low•land *n.* Land that is low and level in relation to the surrounding countryside.

low•ly *adj.* Low in position or rank.

loy•al *adj.* Faithful in allegiance to one's country and government; faithful to a person, cause, ideal, or custom. **loyalty** *n.*

lu•cid *adj.* Easily understood; mentally clear; rational; shining. **lucidity** *n.*

luck *n.* Good fortune; the force or power which controls odds and which brings good fortune or bad fortune. **lucky** *adj.*, **luckily** *adv.*

lu•di•crous *adj.* Amusing or laughable through obvious absurdity; ridiculous.

lug•gage *n.* Suitcases or other traveler's baggage.

luke•warm *adj.* Mildly warm; tepid; unenthusiastic; average.

lull *v.* To cause to rest or sleep; to cause to have a false sense of security. *n.* A temporary period of quiet or rest.

lul•la•by *n.* A song to lull a child to sleep.

lum•ber *n.* Timber, sawed or split into boards.

lum•ber•jack *n.* One who cuts and prepares timber for the sawmill.

lum•ber•yard *n.* A place where lumber and other building materials are sold.

lu•mi•nous *adj.* Emitting or reflecting light; bathed in steady light; illuminated.

lump *n.* A projection; a protuberance; a swelling, as from a bruise or infection. *v.* To group things together.

lu•na•cy *n.* Insanity.

lu•nar *adj.* Of, relating to, caused by the moon.

lu•nar e•clipse *n.* An eclipse where the moon passes partially or wholly through the umbra of the earth's shadow.

lu•na•tic *n.* A crazy person.

lunch•eon *n.* A lunch.

lunch•eon•ette *n.* A modest restaurant at which light meals are served.

lung *n.* One of the two spongy organs that constitute the basic respiratory organ of air-breathing vertebrates.

lunge *n.* A sudden forward movement.

lure *n.* A decoy; something appealing; an artificial bait to catch fish. *v.* To attract or entice with the prospect of reward or pleasure.

lurk *v.* To lie in concealment.

lus•cious *adj.* Very pleasant to smell or taste; appealing to the senses.

lush *adj.* Producing luxuriant growth or vegetation. **lushly** *adv.*, **lushness** *n.*

lust *n.* Intense sexual desire; an intense longing; a craving.

lute *n.* A medieval musical stringed instrument with a fretted finger board, a pear-shaped body, and usually a bent neck.

lux•u•ri•ant *adj.* Growing or producing abundantly; lush; plentiful.

M

M, m The thirteenth letter of the English alphabet; the Roman numeral for 1,000.

mac•a•ro•ni *n.* Dried pasta made into short tubes and prepared as food.

mace *n.* An aromatic spice made by grinding the cover of the nutmeg.

ma•chine *n.* A device or system built to use energy to do work; a political organization. *v.* To produce precision tools.

ma•chine lan•guage *n.* In computers, the system of numbers or instructions for coding input data.

ma•chin•er•y *n.* A collection of machines as a whole; the mechanism or operating parts of a machine.

ma•chin•ist *n.* One skilled in the operation or repair of machines.

mad *adj.* Angry; afflicted with a mental

madam

disorder; insane.

mad·am *n.* A title used to address a married woman; used without a name as a courtesy title when addressing a woman.

made *v.* Past tense of *make*.

mag·a·zine *n.* A publication with a paper cover containing articles, stories, illustrations and advertising; the part of a gun which holds ammunition.

mag·ic *n.* The art which seemingly controls foresight of natural events and forces by means of supernatural agencies.

mag·net *n.* A body having the property of attracting iron and other magnetic material. **magnetism** *n.*

mag·net·ic *adj.* Pertaining to magnetism or a magnet; capable of being attracted by a magnet; having the power or ability to attract. **magnetically** *adv.*

mag·net·ic field *n.* The area in the neighborhood of a magnet or of an electric current, marked by the existence of a detectable magnetic force in every part of the region.

mag·net·ize *v.* To have magnetic properties; to attract by personal charm.

mag·nif·i·cent *adj.* Having an extraordinarily imposing appearance; beautiful; outstanding; exceptionally pleasing.

mag·ni·fy *v.* To increase in size; to cause to seem more important or greater; to glorify or praise someone or something. **magnification, magnifier** *n.*

ma·hog·a·ny *n.* Any of various tropical trees having hard, reddish-brown wood, much used for cabinet work and furniture.

maid *n.* A young unmarried woman or girl; a female servant. **maiden** *n.*

mail *n.* Letter, printed matter, or parcel handled by the postal system.

mail or·der *n.* Goods which are ordered and sent by mail.

main *adj.* Being the most important part of something. *n.* A large pipe used to carry water, oil, or gas. **mainly** *adv.*

main·land *n.* The land part of a country as distinguished from an island.

main·tain *v.* To carry on or to keep in

existence; to preserve in a desirable condition. **maintenance** *n.*

ma·jor *adj.* Greater in importance, quantity, number, or rank; serious; a subject or field of academic study.

ma·jor·i·ty *n.* The greater number of something; more than half; the age at which a person is considered to be an adult, usually 21 years old.

make *v.* To cause something to happen; to create; to produce, as time; to manufacture a line of goods. *n.* A brand name.

mal·a·dy *n.* A chronic disease or sickness.

male *adj.* Of or belonging to the sex that has organs to produce spermatozoa.

mal·func·tion *n.* Failure to function correctly.

mal·ice *n.* The direct intention or desire to harm others.

ma·lign *v.* To speak slander or evil of.

ma·lig·nant *adj.* Of or relating to tumors and abnormal or rapid growth; opposed to benign; causing death or great harm. **malignancy** *n.*, **malignantly** *adv.*

mall *n.* A walk or other shaded public promenade; a street with shops, restaurants, and businesses, closed to vehicles.

mal·lard *n.* A wild duck having brownish plumage, the male of which has a green head and neck.

mal·prac·tice *n.* Improper treatment of a patient by his doctor during surgery or treatment which results in damage or injury; failure to perform a professional duty in a proper or correct fashion, resulting in injury, loss, or other problems.

malt *n.* Grain, usually barley, used chiefly in brewing and distilling; an alcoholic beverage.

ma·ma *n.* Mother.

mam·mal *n.* Any member of a class whose females secrete milk for nourishing their young, including man. **mammalian** *adj.*

mam·ma·ry gland *n.* The milk-producing organ of the female mammal, consisting of small cavity clusters with ducts ending in a nipple.

man *n.* An adult or fully-grown male; the

human race; any human being, regardless of sex [not current].

man•age v. To direct or control the affairs or use of; to organize. **manageability** n., **manageable** adj.

man•ag•er n. One in charge of managing an enterprise or business.

man•da•to•ry adj. Required by; having the nature of, or relating to a mandate; obligatory.

mane n. The long hair growing on the neck of some animals, as the lion, and horse.

ma•neu•ver n. A planned strategic movement or shift, as of warships, or troops; any planned, skillful, or calculated move. **maneuver** v., **maneuverability** n., **maneuverable** adj.

man•ger n. A trough or box which holds livestock feed.

man•gle v. To disfigure or mutilate by bruising, battering, or crushing; to spoil.

man•han•dle v. To handle very roughly.

man•hole n. A circular covered opening usually in a street, through which one may enter a sewer, drain, or conduit.

ma•ni•a n. An extraordinary enthusiasm or craving for something; intense excitement and physical overactivity, often a symptom of manic-depressive psychosis.

man•i•cure n. The cosmetic care of the hands and fingernails. **manicurist** n.

man•i•fes•to n. A public or formal expectation of principles or intentions, usually of a political nature. **manifestos** or **manifestoes** pl.

ma•nip•u•late v. To handle or manage; to control shrewdly and deviously for one's own profit. **manipulation, manipulator** n., **manipulative** adj.

man•kind n. The human race.

manned adj. Operated by a human being.

man•ne•quin n. A life-sized model of a human figure, used to fit or display clothes; a woman who models clothes.

man•ner n. The way in which something happens or is done; an action or style of speech; one's social conduct and etiquette.

mannered adj.

man•or n. A landed estate; the house or hall of an estate. **manorial** adj.

man•sion n. A very large, impressive house.

man•slaugh•ter n. The unlawful killing without malice of a person by another.

man•u•al adj. Used or operated by the hands. n. A small reference book which gives instructions on how to operate or work something. **manually** adv.

man•u•fac•ture v. To make a product; to invent or produce something. **manufacturer** n.

ma•nure n. The fertilizer used to fertilize land, obtained from animal dung.

man•u•script n. A typed or written material copy of an article, book, or document, which is being prepared for publication.

man•y adj. Amounting to a large or indefinite number or amount.

map n. A plane surface representation of a region. v. To plan anything in detail. **mapmaker** n., **mapper** n.

ma•ple n. A tall tree having lobed leaves and a fruit of two joined samaras; the wood of this tree, amber in color when finished, used for furniture and flooring.

mar v. To scratch or deface; to blemish; to ruin; to spoil.

mar•a•thon n. A foot race of slightly more than 26 miles, usually run on the streets of a city; any contest of endurance.

mar•ble n. A limestone which is partly crystallized and irregular in color. pl. A game played with balls of glass.

march v. To walk with measured, regular steps in a solemn or dignified manner; a musical composition for marching.

mare n. The female of the horse and other equine animals.

mar•ga•rine n. A butter substitute made from vegetable oils and milk.

mar•gin n. The edge or border around the body of written or printed text.

ma•rine adj. Of, pertaining to, existing in, or formed by the sea. n. A soldier trained for service on land and at sea.

mar·i·tal *adj.* Pertaining to marriage.

mar·i·time *adj.* Located and situated on or near the sea; pertaining to the sea and its navigation and commerce.

mark *n.* A visible impression, trace, dent, or stain; an identifying seal, inscription, or label.

mar·ket *n.* The trade and commerce in a certain service or commodity; a public place for purchasing and selling merchandise; the possible consumers of a particular product. *v.* To sell. **marketability** *n.*, **marketable** *adj.*

mar·ket·place *n.* A place, such as a public square, where ideas, opinions, and works are traded and tested.

mar·riage *n.* The state of being married; wedlock; the act of marrying or the ceremony entered into by a man and woman so as to live together as husband and wife.

mar·ry *v.* To take or join as husband or wife; to unite closely.

marsh *n.* An area of low, wet land; a swamp. **marshy** *adj.*

marsh·mal·low *n.* A soft, white confection made of sugar, corn syrup, starch, and gelatin and coated with powdered sugar.

mar·su·pi·al *n.* An animal, such as a kangaroo, koala, or opossum, which has no placenta, but which in the female has an abdominal pouch with teats to feed and carry the offspring.

mart *n.* A trading market; a center.

mar·tial *adj.* Of, pertaining to, or concerned with war or the military life.

mar·vel *n.* Anything causing surprise, wonder, or astonishment.

mar·vel·ous or **mar·vel·lous** *adj.* Causing astonishment and wonder; wondrous; excellent; very good, admirable.

mas·cu·line *adj.* Of or pertaining to the male sex; male; the masculine gender. **masculinity** *n.*

mash *n.* A soft, pulpy mass or mixture used to distill alcohol or spirits. *v.* To crush into a soft, pulpy mass.

mask *n.* A covering used to conceal the face in order to disguise or protect. *v.* To hide or conceal.

mass *n.* A body of matter that does not have definite shape but is relatively large in size; physical volume; the measure of a body's resistance to acceleration.

mas·sa·cre *n.* The indiscriminate and savage killing of human beings in large numbers.

mas·sage *n.* The manual or mechanical manipulation of the skin to improve circulation and to relax muscles.

mas·sive *adj.* Of great intensity, degree, or size.

mas·ter *n.* A person with control or authority over others; one who is exceptionally gifted or skilled in an art, science, or craft; the title given for respect or in address. *v.* To learn a skill, craft, or job; to overcome defeat.

mas·ter·piece *n.* Something having notable excellence; an unusually brilliant achievement considered the greatest achievement of its creator.

mat *n.* A flat piece of material made of fiber, rubber, rushes, or other material and used to cover floors.

match *n.* Anything that is similar or identical to another; a short, thin piece of wood, or cardboard with a specially treated tip which ignites as a result of friction. *v.* To equal; to oppose successfully.

mate *n.* A spouse; something matched, joined, or paired with another; in chess, a move which puts the opponent's king in jeopardy. **mate** *v.*

ma·te·ri·al *n.* The substance from which anything is or may be composed or constructed of; anything used in creating, working up, or developing something.

ma·ter·nal *adj.* Relating to a mother or motherhood; inherited from one's mother.

ma·ter·ni·ty *n.* The state of being a mother; the qualities of a mother; the department in a hospital for the prenatal and postnatal care of babies and their mothers.

math *n.* Mathematics.

math·e·mat·ics *n.* The study of form, arrangement, quantity, and magnitude of numbers and operational symbols. **math-ematical** *adj.*, **mathematician** *n.*

mat•i•nee *n.* An afternoon performance of a play, concert, or movie.

mat•ri•mo•ny *n.* The condition of being married; the act, sacrament, or ceremony of marriage. **matrimonial** *adj.*

ma•tron *n.* A married woman or widow of dignity and social position; the woman supervisor in a prison.

mat•ter *n.* Something that makes up the substance of anything; that which is material and physical, occupies space, and is perceived by the senses; something that is sent by mail; something written or print-ed.

mat•tress *n.* A large cloth case filled with soft material and used on or as a bed.

ma•ture *adj.* Completely developed; at full growth; something, as a bond at a bank, that is due and payable. **maturely** *adv.*, **maturity** *n.*

max•im *n.* A brief statement of truth, gen-eral principle, or rule of conduct.

max•i•mize *v.* To increase as greatly as possible; to intensify to the maximum.

max•i•mum *n.* The greatest possible number, measure, degree, or quantity. **maximum** *adj.*

may *v.* To be permitted or allowed; used to express a wish, purpose, desire, contin-gency, or result.

may•be *adv.* Perhaps; possibly.

may•or *n.* The chief magistrate of a town, borough, municipality, or city. **mayoral** *adj.*, **mayoralty, mayorship** *n.*

maze *n.* A complicated, intricate network of passages or pathways; a labyrinth; a state of uncertainty or bewilderment.

me *pron.* The objective case of the pronoun *I*.

mead•ow *n.* A tract of grassland used for grazing or growing hay.

mea•ger or **mea•gre** *adj.* Thin; lean; deficient in quantity, vigor, or fertility.

meal *n.* The edible seeds of coarsely ground grain; any powdery material; the food served or eaten at one sitting at cer-tain times during the day; the time or occasion of taking such food.

mean *v.* To have in mind as a purpose or intent; to have a specified importance or sig-nificance. *adj.* Poor or inferior in appear-ance or quality. *n.* The medium point.

mean•ing *n.* That which is meant or intended; the aim, end, or purpose; the significance; an interpretation. **mean-ingful, meaningfulness** *adj.*

mean•while *adv.* At the same time.

meas•ure *n.* The range, dimension, extent, or capacity of anything; in music, the group of beats marked off by regularly recurring primary accents; the notes and rests between two successive bars on a musical staff. *v.* To determine the range, dimension, extent, volume, or capacity of anything. **measurable** *adj.*, **measura-bly** *adv.*, **measurement** *n.*

meat *n.* The flesh of an animal which is used as food; the core or essential part of something.

me•chan•ic *n.* A person skilled in the making, operation, or repair of machines.

me•chan•i•cal *adj.* Involving or having to do with the construction, operation, or design of tools or machines; produced or operated by a machine.

med•al *n.* A small piece of metal with a commemorative image or inscription pre-sented as an award.

med•i•a *pl. n.* The instruments of news communication, as radio, television, and newspapers.

med•i•cal *adj.* Relating to the study or practice of medicine. **medically** *adv.*

med•i•cine *n.* Any agent or substance used in the treatment of disease or in the relief of pain; the science of diagnosing and treating disease; the profession of medicine.

me•di•e•val or **mediae•val** *adj.* Like or characteristic of the Middle Ages.

me•di•o•cre *adj.* Common; fair; undistin-guished.

me•di•um *n.* Something which occupies a middle position between two extremes;

the means of communicating information or ideas through publishing, radio, or television.

meek *adj.* Showing patience and a gentle disposition; lacking spirit or backbone.

meet *v.* To come upon; to encounter; to come into conjunction or contact with someone or something; to cope or deal with; to handle; to fulfill an obligation of need.

meet·ing *n.* An assembly or gathering of persons; a coming together.

meg·a·byte *n.* Literally, a million bytes. In computers, a measurement of computer and storage disk capacity, or size of a file.

mel·an·chol·y *adj.* Excessively gloomy or sad.

mel·low *adj.* Sweet and soft; rich and full-flavored; rich and soft in quality, as in sounds or colors.

mel·o·dy *n.* An agreeable succession of pleasing sounds. **melodic** *adj.*, **melodically** *adv.*

mel·on *n.* The large fruit of any of various plants of the gourd family, as the watermelon.

melt *v.* To change from a solid to a liquid as a result of pressure or heat.

melt·ing pot *n.* A metaphorical place where immigrants of different cultures or races are assimilated.

mem·ber *n.* A person who belongs to a society, party, club, or other organization.

mem·ber·ship *n.* The state or fact of being a member.

mem·o *n.* A memorandum; a brief communication in writing between business partners.

mem·o·ra·ble *adj.* Worth remembering or noting. **memorably** *adv.*

me·mo·ri·al *n.* Something that serves to keep in remembrance, as a person or event. *adj.* Perpetuating remembrance. **memorialize** *v.*

mem·o·rize *v.* To commit something to memory. **memorization** *n.*

mem·o·ry *n.* The mental function or capacity of recalling or recognizing something that has been previously learned or experienced.

men *pl.* The plural of *man.*

men·ace *n.* Something or someone who threatens; an annoying person. **menacingly** *adv.*

mend *v.* To fix; to repair; to correct.

me·ni·al *adj.* Relating to a household servant or household chores requiring little responsibility or skill.

men·tal *adj.* Relating to or of the mind.

men·tion *v.* To refer to incidentally, in passing, or briefly.

men·u *n.* A list of food or dishes available at a restaurant; in computer science, a list of options displayed on the screen.

me·ow *n.* The cry of a cat.

mer·chan·dise *n.* Commodities or goods that are bought and sold.

mer·chant *n.* A person who operates a retail business for profit.

mer·cy *n.* Compassionate and kind treatment. **merciful, merciless** *adj.*, **mercilessly** *adv.*

mere *adj.* Absolute; no more than what is stated. **merest** *adj.*, **merely** *adv.*

merge *v.* To unite or bring together as one; in computers, to combine two or more files into one.

mer·it *n.* A characteristic act or trait which is worthy of praise. *v.* To earn; to be worthy of.

mer·maid *n.* An imaginary sea creature having the upper body of a woman and the tail of a fish. **merman** *n.*

mer·ry *adj.* Delightful; gay; entertaining; festive; happy; joyous. **merrily** *adv.*, **merriness** *n.*

mess *n.* A disorderly or confused heap; a jumble; a dish or portion of soft or liquid food; a meal eaten by a group of persons, usually in the military.

mes·sage *n.* Any information, command, or news transmitted from one person to another.

mes·sen·ger *n.* A person who carries a message or does an errand for another person or company.

mess•y *adj.* Untidy; upset; dirty; lacking neatness. **messily** *adv.*, **messiness** *n.*

met•al *n.* One of a category of opaque, fusible, ductile, and typically lustrous elements. **metallic** *adj.*, **metallically** *adv.*

met•a•phor *n.* A figure of speech in which the context demands that a word or phrase not be taken literally, as the sun is smiling; a comparison which doesn't use *like* or *as.*

me•te•or *n.* A moving particle in the solar system which appears as a trail or streak in the sky as it comes into contact with the atmosphere of the earth.

me•te•or•ic *adj.* Of or relating to a meteor or meteors; resembling a meteor in speed, brilliance, or brevity.

me•te•or•ite *n.* A stony or metallic mass of a meteor which reaches the earth after partially burning in the atmosphere.

me•te•or•ol•o•gy *n.* The science concerned with the study of weather, weather conditions and weather forecasting. **meteorologic** *adj.*, **meteorologically** *adv.*, **meteorologist** *n.*

me•ter *n.* The arrangement of words, syllables, or stanzas in verse or poetry; a measure equaling 39.37 inches.

meth•od *n.* A manner, a process, or the regular way of doing something; the orderly arrangement, development, or classification.

met•ric *adj.* Of or relating to the metric system. **metrical** *adj.*, **metrication** *n.*

mice *pl.* The plural of *mouse.*

mi•cro•phone *n.* An instrument which converts acoustical waves into electrical signals and feeds them into a recorder, amplifier or broadcasting transmitter. **microphonic** *adj.*

mi•cro•proc•es•sor *n.* In computers, a semiconductor processing unit which is contained on an integrated circuit chip.

mi•cro•scope *n.* An optical instrument consisting of a lens or combination of lenses, used to produce magnified images of very small objects.

mi•cro•wave *n.* A very short electromagnetic wave.

mid•air *n.* A point in the air just above the ground surface.

mid•day *n.* Noon; the middle of the day.

mid•dle *adj.* Being equally distant from extremes or limits; central. *n.* Anything which occupies a middle position; the waist.

mid•dle age *n.* The period of life from about 40 to 60 years.

Mid•dle Ages *pl.* The period of European history from about 500 to 1500.

mid•dle ear *n.* A small membrane-lined cavity between the tympanic membrane and the inner ear through which sound waves are carried.

mid•night *n.* 12 o'clock a.m.; the middle of the night.

midst *n.* The central or middle part or position; a person positioned among others in a group.

might *n.* Force, power, or physical strength. *v.* Past tense of *may;* used to indicate a present condition contrary to fact.

might•y *adj.* Showing or having great power.

mi•grate *v.* To move from one place to another or from one climate to another. **migration** *n.*

mild *adj.* Gentle in manner, behavior, or disposition; not severe or extreme. **mildly** *adv.*, **mildness** *n.*

mile *n.* A unit of measurement equaling 5,280 feet.

mile•age *n.* The distance traveled or measured in miles; an allowance given for traveling expenses at a set rate per mile; the average distance of miles a vehicle will travel on a gallon of gas.

mil•i•tar•y *adj.* Of or related to arms, war, or soldiers. *n.* A nation's armed forces. **militarily** *adv.*

milk *n.* A whitish fluid produced by the mammary glands of all mature female mammals as a source of food for their young. *v.* To draw milk from the breast or udder. **milkiness** *n.*, **milky** *adj.*

Milk•y Way *n.* The broad, luminous galaxy

in which the solar system is located.

mill *n.* A building housing machinery for grinding grain into meal or flour; any of various machines which grind, crush, or press; a unit of money which equals 1/1000 of a U.S. dollar. *v.* To grind.

mill•er *n.* A person who operates, works, or owns a grain mill; a moth whose wings are covered with a powdery substance.

mil•lion *n.* A large number equal to 1,000 x 1,000. **million** *adj.*, **millionth** *n.*, *adj.*

mil•lion•aire *n.* A person whose wealth is estimated at $1,000,000 or more.

mime *v.* To act a part or performance without using words. *n.* An actor who portrays a part, emotion, or situation using only gestures and body language.

mim•ic *v.* To imitate another person's behavior or speech.

mince *v.* To cut or chop something into small pieces.

mind *n.* The element of a human being which controls perception, thought, feeling, memory, and imagination. *v.* To obey; to take care of; to bring; to remember; to object to.

mine *n.* A pit or underground excavation from which metals or coal can be uncovered and removed. **miner** *n.*

mine *pron.* The one that belongs to me.

min•er•al *n.* A solid inorganic substance, such as silver, diamond, or quartz, which is taken from the earth. **mineral** *adj.*

min•gle *v.* To mix or come together.

min•i•a•ture *n.* A copy or model of something that has been greatly reduced in size.

min•i•com•put•er *n.* In computers, a computer designed on a very small scale.

min•i•mum *n.*, *pl.* -**ums** or -**uma** The least, smallest, or lowest amount, degree, number, or position.

min•is•ter *n.* The pastor of a Protestant church; a high officer of state who is in charge of a governmental division.

mi•nor *adj.* Not of legal age; lesser in degree, size, or importance.

mi•nor•i•ty *n.* The smaller in number of two groups constituting a whole; a part of the population that differs, as in race, sex, or religion.

mint *n.* A place where coins are made by a government; any of a variety of aromatic plants used for flavoring; candy flavored by such a plant.

mi•nus *prep.* Reduced by subtraction.

min•ute *n.* The unit of time which equals 60 seconds.

mi•nute *adj.* Extremely small in size.

mir•a•cle *n.* A supernatural event or happening regarded as an act of God.

mi•rage *n.* An optical illusion in which nonexistent bodies of water with reflections of objects are seen.

mire *n.* Soil or heavy mud.

mir•ror *n.* A surface of glass which reflects light, forming the image of an object.

mirth *n.* Merriment or joyousness expressed by laughter.

mis•cel•la•ne•ous *adj.* Consisting of a mixed variety of parts, elements, or characteristics.

mis•chief *n.* Behavior which causes harm, damage, or annoyance.

mis•chie•vous *adj.* Tending to behave in a playfully annoying way.

mis•con•duct *n.* Improper conduct or behavior; bad management.

mis•deed *n.* A wrong or improper act; an evil deed.

mis•er•a•ble *adj.* Very uncomfortable or unhappy; causing misery. **miserableness** *n.* **miserably** *adv.*

mis•er•y *n.* A state of great unhappiness, distress, or pain.

mis•hap *n.* An unfortunate accident; bad luck.

mis•lead *v.* To lead in a wrong direction; to deliberately deceive. **misleading** *adj.*

Miss *n.* The title indicating the unmarried status of a woman or girl. *v.* To fail to hit, reach, or make contact with something; to omit; to feel the absence or loss of.

mis•sile *n.* An object that is thrown or shot at a target.

mis·sion *n.* An instance or the act of sending; an assignment to be carried out.

mis·sion·ar·y *n.* A person sent to do religious or charitable work, usually in a foreign country.

mis·spell *v.* To spell a word incorrectly. **misspelling** *n.*

mis·take *n.* A wrong statement, action, or decision. **mistaken, mistakable** *adj.*, **mistakably** *adv.*, **mistake** *v.*

Mis·ter *n.* A courtesy title used before a man's name, abbreviated to Mr.

mis·treat *v.* To treat badly or wrongly. **mistreatment** *n.*

mite *n.* A very small insect; a small amount of money.

mitt *n.* In baseball, a glove worn to protect the hand while catching; short for mitten.

mix *v.* To blend or combine into one; to come or bring together. **mixable** *adj.*

mix·ture *n.* The state of being mixed; the process or act of mixing; a combination of two or more substances.

mix·up *n.* An instance or state of confusion.

moan *n.* A very low, dull sound indicative of pain or grief.

moat *n.* A deep, wide trench surrounding a castle, usually filled with water.

mob *n.* A large, unruly crowd. *v.* To overcrowd.

mo·bi·lize *v.* To put into motion; to make ready. **mobilization** *n.*

mock *v.* To treat with contempt or scorn; to imitate a mannerism or sound closely; to mimic. *adv.* In an insincere manner. *n.* An imitation; a copy. **mockingly** *adv.*

mock·er·y *n.* Insulting or contemptuous action or speech; a subject of laughter or sport; a false appearance.

mode *n.* A way or method of doing something; a particular manner or form; the value or score that occurs most frequently in a set of data.

mod·el *n.* A small representation of an object; a pattern that something will be based on; a design or type; one serving as an example; one who poses for an artist or photographer. **model** *v.*, **modeler** *n.*

mo·dem *n.* In computers, a digital-to-analog converter for converting telephone lines into conveyers of digitized information.

mod·er·ate *adj.* Not excessive; tending toward the mean or average extent or quality; opposed to extreme political views. **moderate** *v.*, **moderation** *n.*

mod·er·a·tor *n.* A person who moderates; a person who presides over a discussion or meeting but takes no sides.

mod·ern *adj.* Typical of the recent past or the present; advanced or up-to-date. **modernity** *n.*, **modernly** *adv.*

mod·ern·ism *n.* A thought, action, or belief characteristic of modern times. **modernistic** *adj.*

mod·est *adj.* Placing a moderate estimate on one's abilities or worth; retiring or reserved; limited in size or amount. **modesty** *n.*

mod·i·fy *v.* To alter; to make different in character or form; to change to less extreme; to moderate. **modification** *n.*

mod·ule *n.* One of a series of standardized components in a system.

moist *adj.* Slightly wet; damp; saturated with moisture or liquid.

mois·ten *v.* To make or become moist or slightly wet.

mois·ture *n.* Liquid diffused or condensed in a relatively small quantity; dampness. **moisturize** *v.*, **moisturizer** *n.*

mo·lar *n.* A grinding tooth which has a broad surface for grinding food, located in the back of the mouth.

mo·las·ses *n.* A thick, dark syrup produced when sugar is refined.

mold *n.* A superficial, often woolly growth produced on damp or decaying organic matter or on living organisms; a fungus that produces such a growth; crumbling, soft, friable earth suited to plant growth; distinctive nature or character; the frame on or around which an object is constructed; a cavity in which an object is shaped; general shape; form. **moldable** *adj.*

molecular

mo·lec·u·lar *adj.* Of, relating to, or caused by molecules.

mol·e·cule *n.* The simplest structural unit into which a substance can be divided and still retain its identity.

mole·hill *n.* A small ridge of earth thrown up by a mole.

mo·lest *v.* To bother or persecute; to accost sexually. **molestation, molester** *n.*

mo·men·tar·y *adj.* Lasting just a moment; occurring presently or at every moment.

mo·men·tum *n.* A property of a moving body which determines the length of time required to bring it to rest when under the action of a constant force.

mon·arch *n.* A person who reigns over a kingdom or empire; a large orange and black butterfly.

mon·ar·chy *n.* Government by a monarch; sovereign control; a government or nation ruled by a monarch.

mon·ey *n.* Anything which has or is assigned value and is used as a medium of exchange.

mon·i·tor *n.* A student assigned to assist a teacher; a receiver used to view the picture being picked up by a television camera; the image being generated by a computer.

monk *n.* A man who is a member of a religious order and lives in a monastery.

mon·key *n.* A member of the older primates, excluding man, having a long-tail; a small species as distinguished from the larger apes.

mo·nop·o·ly *n.* Exclusive ownership or control, as of a service or commodity, by a single group, person, or company; a group, person, or company having a monopoly; exclusive possession; a service or commodity controlled by a single group.

mon·o·tone *n.* The utterance of sounds, syllables, or words in a single tone.

mo·not·o·nous *adj.* Spoken in a monotone; lacking in variety. **monotonously** *adv.*, **monotony** *n.*

mon·soon *n.* A periodic wind, especially in the Indian Ocean and southern Asia; the season of the monsoon.

mon·ster *n.* An animal or plant having an abnormal form or structure; an animal, plant, or object having a frightening or deformed shape; one unusually large for its kind. **-ity, -ousness** *n.*, **-ous** *adj.*, **-ously** *adv.*

month *n.* One of the twelve divisions of a calendar year.

month·ly *adj.* Occurring, done, or payable each month. *n.* A publication issued once a month. **monthly** *adv.*

mon·u·ment *n.* An object, such as a statue, built as a memorial to a person or an event; a burial vault; an area set aside for public use because of its aesthetic, historical, or ecological significance.

mon·u·men·tal *adj.* Serving as or similar to a monument; massive; extremely important. **monumentally** *adv.*

mood *n.* A conscious yet temporary state of mind or emotion; the prevailing spirit; a verb form or set of verb forms inflected to show the understanding of the person speaking regarding the condition expressed.

mood·y *adj.* Subject to moods, especially depression; gloomy.

moon *n.* The earth's only natural satellite; a natural satellite which revolves around a planet.

moon·beam *n.* A ray of moonlight.

moon·light *n.* The light of the moon. *v.* To hold a second job in addition to a regular one. **moonlighter** *n.*

mope *v.* To be uncaring or dejected; to move in a leisurely manner. **moper** *n.*

mor·al *adj.* Of or pertaining to conduct or character from the point of right and wrong; teaching a conception of right behavior. *n.* The lesson to be learned from a story, event, or teaching. *pl.* Standards of right and wrong. **morally** *adv.*

mo·rale *n.* An individual's state of mind with respect to the tasks he or she is expected to perform.

mo·ral·i·ty *n.* The quality of being

morally right; moral behavior.

mor•bid *adj.* Of, pertaining to, or affected by disease; suggesting an unhealthy mental state of being; gruesome.

more *adj.* Greater number, size, or degree; additional. *n.* An additional or greater number, degree, or amount. *adv.* To a greater extent or degree; in addition. *pron.* Additional things or persons.

more•o•ver *adv.* Furthermore; besides.

morn•ing *n.* The early part of the day; the time from midnight to noon.

mor•sel *n.* A small piece or quantity of food; a tasty dish.

mor•tal *adj.* Having caused or about to cause death; fatal; subject to death; very tedious or prolonged; unrelentingly hostile; of, relating to, or connected with death. *n.* A human being. **mortally** *adv.*

mor•tal•i•ty *n.* The state or condition of being mortal; the death rate; deaths.

mor•tar *n.* A strong vessel in which materials can be crushed or ground with a pestle; a muzzle-loading cannon for firing shells at short ranges and at high angles; a mixed building material, as cement with sand and water, which hardens and is used with masonry or plaster.

mort•gage *n.* A temporary conveyance of property to a creditor as security for the repayment of a debt; a contract or deed defining the terms of a mortgage. *v.* To pledge or transfer by means of a mortgage.

mor•ti•cian *n.* An undertaker.

mor•ti•fy *v.* To destroy the strength or functioning of; to subdue or deaden through pain or self-denial; to subject to severe humiliation; to become gangrenous. **mortification** *n.*

mos•qui•to *n.* Any of various winged insects of which the females suck the blood of animals or humans.

moss *n.* Delicate, small green plants which often form a dense, mat-like growth. **mossiness** *n.*, **mossy** *adj.*

most *adj.* The majority of. *n.* The greatest amount. *pron.* The largest part or number. *adv.* In or to the highest degree.

most•ly *adv.* For the most part.

mo•tel *n.* A temporary, roadside dwelling for motorists with rooms opening directly onto a parking area.

moth *n.* A usually nocturnal insect of the order Lepidoptera, having antennae that are often feathered, duller in color and with wings smaller than the butterflies.

moth•er *n.* A female parent; one who holds a maternal relationship toward another; an old or elderly woman; a woman in a position of authority. *adj.* Of, relating to, or being a mother. *v.* To give birth to; to care for or protect like a mother. **motherhood, motherliness** *n.*, **motherly** *adj.*

mo•tion *n.* The act or process of changing position; a purposeful movement of the body or a bodily part; a formal proposal or suggestion that action be taken. **motion** *v.*, **motionless** *adj.*

mo•tion pic•ture *n.* A sequence of filmed pictures that gives the illusion of continuous movement, when projected on a screen.

mo•ti•vate *v.* Causing to act.

mo•tive *n.* Something, as a need or desire, which causes a person to act; a musical motif.

mo•tor *n.* Any of various devices which develop energy or impart motion.

mo•tor•cy•cle *n.* A two-wheeled automotive vehicle. **motorcycle** *v.*, **motorcyclist** *n.*

mot•to *n.* A sentence, phrase, or word expressing purpose, character, or conduct; an appropriate phrase inscribed on something.

mound *n.* A small hill of earth, sand, gravel or debris; a burial place of primitive cultures.

mount *v.* To rise or ascend; to get up on; climb upon; to increase in amount or extent; to organize and equip; to launch and carry out. *n.* A horse or other animal used for riding; a support to which something is fixed.

moun•tain *n.* A land mass that rises above

its surroundings and is higher than a hill.

moun·tain·eer *n.* An inhabitant of a mountainous region; one who climbs mountains for sport.

mount·ing *n.* A supporting frame or structure of an article.

mourn *v.* To express grief; to feel grief or sorrow; to follow the religious customs and rituals surrounding the death of a loved one.

mouse *n.* A small rodent that frequents human habitations; a timid person.

mouth *n.* The bodily opening through which food is taken in.

move *v.* To set in motion; to change one's place or location; to make a recommendation in a formal manner. **movable, moveable** *adj.*, **moveably** *adv.*

move·ment *n.* The act of moving; a part of a musical composition; a political or ethical organization for change.

mov·er *n.* One that moves; a person employed to help in moving the contents of a home or business.

mov·ie *n.* A motion picture.

mow *v.* To cut down, as with a machine. *n.* The part of the barn where hay or grain is stored. **mower** *n.*

much *adj.* In great amount, quantity, degree, or extent. *adv.* To a great extent.

mud *n.* A mixture of water and earth. **muddily** *adv.*, **muddiness** *n.*, **muddy** *adj.*

mud·dle *v.* To make muddy; to mix up or confuse; to make a mess of; to think or act in a confused way.

muf·fin *n.* A soft, cap-shaped bread that is cooked in a muffin pan.

muf·fle *v.* To wrap up so as to conceal or protect; to deaden the sound of; to suppress.

muf·fler *n.* A scarf worn around the neck; a device which deadens noise, especially as part of the exhaust system of an vehicle.

mug *n.* A large drinking cup; a person's face; a photograph of someone's face. *v.* To make funny faces; to assault viciously, usually with intent to rob. **mugger** *n.*

mug·gy *adj.* Warm, humid and sultry. **muggily** *adv.*, **mugginess** *n.*

mulch *n.* A loose protective covering, as of sawdust, compost, or wood chips spread on the ground to prevent moisture evaporation, to protect roots from freezing, and to retard the growth of weeds.

mule *n.* A hybrid animal that is the offspring of a female horse and a male ass.

mull *v.* To mix or grind thoroughly; to ponder; to think about.

mul·ti·na·tion·al *adj.* Involving or relating to several countries.

mul·ti·ple *adj.* Relating to or consisting of more than one individual, part, or element. *n.* A number into which another number can be divided with no remainders.

mul·ti·ple-choice *adj.* Offering several answers from which the correct one is to be chosen.

mul·ti·pli·ca·tion *n.* The mathematical operation by which a number indicates how many times another number is to be added to itself.

mul·ti·ply *v.* To increase in amount or number; to combine by multiplication.

mum·ble *v.* To speak or utter in a low, confused manner. **mumbler** *n.*

mum·my *n.* A body embalmed or treated for burial in the manner of the ancient Egyptians. **mummies** *pl.*

mur·der *n.* The crime of unlawfully killing a person.

mur·der·ous *adj.* Intending or having the purpose or capability of murder. **murderously** *adv.*

murk *n.* Darkness; gloom. **murkily** *adv.*, **murkiness** *n.*, **murky** *adv.*

mur·mur *n.* A low, indistinct, and often continuous sound; a gentle or soft utterance. **murmur** *v.*

mus·cle *n.* Bodily tissue which consists of long cells that contract when stimulated. **muscular** *adj.*

mush *n.* A thick porridge of cornmeal boiled in water or milk; soft matter. **mushiness** *n.*, **mushy** *adj.*

mush•room *n.* A fungus having an umbrella-shaped cap on a stalk. *v.* To grow or multiply quickly.

mu•sic *n.* Organized tones in sequences and combinations which make up a continuous composition. **musical** *adj.*

mu•si•cian *n.* A composer or performer of music. **musicology** *n.*

musk *n.* A substance with a strong, powerful odor which is secreted by the male musk deer. **muskiness** *n.*, **musky** *adj.*

mus•ket *n.* A heavy, large-caliber shoulder gun with a long barrel. **musketeer** *n.*

musk•mel•on *n.* A sweet melon having a rough rind and juicy, edible flesh.

Mus•lim *n.* A follower of Islam. **Muslim** *adj.*

must *v.* To be forced to; to have to; to be obligated to do something; to be necessary to do something. *n.* A requirement; absolute; something indispensable.

mus•tache or **mous•tache** *n.* The hair growing on the human upper lip.

mus•tard *n.* A condiment or medicinal preparation made from the seeds of the mustard plant.

must•n't *contr.* Must not.

mus•ty *adj.* Moldy or stale in odor or taste.

mute *adj.* Unable to speak. *n.* A person who cannot speak.

mut•ter *v.* To speak or utter in a low voice; to grumble; to complain.

mu•tu•al *adj.* Having the same relationship; received and directed in equal amounts. **mutuality** *n.*

muz•zle *n.* The projecting mouth of certain animals; the open end or mouth of an implement such as the barrel of a gun.

my *adj.* Relating to or of myself or one. *interj.* An expression of surprise, dismay, or pleasure.

myr•i•ad *adj.* Having extremely large, indefinite aspects or elements.

my•self *pron.* The one identical with me; used reflexively; my normal, healthy state or condition.

mys•te•ri•ous *adj.* Relating to or being a mystery; impossible or difficult to comprehend. **mystery** *n.*

mys•tic *adj.* Relating to mystics, mysticism, or mysteries. *n.* A person practicing or believing in mysticism. **mystical** *adj.*, **mystically** *adv.*

mys•ti•fy *v.* To perplex, to bewilder. **mystification** *n.*, **mystifyingly** *adv.*

myth *n.* A traditional story dealing with supernatural ancestors; a person or thing having only an unverifiable or imaginary existence. **mythical, mythic** *adj.*, **mythically** *adv.*

my•thol•o•gy *n.* A body of myths dealing with gods and heroes. **mythological** *adj.*, **mythologist** *n.*

N

N, n The fourteenth letter of the English alphabet.

nab *v.* To seize; to arrest.

nag *v.* To bother by scolding or constant complaining. *n.* A worthless horse.

nail *n.* A thin pointed piece of metal for hammering into wood and other materials to hold pieces together.

nail•brush *n.* A small brush with trim bristles used to clean the hands and nails.

nail file *n.* A small instrument with a rough surface, used to shape the fingernails.

na•ive *adj.* Simple and trusting; not sophisticated. **naiveness, naivete** *n.*

na•ked *adj.* Without clothes on the body; nude. **nakedness** *n.*

name *n.* A title or word by which something or someone is known. *v.* To give a name. **nameable** *adj.*

name•less *adj.* Having no name; anonymous. **namelessly** *adv.*

name•sake *n.* A person named after someone with the same name.

nan•ny *n.* A child's nurse; one who cares for small children.

nap *n.* A short rest or sleep, often during the day. *v.* The surface of a piece of leather or fabric.

na·palm *n.* A mixture of aluminum soaps used in jelling gasoline for use in bombs or by flame throwers.

nape *n.* The back of the neck.

nap·kin *n.* A cloth or soft paper, used at the table for wiping the lips and fingers.

nar·cot·ic *n.* A drug which dulls the senses, relieves pain, and induces a deep sleep; if abused, it can become habit-forming and cause convulsions or comas.

nar·rate *v.* To tell a story or give a description in detail. **narration** *n.*, **narrator** *v.*

nar·row *adj.* Slender or small in width; of less than standard width. **narrowly** *adj.*

nas·ty *adj.* Dirty, filthy, or indecent; unpleasant. **nastily** *adv.*, **nastiness** *n.*

na·tion *n.* A group of people made up of one or more nationalities under one government.

na·tion·al·ism *n.* Devotion to or concern for one's nation.

na·tion·al·i·ty *n.* The fact or condition of belonging to a nation.

na·tion·al·ize *v.* To place a nation's resources and industries under the control of the state.

na·tive *n.* A person born in a country or place.

nat·u·ral *adj.* Produced or existing by nature; a note that is not sharp or flat. **naturalness** *n.*, **naturally** *adv.*

na·ture *n.* The universe and its phenomena; one's own character or temperament.

naught *n.* Nothing; the number 0; zero.

naugh·ty *adj.* Unruly; ill-behaved.

nau·se·a *n.* An upset stomach with a feeling that one needs to vomit. **nauseous** *adj.*, **nauseate** *v.*, **nauseatingly** *adv.*

nau·ti·cal *adj.* Pertaining to ships or seamanship.

na·val *adj.* Of or relating to ships.

na·vel *n.* A small mark on the abdomen where the umbilical cord was attached.

nav·i·ga·ble *adj.* Sufficiently deep and wide enough to allow ships to pass. **navigability** *n.*, **navigably** *adv.*

nav·i·gate *v.* To plan the course of a ship or aircraft; to steer a course. **navigator** *n.*, **navigational** *adj.*

na·vy *n.* One of a nation's organizations for defense; a nation's fleet of ships; a very dark blue.

near *adv.* At, to, or within a short time or distance. **nearness** *n.*

near·by *adj.* or *adv.* Close by; near at hand; adjacent.

near·sight·ed *adj.* Able to see clearly at short distances only. **nearsightedness** *n.*

neat *adj.* Tidy and clean; free from disorder and dirt. **neatly** *adv.*, **neatness** *n.*

neat·en *v.* To make neat; to set in order.

nec·es·sar·y *adj.* Unavoidable; required; essential; needed. **necessarily** *adv.*

ne·ces·si·ty *n.* The condition of being necessary; the condition making a particular course of action necessary.

neck *n.* The part of the body which connects the head and trunk; a narrow part or projection, as of land; a stringed instrument, or bottle.

neck·tie *n.* A narrow strip of material worn around the neck and tied.

need *n.* The lack of something desirable, useful, or necessary.

need·ful *adj.* Necessary.

nee·dle *n.* A slender, pointed steel implement which contains an eye through which thread is passed. *v.* To tease. **needlelike** *adj.*

need·less *adj.* Unnecessary; not needed. **needless** *adv.*, **needlessness** *n.*

need·n't *contr.* Need not.

neg·a·tive *adj.* Expressing denial or disapproval; not positive. *n.* In photography, a negative photo. **negativity** *n.*

ne·glect *v.* To ignore; to pay no attention to; to fail to perform. **neglectful** *adj.*

neg·li·gent *adj.* To neglect what needs to be done.

ne·go·ti·ate *v.* To confer with another person to reach an agreement. **negotiation, negotiator** *n.*

neigh·bor *n.* One who lives near another. **neighboring** *adj.*, **neighbor** *v.*

neigh·bor·hood *n.* A section or small

region that possesses a specific quality.

neigh·bor·ly *adj.* Characteristic of good neighbors; friendly. **neighborliness** *n.*

nei·ther *adj.* Not one or the other. *pron.* Not the one or the other.

ne·on *n.* An inert gaseous element used in lighting fixtures, symbolized by *Ne*; the light from such fixtures.

neph·ew *n.* The son of one's sister, brother, sister-in-law, or brother-in-law.

nerve *n.* The bundles of fibers which convey sensation and originate motion through the body.

nerve·less *adj.* Lacking courage or strength. **nervelessness** *n.*

nerv·ous *adj.* Affecting the nerves or the nervous system; agitated; worried. **nervously** *adv.*, **nervousness** *n.*

nest *n.* A place, shelter, or home built by a bird to hold its eggs and young.

nes·tle *v.* To lie close to.

net *n.* A meshed fabric made of cords, ropes, threads, or other material knotted or woven together; the profit, weight, or price which remains after all additions, subtractions, or adjustments are made.

net·i·quette *n.* In computers, the widely shared informal agreements among users regarding waste, propriety, and fairness in the exchange of electronic information.

net·work *n.* A system of interlacing tracks, channels, or lines; an interconnected system.

neu·ter *adj.* Neither feminine nor masculine.

neu·tral *adj.* Not supporting either side of a debate, quarrel, or party; a color which does not contain a decided hue; in chemistry, neither alkaline nor acid. **neutrality** *n.*

neu·tral·ize *v.* To make or declare neutral.

nev·er *adv.* Not over; absolutely not.

nev·er·the·less *adv.* Nonetheless; however; in spite of this.

new *adj.* Not used before; unaccustomed; unfamiliar. **newness** *n.*

news *pl. n.* Current information and happenings.

news·cast *n.* A television or radio news broadcast.

news·group *n.* In computers, a group of users with a similar interest communicating and sharing information.

news·pa·per *n.* A weekly or daily publication which contains recent information.

news·print *n.* An inexpensive machine-finished paper made from wood pulp and used chiefly for newspapers and some paperback books.

next *adj.* Immediately following or proceeding; nearest in space or position.

nib·ble *v.* To bite a little at a time; to take small bites. **nibble, nibbler** *n.*

nice *adj.* Pleasing; enjoyable; polite and courteous; refined.

nick *n.* A small chip or cut on a surface; the final critical moment.

nick·el *n.* A hard, silver, metallic element used in alloys and symbolized by *Ni*; a U.S. coin worth five cents.

nick·name *n.* The familiar form of a proper name, expressed in a shortened form.

nic·o·tine or **nic·o·tin** *n.* A poisonous alkaloid found in tobacco and used in insecticides and medicine.

niece *n.* The daughter of one's sister, brother, sister-in-law, or brother-in-law.

night *n.* The time between dusk and dawn or the hours of darkness.

night·mare *n.* A frightening and horrible dream.

nim·ble *adj.* Marked by a quick, light movement; quick-witted. **nimbleness** *n.*, **nimbly** *adv.*

nine *n.* The cardinal number that is equal to 8 + 1.

nip *v.* To pinch, bite, or grab something. *n.* To pinch, bite, or grab; a sharp, stinging feeling caused by cold temperatures. **nipper** *n.*

nip·ple *n.* The small projection of a mammary gland through which milk passes; an artificial teat usually made from a type of rubber from which a bottle-fed baby nurses.

no *adv.* Used to express rejection, disagreement, or denial; not so; not at all.

noble

no•ble *adj.* Morally good; superior in character or nature. *n.* A person of rank or noble birth. **noblemen, nobleness** *n.*, **nobly** *adv.*

no•bod•y *pron.* Not anybody; no person.

noc•tur•nal *adj.* Pertaining to or occurring during the night.

nod *n.* A quick downward motion of the head as one falls off to sleep; a downward motion of the head indicating acceptance or approval.

node *n.* A swollen or thickened enlargement.

no•el *n.* A Christmas carol.

noise *n.* A sound which is disagreeable or loud; in computers, unwanted data in an electronic signal. **noisy** *adj.*, **noisily** *adv.*

no•mad *n.* A member of a group of people who wander from place to place. **nomadic** *adj.*, **nomadism** *n.*

nom•i•nate *v.* To select a candidate for an elective office. **-tion, -tor** *n.*

non•cha•lant *adj.* Giving an effect of casual unconcern. **nonchalance** *n.*, **nonchalantly** *adv.*

none *pron.* Not any; not one.

non•sense *n.* Something that seems senseless or foolish. **nonsensical** *adj.*

noo•dle *n.* A flat strip of dried dough made with eggs and flour.

nook *n.* A corner, recess, or secluded place.

noon *n.* The middle of the day; 12:00 o'clock.

noose *n.* A loop of rope secured by a slipknot, allowing it to decrease in size as the rope is pulled.

nor *conj.* Not either; not.

norm *n.* A rule, model, or pattern typical for a particular group.

nor•mal *adj.* Ordinary, average, usual; having average intelligence. **normalcy, normality** *n.*, **normally** *adv.*

north *n.* The direction to a person's left while facing east.

nose *n.* The facial feature containing the nostrils; the sense of smell.

nos•tril *n.* The external openings of the nose.

nos•y or **nos•ey** *adj.* Prying; inquisitive.

not *adv.* In no manner; used to express refusal or denial.

no•ta•ble *adj.* Remarkable, distinguished. **notably** *adv.*

no•ta•tion *n.* A process or system of figures or symbols used in specialized fields to represent quantities, numbers, or values. **notational** *adj.*

notch *n.* A v-shaped indentation or cut.

note *n.* A record or message in short form; a musical tone or written character. **note** *v.*

not•ed *adj.* Famous; well-known.

noth•ing *n.* Not anything; no part or portion.

no•tice *n.* An announcement; a notification. **noticeable** *adj.*, **noticeably** *adv.*

no•ti•fy *v.* To give notice of; to announce. **notifier, notification** *n.*

no•tion *n.* An opinion; a general concept; an idea.

no•to•ri•ous *adj.* Having a widely known and usually bad reputation.

not•with•stand•ing *prep.* In spite of. *adv.* Nevertheless; anyway. *conj.* Although.

noun *n.* A word which names a person, place, or thing.

nour•ish *v.* To furnish with the nutriment and other substances needed for growth and life; to support. **nourishing** *adj.*, **nourishment** *n.*

nov•el *n.* An inventive narrative dealing with human experiences; a book. **novelist** *n.*

nov•el•ty *n.* Something unusual or new.

nov•ice *n.* A person who is new and unfamiliar with an activity or business.

now *adv.* At the present time; immediately.

no•where *adv.* Not in or at any place.

nox•ious *adj.* Harmful; obnoxious; corrupt.

noz•zle *n.* A projecting spout or vent.

nu•ance *n.* A slight variation.

nub *n.* A knob; a small piece or lump.

nu•cle•ar *adj.* Pertaining to and

resembling a nucleus; relating to atomic energy.

nu·cle·us *n.* A central element around which other elements are grouped. **nuclei** *pl.*

nude *adj.* Unclothed; naked. **nudity, nudist** *n.*

nudge *v.* To poke or push gently.

nug·get *n.* A lump, as of precious metal.

nui·sance *n.* A source of annoyance.

nul·li·fy *v.* To counteract.

numb *adj.* Lacking physical sensation. **numb** *v.,* **numbness** *n.*

num·ber *n.* A word or symbol which is used in counting or which indicates how many or which one in a series.

num·ber·less *adj.* Too many to be counted.

nu·mer·al *n.* A symbol, figure, letter, word, or a group of these which represents a number.

nu·mer·a·tor *n.* The term in mathematics indicating how many parts are to be taken; the number in a fraction which appears above the line.

nun *n.* A woman who has joined a religious group and has taken vows to give up worldly goods and never to marry.

nup·tial *adj.* Of or pertaining to a wedding.

nup·tials *pl. n.* A wedding.

nurse *n.* A person who is specially trained to care for disabled or sick persons. *v.* To feed a baby from a mother's breast.

nurs·er·y *n.* A room reserved for the special use of infants or small children; a business or place where trees, shrubs, and flowers are raised.

nur·ture *n.* The upbringing, care, or training of a child. **nurture** *v.,* **nurturer** *n.*

O

O, o The fifteenth letter of the English alphabet.

oaf *n.* A stupid or clumsy person. **oafish** *adj.,* **oafishly** *adv.*

oar *n.* A long pole, flat at one end, used in rowing a boat.

o·a·sis *n.* A fertile section in the desert which contains water. **oases** *pl.*

oat *n.* A cultivated cereal grass whose grain or seed is used as food.

oath *n.* A solemn promise in the name of God or on a Bible that a person will speak only the truth.

oat·meal *n.* A cooked cereal made from rolled oats.

o·be·di·ent *adj.* Obeying or willing to do what one is told. **obedience** *n.*

o·bese *adj.* Very fat. **obesity** *n.*

o·bey *v.* To carry out instructions; to be guided or controlled; to follow directions.

o·bit·u·ar·y *n.* A published announcement that a person has died, often containing a short biography. **obituary** *adj.*

ob·ject *v.* To voice disapproval; to protest. *n.* Something visible which can be touched; a word in a sentence which explains who or what is acted upon.

ob·jec·tion *n.* A feeling of opposition or disagreement; the reason for a disagreement.

ob·jec·tive *adj.* Pertaining to or dealing with material objects rather than mental concepts. *n.* Something that one works toward, a goal; a purpose. **objectivity** *n.*

ob·li·ga·tion *n.* A promise or feeling of duty; something one must do because one's conscience or the law demands it; a debt which must be repaid.

o·blige *v.* To constrain; to put in one's debt by a service or favor; to do a favor. **obliger** *n.,* **obligingly** *adv.*

o·blique *adj.* Inclined; not level or straight up and down; slanting; indirect. **obliqueness, obliquity** *n.*

ob·liv·i·on *n.* The condition of being utterly forgotten; the act of forgetting.

ob·long *adj.* Rectangular; longer in one direction than the other; normally, the horizontal dimension; the greater in length. **oblong** *n.*

ob·nox·ious *adj.* Very unpleasant; repugnant. **obnoxiousness** *n.*

ob·scene *adj.* Indecent; disgusting.

obscure

obscenity *n.*

ob•scure *adj.* Remote; not clear; faint. *v.* To make dim; to conceal by covering. **obscurity**, **obscureness** *n.*

ob•ser•va•tion *n.* The act of observing something; that which is observed; a judgment or opinion. **observational** *adj.*, *adv.*

ob•serve *v.* To pay attention; to watch. **observable**, **observant** *adj.*, **observably** *adv.*, **observer** *n.*

ob•so•lete *adj.* No longer in use; out-of-date. **obsolescence** *n.*, **obsolescent** *adj.*

ob•sta•cle *n.* An obstruction; anything which opposes or stands in the way.

ob•sti•nate *adj.* Stubbornly set to an opinion or course of action; difficult to control or manage; hardheaded. **obstinacy** *n.*, **obstinately** *adv.*

ob•struct *v.* To block, hinder or impede. **obstructor**, **obstruction** *n.*

ob•tain *v.* To acquire or gain possession of. **obtainable** *adj.*, **obtainer** *n.*

ob•vi•ous *adj.* Easily seen, discovered, or understood. **obviously** *adv.*

oc•ca•sion *n.* The time an event occurs; the event itself; a celebration.

oc•ca•sion•al *adj.* Appearing or occurring irregularly or now and then; intended, made, or suitable for a certain occasion; incidental.

oc•cu•pant *n.* A person who acquires title by occupancy.

oc•cu•pa•tion *n.* A job, profession, or vocation; a foreign military force which controls an area.

oc•cu•py *v.* To take and retain possession of; to live in. **occupier** *n.*

oc•cur *v.* To suggest; to have something come to mind; to happen. **occurrence** *n.*, **occurrent** *adj.*

o•cean *n.* An immense body of salt water which covers three fourths of the earth's surface; one of the oceans. **oceanic** *adj.*

oc•ta•gon *n.* A polygon with eight angles and eight sides. **octagonal** *adj.*

odd *adj.* Unusual; strange; singular; left over; not even. **oddly** *adv.*, **oddness** *n.*

ode *n.* A lyric poem usually honoring a person or event.

o•dor *n.* A smell; a sensation which occurs when the sense of smell is stimulated.

of *prep.* Proceeding; composed of; relating to.

off *adv.* From a position or place; no longer connected or on. *adj.* Canceled. *prep.* Away from.

of•fend *v.* To make angry; to arouse resentment; to break a law. **offender** *n.*

of•fense *n.* A violation of a duty, rule, or a propriety; the act of causing displeasure; the act of assaulting or attacking.

of•fer *v.* To present for acceptance or rejection; to present as an act of worship; to make available; to present in order to satisfy a requirement.

of•fer•ing *n.* The act of one who offers; a contribution, as money, given to the support of a church.

off•hand *adv.* or *adj.* Without preparation or premeditation.

of•fice *n.* A place where business or professional duties are conducted; an important job, duty, or position.

of•fi•cer *n.* A person who holds a title, position, or office; a policeman.

of•fi•cial *adj.* Something derived from proper authority. *n.* One who holds a position or office; a person who referees a game such as football, basketball, or soccer. **officialism** *n.*, **officially** *adv.*

off•spring *n.* The descendants of a person, plant, or animal.

of•ten *adv.* Frequently; many times.

oh *interj.* Used to express surprise, fear, or pain.

oil *n.* Any of various substances, usually thick, which can be burned or easily melted; a lubricant. *v.* To lubricate.

oint•ment *n.* An oily substance used on the skin as an aid to healing or to soften the skin.

old *adj.* Having lived or existed for a long time; of a certain age. *n.* Former times.

o•men *n.* A phenomenon thought of as a

sign of something to come, whether good or bad.

o•mit *v.* To neglect; to leave out; to over-look.

on *prep.* Positioned upon; indicating proximity; indicating direction toward; with respect to. *adv.* In a position of covering; forward.

once *adv.* A single time; at any one time. *conj.* As soon as.

one *adj.* Single; undivided. *n.* A single person; a unit; the first cardinal number (1).

one•self *pron.* One's own self.

on•line or **on-line** *adj.* or *adv.* In computers, connected with a network of other users and therefore capable of contact and exchange of electronic information.

on•ly *adj.* Sole; for one purpose alone. *adv.* Without anyone or anything else. *conj.* Except; but.

on•shore *adj.* Moving or coming near or onto the shore.

on•to *prep.* To a position or place; aware of.

on•ward *adv.* Moving forward in time or space. **onwards** *adj.*

o•paque *adj.* Not transparent; dull; obscure. **opacity, opaqueness** *n.*

o•pen *adj.* Having no barrier; not covered, sealed, locked, or fastened. *n.* A contest for both amateurs and professionals. *v.* To begin. **openness** *n.,* **openly** *adv.*

op•er•a *n.* A drama having music as a dominant factor, an orchestral accompaniment, acting, and scenery.

op•er•ate *v.* To function, act, or work effectively; to perform an operation, as surgery. **operative** *adj.*

op•er•a•tion *n.* The system or method of operating; a series of acts to effect a certain purpose; a process; a procedure performed on the human body with surgical instruments to restore health.

o•pin•ion *n.* A judgment held with confidence; a conclusion held without positive knowledge.

op•po•nent *n.* An adversary; one who opposes another.

op•por•tu•ni•ty *n.* A favorable position; a chance for advancement.

op•pose *v.* To be in direct contention with; to resist; to be against. **opposable** *adj.,* **opposition** *n.*

op•po•site *adj.* Situated or placed on opposing sides. **oppositeness** *n.*

op•tic *adj.* Pertaining or referring to sight or the eye.

op•tion *n.* The act of choosing or the power of choice; a choice. **optionally** *adv.*

or *conj.* A word used to connect the second of two choices or possibilities, indicating uncertainty.

o•ral *adj.* Spoken or uttered through the mouth; taken or administered through the mouth. **orally** *adv.*

or•ange *n.* A citrus fruit round and orange in color. *adj.* Yellowish red.

or•bit *n.* The path of a celestial body or a man-made object. *v.* To revolve or move in an orbit; to circle. **orbital** *adj.*

or•chard *n.* Land devoted to the growing of fruit trees.

or•ches•tra *n.* A group of musicians performing together on various instruments. **orchestral** *adj.*

or•der *n.* A condition where there is a logical arrangement or disposition of things; sequence or succession; method; an instruction for a person to follow; a request for certain objects. *v.* To command; to demand.

or•di•nar•y *adj.* Normal; having no exceptional quality; common; average; plain.

ore *n.* A natural underground substance, as a mineral or rock, from which valuable matter is extracted.

or•gan *n.* A musical instrument of pipes, reeds, and keyboards which produces sound by means of compressed air; a part of an animal, human, or plant that performs a definite function, as the heart or kidney.

or•gan•ic *adj.* Pertaining to the organs of an animal or plant; of or relating to the process of growing plants with natural fertilizers with no chemical additives.

organically *adv.*

or·gan·i·za·tion *n.* The state of being organized or the act of organizing; a group of people united for a particular purpose. **organizational** *adj.*, **organize** *v.*

or·i·gin *n.* The cause or beginning of something; the source; a beginning place.

o·rig·i·nal *adj.* Belonging to the first or beginning. *n.* A new idea produced by one's own imagination; the first of a kind. **originality** *n.*, **originally** *adv.*

or·na·ment *n.* A decoration. *v.* To adorn or beautify. **ornamental** *adj.*, **ornamentally** *adv.*, **ornamentation** *n.*

or·nate *adj.* Excessively ornamental; elaborate; showy, as a style of writing.

or·phan *n.* A child whose parents are deceased. **orphan** *v.*, **orphanage** *n.*

oth·er *adj.* Additional; alternate; different from what is implied or specified. *pron.* A different person or thing.

oth·er·wise *adv.* Under different conditions or circumstances.

ouch *interj.* An exclamation to express sudden pain.

ought *v.* Used to show or express a moral duty or obligation; to be advisable or correct.

ounce *n.* A unit of weight which equals 1/16 of a pound.

our *adj.* Of or relating to us; ourselves. *pron.* The possessive case of the pronoun *we*.

oust *v.* To eject; to remove with force.

out *adv.* Away from the center or inside. *adj.* Away. *n.* A means of escape. *prep.* Through; forward from.

out·cast *n.* A person who is excluded; a homeless person.

out·come *n.* A consequence or result.

out·dat·ed *adj.* Old-fashioned; obsolete.

out·do *v.* To excel in achievement.

out·fit *n.* The equipment or tools required for a specialized purpose; the clothes a person is dressed in. *v.* To supply.

out·law *n.* A person who habitually defies or breaks the law; a criminal. *v.* To ban; prohibit; to deprive of legal protection.

out·let *n.* An exit.

out·line *n.* A rough draft showing the main features of something. **outline** *v.*

out·look *n.* A person's point of view; an area offering a view of something.

out·num·ber *v.* To go over or exceed in number.

out·rage *n.* An extremely violent act of violence or cruelty; the violent emotion such an act engenders. **outrageous** *adj.*, **outrage** *v.*

out·side *n.* The area beyond the boundary lines or surface; extreme. **outdoors** *adv.*

out·spo·ken *adj.* Spoken without reserve; candid. **outspokenly** *adv.*

out·stand·ing *adj.* Excellent; prominent; unsettled, as a bill owed; projecting.

out·ward *adj.* Pertaining to the outside or exterior; superficial. **outwards** *adv.*

out·wit *v.* To trick, baffle, or outsmart.

o·val *adj.* Having the shape of an egg; an ellipse.

ov·en *n.* An enclosed chamber used for baking, drying, or heating.

o·ver *prep.* Above; across; upon. *adv.* Covering completely; thoroughly; again; repetition. *adj.* Higher; upper. *prefix* Excessive, beyond normal boundaries.

o·ver·act *v.* To act in an exaggerated way.

o·ver·all *adj.* Including or covering everything; from one side or end to another; generally. *pl.* Pants with a bib and shoulder straps.

o·ver·board *adv.* Over the side of a boat or ship into the water.

o·ver·cast *adj.* Gloomy; obscured; clouds covering more than nine tenths of the sky.

o·ver·coat *n.* A coat worn over a suit for extra warmth.

o·ver·come *v.* To prevail; to conquer or defeat. **overcomer** *n.*

o·ver·do *v.* To do anything excessively.

o·ver·dose *v.* To take an excessive dose of medication, especially narcotics.

o·ver·due *adj.* Past the time of return or payment.

o·ver·look *v.* To disregard or fail to notice something purposely; to ignore.

o·ver·rule *v.* To put aside by virtue of

higher authority.

o•ver•seas *adv.* Abroad; across the seas. **overseas** *adj.*

owe *v.* To be in debt for a certain amount; to have a moral obligation.

owl *n.* A predatory nocturnal bird, having large eyes, a short hooked bill, and long powerful claws. **owlish** *adj.*

own *adj.* Belonging to oneself. *v.* To possess; to confess; to admit. **owner** *n.*

ox *n.* A bovine animal used domestically in much the same way as a horse; an adult castrated bull. **oxen** *pl.*

oys•ter *n.* An edible marine mollusk.

o•zone *n.* A pale blue gas formed of oxygen with an odor like chlorine, formed by an electrical discharge in the air.

P

P, p The sixteenth letter of the English alphabet.

pace *n.* A person's step or length of a step; stride; the gait of a horse in which the legs on the same side are moved at the same time. **pace** *v.,* **pacer** *n.*

pace•mak•er *n.* The person who sets the pace for another in a race; a surgically implanted electronic instrument used to stabilize or stimulate the heartbeat.

pac•er *n.* One that sets a particular speed.

pac•i•fy *v.* To quiet or soothe anger or distress; to calm. **pacification** *n.*

pack *n.* A bundle; a group of things tied or wrapped up; a full set of associated or like things, such as a pack of cards; a group of wolves or wild dogs that hunt together. *v.* To put things together in a trunk, box, or suitcase; to put away for storage.

pack•age *n.* Something tied up, wrapped or bound together.

pack an•i•mal *n.* An animal used to carry heavy packs.

pad *n.* Anything stuffed with soft material and used to protect against blows; a cushion; a drawing or writing tablet of paper gummed together at one edge. *v.* To

stuff, line, or protect with soft material; to extend or lengthen something by inserting unnecessary matter.

pad•dle *n.* A broad-bladed implement usually made from wood, used to steer and propel a small boat; a tool used for mixing, turning, or stirring.

pad•dle•wheel *n.* A wheel with boards for propelling vessels.

page *n.* A person hired to deliver messages or run errands; one side of the leaf of a book or letter. *v.* To call or summon a person.

pag•eant *n.* An elaborate exhibition or spectacular parade for public celebration. **pageantry** *n.*

paid *v.* Past tense of *pay.*

pail *n.* A cylindrical container usually having a handle; a bucket.

pain *n.* The unpleasant feeling resulting from injury or disease; any distress or suffering of the mind; sorrow. *v.* To cause or experience pain. **painful, painless** *adj.*

paint *n.* A mixture of colors or pigments spread on a surface as protection or as a decorative coating. *v.* To apply paint to a surface; to express oneself creatively on canvas. **painter, painting** *n.*

pair *n.* Two things similar and used together; something made of two parts used together; two persons or animals which live or work together.

pa•ja•mas *pl. n.* A garment for sleeping, consisting of a jacket and pants.

pal•ace *n.* The residence of a sovereign, as of a king; a mansion. **palatial** *adj.*

pale *n.* The pointed stake of a fence; a picket; an area enclosed within bounds. *adj.* Having a whitish or lighter than normal complexion; pallid; weak.

pal•ette *n.* A thin oval board with a hole for the thumb, on which an artist lays and mixes colors.

palm *n.* The inner area of the hand between the fingers and the wrist; any of a large group of tropical evergreen trees, having an unbranched trunk with a top or crown of fan-like leaves. *v.* To hide something small in or about the hand.

pam·per *v.* To treat with extreme care.

pam·phlet *n.* A brief publication.

pan·cake *n.* A thin, flat cake made from batter and fried on a griddle, served with butter, syrup, and other toppings.

pan·da *n.* A large bear-like animal of China and Tibet with black and white fur and rings around the eyes; a raccoon-like animal of the south-eastern Himalayas with a ringed tail and reddish fur.

pan·el *n.* A flat, rectangular piece of material, often wood, which forms a part of a surface; a group of people selected to participate in a discussion group or to serve on a jury. **panelist** *n.*, **panel** *v.*

pan·ic *n.* A sudden unreasonable fear which overpowers. *v.* To cause or to experience panic. **panicky** *adj.*

pan·o·rama *n.* An unlimited or complete view in all directions of what is visible.

pant *v.* To breathe in rapid or short gasps; to yearn. *n.* A short breath.

pan·to·mime *n.* Communication done solely by means of facial and body gestures. *v.* To express or act in pantomime.

pants *pl. n.* Trousers; underpants.

pap *n.* A soft food for invalids or babies.

pa·per *n.* A substance made of pulp from wood and rags, formed into sheets for printing, wrapping and writing.

par·a·ble *n.* A short, fictitious story which illustrates a moral lesson.

par·a·chute *n.* A folding umbrella-shaped apparatus of light fabric used to make a safe landing after a free fall from an airplane. **parachute** *v.*, **parachutist** *n.*

pa·rade *n.* An organized public procession; a march. **parader** *n.*

par·a·dise *n.* A state or place of beauty, bliss or delight; heaven.

par·a·dox *n.* A statement which seems opposed to common sense or contradicts itself, but is perhaps true. **paradoxical** *adj.*, **paradoxically** *adv.*

par·a·graph *n.* A section of a composition dealing with a single idea, containing one or more sentences with the first line usu-

ally indented.

par·a·keet *n.* A small parrot with a long, wedge-shaped tail.

par·al·lel *adj.* Moving in the same direction but separated by a distance, as railroad tracks. *n.* A parallel curve, line, or surface; a comparison; one of the imaginary lines which circle the earth paralleling the equator and mark the latitude. **parallel** *v.*, **parallelism** *n.*

par·al·lel·o·gram *n.* A four-sided figure having parallel, opposite, equal sides.

pa·ral·y·sis *n.* Complete or partial loss of the ability to feel any sensation or to move. **paralytic** *adj.*

par·a·lyze *v.* To cause to be inoperative or powerless.

par·a·phrase *v.* To put something written or spoken into different words while retaining the same meaning.

par·a·site *n.* An organism which lives, grows, feeds, and takes shelter in or on another organism; a person depending entirely on another without providing something in return.

par·cel *n.* A wrapped package; a bundle; a portion or plat of land. **parcel** *v.*

parch·ment *n.* Goatskin or sheepskin prepared with a pumice stone and used as a material for writing or drawing.

par·don *v.* To forgive someone for an offense; in law, to allow a convicted person freedom from the penalties of an office or crime. **pardonable** *adj.*, **pardonably** *adv.*, **pardon** *n.*

pare *v.* To cut away or remove the outer surface gradually.

par·ent *n.* A mother or father; a forefather; an ancestor; a source; a cause. **parentage**, **parenthood** *n.*, **parental** *adj.*

pa·ren·the·sis *n.* One of a pair of curved lines ( ) used to enclose a qualifying or explanatory remark. **parentheses** *pl.*

park *n.* A tract of land used for recreation. *v.* To leave something temporarily in a parking garage or lot, as a car. **parker** *n.*

par·ka *n.* A jacket with an attached hood.

par·lia·ment *n.* The assembly which

constitutes the lawmaking body of various countries, as the United Kingdom.

par•lor *n.* A room for entertaining visitors or guests; a business offering a personal service, such as beauty parlor, ice cream parlor, or funeral parlor.

par•o•dy *n.* A composition, song, or poem which mimics another in a ridiculous way.

pa•role *n.* The conditional release of a prisoner before his sentence expires. **parole** *v.*

par•rot *n.* A brightly colored, semi-tropical bird with a strong, hooked bill. *v.* To imitate or repeat.

parse *v.* To identify the parts of speech in a sentence and to indicate their relationship to each other.

par•son *n.* A pastor or clergyman.

par•son•age *n.* The home provided by a church for its parson.

part *n.* A segment, portion, or division of a whole; a component for a machine; the role of a character, as in a play; the line which forms where the hair is parted by combing or brushing. *v.* To leave or go away from; to be separated into pieces; to give up control or possession.

par•tial *adj.* Incomplete; inclined to favor one side more than the other. **partiality** *n.*, **partially** *adv.*

par•tic•i•pate *v.* To join in or share; to take part. **participant, participation, participator** *n.*, **participatory** *adj.*

par•ti•cle *n.* A very small piece of solid matter; a group of words, such as articles, prepositions, and conjunctions which convey very little meaning but help to connect, specify, or limit the meanings of other words.

par•tic•u•lar *adj.* Having to do with a specific person, group, thing, or category; noteworthy; precise. **particularly** *adv.*

par•ti•tion *n.* A separation or division. *v.* To divide.

part•ner *n.* One who shares something with another.

part•ner•ship *n.* Two or more persons who run a business together and share in the profits and losses.

par•ty *n.* A group of persons who gather for pleasure or entertainment; a group of persons associated together for a common purpose; a group which unites to promote or maintain a policy or a cause.

pass *v.* To proceed; to move; to transfer; to go away or come to an end; to get through a course, trial or test; to approve; to vote for; to give as an opinion or judgment; to hit or throw a ball to another player. *n.* A ticket or note that allows a person to come and go freely.

pas•sage *n.* The act of going, proceeding, or passing; a small portion or part of a whole book or speech; something, as a path or channel, through, over or along which something else may pass.

pas•sen•ger *n.* One who travels in a vehicle, car, plane, boat, or other conveyance.

pas•sion *n.* A powerful feeling; sexual desire; an outburst of strong feeling; violence or anger. **passionless, passionate** *adj.*

pas•sive *adj.* Not working, acting, or operating; inactive; acted upon, influenced, or affected by something external; designating the form of a verb which indicates the subject is receiving the action. **passively** *adv.*, **passivity, passiveness** *n.*

past *adj.* Having to do with or existing at a former time. *n.* Before the present time; a person's history or background. *adv.* To go by. *prep.* After; beyond in time; beyond the power, reach, or influence.

paste *n.* A mixture usually made from water and flour, used to stick things together; dough used in making pastry; a brilliant glass used in imitating precious stones. **paste** *v.*

pas•tel *n.* A crayon made of ground pigments; a drawing made with crayons of this kind. *adj.* Pale and light in color or shade.

pas•ture *n.* An area for grazing of domestic animals.

pat *v.* To tap lightly with something flat. *n.* A soft, caressing stroke.

patch

patch *n.* A piece of fabric used to repair a weakened or torn area in a garment; a piece of cloth with an insignia which represents an accomplishment. *v.* To repair or put together hastily. **patchy** *adj.*

pa•ter•nal *adj.* Relating to or characteristic of a father; inherited from a father. **paternally** *adv.*, **paternalism** *n.*

path *n.* A track or course; a route; a course of action or life.

pa•thet•ic *adj.* Arousing pity, tenderness, or sympathy. **pathetically** *adv.*

pa•tience *n.* The quality, state, or fact of being patient; the ability to be patient.

pa•tient *adj.* Demonstrating uncomplaining endurance under distress *n.* A person under medical care.

pa•tri•ot *n.* A person who loves and defends his country. **patriotic** *adj.*, **patriotism** *n.*

pa•trol *n.* Walking around an area for the purpose of maintaining or observing security; a person or group carrying out this action. **patrol** *v.*

pa•tron *n.* A person who fosters, protects, or supports some person, enterprise, or thing; a regular customer. **patroness** *n.*

pat•tern *n.* Anything designed or shaped to serve as a guide in making something else; a sample. *v.* To make according to a pattern.

pause *v.* To linger, hesitate, or stop for a time.

pave *v.* To surface with gravel, concrete, asphalt, or other material.

pave•ment *n.* A paved surface.

paw *n.* The foot of an animal. *v.* To handle clumsily or rudely.

pawn *n.* Something given as security for a loan; a hostage; a chessman of little value.

pay *v.* To give a person what is due for a debt, purchase, or work completed; to compensate; to suffer the consequences.

pay•ment *n.* The act of paying.

pay•roll *n.* The amount of money to be paid to a list of employees.

pea *n.* A round edible seed contained in a pod and grown on a vine.

peace *n.* A state of physical or mental tranquillity; calm; serenity; the absence of war; the state of harmony between people.

peach *n.* A round, sweet, juicy fruit having a thin, downy skin, a pulpy yellow flesh, and a hard, rough single seed.

pea•cock *n.* A male bird with brilliant blue or green plumage and a long iridescent tail that fans out to approximately six feet.

peak *n.* A projecting edge or point; the summit of a mountain; the top. *v.* To bring to the maximum.

pea•nut *n.* A nut-like seed which ripens underground; the plant bearing this nut.

pear *n.* A juicy, edible fruit.

pearl *n.* A smooth, rounded deposit formed around a grain of sand in the shell of various mollusks, especially the oyster; anything precious or rare. **pearly** *adj.*

peas•ant *n.* A farmhand or rustic workman; a person of the lowest class.

peat *n.* The black substance formed when plants begin to decay in wet ground, as bogs. **peaty** *adj.*

peat moss *n.* A moss which grows in very wet areas, used as plant food and mulch.

peb•ble *n.* A small, smooth stone.

pe•can *n.* A large tree of the central and southern United States with an edible oval, thin-shelled nut.

peck *v.* To strike with the beak; to eat taking only small bites. *n.* A measure which equals one fourth of a bushel.

pe•cu•liar *adj.* Odd; strange. **peculiarity** *n.*, **peculiarly** *adv.*

ped•al *n.* A lever usually operated by the foot.

ped•dle *v.* To travel around in an attempt to sell merchandise.

pe•des•tri•an *n.* A person traveling by foot.

pe•di•at•rics *n.* The branch of medicine dealing with the care of children and infants. **pediatric** *adj.*, **pediatrician** *n.*

ped•i•gree *n.* A line of ancestors, especially of an animal of pure breed.

peek *v.* To look shyly or quickly from a place of hiding; to glance. **peek** *n.*

peel *n.* The natural rind or skin of a fruit. *v.* To pull or strip the skin or bark off; to remove in thin layers.

peep *v.* To utter a very small and weak sound, as of a young bird.

peer *v.* To look searchingly; to come partially into one's view. *n.* An equal; a member of the British nobility, as a duke or earl.

peg *n.* A small pin, usually of wood or metal; a projecting pin on which something may be hung. *slang* An artificial leg, often made of wood.

pel·i·can *n.* A large, web-footed bird with a large pouch under the lower bill for the temporary storage of fish.

pel·let *n.* A small round ball made from paper or wax; a small bullet or shot.

pelt *n.* The skin of an animal with the fur.

pen *n.* An instrument used for writing.

pen·al·ty *n.* The legal punishment for an offense or crime; something forfeited when a person fails to meet a commitment; in sports, a punishment or handicap imposed for breaking a rule.

pen·ance *n.* A voluntary act to show sorrow or repentance for sin.

pen·cil *n.* A writing or drawing implement made from graphite. *v.* To make, write, or draw with a pencil.

pen·du·lum *n.* A suspended object free to swing back and forth.

pen·e·trate *v.* To force a way through or into; to pierce; to enter; to pass through something. **penetrable, penetrating** *adj.*, **penetration** *n.*

pen·guin *n.* A web-footed, flightless, marine bird of the southern hemisphere.

pen·i·cil·lin *n.* A powerful antibiotic derived from mold and used to treat certain types of bacterial infections.

pen·in·su·la *n.* A piece of land projecting into water from a larger land mass. **peninsular** *adj.*

pen·ny *n.* A U.S. coin worth one hundredth of a dollar.

pen·sion *n.* The amount of money a person receives regularly after retirement.

pensioner *n.*

pen·ta·gon *n.* Any object or building having five sides and five interior angles.

peo·ple *n.* Human beings; a body of persons living in the same country, under the same government, and speaking the same language; one's relatives or family.

pep·per *n.* A strong, aromatic condiment. *v.* To pelt or sprinkle.

per·ceive *v.* To become aware of by the senses; to understand; to feel or observe.

per·cent·age *n.* The rate per hundred; a part or proportion in relation to a whole.

perch *n.* A place on which birds rest or alight; any place for standing or sitting; a small, edible freshwater fish.

per·cus·sion *n.* The sharp striking together of one body against another; the striking of a cap in a firearm; an instrument which makes music when it is struck, as a drum or cymbal.

per·fect *adj.* Having no defect or fault; flawless; accurate; absolute. *v.* To make perfect. **perfectness, perfection** *n.*

per·form *v.* To execute or carry out an action; to act or function in a certain way; to act; to give a performance or exhibition. **performer, performance** *n.*

per·fume *n.* A fragrant substance which emits a pleasant scent; one distilled from flowers. **perfume** *v.*

per·haps *adv.* Possibly; maybe; not sure.

per·il *n.* A source of danger; exposure to the chance of injury; danger. **perilous** *adj.*, **perilously** *adv.*

pe·ri·od *n.* An interval of time marked by certain conditions; an interval of time regarded as a phase in development; the punctuation mark which indicates the end of a sentence or an abbreviation.

per·ish *v.* To ruin or spoil; to suffer an untimely or violent death.

per·ma·nent *adj.* Continuing in the same state; lasting indefinitely; enduring. *n.* A hair wave which gives long-lasting curls or body to the hair. **permanence, permanency** *n.*, **permanently** *adv.*

per·mis·sion *n.* The act of permitting

something; consent.

per•mit *v.* To consent to; to allow. *n.* An official document giving permission.

per•pen•dic•u•lar *adj.* Being at right angles to the plane of the horizon; in math, meeting a plane or given line at right angles.

per•pet•u•al *adj.* Lasting or continuing forever or an unlimited time.

per•se•cute *v.* To harass or annoy persistently; to oppress because of one's religion, beliefs, or race. **persecution, persecutor** *n.*, **persecutive** *adj.*

per•se•vere *v.* To persist in any purpose or idea; to strive in spite of difficulties. **perseverance** *n.*, **perseveringly** *adv.*

per•sist *v.* To continue firmly despite obstacles; to endure. **persistence** *n.*, **persistent** *adj.*, **persistently** *adv.*

per•son *n.* A human being; an individual; the personality of a human being.

per•son•al *adj.* Belonging to a person or persons; of the body or person; relating to oneself; done by oneself.

per•spire *v.* To give off perspiration.

per•suade *v.* To cause to convince or believe by means of reasoning or argument. **persuasion** *n.*, **persuasive** *adj.*

pes•si•mism *n.* The tendency to take a gloomy view of affairs or situations and to anticipate the worst.

pest *n.* A person or thing which is a nuisance; an annoying person or thing; a destructive insect, plant, or animal.

pes•ter *v.* To harass with persistent annoyance; to bother.

pes•ti•cide *n.* A chemical substance used to destroy rodents, insects, and pests. **pesticidal** *adj.*

pet *n.* An animal, bird, or fish one keeps for companionship; any favorite or treasured thing. *adj.* Treated or tamed as a pet. *v.* To stroke or caress gently.

pe•ti•tion *n.* A solemn request or prayer; a written request addressed to a group or person in authority. **petitioner** *n.*

pet•ri•fy *v.* To convert into a stony mass; to make fixed or immobilize, as in the face of

danger or surprise. **petrification** *n.* **petrifactive, petrified** *adj.*

pe•tro•le•um *n.* An oily, thick liquid which develops naturally below the ground surface, used in products such as gasoline, fuel oil, and kerosene.

pet•ty *adj.* To have little importance or value; insignificant; trivial; having a low position or rank; minor; small-minded. **pettiness** *n.*

pet•ty cash *n.* Cash held on hand for minor bills or expenditures.

pew•ter *n.* An alloy of tin with copper, silver-gray in color and used for tableware and kitchen utensils.

phan•tom *n.* Something which exists but has no physical reality; a ghost. **phantom** *adj.*

phar•ma•cy *n.* A place of business which specializes in preparing, identifying, and disbursing drugs; a drugstore.

phase *n.* Any decisive stage in development or growth.

pheas•ant *n.* A long-tailed game bird noted for the plumage of the male.

phe•nom•e•non *n.* Something that can be observed or perceived; a rare occurrence; an outstanding person with remarkable power, ability, or talent. **phenomena** *pl.*

phi•los•o•phy *n.* The logical study of the nature and source of human knowledge or human values; the set of values, opinions, and ideas of a group or individual.

pho•bi•a *n.* A compulsive fear of a specified situation or object.

phone *n.* A telephone. *v.* To call or communicate by telephone.

phon•ic *adj.* Pertaining to sounds in speech; using the same symbol for each sound. **phonetics** *n.*

pho•ny *adj. informal* Counterfeit; fraudulent; not real or genuine.

pho•to *n.* A photograph.

pho•to•cop•y *v.* To reproduce printed material using a photographic process. **photocopier, photocopy** *n.*

pho•to•graph *n.* A picture or image

pinch

recorded by a camera and reproduced on photosensitive paper. **photography** *n.*

pho·to·syn·the·sis *n.* The chemical process by which plants use light to change carbon dioxide and water into carbohydrates, releasing oxygen as a by-product.

phrase *n.* A brief or concise expression which does not contain both a predicate and a subject.

phys·i·cal *adj.* Relating to the human body apart from the mind or emotions; pertaining to material rather than imaginary subjects. *n.* A medical exam to determine a person's physical condition. **physically** *adv.*

phy·si·cian *n.* A person licensed to practice medicine.

phys·ics *n.* The scientific study which deals with energy, matter, motion, and related areas of science.

phys·i·ol·o·gy *n.* The scientific study of living animals, plants, and their activities and functions; the vital functions and processes of an organism. **physiological, physiologic** *adj.*, **physiologist** *n.*

pi·an·o *n.* A musical instrument with a manual keyboard and felt-covered hammers which produce musical tones when struck upon steel wires.

pic·co·lo *n.* A small flute with a brilliant sound pitched an octave above the flute.

pick *v.* To select or choose from a number or group; to remove the outer area of something with the fingers or a pointed instrument; to remove by tearing away little by little; to open a lock without using a key; to harass or tease someone or something; to pluck a musical instrument. *n.* A pointed metal tool sharpened at both ends, used to break up hard surfaces; a small flat piece of plastic or of bone, used to pluck or strum the strings of an instrument, as a guitar or banjo.

pick·et *n.* A pointed stake driven into the ground as support for a fence; a person positioned outside of a place of employment during a strike.

pick·le *n.* A cucumber preserved in a solution of brine or vinegar.

pic·nic *n.* An outdoor social gathering where food is provided usually by the people attending. **picnicker** *n.*

pic·ture *n.* A visual representation on a surface, printed, drawn or photographed; the mental image or impression of an event or situation.

piece *n.* An element, unit, or part of a whole; a musical or literary work.

pier *n.* A structure extending into the water, used to secure, protect, and provide access to vessels.

pierce *v.* To penetrate or make a hole in something; to force into or through. **piercing** *adj.*

pi·e·ty *n.* Devoutness toward God.

pig *n.* A cloven-hoofed mammal with short legs, bristly hair, and a snout for rooting; the edible meat of a pig; pork.

pi·geon *n.* A bird with short legs, a sturdy body, and a small head.

pig·ment *n.* A material used as coloring matter, suitable for making paint.

pile *n.* A quantity of anything thrown in a heap; a massive or very large building or a group of buildings.

pil·grim *n.* A person who travels to a sacred place; a wanderer.

pill *n.* A small tablet containing medicine taken by mouth; someone or something disagreeable but that must be dealt with.

pil·lar *n.* A freestanding column which serves as a support.

pil·low *n.* A cloth case filled with feathers or other soft material, used to cushion the head during sleep.

pi·lot *n.* A person licensed to operate an aircraft; someone trained and licensed to guide ships in and out of port. *v.* To act or serve as a pilot.

pin *n.* A small, stiff piece of wire with a blunt head and a sharp point, used to fasten something, usually temporarily.

pinch *v.* To squeeze between a finger and thumb causing pain or discomfort; to be miserly. *n.* The small amount that can be held between the thumb and forefinger.

pine *n.* Any of various cone-bearing evergreen trees; the wood of such a tree.

pine·ap·ple *n.* A tropical American plant with spiny, curved leaves bearing a large edible fruit.

pink *n.* Any of various plants related to the carnation, having fragrant flowers; a light or pale hue of crimson; the highest or best possible degree.

pint *n.* A liquid or dry measurement equal to half of a quart or two cups.

pi·o·neer *n.* One of the first settlers of a new region or country; the first developer or investigator in a new field of enterprise, research, or other endeavor.

pi·ous *adj.* Reverently religious; devout. **piously** *adv.*, **piousness, piety** *n.*

pipe *n.* A hollow cylinder for conveying fluids; a small bowl with a hollow stem for smoking tobacco.

pipe-line *n.* A pipe used to transfer gas or oil over long distances; a smoking container; a means for conveying information.

pi·rate *n.* A robber of the high seas; someone who uses or reproduces someone else's work without authorization. **piracy** *n.*

pis·tol *n.* A small hand-held firearm.

pis·ton *n.* A solid cylinder fitted into a larger cylinder, moving back and forth under liquid pressure.

pit *n.* An artificial or manmade hole in the ground; a slight indentation in the skin, as a scar from the chicken pox; an area for refueling or repair at a car race; the stone in the middle of some fruit, as peaches.

pitch *n.* A thick, sticky, dark substance which is the residue of the distillation of petroleum or coal tar; the degree of slope of an incline; the property of a musical tone which makes it high or low. *v.* To cover with pitch; to throw; to throw out; to slope.

pitch·er *n.* The person who throws the ball to the batter; a container for holding and pouring liquids.

pitch·fork *n.* A large fork with a wide prong span, used as a garden or farm tool.

pit·y *n.* A feeling of compassion or sorrow for another's misfortune. **pit·i·ful** *adj.*, **pitifully** *adv.*

piv·ot *n.* A thing or person upon which development, direction, or effect depends. *v.* To turn.

piz·za *n.* An Italian food consisting of a doughy crust covered with tomato sauce, cheese, and toppings and then baked.

place *n.* A region; an area; a building or location used for a special purpose; the position of something in a series or sequence. *v.* To put in a particular order or place.

place·ment *n.* The act of being placed; a business or service which finds positions of employment for applicants.

plague *n.* Anything troublesome; a highly contagious and often fatal epidemic disease, as the bubonic plague.

plain *adj.* Level; flat; clear; open, as in view; not rich or luxurious; not highly gifted or cultivated. **plainly** *adv.*, **plainness** *n.*

plan *n.* A scheme or method for achieving something; a drawing to show proportion and relationship to parts. *v.* To have in mind as an intention or purpose.

plane *n.* A tool for smoothing or leveling a wood surface; a surface on which any two points can be joined with a straight line; an airplane.

plan·et *n.* A celestial body illuminated by light from the star around which it revolves.

plant *n.* A living organism belonging to the vegetable kingdom, having cellulose cell walls. *v.* To place a living organism in the ground for growing; to place so as to deceive or to spy.

plas·ma *n.* The clear fluid part of blood, used for transfusions.

plas·tic *adj.* Pliable; capable of being molded. *n.* A synthetic material molded and then hardened into objects.

plate *n.* A flat flexible, thin piece of material, as metal; a shallow, flat vessel made from glass, crockery, plastic, or other material from which food is eaten.

pla·teau *n.* An extensive level expanse of elevated land; a period of stability.

plat·form *n.* Any elevated surface used by speakers, or by other performers or for display purposes; a formal declaration of principles or policy of a political party.

plat·ter *n.* A large, oblong, shallow dish for serving food.

plau·si·ble *adj.* Seeming to be probable; appearing to be trustworthy or believable.

play *v.* To amuse or entertain oneself, as in recreation; to take part in a game; to perform in a dramatic role; to perform with a musical instrument; in fishing, to allow a hooked fish to tire itself out; to pretend to do something. *n.* A dramatic presentation.

play·ful *adj.* Lightly humorous; full of high spirits.

play·ground *n.* The area set aside for children's recreation.

pla·za *n.* An open-air marketplace or square; a shopping mall.

plea *n.* An urgent request; a legal allegation made by either party in a lawsuit.

plead *v.* To argue for or against something in court; to ask earnestly.

pleas·ant *adj.* Giving or promoting the feeling of pleasure; very agreeable. **pleasantly** *adv.*, **pleasantness** *n.*

please *v.* To make happy; to give pleasure; to be the will or wish of; to prefer.

pleas·ur·a·ble *adj.* Pleasant; gratifying.

pleas·ure *n.* A feeling of satisfaction or enjoyment; one's preference or wish.

pleat *n.* A fold in a cloth made by doubling the cloth back and fastening it down.

pledge *n.* A solemn promise; a deposit of something as security for a loan; a promise to join a fraternity; a person who is pledged to join a fraternity. *v.* To promise or vow.

plen·ti·ful *adj.* Having great abundance. **plentifully** *adv.*, **plentifulness** *n.*

plen·ty *n.* An ample amount; prosperity or abundance.

plight *n.* A distressing circumstance, situation, or condition. ·

plod *n.* To walk in a heavy, slow way.

plot *n.* A small piece of ground usually used for a special purpose; the main story line in a piece of fiction; a plan; an intrigue; a conspiracy. *v.* To represent something by using a map or chart; to scheme secretly. **plotter** *n.*

plow *n.* An implement for breaking up or turning over the soil. *v.* To dig out. *slang* To hit with force.

pluck *v.* To remove by pulling out or off; to pull and release the strings on a musical instrument.

plug *n.* Anything used to stop or close a hole or drain; a two-pronged device attached to a cord and used in a jack or socket to make an electrical connection.

plum *n.* A small tree bearing an edible fruit with a smooth skin and a single hard seed; the fruit from such a tree.

plum·age *n.* The feathers of a bird.

plumb *n.* A lead weight tied to the end of a string, used to test the exact perpendicular line of something.

plumb·er *n.* A person who repairs or installs plumbing in a home or business.

plumb·ing *n.* The profession or trade of a plumber; the connecting of pipes and fixtures used to carry water and waste.

plume *n.* A feather used as an ornament.

plun·der *v.* To deprive of goods or property in a violent way. **plunderer** *n.*

plunge *v.* To thrust or cast something, as into water; to submerge; to descend sharply or steeply.

plu·ral *adj.* Consisting of or containing more than one. **plural** *n.*

ply *v.* To mold, bend, or shape. *n.* A layer of thickness; the twisted strands of thread, yarn, or rope.

pock·et *n.* A small pouch within a garment, having an open top and used for carrying items. *v.* To put in or deposit in a pocket.

pod *n.* A seed vessel, as of a bean or pea. A separate and detachable compartment in a spacecraft.

po·em *n.* A composition in verse with

language selected for its beauty and sound. **poet** *n.*

po•et•ry *n.* The art of writing stories, poems, and thoughts into verse.

point *n.* The sharp or tapered end of something; a mark of punctuation, as a period; a geometric object which does not have property or dimensions other than location; a degree, condition, or stage; a particular or definite spot in time. *v.* To aim; to indicate direction by using the finger.

poise *v.* To bring into or hold one's balance. *n.* Equilibrium; self-confidence; the ability to stay calm in all social situations.

poi•son *n.* A substance which kills, injures, or destroys. **poisoner** *n.*, **poisonous** *adj.*

poke *v.* To push or prod at something with a finger or other implement.

po•lar *adj.* Having to do with the poles of a magnet or sphere; relating to the geographical poles of the earth.

pole *n.* A long, slender rod; either of the two ends of the axis of a sphere, as the earth; the two points called the North and South Poles, where the axis of the earth's rotation meets the surface.

po•lice *n.* A division or department organized to maintain order; the members of such a department; a law enforcement officer. *v.* To patrol; to enforce the law and maintain order. **policeman, police-woman** *n.*

pol•i•cy *n.* Any plan or principle which guides decision making.

pol•ish *v.* To make lustrous and smooth by rubbing; to become refined or elegant.

po•lite *adj.* Refined, mannerly, and courteous.

po•lit•i•cal *adj.* Pertaining to government; involved in politics.

poll *n.* The recording of votes in an election; a public survey taken on a given topic. **poll** *v.*

pol•lute *v.* To contaminate; to make unclear or impure; to dirty. **pollution** *n.*

pond *n.* A body of still water, smaller in size than a lake.

pon•der *v.* To weigh or think about very carefully; to meditate.

pon•der•ous *adj.* Massive; having great weight.

po•ny *n.* A small horse.

pool *n.* A small body of water; the collective stake in gambling games.

poor *adj.* Lacking possessions and money; not satisfactory; broke; needy; destitute.

pop *v.* To cause something to burst; to make a sharp, explosive sound. *n.* Soda; a carbonated sweet drink.

pop•corn *n.* A type of corn which explodes when heated, forming white puffs.

pop•lar *n.* A rapidly growing tree having a light, soft wood.

pop•u•lar *adj.* Approved of; widely liked; suited to the means of the people.

pop•u•la•tion *n.* The total number of people in a given area, country, or city.

por•ce•lain *n.* A hard, translucent ceramic which has been fired and glazed.

porch *n.* A covered structure forming the entrance to a house.

pork *n.* The edible flesh of swine. *informal* Favors given by a government for political reasons and not public necessity.

por•poise *n.* An aquatic mammal with a blunt, rounded snout.

port *n.* A city or town with a harbor for loading and unloading cargo from ships; the left side of a ship; a dark-red, sweet, fortified wine; in computers, the hardware connection by which elements of a computer system are physically linked to enable electronic transfer among devices.

port•a•ble *adj.* Capable of being moved easily.

por•ter *n.* A person hired to carry baggage.

por•tion *n.* A section or part of a whole; a share. *v.* To allot; to assign.

por•tray *v.* To represent by drawing, writing, or acting.

pose *v.* To place or assume a position, as for a picture.

po•si•tion *n.* The manner in which something is placed; an attitude; a viewpoint; a job. *v.* To place in proper order.

pos·i·tive *adj.* Containing, expressing, or characterized by affirmation; very confident; absolutely certain; not negative. **positively** *adv.*, **positiveness** *n.*

pos·ses·sion *n.* The fact or act of possessing property; the state of being possessed, as by an evil spirit.

pos·ses·sive *adj.* Having a strong desire to possess; not wanting to share. *n.* The noun or pronoun case which indicates ownership.

pos·si·ble *adj.* Capable of being true, happening, or being accomplished. **possibility** *n.*, **possibly** *adv.*

post *n.* An upright piece of wood or metal support; a position of employment. *v.* To put up information in a public place.

post·age *n.* The charge or fee for mailing something.

post·pone *v.* To put off; to defer to a later time. **postponement, postponer** *n.*

pos·ture *n.* The position of the body.

pot *n.* A rounded, deep container used for cooking and other domestic purposes.

po·tent *adj.* Having great strength or physical powers; having a great influence on the mind or morals; sexually competent.

po·ten·tial *adj.* Possible, but not yet actual; having the capacity to be developed; the energy of an electric charge that depends on its position in an electric field. **potentiality** *n.*, **potentially** *adv.*

pot·ter·y *n.* Objects molded from clay and fired by intense heat.

poul·try *n.* Domestic fowl as ducks and hens, raised for eggs or meat.

pound *n.* A measure of weight equal to sixteen ounces; a public enclosure where stray animals are fed and housed. *v.* To strike repeatedly or with force; to throb or beat violently or rapidly.

pov·er·ty *n.* The condition or state of being poor and needing money.

pow·der *n.* A dry substance which has been finely ground or pulverized; dust; an explosive, such as gunpowder. *v.* To dust

or cover.

pow·er·ful *adj.* Possessing energy or great force; having authority.

prac·ti·cal *adj.* Serving an actual use or purpose; inclined to act instead of thinking or talking about something; useful.

prac·tice *n.* A custom or habit of doing something. *v.* To work at a profession; to apply; to put into effect; to rehearse.

prai·rie *n.* A wide area of level or rolling land with grass and weeds but no trees.

praise *v.* To express approval; to glorify.

prank *n.* A mischievous, playful action or trick. **prankster** *n.*

pray *v.* To address prayers to God; to ask or request.

pray·er *n.* A devout request; the act of praying; a formal or set group of words used in praying.

preach *v.* To advocate; to proclaim; to deliver a sermon. **preacher, preachment** *n.*, **preachy** *adj.*

pre·am·ble *n.* An introduction to something, as a law, which states the purpose and reasons for the matter which follows.

pre·cau·tion *n.* A measure of caution taken in advance to guard against harm.

pre·cious *adj.* Having great worth or value; beloved; cherished.

pre·cip·i·ta·tion *n.* Condensed water vapor which falls as snow, rain, sleet, or hail; the act of causing crystals to separate and fall to the bottom of a liquid.

pre·cise *adj.* Exact; definite; strictly following rules; very strict.

pre·ci·sion *n.* Exactness; the quality of being precise; accuracy.

pred·a·tor *n.* A person who steals from others; an animal that survives by killing and eating other animals.

pred·i·cate *n.* The word or words which say something about the subject of a clause or sentence; the part of a sentence which contains the verb. *v.* To establish.

pre·dict *v.* To tell beforehand; to foretell; to forecast. **predictability, prediction** *n.*, **predictable** *adj.*

pref·ace *n.* The introduction at the

eginning of a book or speech.

pre•fer v. To select as being the favorite; to promote; to present.

pref•er•ence n. A choice; a special liking for something. **preferential** adj.

pre•fix v. To put at the beginning; to put before.

preg•nant adj. Carrying an unborn fetus; significant. **pregnancy** n.

prej•u•dice n. A biased opinion based on emotion rather than reason; bias against a group, race, or creed.

pre•lim•i•nar•y adj. Leading up to the main action. **preliminaries** n. pl.

prel•ude n. An introductory action; the movement at the beginning of a piece of music.

pre•ma•ture adj. Occurring or born before the natural time. **prematurely** adv.

pre•mi•um n. An object offered free as an inducement to buy; the fee or amount payable for insurance; an additional amount charged above the nominal value.

prep•a•ra•tion n. The process of preparing for something.

pre•pare v. To make ready or qualified; to equip. **preparedly** adv.

prep•o•si•tion n. A word placed in front of a noun or pronoun to show a connection with or to something or someone.

pre•school adj. Of or for children usually between the ages of two and five. **pre-schooler** n.

pre•scrip•tion n. A physician's written order for medicine.

pres•ence n. The state of being present; the immediate area surrounding a person or thing; poise.

pres•ent adj. Now going on; not past or future; denoting a tense or verb form which expresses a current state or action. v. To bring into the acquaintance of another; to introduce; to make a gift of. n. A gift.

pres•en•ta•tion n. A formal introduction of one person to another; to present something as an exhibition, show, or product.

pre•serve v. To keep or save from destruc-

tion or injury; to prepare fruits or vegetables to prevent spoilage or decay. n. pl. Fruit preserved with sugar.

pres•i•dent n. The chief executive officer of a government, corporation, or association. **presidency** n.

press v. To act upon or exert steady pressure or force; to squeeze out or extract by pressure; to smooth by heat and pressure; to iron clothes. n. A machine used to produce printed material.

pres•sure n. The act of or state of being pressed; a constraining moral force; any burden, force, painful feeling, or influence; a depressing feeling or influence; the depressing effect of something.

pre•sume v. To take for granted; to take upon oneself without permission; to proceed overconfidently. **presumably** adv.

pre•sump•tion n. Arrogant conduct or speech; something that can be logically assumed true until disproved.

pre•tend v. To make believe; to act in a false way. **pretender** n.

pre•tense n. A deceptive and false action or appearance; a false purpose.

pret•ty adj. Pleasant; attractive; characterized by gracefulness; pleasing to look at; informal Sitting pretty; in a favorable position; good circumstances. **prettier**, **prettiest** adj.

pre•vent v. To keep something from happening; to keep from doing something.

pre•view n. An advance showing or viewing to invited guests.

pre•vi•ous adj. Existing or occurring earlier. **previously** adv.

price n. The set amount of money expected or given for the sale of something.

prick n. A small hole made by a sharp point. v. To pierce something lightly.

pride n. A sense of personal dignity; a feeling of pleasure because of something achieved, done, or owned.

pri•ma•ry adj. First in origin, time, series, or sequence; basic; fundamental.

prime adj. First in importance, time, or rank. n. A period of full vigor, success, or beauty. *v.* To make ready by putting something on before the final coat.

prim•i•tive *adj.* Of or pertaining to the beginning or earliest time; resembling the style or manners of an earlier time.

prince *n.* The son of a king; a king.

prin•cess *n.* The daughter of a king.

prin•ci•pal *adj.* Chief; most important. *n.* The principal administrator; the headmaster or chief official of a school; a sum of money invested or owed separate from the interest.

prin•ci•ple *n.* The fundamental law or truth upon which others are based; a moral standard.

print *n.* An impression or mark made with ink; the design or picture transferred from an engraved plate or other impression. *v.* To stamp designs; to publish something.

print•er *n.* A person whose occupation is printing.

print•out *n.* The output of a computer, printed on paper; hard copy.

pri•or *adj.* Previous in order or time.

pri•or•i•ty *n.* Something which takes precedence; something which must be done or taken care of first.

pris•on *n.* A place of confinement where people are kept while waiting for a trial or while serving time for breaking the law; jail. **prisoner** *n.*

pri•vate *adj.* Secluded or removed from the public view; secret; intimate; owned or controlled by a group or person rather than by the public or government. *n.* An enlisted person holding the lowest rank in military service.

priv•i•lege *n.* A special right or benefit granted to a person. **privileged** *adj.*

prize *n.* An award or something given to the winner of a contest; something exceptional or outstanding.

pro *n.* An argument in favor of something.

prob•a•ble *adj.* Likely to become a reality, but not certain or proved.

pro•ba•tion *n.* A period used to test the qualifications and character of a new employee; the early release of lawbreakers who must be under supervision.

prob•lem *n.* A perplexing situation or question; a question presented for consideration or solution. **problematic** *adj.*

pro•ce•dure *n.* A certain pattern or way of doing something; the normal methods or forms to be followed.

pro•ceed *v.* To carry on or continue an action or process.

proc•ess *n.* The course, steps, or methods toward a desired result. *v.* To compile, compute, or assemble data.

pro•ces•sion *n.* A group which moves along in a formal manner; a parade.

proc•la•ma•tion *n.* An official public declaration or announcement.

prod *v.* To arouse mentally; to poke with a pointed instrument. *n.* A pointed implement used to prod or poke.

pro•duce *v.* To bear or bring forth by a natural process; to manufacture; to make; to present or bring into view.

prod•uct *n.* Something produced, manufactured, or obtained; the answer obtained by multiplying.

pro•duc•tion *n.* The process or act of producing; something produced, as a play.

pro•fess *v.* To admit or declare openly; to make an open vow.

pro•fes•sor *n.* A faculty member of the highest rank in a college or university; a highly skilled teacher.

pro•fi•cient *adj.* Highly skilled in a field of knowledge. **proficiency** *n.*

pro•file *n.* The outline of a person's face or figure as seen from the side; a short biographical sketch.

prof•it *n.* The financial return after all expenses have been accounted for. *v.* To gain an advantage or a financial reward. **profitable** *adj.*

pro•found *adj.* Deeply held or felt; intellectually penetrating.

pro•gram *n.* Any prearranged plan or course; a show or performance; a sequence of commands which tell a computer how to perform a task or sequence of tasks. **program** *v.*

prog•ress *n.* Forward motion or advancement to a higher goal; an advance; steady improvement.

pro•hib•it *v.* To forbid legally; to prevent.

pro•ject *n.* A plan or course of action; a proposal; a large job. *v.* To give an estimation on something.

pro•logue *n.* An introductory statement at the beginning of a poem, song, or play.

pro•long *v.* To extend or lengthen in time.

prom•i•nent *adj.* Jutting out; widely known; held in high esteem.

prom•ise *n.* An assurance given that one will or will not do something; a pledge. **promise** *v.*

prompt *adj.* Arriving on time; punctual; immediate. *v.* To suggest or inspire.

prone *adj.* Lying flat; face down.

pro•noun *n.* A word used in the place of a noun or noun phrase.

pro•nounce *v.* To deliver officially; to articulate the sounds.

proof *n.* The establishment of a fact by evidence; the act of showing that something is true; a trial impression from the negative of a photograph. *v.* To proofread.

prop *n.* A support to keep something upright. *v.* To sustain.

prop•er *adj.* Appropriate; especially adapted or suited; conforming to social convention; correct.

prop•er•ty *n.* Any object of value owned or lawfully acquired; a piece of land.

proph•e•cy *n.* A prediction made under divine influence.

proph•et *n.* One who delivers divine messages; one who foretells the future. **prophetess** *n.*

pro•por•tion *n.* The relation of one thing to another in size, degree, or amount. *v.* To adjust or arrange with balance and harmony.

pro•pose *v.* To present or put forward for consideration or action; to suggest someone for an office or position; to make an offer; to offer marriage. **proposal** *n.*

prose *n.* Ordinary language, speech, or writing which is not poetry.

pros•e•cute *v.* To carry on; in law, to bring suit against a person; to seek enforcement for legal process. **prosecution** *n.*

pros•pect *n.* Something that has the possibility of future success; a possible customer. *v.* To explore. **prospective** *adj.*

pros•per *v.* To be successful; to achieve success. **prosperous** *adj.*

pro•tect *v.* To guard or shield from attack or injury; to shield. **protective** *adj.*, **protectively** *adv.*

pro•tein *n.* Any of a very large group of highly complex nitrogenous compounds occurring in living matter and composed of amino acids essential for tissue repair and growth.

pro•test *v.* To make a strong formal objection; to object to. *n.* The act of protesting. **protester** *n.*

pro•to•col *n.* In computers, an electronically defined set of transmission and communication rules, by which various software devices can be interchanged.

proud *adj.* Showing or having a feeling that one is better than the others; having a feeling of satisfaction; having proper self-respect or proper self-esteem.

prove *v.* To show with valid evidence that something is true. **provable** *adj.*

prov•erb *n.* An old saying which illustrates a truth.

pro•vide *v.* To supply or furnish with what is needed.

pro•voke *v.* To cause to be angry; to annoy. **provocation** *n.*

prude *n.* A person who is very modest, especially in matters related to sex. **prudery, prudishness** *n.*, **prudish** *adj.*

prune *n.* The dried fruit of a plum. *v.* To cut off that which is not wanted or not necessary.

psy•chol•o•gy *n.* The science of emotions, behavior, and the mind. **psychological** *adj.*, **psychologist** *n.*

pu•ber•ty *n.* The stage of development in which sexual reproduction can first occur; the process of the body which culminates in sexual maturity.

pub•lic *adj.* Pertaining to or affecting the people or community; for everyone's use; widely or well known.

pub•li•ca•tion *n.* The business of publishing; any pamphlet, book, or magazine.

pub•lic•i•ty *n.* The state of being known to the public; common knowledge.

pub•lish *v.* To print and distribute a book, magazine, or any printed matter to the public. **publisher** *n.*

pud•dle *n.* A small pool of water or other liquid.

puff *n.* A brief discharge of air or smoke. *v.* To breathe in short heavy breaths.

pull *v.* To apply force; to cause motion toward or in the same direction of; to remove from a fixed place; to stretch.

pulp *n.* The soft juicy part of a fruit; a soft moist mass; inexpensive paper.

pump *n.* A mechanical device for moving a gas or liquid. *v.* To raise with a pump; to obtain information through persistent questioning.

punch *n.* A tool used for perforating or piercing; a blow with the fist; a drink made of an alcoholic beverage and a fruit juice or other non-alcoholic beverage. *v.* To use a punch on something; to hit sharply with the hand or fist.

pun•ish *v.* To subject a person to confinement or impose a penalty for a crime.

pun•ish•ment *n.* A penalty imposed for breaking the law or a rule.

pup *n.* A puppy, young dog, or the young of other animals.

pu•pil *n.* A person who attends school and receives instruction by a teacher.

pup•pet *n.* A small figure of an animal or person manipulated by hand or by strings. **puppeteer, puppetry** *n.*

pur•chase *v.* To receive by paying money as an exchange. **purchaser** *n.*

pure *adj.* Free from anything that damages, weakens, or contaminates; innocent; clean.

pu•ri•fy *v.* To make clean or pure. **purification, purifier** *n.*

pu•ri•ty *n.* The quality of being pure; freedom from guilt or sin.

pur•pose *n.* A desired goal; an intention. **purposeful, purposeless** *adj.*, **purposely** *adv.*

purr *n.* The low, murmuring sound characteristic of a cat.

purse *n.* A small pouch or bag for money; a handbag; a pocketbook; the sum of money offered as a prize.

pur•sue *v.* To seek to achieve; to follow in an attempt to capture. **pursuer** *n.*

pur•suit *n.* The act of pursuing an occupation.

push *v.* To move forward by exerting force; to force oneself through a crowd; to sell illegally.

put *v.* To cause to be in a location; to bring into a specific relation or state; to bring forward for debate or consideration.

puz•zle *v.* To bewilder; to confuse. *n.* A toy, board game, or word game which tests one's patience and skills.

Q, q The seventeenth letter of the English alphabet.

quack *n.* The harsh, croaking cry of a duck; someone who pretends to be a doctor. **quackery** *n.*

quad•ri•ceps *n.* The great muscle of the front of the thigh.

quad•ril•lion *n.* A thousand trillions; one followed by fifteen zeros.

quad•ru•ple *adj.* Consisting of four parts; multiplied by four.

quaff *v.* To drink in abundance.

quag•mire *n.* An area of soft muddy land that gives away underfoot; a marsh.

quail *n.* A small game bird.

quaint *adj.* Pleasing in an old-fashioned, unusual way.

quake *v.* To shake or tremble violently.

qual•i•fi•ca•tion *n.* An act of qualifying; the ability, skill, or quality which makes something suitable for a given position.

qual•i•fy *v.* To prove something able.

qual·i·ty *n.* A distinguishing character which makes something such as it is; a high degree of excellence.

qualm *n.* A sudden feeling of sickness; sensation of uneasiness or doubt.

quan·ti·ty *n.* Number; amount; bulk; weight; a portion; as a large amount.

quar·an·tine *n.* A period of enforced isolation for a period of time used to prevent the spread of a contagious disease.

quar·rel *n.* An unfriendly, angry disagreement.

quart *n.* A unit of measurement equaling four cups.

quar·ter *n.* One of four equal parts into which anything may be divided; a place of lodging, as a barracks; a U.S. coin equal to one fourth of a dollar.

quar·tet *n.* A musical composition for four voices or instruments; any group or set of four.

quartz *n.* A hard, transparent crystallized mineral.

qua·sar *n.* One of the most distant and brightest bodies in the universe; a quasar producing intense visible radiation but not emitting radio signals.

quea·sy *adj.* Nauseated; sick. **queasiness** *n.*

queen *n.* The wife of a king; a woman sovereign; in chess, the most powerful piece on the board, which can move any number of squares in any direction; the fertile female in a colony of social insects.

queer *adj.* Strange; unusual; different from the normal.

quell *v.* To put down with force; to quiet.

quench *v.* To extinguish or put out; to cool metal by thrusting into water; to drink to satisfy a thirst.

que·ry *n.* An inquiry; a question. *v.* To question.

quest *n.* A search; pursuit; an expedition to find something.

ques·tion *n.* An expression of inquiry which requires an answer; a problem; an unresolved matter; the act of inquiring.

ques·tion mark *n.* A mark of punctuation used in writing to indicate a question.

ques·tion·naire *n.* A written series of questions to gather statistical information.

queue *n.* A waiting line; any linear arrangement; in computers, a sequence of stored programs or data on hold for processing.

quib·ble *v.* To raise a trivial objection. **quibble, quibbler** *n.*

quick *adj.* Moving swiftly; occurring in a short time; responding, thinking, or understanding something rapidly and easily. **quickly** *adv.*, **quickness** *n.*

quick·sand *n.* A bog of very fine, wet sand of considerable depth, that engulfs and sucks down objects, people, or animals.

qui·et *adj.* Silent; making very little sound; still; tranquil; calm. *v.* To become or make quiet. *n.* The state of being quiet.

quin·tes·sence *n.* The most essential and purest form of anything.

quin·tet *n.* A musical composition written for five people; any group of five.

quin·til·lion *n.* A thousand quadrillions, one followed by eighteen zeros.

quin·tu·ple *adj.* Increased five times; multiplied by five; consisting of five parts.

quip *n.* A sarcastic remark. **quipster** *n.*

quirk *n.* A sudden, sharp bend or twist; a personal mannerism.

quit *v.* To cease; to give up; to depart; to abandon; to resign from a job or position.

quite *adv.* To the fullest degree; really; actually; to a great extent.

quiz *v.* To question, as with an informal oral or written examination. **quiz** *n.*

quiz·zi·cal *adj.* Being odd; teasing; questioning.

quo·rum *n.* The number of members needed in order to validate a meeting.

quo·ta *n.* An allotment or proportional share.

quote *v.* To repeat exactly what someone else has previously stated.

quo·tient *n.* In math, the amount or number which results when one number is divided by another.

R

R, r The eighteenth letter of the English alphabet.

rab•bit *n.* A burrowing mammal related to but smaller than the hare.

ra•bies *n.* An infectious viral disease of the central nervous system, often fatal, transmitted by the bite of an infected animal.

rac•coon *n.* A nocturnal mammal with a black, mask-like face and a black-and-white ringed, bushy tail.

race *n.* The zoological division of the human population having common origin and other physical traits, such as hair, form and pigmentation; a contest judged by speed; any contest, such as a race for an elective office. **raced, racer** *n.*

ra•cial *adj.* A characteristic of a race of people.

rac•ism *n.* A thought or belief that one race is better than another race.

rack *n.* An open framework or stand for displaying or holding something; an instrument of torture used to stretch the body; a triangular frame used to arrange the balls on a pool table.

ra•dar *n.* A system which uses radio signals to detect the presence or speed of an object.

ra•di•al *adj.* Pertaining to or resembling a ray or radius; developing from a center axis.

ra•di•ant *adj.* Emitting rays of heat or light; beaming with kindness or love; projecting a strong quality.

ra•di•ate *v.* To move out in rays, such as heat moving through the air. **radiation** *n.*

rad•i•cal *adj.* Making extreme changes in views, conditions, or habits; carrying theories to their fullest application.

ra•di•o *n.* The technique of communicating by radio waves; the business of broadcasting programmed material to the public via radio waves.

ra•di•o•ac•tive *adj.* Exhibiting radioactivity.

rad•ish *n.* The edible root of the radish plant.

ra•di•us *n.* A line from the center of a circle to its surface or circumference. **radii, radiuses** *pl.*

raf•fle *n.* A game of chance; a lottery in which one buys chances to win something.

raft *n.* A floating structure made from logs or planks.

raft•er *n.* A timber of a roof which slopes.

rag *n.* A useless cloth sometimes used for cleaning purposes.

rage *n.* Violent anger.

rag•ged *adj.* To be torn or ripped.

raid *n.* A sudden invasion or seizure.

rail *n.* A horizontal bar of metal, wood, or other strong material supported at both ends or at intervals; the steel bars used to support a track on a railroad.

rail•ing *n.* A barrier of wood.

rain *n.* The condensed water from atmospheric vapor, which falls to earth in the form of drops.

rain•bow *n.* An arc containing bands of colors of the spectrum formed opposite the sun and reflecting the sun's rays.

raise *v.* To cause to move upward; to build; to make greater in size, price, or amount; to increase the status; to grow.

rake *n.* A tool with a long handle at the end and a set of teeth at the other end used to gather leaves and other matter; a slope or incline. **rake** *v.*

ram *n.* A male sheep; an implement used to drive or crush by impact; to cram or force into place.

ram•ble *v.* To stroll or walk without a special destination in mind; to talk without a sequence of ideas.

ramp *n.* An incline which connects two different levels.

ranch *n.* A large establishment for raising cattle, sheep, or other livestock; a large farm that specializes in a certain crop or animals.

ran•dom *adj.* Done or made in a way that has no specific pattern or purpose.

range *n.* An area over which anything moves; an area of activity; a tract of land for animal grazing; an extended line or row especially of mountains.

rank *n.* A degree of official position or status. *v.* To place in order, class, or rank.

ran•som *n.* The price demanded or paid for the release of a kidnapped person; the payment for the release of a person or property detained.

rap•id *adj.* Having great speed; completed quickly or in a short time.

rare *adj.* Scarce; infrequent; held in high esteem or admiration because of infrequency.

ras•cal *n.* A person full of mischief; a dishonest person.

rash *adj.* Acting without consideration or caution. *n.* A skin irritation or eruption.

rat *n.* A rodent similar to the mouse, but having a longer tail.

rate *n.* The measure of something to a fixed unit; the degree of value; a fixed ratio or amount. *v.* To appraise. **rating** *n.*

rath•er *adv.* Preferably; with more reason or justice; more accurate or precise.

ra•ti•o *n.* The relationship between two things in amount, size, degree, expressed as a proportion.

ra•tio•nal *adj.* Having the faculty of reasoning; being of sound mind.

rat•tle *v.* To make a series of rapid, sharp noises in quick succession; to talk rapidly; chatter. *n.* A baby's toy made to rattle when shaken.

rave *v.* To speak incoherently; to speak with enthusiasm. *n.* The act of raving.

ra•ven *n.* A large bird, with shiny black feathers. *adj.* Of or relating to the glossy sheen or color of the raven.

ra•vine *n.* A deep gorge with steep sides in the earth's surface, usually created by flowing water.

raw *adj.* Uncooked; in natural condition; not processed; inexperienced; damp,

sharp, or chilly.

ray *n.* A thin line of radiation or light; a small trace or amount; one of several lines coming from a point.

ra•zor *n.* A sharp cutting instrument used especially for shaving.

reach *v.* To stretch out; to be able to grasp. *n.* The act of stretching out.

re•act *v.* To act in response to; to undergo a chemical change; to experience a chemical reaction.

read *v.* To visually go over something as a book, and to understand its meaning; to learn or be informed.

read•y *adj.* Prepared for use or action; quick or prompt; willing.

real *adj.* Something existing; genuine; true.

re•al•ism *n.* Concern or interest with actual fads and things as they really are.

re•al•i•ty *n. pl.* The fact or state of being real or genuine; an actual situation or event.

re•al•ize *v.* To understand correctly; to make real.

re•al•ly *adv.* Actually; truly; indeed.

rear *n.* The back. *adj.* Of or at the rear. *v.* To raise up on the hind legs; to raise as an animal or child.

rea•son *n.* A statement given to confirm or justify a belief, promise, or excuse; the ability to decide things, to obtain ideas, to think clearly, and to make logical and rational choices and decisions. *v.* To discuss something logically; reasoning.

re•bel *v.* To refuse allegiance; to resist any authority; to react with violence.

re•bound *v.* To spring back; to recover from a setback or frustration. *n.* Recoil.

re•build *v.* To make extensive repairs to something; to reconstruct; remodel.

re•call *v.* To order or summon to return; to ask for something to be returned, so that defects can be fixed or repaired; to remember; to recollect.

re•ceipt *n.* The written acknowledgment of something received.

re•ceive *v.* To take or get something; to greet customers or guests; to accept as true or correct.

re·cent *adj.* Happening at a time just before the present.

re·cess *n.* A break in the normal routine; a depression or niche in a smooth surface.

rec·i·pe *n.* The directions and a list of ingredients for preparing food.

re·cite *v.* To repeat from memory; to give an account of something in detail.

reck·less *adj.* State of being careless and rash when doing something.

rec·og·nize *v.* To experience or identify something or someone as having been known previously; to appreciate.

rec·om·mend *v.* To suggest to another as desirable; advise.

re·cord *v.* To write down for future use or permanent reference; to preserve sound on a tape or disk for replay; a phonograph record.

re·cov·er *v.* To regain something which was lost; to be restored to good health.

rec·re·a·tion *n.* Refreshment of body and mind; a pleasurable occupation or exercise.

rec·tan·gle *n.* A parallelogram with all right angles.

re·duce *v.* To decrease; lessen in number, degree, or amount; to put into order; to lower in rank; to lose weight by dieting.

reed *n.* Tall grass with a slender stem, which grows in wet areas; a thin tongue of wood, metal, cane, or plastic; placed in the mouthpiece of an instrument to produce sounds by vibrating.

reef *n.* A chain of rocks, coral, or sand at or near the surface of the water.

reel *n.* A device which revolves on an axis, used for winding up or letting out fishing line, rope, or other string-like material.

re·en·ter *v.* To enter a room or area again.

re·fer *v.* To direct for treatment, information, or help.

ref·er·ence *n.* The act of referring someone to someplace or to something.

re·fill *v.* To fill something again.

re·fine *v.* To purify by removing unwanted substances or material; to improve.

re·flect *v.* To throw back rays of light from a surface; to give an image, as from a mirror; to ponder or think carefully.

re·for·est *v.* To replant a forest.

re·form *v.* To reconstruct, make over, or change something for the better; improve; to abandon or give up evil ways.

re·frain *v.* To hold back.

re·fresh *v.* To freshen something again.

re·fresh·ment *n.* Something which will refresh, such as a cold drink or snack.

re·frig·er·ate *v.* To chill; to preserve food by chilling; to place in a refrigerator.

re·frig·er·a·tor *n.* A box-like piece of equipment which chills food and other matter.

re·fund *v.* To return or pay back; to reimburse.

re·fuse *v.* To decline; to reject; to deny.

ref·use *n.* Rubbish; trash.

re·gain *v.* To recover; to reach again.

re·gal *adj.* Of or appropriate for royalty.

re·gard *v.* To look upon closely; to consider; to have great affection for. *n.* Careful attention or thought; esteem or affection. *pl.* Greetings of good wishes.

re·gard·less *adj.* State of being careless or showing no regard toward something or someone.

re·gion *n.* An administrative, political, social, or geographical area.

re·gret *v.* To feel disappointed or distressed about. *n.* A sense of loss or expression of grief; a feeling of sorrow.

reg·u·lar *adj.* Usual; normal; conforming to set principles or procedures.

re·hears·al *n.* The act of practicing for a performance.

reign *n.* The time when the monarch rules over an area.

re·im·burse *v.* To repay.

re·in·force *v.* To support; to strengthen with additional people or equipment.

re·ject *v.* To refuse; to discard as useless.

re·joice *v.* To fill with joy; to be filled with joy.

re·late *v.* To tell the events of; to narrate; to bring into natural association.

re·lat·ed *adj.* To be in the same family; connected to each other by blood or by marriage.

re·la·tion·ship *n.* A connection by blood or family; kinship; friendship; a natural association.

rel·a·tive *adj.* Relevant; connected; considered in comparison or relationship to other. *n.* A member of one's family.

re·lax *v.* To make loose or lax; to relieve something from effort or strain; to become less formal or less reserved.

re·lease *v.* To set free from confinement; to unfasten; to free; to relinquish a claim on something.

re·lief *n.* Anything which decreases or lessens anxiety, pain, discomfort, or other unpleasant conditions or feelings.

re·lig·ion *n.* An organized system of beliefs, rites, and celebrations centered on a supernatural being; belief pursued with devotion. **religious** *adj.*

re·main *v.* To continue without change; to stay after the departure of others.

re·main·der *n.* Something left over.

re·mem·ber *v.* To bring back or recall to the mind; to retain in the mind carefully.

re·mind *v.* To cause or help to remember.

re·move *v.* To get rid of; to extract; to dismiss from office; to change one's business or residence.

re·new *v.* To make new or nearly new by restoring; to resume.

ren·o·vate *v.,* To return or to restore to a good condition.

re·nown *n.* The quality of being widely honored.

rent *n.* The payment made for the use of another's property. *v.* To obtain occupancy in exchange for payment.

re·pair *v.* To restore to good or usable condition; to renew; refresh.

re·pay *v.* To pay back money; to do something in return.

re·peat *v.* To utter something again; to do an action again.

re·pel *v.* To discourage; to force away; to create aversion.

re·pent *v.* To feel regret for something which has occurred; to change one's sinful way.

rep·e·ti·tion *n.* The act of doing something over and over again.

re·place *v.* To return something to its previous place.

re·plen·ish *v.* To add to something; to replace what has gone or been used.

rep·li·ca *n.* A reproduction or copy.

re·ply *v.* To give an answer.

re·port *n.* A detailed account; usually in a formal way. *v.* To tell about.

re·port card *n.* The report of a student's progress.

re·pos·sess *v.* To restore ownership.

rep·re·hend *v.* To show or express disapproval of.

rep·re·sent *v.* To stand for something; to serve as the official representative for. **representative** *n.*

rep·ri·mand *v.* To censure severely; rebuke.

re·pro·duce *v.* To produce an image or copy; to produce an offspring; to recreate.

rep·tile *n.* A cold-blooded, egg-laying vertebrate.

re·pub·lic *n.* A political unit or state where representatives are elected to exercise the power.

re·pu·ta·tion *n.* The commonly held evaluation of a person's character.

re·quest *v.* To ask for something.

re·quire *v.* To demand or insist upon.

re·sale *n.* The act of selling something again.

res·cue *v.* To free from danger.

re·search *n.* A scientific or scholarly investigation.

re·sem·ble *v.* To have similarity to something.

re·sent *v.* To feel angry about.

res·er·va·tion *n.* The act of keeping something back.

re·serve *v.* To save for a special reason; to set apart; to retain; to put off.

res·er·voir *n.* A body of water stored for the future; large reserve; a supply.

re•side v. To dwell permanently; to exist as a quality or attribute.

re•sign v. To give up; to submit to something as being unavoidable; to quit.

res•in n. A substance from certain plants and trees used in varnishes and lacquers.

re•sist v. To work against or actively oppose; to withstand.

res•o•lute adj. Coming from or characterized by determination.

re•solve v. To make a firm decision on something; to solve.

re•sort v. To fall back upon. n. A place, or recreation, for rest, and for a vacation.

re•sound v. To be filled with echoing sounds; to reverberate; to ring or sound loudly.

re•source n. A source of aid or support which can be drawn upon if needed.

re•spect v. To show consideration or esteem for; to relate to. n. Courtesy or considerate treatment.

re•spond v. To answer or reply; to act when prompted by something or someone.

re•sponse n. A reply; the act of replying.

re•spon•si•ble adj. Trustworthy; in charge; having authority. **responsibility** n.

rest n. A cessation of all work, activity, or motion. v. To stop work.

res•tau•rant n. A place which serves meals to the public.

re•store v. To bring back to a former condition.

re•strict v. To confine within limits. **restriction** n.

re•sult v. To happen or exist in a particular way. n. The consequence of an action, course, or operation.

re•sume v. To start again after an interruption.

res•u•me n. A summary of one's personal history, background, work, and education.

re•tail n. The sale of goods or commodities to the public. v. To sell to the consumer.

re•tain v. To hold in one's possession; to remember; to employ someone.

re•tard v. To delay or slow the progress of.

re•ten•tion n. The act or condition of being retained.

re•tire v. To depart for rest; to remove oneself from the daily routine of working. **retirement** n.

re•trace v. To go back over.

re•treat n. The act of withdrawing from danger; a time of study and meditation in a quiet; isolated location.

re•trieve v. To regain; to find something and carry it back.

re•turn v. To come back to an earlier condition; to reciprocate. n. The act of sending, bringing, or coming back. pl. A yield or profit from investments; a report on the results of an election.

re•un•ion n. The coming together of a group which has been separated for a period of time.

re•veal v. To disclose; to expose.

re•venge v. To impose injury in return for injury received.

re•verse adj. Turned backward in position. n. The opposite of something; change or turn to the opposite direction; to transpose or exchange the positions of.

re•view v. To study or look over something again; to give a report on. n. A study which gives a critical estimate of something.

re•vise v. To look over something again with the intention of improving or correcting it.

re•viv•al n. The act or condition or reviving; the return of a film or play which was formerly presented, a meeting whose purpose is religious reawakening.

re•vive v. To restore, refresh, or recall; to return to consciousness or life.

re•voke v. To nullify or make void by recalling.

re•volt v. To try to overthrow authority; to fill with disgust.

rev•o•lu•tion n. The act or state of orbital motion around a point; the abrupt overthrow of a government; a sudden change in a system.

re•volve *v.* To move around a central point; to spin; to rotate.

re•ward *n.* Something given for a special service. *v.* To give a gift for a good performance or deed.

rhap•so•dy *n.* An extreme display of enthusiasm.

rhet•o•ric *n.* Effective expression in writing or speech.

rhi•noc•er•os *n.* A very large mammal with one or two upright horns on the snout.

rhyme *n.* A word or verse whose terminal sound corresponds with another.

rhy•thm *n.* Music, speech, or movements characterized by equal or regularly alternating beats.

rib *n.* One of a series of curved bones enclosed in the chest of man and animals.

rib•bon *n.* A narrow band or strip of fabric.

rice *n.* A cereal grass grown extensively in warm climates.

rich *adj.* Having great wealth; of great value; satisfying and pleasing in voice, color, tone, or other qualities.

rid *v.* To make free from anything objectionable.

rid•dle *v.* To perforate with numerous holes. *n.* A puzzling problem or question which requires a clever solution.

ride *v.* To travel in a vehicle or on an animal. **rider** *n.*

ridge *n.* A long, narrow crest; a horizontal line formed where two sloping surfaces meet.

ri•dic•u•lous *adj.* Causing derision or ridicule.

ri•fle *n.* A firearm having a grooved bore designed to be fired from the shoulder.

rift *n.* A fault; disagreement; a lack of harmony.

rig *v.* To outfit with necessary equipment. *n.* The arrangement of sails, masts, and other equipment on a ship.

right *adj.* In accordance with or conformable to law, justice, or morality; proper and fitting; properly adjusted, disposed, or placed; orderly; sound in body or mind. *n.*

The right side, hand, or direction; the direction opposite left. *adv.* Immediately; completely; according to justice, morality, or law.

right an•gle *n.* An angle of 90 degrees; an angle with two sides perpendicular to each other.

rig•id *adj.* Not bending; inflexible; severe; stern.

rig•or *n.* The condition of being rigid or stiff; stiffness of temper; harshness.

rind *n.* A tough outer layer which may be peeled off.

ring *n.* A circular mark, line, or object; a small circular band worn on a finger. *v.* To make a clear resonant sound.

rink *n.* A smooth area covered with ice used for ice-skating.

rinse *v.* To wash lightly with water. *n.* A hair coloring or conditioning solution.

ri•ot *n.* A turbulent public disturbance.

rip *v.* To tear apart violently; to move violently or quickly. *n.* A torn place.

rip•cord *n.* A cord which, when pulled, releases a parachute from its pack.

ripe *adj.* Fully developed or aged, mature.

rip•ple *v.* To cause to form small waves on the surface of water; to waver gently.

rise *v.* To move from a lower position to a higher one; to extend upward; to meet a challenge. *n.* The act of going up or rising; an elevation in condition or rank. **riser** *n.*

risk *n.* A chance of suffering or encountering harm or loss.

rite *n.* A formal religious ceremony; any formal custom or practice.

rit•u•al *n.* A prescribed method for performing a religious ceremony.

ri•val *n.* One who strives to compete with another; one who equals or almost equals another.

riv•er *n.* A large natural stream of water, usually fed by another body of water.

ri•vet *n.* A metal bolt used to secure two or more objects.

road *n.* A public highway used for vehicles, people, and animals; a path or course.

roam *v.* To travel aimlessly.

roar *v.* To utter a deep prolonged sound of excitement; to laugh loudly.

roast *v.* To cook meat by using dry heat in an oven. *n.* A cut of meat.

rob *v.* To take property unlawfully from another person. **robber** *n.*, **robbery** *n.*

robe *n.* A long loose garment usually worn over night clothes; a long flowing garment worn on ceremonial occasions.

ro•bot *n.* A machine capable of performing human duties.

ro•bust *adj.* Full of strength and health; rich; vigorous.

rock *n.* A hard naturally formed material.

rock•er *n.* A curved piece, usually of wood, on which a cradle or chair rocks.

rock•et *n.* A device propelled with the thrust from a gaseous combustion. *v.* To move rapidly.

rode *v.* Past tense of *ride*.

ro•dent *n.* A mammal, such as a rat, mouse, or beaver having large incisors used for gnawing.

ro•de•o *n.* A public show, contest, or demonstration of ranching skills.

rogue *n.* A scoundrel or dishonest person; an innocent or playful person.

roll *v.* To move in any direction by turning over and over; to sway or rock from side to side, as a ship; to make a deep prolonged sound, as thunder. *n.* A list of names.

roll•er *n.* A cylinder for crushing, smoothing or rolling something.

ro•mance *n.* A love affair characterized by ideals of devotion and purity; a fictitious story filled with extravagant adventures.

Ro•man nu•mer•al *n.* The letter or letters of the Roman system of numbering.

romp *v.* To play or frolic in a carefree way.

rook•ie *n.* An untrained person; a novice or inexperienced person.

room *n.* A section or area of a building set off by partitions or walls. *v.* To occupy or live in a room.

roost *n.* A place or perch on which birds sleep or rest.

root *n.* The part of a plant which grows in the ground. *v.* To search or rummage for something.

rope *n.* A heavy cord of twisted fiber.

rose *n.* A shrub or climbing vine having sharp prickly stems and variously colored fragrant flowers.

ros•ter *n.* A list of names.

ro•tate *v.* To turn on an axis; to alternate something in sequence.

rot•ten *adj.* Decomposed, morally corrupt; very bad.

ro•tund *adj.* Plump; rounded.

rouge *n.* A cosmetic coloring for the cheeks.

rough *adj.* Having an uneven surface; violent or harsh. *n.* The part of a golf course with tall grass.

round *adj.* Curved; circular; spherical. *v.* To become round; to surround.

route *n.* A course of travel. *v.* To send in a certain direction.

rout•er *n.* In computers, a distribution device allowing connections among several networks via a system of electronic channels.

rou•tine *n.* Activities done regularly. *adj.* Ordinary.

rove *v.* To wander over a wide area.

row *n.* A number of things positioned next to each other; a continuous line. *v.* To propel a boat with oars.

roy•al *adj.* Relating to a king or queen.

roy•al•ty *n.* Monarchs and or their families; a payment to someone for the use of copyright or services.

rub *v.* To move over a surface with friction and pressure; to cause to become worn or frayed.

rub•ber *n.* A resinous elastic material obtained from tropical plants or produced synthetically.

rub•bish *n.* Worthless trash; nonsense.

rub•ble *n.* The pieces of broken material or stones.

rude *adj.* Discourteous; offensively blunt.

rug *n.* A heavy textile fabric used to cover a floor.

rug•ged *adj.* Strong; rough; having an

uneven or rough surface.

ru•in n. Total destruction. v. To destroy. **ruination** n.

rule n. Controlling power; an authoritative direction or statement. v. To have control over; to be in command.

rum•ble v. To make a heavy, continuous sound. n. A long, deep rolling sound.

rum•mage v. To look or search thoroughly by digging or turning things over; to ransack.

ru•mor n. An uncertain truth circulated from one person to another; gossip. v. To spread by rumor.

run v. To hurry busily from place to place; to move quickly in such a way that both feet leave the ground for a portion of each step; to be a candidate seeking an office; to drain or discharge.

run•down adj. The state of being worn down.

rung n. A bar or board which forms a step of a ladder.

ru•ral adj. Pertaining to the country.

rush v. To move quickly; to hurry; to be in a hurry.

rust n. Ferric oxide which forms a coating on iron material exposed to moisture and oxygen.

rus•tle v. To move making soft sounds.

ruth•less adj. Merciless.

rye n. A cultivated cereal grass whose seeds are used to make flour and whiskey.

S

S, s The nineteenth letter of the English alphabet.

sack n. A strong bag for holding articles; dismissal from a position or job; sleeping bag or bed.

sa•cred adj. Dedicated to worship; holy.

sac•ri•fice n. The practice of offering something, as an animal's life, to a deity. v. To give up something of value for something else.

sac•ri•lege n. A technical violation of what

is sacred because it is consecrated to God.

sad adj. Marked by sorrow; unhappy; causing sorrow; deplorable.

sad•dle n. A seat for a rider, as on the back of a horse or bicycle. v. To put a saddle on; to load down; to burden.

sa•fa•ri n. A trip or journey; a hunting expedition in Africa.

safe adj. Secure from danger, harm, or evil; not likely to cause harm. n. A strong metal container used to protect and store important documents or money.

safe•guard n. A precautionary measure.

safe•ty n. A condition of being safe from injury or hurt.

safe•ty pin n. A type of pin with a clasp that has a guard to cover its point.

sag v. To droop; to sink from pressure or weight; to lose strength.

sa•ga n. A long heroic story.

sage n. A person recognized for judgment and wisdom.

said v. Past tense of *say*.

sail n. A strong fabric used to catch the wind and cause a ship to move v. To travel on a sailing vessel.

sail•boat n. A boat propelled with a sail.

sail•fish n. A type of fish that has a large dorsal fin.

sail•ing n. The skill of managing a ship.

sail•or n. The person that sails a boat or a ship.

saint n. A person of great purity who has been officially recognized as such by the Roman Catholic Church. **saintly** adj.

sake n. Motive or reason for doing something.

sal•ad n. A dish usually made of green vegetables, fruit, or meat tossed with dressing.

sa•la•ry n. A set compensation paid on a regular basis for services rendered. **salaried** adj.

sale n. An exchange of goods for a price; disposal of items at reduced prices.

salt n. A white crystalline solid, mainly sodium chloride, found in the earth and sea water, used as a preservative and a seasoning. **salty** adj.

salt•wa•ter *adj.* Seawater.

sa•lute *v.* To show honor to a superior officer by raising the right hand to the forehead. *n.* An act of respect or greeting.

sal•vage *n.* The act of rescuing a ship, its cargo, or its crew; property which has been saved. *v.* To save from destruction.

sal•va•tion *n.* The means which effect salvation; deliverance from the effects of sin.

salve *n.* A medicated ointment used to soothe the pain of a burn or wound.

sa•mar•i•tan *n.* A person who is ready to help others in need.

same *adj.* Identical; exactly alike; similar; not changing. *pron.* The very same one or thing.

sam•ple *n.* A portion which represents the whole. *v.* To try a little. **sampler** *n.*

sam•pling *n.* A small section, part, or portion collected as a sample or analysis.

sanc•ti•fy *v.* To make holy.

sanc•tu•ar•y *n.* A sacred, holy place, as the part of a church, where services are held; a safe place; a refuge.

sand *n.* Fine grains of disintegrated rock found in deserts and on beaches. *v.* To smooth or polish with sandpaper.

san•dal *n.* A shoe fastened to the foot by straps attached to the sole.

sand•bag *n.* A sand-filled bag.

sand•bar *n.* A sand ridge which has been built by currents of the water.

sand•pa•per *n.* A type of paper covered on one side with sand used for the purpose of smoothing rough edges.

sand•wich *n.* Two or more slices of bread between which a filling, such as cheese or meat, is placed.

sand•y *adj.* Containing or consisting of sand.

sane *adj.* Having a healthy, sound mind; showing good judgment. **sanity** *n.*

san•i•tar•y *adj.* Free from bacteria or filth which endanger health.

san•i•ta•tion *n.* The process of making something sanitary.

san•i•tize *v.* To make sanitary; to make clean or free of germs.

sank *v.* Past tense of *sink*.

sap *n.* The liquid which flows or circulates through plants and trees. *v.* To weaken or wear away gradually.

sar•casm *n.* An insulting or mocking statement or remark.

sar•dine *n.* A small edible fish of the herring family, often canned in oil.

sash *n.* A band worn over the shoulder or around the waist.

sat•el•lite *n.* A natural or man-made object which orbits a celestial body.

sat•in *n.* A smooth, shiny fabric made of silk, nylon, or rayon, having a glossy face and dull back.

sat•ire *n.* The use of mockery, sarcasm, or humor in a literary work to ridicule or attack human vice.

sat•is•fac•tion *n.* Anything which brings about a happy feeling; the fulfillment of a need, appetite, or desire; a source of gratification.

sat•is•fy *v.* To fulfill; to give assurance to.

sat•u•rate *v.* To make completely wet; to soak or load to capacity.

sauce *n.* A liquid or dressing served as an accompaniment to food.

sau•cer *n.* A small shallow dish for holding a cup.

sau•na *n.* A steam bath in which one is subjected to heat produced by water poured over heated rocks.

sau•sage *n.* Chopped meat, usually pork, highly seasoned, stuffed into a casing and cooked.

save *v.* To rescue from danger, loss, or harm; to prevent loss or waste; to keep for another time in the future; to be delivered from sin.

sa•vor *n.* The taste or smell of something. *v.* To have a particular smell; to enjoy.

saw *n.* A tool with a sharp metal blade edged with teeth-like points for cutting. *v.* Past tense of see; to cut with a saw.

sax•o•phone *n.* A brass wind instrument having finger keys and a reed mouthpiece.

say *v.* To speak aloud; to express oneself in words; to indicate; to show. *n.* The chance to speak; the right to make a decision.

scab *n.* The stiff, crusty covering which forms over a healing wound.

scaf•fold *n.* A temporary support of metal or wood erected for workers who are building or working on a large structure

scaf•fold•ing *n.* The system of scaffolds.

scald *v.* To burn with steam or a hot liquid; to heat a liquid to a temperature just under boiling.

scale *n.* A flat plate which covers certain animals, especially fish and reptiles; a device for weighing; a series of marks indicating the relationship between a map or model and the actual dimensions.

sca•lene *adj.* Having three sides not equal in their lengths.

scalp *n.* The skin which covers the top of the human head where hair normally grows. *v.* To remove the scalp from.

scal•pel *n.* A small, straight knife with a narrow, pointed blade, used in surgery.

scamp•er *v.* To run playfully about.

scan *v.* To examine all parts closely; to look at quickly; to analyze the rhythm of a poem.

scan•dal *n.* Something which brings disgrace when exposed to the public; gossip.

scan•dal•ous *adj.* Being offensive to morality.

scan•ner *n.* The device for sensing recorded data.

scant *adj.* Not plentiful or abundant; inadequate.

scar *n.* A permanent mark which remains on the skin after a sore has healed.

scarce *adj.* Not common or plentiful.

scare *v.* To become scared or to frighten someone suddenly.

scare•crow *n.* A human figure usually placed in a garden for the purpose of scaring off animals and preventing them from eating what is being grown.

scared *adj.* The state of fear one may be thrown into.

scarf *n.* A wide piece of cloth worn around the head, neck, and shoulders for warmth.

scar•let *n.* A bright or vivid red.

scat•ter *v.* To spread around; to distribute in different directions.

scav•en•ger *n.* An animal, as a vulture, which feeds on decaying or dead animals or plant matter.

scene *n.* A view; the time and place where an event occurs; a public display of temper; a part of a play.

scen•er•y *n.* Printed scenes or other accessories used with a play.

sce•nic *adj.* Pertaining to natural scenery.

scent *n.* A smell; an odor. *v.* To smell; to give something a scent.

sched•ule *n.* A list or written chart which shows the times at which events will happen, including specified deadlines.

scheme *n.* A plan of action; an orderly combination of related parts; a secret plot.

schol•ar *n.* A student with a strong interest in learning.

schol•ar•ly *adj.* Suitable to learned persons.

schol•ar•ship *n.* A grant given to a student to enable them to go to school.

school *n.* A place for teaching and learning; a group of persons devoted to similar principles.

school•ing *n.* The instruction given in school.

school•room *n.* A classroom used for teaching.

school•work *n.* The lessons done in school.

sci•ence *n.* The study and explanation of natural phenomena in an orderly way.

scis•sors *pl. n.* A cutting tool consisting of two blades joined and pivoted so that the edges are close to each other.

scoff *n.* The expression of derision or scorn.

scold *v.* To accuse or reprimand harshly.

scoop *n.* A small, shovel-like tool. *v.* To lift up or out.

scoot *v.* To go suddenly and quickly.

scoot•er *n.* Type of child's foot-operated toy consisting of a board mounted between two wheels.

scope *n.* The range or extent of one's

actions; the space to function or operate in.

scorch *v.* To burn slightly, changing the color and taste of something; to parch with heat. **scorched** *adj.*

score *n.* A numerical record of total points won in a game or other contest; the result of an examination; a grouping of twenty items; a written musical composition which indicates the part to be performed by each person; a groove made with a pointed tool. *v.* To achieve or win; to arrange a musical score for.

score•board *n.* A board used to display the score of a game.

scorn *n.* Contempt; disdain. *v.* To treat with scorn.

scorn•ful *adj.* Being full of scorn.

scor•pi•on *n.* An arachnid having an upright tail tipped with a poisonous sting.

scoun•drel *n.* A villain or a robber.

scour *v.* To clean by rubbing with an abrasive agent; to clean thoroughly.

scout *v.* To observe activities in order to obtain information. *n.* A person whose job is to obtain information; a member of the Boy Scouts or Girl Scouts.

scout•ing *n.* The action of one who scouts.

scowl *v.* To have an angry look; to frown.

scrab•ble *v.* To scratch about frantically, as if searching for something.

scram•ble *v.* To move with panic.

scrap *n.* A small section or piece. *v.* To throw away waste.

scrap•book *n.* A book for collecting various paper items or other flat objects.

scrape *v.* To rub a surface with a sharp object in order to clean.

scratch *v.* To mark or make a slight cut on; to mark with the fingernails. *n.* The mark made by scratching; a harsh, unpleasant sound.

scrawl *n.* To write or draw quickly and often illegibly.

scraw•ny *adj.* Very thin; skinny.

scream *v.* To utter a long, sharp cry, as of fear or pain. *n.* A long piercing cry.

screech *v.* To make a shrill, harsh noise.

screen *n.* A movable object used to keep something from view, to divide, or to decorate; a flat reflecting surface on which a picture is projected. *v.* To keep from view.

screen•ing *n.* A metal mesh that may be used to cover a window.

screw *n.* A metal piece that resembles a nail, having a spiral thread used for fastening things together; a propeller on a ship. *v.* To join by twisting.

screw•driv•er *n.* A type of tool used for turning screws.

scribe *n.* A person whose profession is to copy documents and manuscripts.

script *n.* The written text of the play.

scrip•ture *n.* A sacred writing.

scroll *n.* A roll of parchment or similar material used in place of paper.

scrooge *n.* A person who is miserly.

scrub *v.* To clean something by rubbing. *slang* To cancel.

scruff *n.* The region on the back of the neck.

scru•ti•nize *v.* To look at or to examine something very carefully.

scuff *v.* To drag or scrape the feet while walking. *n.* A rough spot.

scuf•fle *v.* To struggle in a confused manner.

sculpt *v.* To carve; to make a sculpture.

sculp•tor *n.* A person who creates statues from clay, marble, or other material.

sculp•ture *n.* The art of processing a hard or soft material into another form, such as a statue; the result of this act.

scum *n.* A thin layer of waste matter floating on top of a liquid.

sea *n.* The body of salt water which covers most of the earth; a large body of salt water.

sea•coast *n.* Land that borders the sea.

seal *n.* A device having a raised emblem, displaying word or symbol, used to certify a signature or the authenticity of a document; a tight closure which secures; a large aquatic mammal with a sleek body and large flippers; the fur or pelt of a seal.

sea lev•el *n.* The level of the sea's surface, used as a standard reference point in measuring the height of land or the depth of the sea.

seam *n.* The line formed at the joint of two pieces of material.

sear *v.* To wither or dry up; to shrivel; to burn or scorch.

search *v.* To look over carefully; to find something; to probe. **searcher** *n.*

sea•son *n.* One of the four parts of the year: spring, summer, fall or autumn, and winter; a time marked by particular activities or celebrations. *v.* To add flavorings or spices; to add interest or enjoyment.

seat *n.* A place or spot, as a chair, stool, or bench, on which to sit; the part of the body used for sitting; the buttocks.

se•clude *v.* To isolate; to keep apart.

sec•ond *n.* A unit of time equal to 1/60 of a minute; a very short period of time; an object which does not meet first class standards.

sec•on•dar•y *adj.* Not being first in importance; inferior; pertaining to a secondary school; high school.

se•cret *n.* Knowledge kept from others; a mystery.

sec•re•tar•y *n.* A person hired to write and keep records for an executive or an organization; the head of a government department. **secretarial** *adj.*

sec•tion *n.* A part or division of something; a separate part. *v.* To divide or separate into sections.

se•cure *adj.* Safe and free from doubt or fear; sturdy or strong; not likely to fail. *v.* To tie down, fasten, lock, or otherwise protect from risk or harm; to ensure.

se•cu•ri•ty *n.* The state of being safe and free from danger or risk; protection; an object given to assure the fulfillment of an obligation.

see *v.* To have the power of sight; to understand; to experience; to imagine; to predict.

seed *n.* A fertilized plant ovule with an embryo, capable of producing an offspring. *v.* To plant seeds; to remove the seeds from.

seek *v.* To search for; to try to reach; to attempt.

seem *v.* To appear to be; to have the look of.

see•saw *n.* A board supported in the center which allows children to alternate being up and down.

seg•ment *n.* Any of the parts into which a thing is divided.

sel•dom *adv.* Not often.

se•lect *v.* To choose from a large group; to make a choice.

self *n.* The complete and essential being of a person; personal interest, advantage or welfare. **selves** *pl.*

sell *v.* To exchange a product or service for money; to offer for sale.

se•mes•ter *n.* One of two periods of time in which a school year is divided.

sem•i•co•lon *n.* A punctuation mark, used to separate clauses, having a degree of separation stronger than a comma but less than a period.

send *v.* To cause something to be conveyed from one place to another; to dispatch.

sen•ior *adj.* Of higher office or rank; referring to the last year of high school or college. *n.* One who is older or of higher rank.

sense *n.* Sensation; feeling; the physical ability which allows a person to be aware of things around him; the five senses: taste, smell, touch, sight, and hearing. *v.* To feel through the senses; to have a feeling about.

sen•tence *n.* A series of words arranged to express a complete thought; a prison term for a person, decided by a judge or jury. *v.* To set the terms of punishment.

sep•a•rate *v.* To divide or keep apart by placing a barrier between; to go in different directions; to set apart from others. *adj.* Single; individual.

se•ri•ous *adj.* Sober; grave; not trivial; important.

ser•mon *n.* A message or speech delivered by a clergyman during a religious service.

ser•pent *n.* A snake.

ser•vant *n.* One employed to care for someone or his property.

serve *v.* To take care of; to wait on; to prepare and supply; to complete a term of duty; to act in a certain capacity; to start the play in some sports.

serv•er *n.* In computers, an electronic program or device designed to deliver information as a service to clients.

serv•ice *n.* Help given to others; a religious gathering; the military; a set of dishes or utensils. *v.* To repair; to furnish a service to something or someone.

set *v.* To put or place; to cause to do; to regulate; to adjust; to arrange; to place in a frame or mounting; to go below the horizon; to establish or fix. *n.* A group of things which belong together; a piece of equipment made up of many pieces; a young plant. *adj.* Established; ready.

set•ting *n.* The act of putting something somewhere; the scenery for a show or other production; the place where a novel, play, or other fictional work takes place.

set•tle *v.* To arrange or put in order; to restore calm or tranquillity to; to come to an agreement on something; to resolve a problem or argument; to establish in a new home or business.

sev•er•al *adj.* More than one or two, but not many; separate.

se•vere *adj.* Strict; stern; hard; not fancy; extremely painful; intense.

sew *v.* To fasten or fix; to make stitches with thread and needle.

sew•age *n.* The solid waste material carried away by a sewer.

sew•er *n.* A conduit or drain pipe used to carry away waste.

sex *n.* One of two divisions, male and female, into which most living things are grouped; sexual intercourse.

shab•by *adj.* Worn-out; ragged.

shack *n.* A small, poorly built building.

shade *n.* A shadow that will gather with the coming of darkness; a comparative darkness due to the interception of the rays of the sun by an object. **shady** *adj.*

shad•ow *n.* An area from which light is blocked; a shaded area. *v.* To cast or throw a shadow on.

shaft *n.* A long, narrow part of something; a beam or ray of light; a long, narrow underground passage; a tunnel; a vertical opening in a building for an elevator.

shag•gy *adj.* Covered with long, matted, or coarse hair.

shake *v.* To move or to cause a back and forth or up and down motion; to tremble; to clasp hands with another, as to welcome or say farewell; to upset or disturb.

shall *v.* *Will* in the first person future tense, used with the pronouns *I* or *we* to express future tense; with other nouns or pronouns to indicate promise, determination, or a command.

shal•low *adj.* Not deep; lacking intellectual depth.

shame *n.* A painful feeling of embarrassment or disgrace brought on by doing something wrong; dishonor; disgrace; a disappointment.

shape *n.* The outline or configuration of something; the condition of something; the finished form in which something may appear. *v.* To cause to take a particular form.

shape•less *adj.* Having no real or definite shape.

share *n.* A part or portion given to or by one person; one of equal parts, as the capital stock in a corporation.

share•ware *n.* In computers, software distributed without charge on a trial basis, in expectation of fair payment to the author by eventual users.

shark *n.* A large marine fish which eats other fish and is dangerous to man; a greedy, crafty, person.

sharp *adj.* Having a thin edge or a fine point; capable of piercing or cutting; clever; quick-witted; intense; painful.

sharp•en *v.* To make something sharp.

shat•ter *v.* To burst suddenly into pieces.

shave *v.* To remove a thin layer; to cut body hair, as the beard, by using a razor; to come close to.

she *pron.* A female previously indicated by name.

shed *v.* To pour out or cause to pour; to throw off without penetrating; to cast off or leave behind. *n.* A small building for shelter or storage.

sheep *n.* A cud-chewing thick-fleeced mammal, domesticated for meat and wool; a meek or timid person. **sheep** *pl.*

sheer *adj.* Very thin; almost transparent; complete; absolute; very steep, almost perpendicular.

sheet *n.* A large piece of cloth for covering a bed; a single piece of paper; a continuous, thin piece of anything.

shelf *n.* A flat piece of wood, metal, plastic, or other rigid material attached to a wall or within another structure, used to hold or store things. **shelves** *pl.*

shell *n.* The hard outer covering of certain organisms; something light and hollow which resembles a shell; the framework of a building under construction; a case containing explosives fired from a gun.

shel•ter *n.* Something which gives protection or cover. *v.* To give protection.

shep•herd *n.* A person who takes care of a flock of sheep; a person who takes care of others.

sher•iff *n.* A high ranking law-enforcement officer.

shield *n.* A piece of protective metal or wood held in front of the body; anything which serves to conceal or protect; a badge or emblem.

shift *n.* A group of people who work together; a woman's loose-fitting dress. *v.* To change direction or place; to change or move the gears in an automobile.

shine *v.* To give off light; to direct light; to make bright or glossy; to polish shoes. *n.* Brightness.

shin•er *n.* A black eye.

shin•gle *n.* A thin piece of material, as asbestos, used to cover a roof or side of a house. *v.* To apply shingles to.

ship *n.* A large vessel for deep-water travel or transport. *v.* To send or transport.

ship•ment *n.* The process of shipping goods from one port to another.

ship•wreck *n.* The loss of a ship; destruction; ruin.

shirt *n.* A garment worn on the upper part of the body.

shiv•er *v.* To tremble or shake with excitement or chill.

shock *n.* A sudden blow or violent impact; an unexpected, sudden upset of mental or emotional balance; a serious weakening of the body caused by the loss of blood pressure or sudden injury. *v.* To strike with great surprise, disgust, or outrage; to give an electric shock.

shoe *n.* An outer cover for a foot; the part of a brake which presses against the drum or wheel to slow or stop the motion. *v.* To put on shoes.

shoe•lace *n.* A string used to fasten a shoe.

shoot *v.* To kill or wound with a missile, as a bullet, fired from a weapon; to discharge or throw rapidly; to push forward or begin to grow by germinating.

shop *n.* A small business or small retail store; a place where certain goods are produced. *v.* To visit a store in order to examine or buy things.

shore *n.* The land bordering a body of water.

shore•line *n.* A line or location where a body of water and the shore meet.

short *adj.* Having little height or length; less than normal in distance, time, or other qualities; less than the needed amount.

short•age *n.* A lack in the amount needed.

short•cut *n.* A type of route more direct than the one usually taken.

shorts *n.* Underpants or outer-pants which end at the knee or above.

shot *n.* The discharging of a gun, rocket, or other device; an attempt; a try; an injection; a photograph.

should *v.* Past tense of *shall*, used to express obligation, duty, or expectation.

shoul•der *n.* The part of the body located between the neck and upper arm; the side of the road. *v.* To use the shoulder to push or carry something; to take upon oneself.

should•n't *contr.* Should not.

shout *v.* To yell. *n.* A loud cry.

shove *v.* To push something or someone in a manner that may be rough.

shov•el *n.* A tool with a long handle and a scoop, used for picking up material or for digging. *v.* To move, dig, or scoop up with a shovel; to push or move large amounts rapidly.

show *v.* To put within sight; to point out; to explain; to put on display. *n.* A display; a movie, play or similar entertainment.

show•er *n.* A short period of rain; a party with gifts given in honor of someone; a bath with water spraying down on the bather. *v.* To take a shower; to be extremely generous.

shred *n.* A narrow strip or torn fragment; a small amount *v.* To rip, tear, or cut into shreds.

shrink *v.* To make or become less or smaller; to pull back from; to flinch.

shrub *n.* A woody plant which grows close to the ground and has several stems beginning at its base.

shrug *v.* To raise the shoulders briefly to indicate indifference.

shud•der *v.* To tremble uncontrollably, as from fear.

shuf•fle *v.* To drag or slide the feet; to mix together in a haphazard fashion; to rearrange or change the order of cards.

shut *v.* To move a door, drawer, or other object to close an opening; to block an entrance; to lock up; to cease or halt operations.

shut•tle *n.* A device used to move thread in weaving; a vehicle, as a train or plane, which travels back and forth from one location to another.

shy *adj.* Bashful; timid; easily frightened. *v.* To move suddenly from fear.

sib•ling *n.* One of two or more children from the same parents.

sick *adj.* In poor health; ill; nauseated.

sick•le *n.* A tool with a curved blade attached to a handle, used for cutting grass or grain.

sick•ly *adj.* Somewhat unwell.

side *n.* A surface between the front and back or top and bottom of an object; either surface of a flat object; an opinion or point of view the opposite of another. *v.* To take a stand and support the opinion of a particular side.

side•walk *n.* A type of paved walk used by pedestrians at the side of the street.

siege *n.* The action of surrounding a town or port in order to capture it; a prolonged sickness.

sift *v.* To separate coarse particles from small or fine ones by passing through a sieve.

sigh *v.* To exhale a long, deep breath, usually when tired or sad.

sight *n.* The ability to see with the eyes; the range or distance one can see; a view; a device on a firearm used to guide the aim.

sign *n.* A piece of paper, wood, metal, etc., with information written on it; a gesture that tells or means something. *v.* To write one's name on.

sig•nal *n.* A sign which gives a warning; the image or sound sent by television or radio.

sig•na•ture *n.* The name of a person, written by that person; a distinctive mark which indicates identity.

sig•ni•fy *v.* To express or make known by a sign; to indicate. **significant** *adj.*

si•lence *n.* The state or quality of being silent; quiet. *v.* To make quiet.

si•lent *adj.* Making no sound; not speaking; mute; unable to speak.

silk *n.* A soft, thread-like fiber spun by silkworms; thread or fabric made from silk.

sil•ly *adj.* Foolish; lacking good sense, seriousness, or substance.

si•lo *n.* A tall, cylindrical structure for storing food for farm animals; an underground shelter for guided missiles.

silt *n.* A deposit of soil and sediment that may have been caused by a river.

silver

sil•ver *n.* A soft, white metallic element used in tableware, jewelry, and coins, symbolized by *Ag. adj.* Of the color silver.

sil•ver•smith *n.* A person who makes goods and articles out of silver.

sim•i•lar *adj.* Almost the same, but not identical.

sim•i•le *n.* A part of speech used for the purpose of comparing two things often unalike.

sim•mer *v.* To cook just below boiling; to be near the point of breaking, as with emotion.

sim•ple *adj.* Easy to do or understand; not complicated; ordinary; not showy; lacking intelligence or education.

sim•plic•i•ty *n.* The state of being easy to understand; naturalness; sincerity.

sim•pli•fy *v.* To make easy or simple. **simplification** *n.*

si•mul•ta•ne•ous *adj.* Occurring at exactly the same time.

sin *n.* The breaking of a religious law or a law of God. *v.* To do something morally wrong.

since *adv.* At a time before the present. *prep.* During the time later than; continuously from the time when something occurs.

sin•cere *adj.* Honest; genuine; true.

sin•cer•i•ty *n.* The state of being sincere.

sing *v.* To use the voice to make musical tones; to make a humming or whistling sound.

sin•gle *adj.* Of or referring to only one; separate; individual; unmarried. *n.* A separate, individual person or item; a dollar bill.

sin•gu•lar *adj.* Separate; one; extraordinary; denoting a single unit, thing or person.

sin•is•ter *adj.* Evil or causing evil.

sink *v.* To submerge beneath a surface; to go down slowly; to become less forceful or weaker. *n.* A basin for holding water connected to a drain.

sip *v.* To drink in small amounts.

sir *n.* A respectful term used when addressing a man.

sire *n.* A man who has rank and authority.

si•ren *n.* A whistle which makes a loud wailing noise, as a warning or signal; a seductive woman.

sis•ter *n.* A female having the same parents as another; a woman in membership with others.

sit *v.* To rest the body with the weight on the buttocks; to cover eggs for hatching; to pose for a portrait.

site *n.* A location of planned buildings.

sit•ting *n.* An act of one who sits; a photography session.

sit•ting duck *n.* A defenseless target.

sit•u•a•tion *n.* The way in which something or someone is placed within its surroundings.

size *n.* The measurement or dimensions of something.

siz•zle *v.* To make a hissing sound, as of fat frying.

skate *n.* A device with rollers which attaches to the shoe and allows one to glide over ice or roll over a wooden or cement surface. **skater** *n.*

skat•ing *n.* The action or the art of gliding on skates.

skate•board *n.* A narrow piece of wood with wheels attached.

skel•e•ton *n.* The framework of bones that protects and supports the soft tissues and organs. **skeletal** *adj.*

skep•tic *n.* A person who doubts or questions.

sketch *n.* A rough drawing or outline; a brief literary composition.

sketch•book *n.* A kind of book used for the purpose of sketching things.

skew *v.* To turn or slant. *n.* A slant.

skew•er *n.* A piece of metal used as a pin for the purpose of fastening foods together in order to broil them on a grill.

ski *n.* One of a pair of long, narrow pieces of wood worn on the feet for gliding over snow or water. *v.* To travel on skis. **skis** *pl.*

skid *v.* To slide to the side of the road; to

slide along without rotating.

ski•ing *n.* The sport of jumping and moving on skis.

skill *n.* Ability gained through practice; expertise.

skilled *adj.* To have acquired a skill for something.

skill•ful *adj.* Displaying a skill.

skim *v.* To remove the top layer; to remove floating matter; to read over material quickly; to travel over lightly and quickly.

skin *n.* The tough, outside covering of man and some animals; the outside layer of a vegetable or fruit; the fur or pelt of an animal.

skin•ny *adj.* Lacking a sufficient amount of flesh on the body, making one look thin.

skip *v.* To move in light jumps or leaps; to go from one place to another, missing what is between.

skirt *n.* A piece of clothing that extends down from the waist. *v.* To extend along the boundary; to avoid the issue.

ski-run *n.* The trail used for skiing.

skit *n.* A type of humorous story.

skull *n.* The bony part of the skeleton which protects the brain.

skunk *n.* A black mammal with white streaks down its back, which sprays an unpleasant smelling liquid when annoyed or frightened.

sky *n.* The upper atmosphere above the earth; the celestial regions. **skies** *pl.*

sky•light *n.* A large window in the ceiling of a building.

sky•line *n.* The outline of a building or other very large object against the sky.

sky•scrap•er *n.* A type of building which is very tall and therefore seems to scrape the sky.

slab *n.* A thick piece or slice.

slack *adj.* Not taut or tense; sluggish; lacking in strength. *v.* To make slack. *n.* A part of something which hangs loose.

slack•er *n.* One who shirks an obligation.

slacks *n.* Long pants or trousers.

slain *v.* Past perfect tense of *slay*.

slam *v.* To shut with force; to strike with a loud impact. *n.* A loud noise produced by an impact.

slang *n.* Informal language that contains made-up words or common words used in a different or uncommon way.

slant *v.* To lie in an oblique position; to slope; to report on something giving only one viewpoint. *n.* An incline or slope.

slap *n.* A sharp blow with an open hand.

slash *v.* To cut with a fast sweeping stroke; to reduce or limit greatly. *n.* A long cut.

slate *n.* A fine grained rock that splits into thin layers, often used as a writing surface or roofing material.

slaugh•ter *v.* To kill livestock for food; to kill in great numbers.

slave *n.* A person held against his will and made to work for another.

slay *v.* To kill or to destroy something in a violent manner.

sled *n.* A vehicle with runners, used to travel on snow or ice.

sleek *adj.* Smooth and shiny; neat and trim.

sleep *n.* A natural state of rest for the mind and body. *v.* To rest in sleep. **sleepy** *adj.*

sleep•walk•er *n.* A person who is able to walk while still asleep.

sleet *n.* Rain, partially frozen.

sleeve *n.* The part of a garment which covers the arm; a case for something.

sleigh *n.* A vehicle on runners usually pulled over ice and snow by horses.

sleigh bell *n.* A type of bell attached to a sleigh.

slen•der *adj.* Slim; inadequate in amount.

slept *v.* Past tense of *sleep*.

slice *n.* A thin cut; a portion or share; in golf, a ball in flight that curves off to the right of its target. *v.* To cut into slices.

slick *adj.* Smooth and slippery; quick; clever; attractive for the present time but without quality or depth. *n.* Water with a thin layer of oil floating on top.

slide *v.* To move smoothly across a surface without losing contact. *n.* The act of sliding; a slanted smooth surface usually found on playgrounds; a transparent picture which can be projected on a screen; a small glass plate for examining specimens under a microscope.

slight *adj.* Minor in degree; unimportant. *v.* To ignore.

slim *adj.* Slender; meager; not much.

slime *n.* A wet, slippery substance.

sling *n.* A piece of material, as leather, or a strap which secures something; a piece of fabric worn around the neck used to support an injured hand or arm; a weapon made of a strap, used to throw a stone.

sling•shot *n.* A type of v-shaped device which has an elastic band and is used to propel objects such as rocks through the air.

slip *v.* To move in a smooth, quiet way; to fail or lose one's balance. *n.* The action of slipping; the place between two piers used for docking a boat; a woman's undergarment; a small piece of paper; a portion of a plant used for grafting.

slip•per•y *adj.* To cause something to slip.

slit *v.* To cut a slit into something. *n.* A narrow opening or cut into something.

slith•er *v.* To slide or slip in an indirect manner; to move like a snake.

sliv•er *n.* A thin, narrow piece of something that has been broken off.

slob *n.* One who is slovenly.

slob•ber *v.* To dribble from the mouth.

slo•gan *n.* A phrase used to express the aims of a cause.

slop *n.* A tasteless liquid food.

slope *v.* To slant upward or downward. *n.* An upward or downward incline.

slop•py *adj.* Wet, muddy, or slippery, as in weather conditions; careless, unkempt, or disheveled in appearance.

slot *n.* A narrow, thin groove or opening.

sloth *n.* Laziness; a slow mammal found in South America.

slov•en•ly *adj.* Untidy, as in one's personal appearance.

slow *adj.* Moving at a low rate of speed; requiring more time than usual; not lively; sluggish; not interesting. *adv.* At less speed; in a slow manner; slowly.

slug *n.* A slow animal related to the snail; a

bullet or a lump of metal. *v.* To strike forcefully with the fist or a heavy object.

slug•gish *adj.* Slow to respond to a treatment or to a stimulation.

slum *n.* A crowded urban neighborhood marked by poverty.

slum•ber *v.* To sleep; to doze.

slump *v.* To fall or sink suddenly.

slush *n.* Melting snow; snow that is partially melted.

sly *adj.* Cunning; clever; sneaky.

smack *v.* To slap; to press and open the lips with a sharp noise. *n.* The act or noise of slapping something.

small *adj.* Little in size, quantity, or extent; unimportant.

smart *adj.* Intelligent; clever.

smash *v.* To break into small pieces; to move forward violently, as to shatter; to ruin. *n.* The act or sound of crashing. *adj.* Outstanding.

smear *v.* To spread or cover with a sticky, oily, or moist substance.

smell *v.* To notice an odor by means of the olfactory sense organs. *n.* An odor; the ability to perceive an odor; the scent of something. **smelly** *adj.*

smile *n.* A grin; a facial expression in which the corners of the mouth turn upward, indicating pleasure.

smirk *v.* To smile in a conceited way.

smith *n.* One who repairs or shapes metal.

smock *n.* A loose-fitting garment worn to protect one's clothes while working.

smog *n.* A mixture of smoke and fog.

smoke *n.* A cloud of vapor released into the air when something is burning. *v.* To preserve or flavor meat by exposing it to smoke.

smooth *adj.* Not irregular; flat; without lumps, as in gravy; without obstructions or impediments. *adv.* Evenly. *v.* To make less difficult; to remove obstructions; to remove wrinkles.

smoth•er *v.* To fail to receive enough oxygen to survive; to conceal; to be overly protective.

smudge *v.* To soil by smearing with dirt. *n.* A dirty mark or smear.

smug *adj.* Complacent with oneself, self-satisfied.

smug•gle *v.* To import or export goods illegally without paying duty fees.

smug•ly *adv.* Done in a smug manner.

snack *n.* A small amount of food taken between meals.

snag *n.* A stump or part of a tree partly hidden under the surface of water; a pull in a piece of fabric. *v.* To tear on a rough place.

snail *n.* A type of gastropod mollusk that can live in a spiral shell.

snake *n.* Any of a large variety of scaly reptiles, having a long tapering body.

snap *v.* To break suddenly with a sharp, quick sound; to fly off under tension; to snatch something suddenly.

snap•shot *n.* A type of photograph made by an amateur with a small camera.

snare *n.* Anything that entangles or entraps; a trap with a noose, used to catch small animals.

snarl *v.* To speak in an angry way; to cause confusion; to tangle or be tangled. *n.* A growl.

snatch *v.* To seize or grasp something suddenly. *n.* The act of taking something; a brief or small part.

sneak *v.* To act or move in a quiet, sly way. *n.* A person who acts in a secret, underhanded way.

sneak•y *adj.* Marked by shiftiness.

sneer *v.* To express scorn by the look on one's face.

sneeze *v.* To expel air from the nose suddenly and without control.

sniff *v.* To inhale through the nose in short breaths.

snip *v.* To cut off in small pieces and with quick strokes. *n.* A small piece.

snob *n.* A person who considers himself better than anyone else and who looks down on those he sees as his inferiors.

snooze *v.* To sleep for a short time.

snore *v.* To breathe with a harsh noise while sleeping.

snort *v.* To force air through the nostrils with a loud, harsh noise.

snout *n.* The nose of an animal.

snow *n.* Vapor that forms crystals in cold air and falls to the ground in white flakes.

snow•ball *n.* A mass of snow usually round in shape and pressed together.

snow•man *n.* A figure made out of snow usually resembling a man or woman.

snow•y *adj.* Covered by snow.

snub *v.* To treat with contempt or in an unfriendly way. **snub** *n.*

snug *adj.* Warm, pleasant, comfortable.

snug•gle *v.* To curl up to someone in an affectionate manner.

so *adv.* To a degree or extent as a result; likewise; also; indeed. *conj.* In order that; therefore.

soak *v.* To be thoroughly wet; to penetrate.

soap *n.* A cleansing agent made of an alkali and fat, and used for washing. *v.* To rub with soap.

soap•box *n.* A platform used by an informal orator.

soar *v.* To glide or fly high without any noticeable movement; to rise higher than usual.

sob *v.* To weep with short, quick gasps.

so•ber *adj.* Not drunk or intoxicated; serious; solemn; quiet.

soc•cer *n.* A game in which two teams of eleven men each try to kick a ball into the opposing team's goal.

so•cia•ble *adj.* Capable of friendly social relations; enjoying the company of others.

so•cial *adj.* Having to do with people living in groups; enjoying friendly companionship with others. *n.* An informal party or gathering.

so•cial•ism *n.* A system in which people as a whole, and not individuals, control and own all property.

so•ci•e•ty *n.* People working together for a common purpose; companionship.

so•ci•ol•o•gy *n.* The study of society and the development of human society. **soci-ologic, sociological** *adj.*

sock *n.* A short covering for the foot, ankle, and lower part of the leg; a hard blow.

sock•et *n.* A hollow opening into which something is fitted.

so•da *n.* Sodium carbonate; a flavored, carbonated drink.

so•fa *n.* An upholstered couch with arms and a back.

soft *adj.* Not stiff or hard; not glaring or harsh; mild or pleasant; gentle in sound.

soft•ball *n.* A game played on a smaller diamond than baseball, with a larger, softer ball.

soft•ware *n.* In computer science, data, as routines, programs and languages, essential to the operation of computers.

sog•gy *adj.* Saturated with a liquid or moisture.

sol•ace *n.* Comfort in a time of trouble, grief, or misfortune. **solacer** *n.*

so•lar *adj.* Relating to or connected with the sun; utilizing the sun for power or light; measured by the earth's movement around the sun.

sol•dier *n.* An enlisted person who serves in the military.

sole *n.* The bottom of a foot or shoe; single, the only one; a flat fish.

sol•emn *adj.* Very serious; characterized by dignity; sacred.

so•lic•it *v.* To try to obtain; to ask earnestly; to beg or entice a person persistently. **solicitation** *n.*

sol•id *adj.* Having a definite firm shape and volume; having no crevices; not hollow; having height, weight and length; without interruption; reliable, sound and upstanding. *n.* A solid substance.

sol•i•taire *n.* A single gemstone set by itself; a card game played by one person.

sol•i•tude *n.* The act of being alone or secluded; isolation.

so•lo *n.* A musical composition written for and performed by one single person or played by one instrument.

sol•u•ble *adj.* Capable of being dissolved; able to be solved or explained.

solve *v.* To find the answer to.

som•ber *adj.* Dark; gloomy; melancholy.

some *adj.* Being an indefinite number or quantity; unspecified. *pron.* An undetermined or indefinite quantity. *adv.* An approximate degree.

some•bod•y *n.* A person unknown.

some•day *adv.* At an unspecified future time.

some•how *adv.* In a way.

som•er•sault *n.* The act or acrobatic stunt in which one rolls the body in a complete circle, with heels over head.

son *n.* The male child of a man or woman.

song *n.* A piece of poetry put to music; the act or sound of singing.

son•net *n.* A poem made up of fourteen lines.

soon *adv.* In a short time; in the near future; quickly.

soot *n.* The black powder generated by incomplete combustion of a fuel.

soothe *v.* To make comfortable; to calm.

soph•o•more *n.* A second year college or high school student.

so•pran•o *n.* The highest female singing voice.

sor•cer•y *n.* The use of supernatural powers.

sore *adj.* Tender or painful to the touch, as an injured part of the body; severe or extreme. *n.* A place on the body which has been bruised, inflamed, or injured in some way. **sorely** *adv.*

so•ror•i•ty *n.* A social organization for women.

sor•row *n.* Anguish; mental suffering; an expression of grief. **sorrowful** *adj.,* **sorrowfully** *adv.*

sor•ry *adj.* Feeling or showing sympathy or regret; worthless.

sort *n.* A collection of things having common attributes or similar qualities. *v.* To arrange according to class, kind, or size.

soul *n.* The spirit in man believed to be separate from the body and the source of a person's emotional, spiritual, and moral nature.

sound *n.* A sensation received by the ears from air, water, noise, and other sources. *v.* To make a sound; to make noise. *adj.*

Free from flaw, injury, disease, or damage.

soup *n.* A liquid food made by boiling meat and/or vegetables, in water.

sour *adj.* Sharp to the taste; acid; unpleasant; disagreeable. *v.* To become sour or spoiled. **sourly** *adv.*

source *n.* Any point of origin or beginning; the beginning or place of origin of a stream or river.

south *n.* The direction opposite of north. *adv.* To or towards the south.

sou·ve·nir *n.* An item kept as a remembrance of something or someplace.

sov·er·eign *n.* A ruler with supreme power; a monarch. *adj.* Possessing supreme jurisdiction or authority.

sow *v.* To scatter or throw seeds on the ground for growth. *n.* A female pig.

space *n.* The unlimited area in all directions in which events occur and have relative direction; an interval of time; the area beyond the earth's atmosphere.

spade *n.* A tool with a flat blade used for digging, heavier than a shovel.

spam *n.* In computers, unwanted commercial messages sent electronically to a large mailing list without solicitation. *v.* To engage in such practice.

span *n.* The extent of space from the end of the thumb to the end of the little finger of a spread hand; the section between two limits or supports. *v.* To extend across.

spank *v.* To strike or slap the buttocks with an open hand as a means of punishment.

spare *v.* To refrain from injuring, harming or destroying; to refrain from using; to do without. *n.* An extra, as a spare tire.

spark *n.* A glowing or incandescent particle, as one released from a piece of burning wood. *v.* To give off sparks.

spar·row *n.* A small bird with grayish or brown plumage.

sparse *adj.* Scant; thinly distributed. **sparsely** *adv.*, **sparsity** *n.*

spasm *n.* An involuntary muscle contraction.

speak *v.* To utter words; to express a thought in words.

speak·er *n.* A person who speaks, usually before an audience.

spear *n.* A weapon with a long shaft and a sharply pointed head. *v.* To strike, pierce, or stab with a spear.

spe·cial·ist *n.* A person who devotes his practice to one particular field.

spe·cial·ize *v.* To focus one's efforts or interests in one field of activity or study.

spec·i·men *n.* A sample; a representative of a particular thing.

spec·ta·cle *n.* A public display of something unusual. *pl.* Eyeglasses.

spec·u·late *v.* To reflect and think deeply; to take a chance on a business venture in hopes of making a large profit.

speech *n.* The ability, manner, or act of speaking; a talk before the public.

speed *n.* Rate of action or movement; quickness; rapid motion.

spell *v.* To say out loud or write in proper order the letters which make up a word; to relieve. *n.* The state of being controlled by magic; a short period of time; a time or period of illness; an attack.

spend *v.* To give out; to use up; to pay; to exhaust.

sphere *n.* A round object with all points the same distance from a given point; globe, ball, or other rounded object. **spherical** *adj.* **spherically** *adv.*

spice *n.* A pungently aromatic plant used as flavoring in food, such as nutmeg, cinnamon, or pepper. **spice** *v.*, **spicy** *adj.*

spi·der *n.* An eight-legged arachnid with a body divided into two parts, spinning webs as a means of capturing and holding its prey.

spike *n.* A large, thick nail; a pointed metal piece on the sole of a shoe to prevent slipping, as on a sports shoe.

spill *v.* To allow or cause something to flow or run out of something.

spin *v.* To draw out fibers and twist into thread; to run something around and around; to revolve.

spine *n.* The spinal column; the backbone; the back of a bound book.

spir·it *n.* The vital essence of man, considered divine in origin; the part of a human being characterized by personality and self-consciousness; the mind; the Holy Ghost; the creative power of God; a supernatural being, as a ghost or angel.

spir·i·tu·al *adj.* Of, like, or pertaining to the nature of spirit; relating to religion; sacred. *n.* A religious song originating among the Negroes of the southern United States.

spite *n.* Hatred or malicious bitterness; a grudge. **spiteful** *adj.*, **spitefully** *adv.*

splash *v.* To spatter a liquid; to wet or soil with liquid; to make a splash. **splash** *n.*, **splashy** *adj.*

splice *v.* To join together by wearing, overlapping, and binding the ends. **splice** *n.*

spoil *v.* To destroy the value, quality, or usefulness; to overindulge as to harm the character.

spoke *n.* One of the rods that serve to connect and support the rim of a wheel. *v.* Past tense of *speak.*

sponge *n.* Any of a number of marine creatures with a soft, porous skeleton which soaks up liquid. *v.* To clean with a sponge.

spon·ta·ne·ous *adj.* Done from one's own impulse without apparent cause.

spoon *n.* An eating or cooking utensil; a shiny metallic fishing lure.

sport *n.* An interesting diversion; a particular game or physical activity with set rules; a person who leads a fast life.

sports·man·ship *n.* Fair play; the ability to win or lose graciously.

spot *n.* A small area that differs in size, portion, or color.

spot·light *n.* A powerful light thrown directly at one area.

spouse *n.* One's husband or wife.

spout *v.* To pour out forcibly, as under pressure; to cause to shoot forth; to orate pompously; to declaim. **spouter** *n.*

sprain *n.* A wrenching or twisting of a muscle or joint.

sprawl *v.* To sit or lie in an ungraceful manner; to develop haphazardly. **sprawl**, **sprawler** *n.*

spray *n.* A liquid dispersed in a fine mist or droplets. **sprayer** *n.*

spread *v.* To unfold or open fully; to apply or distribute over an area; to force apart; to extend or expand.

spree *n.* An excessive indulgence in an activity; a binge.

spright·ly *adj.* Vivacious, lively.

sprint *n.* A short, fast race. **sprinter** *n.*

sprung *v.* Past perfect tense of *spring.*

spry *adj.* Quick; brisk; energetic.

spy *n.* A secret agent who obtains information; one who watches other people secretly.

squab·ble *v.* To engage in a petty argument.

squad *n.* A small group organized to perform a specific job.

squal·id *adj.* Marked by degradation, poverty, or neglect.

squall *v.* To cry out. *n.* A brief but violent wind storm at sea.

squan·der *v.* To spend extravagantly or wastefully.

square *n.* A parallelogram with four equal sides; an implement having a T or L shape used to measure right angles; in math, to multiply a number by itself.

square root *n.* A number which when multiplied by itself gives the given number.

squat *v.* To sit on the heels; to crouch; to settle on a piece of land in order to obtain legal title.

squeak *v.* To utter a sharp, penetrating sound. **squeak** *n.*, **squeaky** *adj.*

squeal *v.* To produce or to make a shrill cry. **squealer** *n.*

squeam·ish *adj.* Easily shocked or nauseated. **squeamishly** *adv.*

squeeze *v.* To press together; to extract by using pressure. *n.* An instance of squeezing for pleasure; a hug.

squint *v.* To view something through partly closed eyes; to close the eyes in this manner. **squint** *n.*

squire *n.* An old-fashioned title for a rural justice of the peace, lawyer, or judge; a man who escorts a woman; a young man who ranks just below a knight. **squire** *v.*

squirm *v.* To twist the body in a wiggling motion.

squir•rel *n.* A rodent with gray or brown fur, having a long bushy tail and dark eyes.

squirt *v.* To eject in a thin stream or jet; to wet with a squirt. *n.* The act of squirting.

squish•y *adj.* Soft and damp.

sta•bi•lize *v.* To make firm; to keep from changing.

sta•ble *n.* A building for lodging and feeding horses or other farm animals. *adj.* Standing firm and resisting change.

stac•ca•to *adj.* Marked by sharp emphasis.

stack *n.* A large pile of straw or hay; any systematic heap or pile; a chimney. *v.* To fix cards so as to cheat.

sta•di•um *n.* A large structure for holding athletic events or other large gatherings.

staff *n.* A pole or rod used for a specific purpose; the people employed to assist in the day-to-day affairs of running a business, organization, or government; a group of people on an executive or advisory board; the horizontal lines on which notes are written. **staff** *v.*, **staffs, staves** *pl.*

stag *n.* The adult male of various animals; a man who attends a social gathering without a woman companion.

stag•ger *v.* To walk unsteadily; to totter.

stag•nant *adj.* Not flowing; standing still; foul from not moving; inactive.

stair *n.* A step or a series of steps.

stair•case *n.* A series or a flight of steps that connect one level to another.

stake *n.* A bet placed on a game of chance; a sharpened piece of wood for driving into the ground. **stake** *v.*

stale *adj.* Having lost freshness; deteriorated; lacking in interest; dull; inactive.

stale•mate *n.* A position in chess when a player cannot move without placing his king in check.

stalk *n.* The main axis of a plant. *v.* To approach in a stealthy manner.

stall *n.* An enclosure in a barn, used as a place to feed and confine animals; a sudden loss of power in an engine; a booth used to display and sell. *v.* To try to put off doing something; to delay.

stal•lion *n.* An uncastrated, fully grown male horse.

stam•i•na *n.* Physical or moral endurance.

stam•mer *v.* To make involuntary halts or repetitions of a sound or syllable while speaking. **stammerer** *n.*

stamp *v.* To put the foot down with force; to imprint or impress with a die, mark, or design. *n.* The act of stamping; the impression or pattern made by a stamp; a postage stamp.

stam•pede *n.* A sudden rush of panic, as of a herd of horses or cattle. *v.* To cause a stampede.

stance *n.* The posture or position of a standing person or animal.

stand *v.* To be placed in or maintain an erect or upright position; to take an upright position; to remain unchanged; to maintain a conviction; to resist. *n.* The act of standing; a device on which something rests; a booth for selling items.

stand•ard *n.* A model which stands for or is accepted as a basis for comparison. **standard** *adj.*

stand•ing *n.* A status, reputation, or achievement; a measure of esteem. *adj.* Unchanging; stationary; not moving.

sta•ple *n.* A principle commodity grown in an area; a major element; a metal fastener designed to hold materials such as cloth or paper. **stapler** *n.*

star *n.* A self-luminous body that is a source of light; any of the celestial bodies that can be seen in the night sky; a symbol having five or six points and resembling a star; a famous celebrity.

starch *n.* Nutrient carbohydrates found in foods such as rice and potatoes. *v.* To stiffen clothing by using starch.

stare *v.* To look with an intent, direct gaze. **stare, starer** *n.*

stark *adj.* Bare; total; complete; forbidding

in appearance.

star·tle *v.* To cause a sudden surprise; to shock. **startle** *n.*

starve *v.* To suffer or die from not having food; to suffer from the need of food, love, or other necessities.

state *n.* A situation, mode, or condition of something; a nation; the governing power or authority of; one of the subdivisions or areas of a federal government. *v.* To make known verbally.

stat·ic *adj.* Not moving. *n.* A random noise heard on a radio.

sta·tion *n.* The place where someone or something is directed to stand; a scheduled stopping place; the place from which radio and television programs are broadcast.

sta·tion·ar·y *adj.* Not movable; unchanging.

sta·tion·er·y *n.* Writing paper and envelopes.

sta·tis·tic *n.* An estimate using an average or mean on the basis of a sample taken; numerical data.

stat·ue *n.* A form sculpted from wood, clay, metal, or stone.

stay *v.* To remain; to pause; to maintain a position; to halt or stop; to postpone or delay an execution. *n.* A short visit.

stead·fast *adj.* Not changing or moving; firm in purpose; true.

stead·y *adj.* Firmly placed, fixed or set; not changing; constant; uninterrupted.

steal *v.* To take another person's property; to move in a sly way; to move secretly.

steam *n.* Water in the form of vapor; the visible mist into which vapor is condensed by cooling. **steamy** *adj.*

steel *n.* A various mixture of iron, carbon, and other elements; a strong material that can be shaped when heated. **steely** *adj.*

stem *n.* The main stalk of a plant; the main part of a word to which prefixes and suffixes may be added. *v.* To stop or retard the progress or flow of something.

step *n.* A single completed movement in walking, dancing, or running; the distance of such a step; the part of a ladder that one places the feet on.

ster·ile *adj.* Free from microorganisms; sanitary; unable to reproduce.

stern *adj.* Inflexible; harsh. *n.* The rear of a boat or ship. **sternly** *adv.*

stew *v.* To cook slowly; to simmer; to boil; to worry. *n.* A dish of stewed meat and potatoes.

stick *n.* A slender piece of wood; a club, rod, or walking stick. *v.* To put a hole in something; to pierce; to cling; to become jammed.

stiff *adj.* Not flexible; not easily bent; awkward.

sti·fle *v.* To suffocate; to cut off; to suppress; to keep back.

still *adj.* Silent; calm; peaceful; until now or another time. **still** *v.,* **stillness** *n.*

stim·u·late *v.* To excite to a heightened activity; to quicken. **stimulation** *n.*

sting *v.* To prick with something sharp; to feel or cause to feel a smarting pain; to cause or feel sharp pain, either physical or mental. *n.* The act of stinging; the injury or pain caused by the stinger of a bee or wasp. **stinger** *n.*

stin·gy *adj.* Not giving freely; cheap.

stink *v.* To give off a foul odor that is highly offensive.

stir *v.* To mix a substance by moving round and round; to agitate or provoke.

stitch *n.* In sewing, a single loop formed by a needle and thread; the section of loop of thread, as in sewing. *v.* To join with a stitch.

stock *n.* A supply of goods kept on hand; animals living on a farm; a share in ownership, as in a company or corporation; the raw material or the base used to make something. *v.* To provide with stock. *adj.* Regular, common, or typical.

stock·ing *n.* A knitted covering for the foot.

stock·y *adj.* Short and plump; built sturdily.

stom·ach *n.* The organ into which food passes from the esophagus; one of the primary organs of digestion. *v.* To tolerate or stand; to put up with.

stone *n.* Rock; compacted earth or mineral matter; a gem or jewel; the seed or pit of certain fruits.

stool *n.* A seat without a backrest and arms; a small version of this on which to rest the feet; a bowel movement.

stoop *v.* To bend the body forward and downward from the waist. *n.* A porch attached to a house.

stop *v.* To cease; to halt; to refrain from moving, operating, or acting; to block or obstruct; to visit for a short time. *n.* A location where a bus, train, or other means of mass transportation may pick up or drop off passengers.

stor•age *n.* The act of storing or keeping; in computers, the part of a computer in which all information is held; the memory.

store *n.* A business offering merchandise for sale; a supply to be used in the future. *v.* To supply; to accumulate.

stork *n.* A large, wading bird.

storm *n.* An atmospheric condition marked by strong winds with rain, sleet, hail, or snow. *v.* To charge or attack with a powerful force. **stormy** *adj.*

sto•ry *n.* A narration of a fictional tale or account; a lie; a level in a building or house.

stout *adj.* Strong; sturdy; substantial; courageous. **stoutly** *adv.*

stove *n.* An apparatus in which oil, electricity, gas, or other fuels are consumed to provide the heat for cooking.

stow *v.* To pack or put away.

strad•dle *v.* To sit or stand with the legs on either side of something; to favor both sides of an issue. **straddler** *n.*

straight *adj.* Being without bends, angles, or curves; upright; erect; honest; undiluted; unmodified. *n.* In poker, a numerical sequence of five cards not of the same suit.

strain *v.* To stretch beyond a proper limit, to injure by putting forth too much effort; to pass through a sieve to separate small particles from larger ones.

strange *adj.* Not previously known or experienced; odd; peculiar; alien.

stran•ger *n.* A person unknown; a newcomer.

stran•gle *v.* To kill by choking.

strap *n.* A long, narrow strip of leather or other material used to secure objects.

strat•e•gy *n.* The skillful planning and managing of an activity.

straw *n.* A stalk of dried, threshed grain; a slender, plastic or paper straw used to suck up a liquid. *adj.* Yellowish brown.

stray *v.* To roam or wander. *n.* A lost or wandering animal or person. **strayer** *n.*

stream *n.* A small body of flowing water; a steady or continuous succession or procession. *v.* To flow in or like a stream.

street *n.* A public thoroughfare in a town or city with buildings on either or both sides.

strength *n.* The quality of being strong; power in general; degree of concentrated potency.

stren•u•ous *adj.* Necessitating or characterized by vigorous effort or exertion. **strenuously** *adv.*

stress *n.* Special significance; an emphasis given to a specific syllable, word, action, or plan; strain or pressure.

stretch *v.* To extend fully; to extend forcibly beyond proper limits; to prolong. *n.* The state or act of stretching.

strick•en *adj.* Suffering, as from an emotion, illness, or trouble.

strict *adj.* Holding to or observing rules exactly; imposing absolute standards. **strictly** *adv.* **strictness** *n.*

stride *v.* To walk with a long step.

strike *v.* To hit with the hand; to ignite, as with a match; to afflict suddenly with a disease; to discover; to conclude or make; to stop working as a protest against something or in favor of rules or demands presented to an employer. **strike** *n.*

string *n.* A strip of thin twine, wire, or catgut used on stringed musical instruments; a series of ads, items, or events.

strip *v.* To take off the outer covering; to divest or pull rank, to remove one's clothes; to rob.

stripe *n.* A streak, band, or strip of a different color or texture; a piece of material or cloth worn on the sleeve of a uniform to indicate rank, award, or service.

stroke *n.* The movement of striking; a sudden action with a powerful effect; a single movement made by the hand or as if by a brush or pen; a sudden interruption of the blood supply to the brain. *v.* To pass the hand over gently.

stroll *v.* To walk in a slow, leisurely way.

strong *adj.* Exerting or possessing physical power; durable; difficult to break. **strongly** *adv.*

struc•ture *n.* A construction made up of a combination of related parts. **structural** *adj.*

strug•gle *v.* To put forth effort against opposition.

stub *n.* A short, projecting part; the short end of something after the main part has been removed or used.

stub•born *adj.* Inflexible; difficult to control, handle, or manage.

stu•dent *n.* A person who studies at a school or college.

stu•di•o *n.* The place of work for an artist, photographer, or other creative person; a place for filming movies.

stud•y *n., pl.* **-ies** The process of applying the mind to acquire knowledge.

stum•ble *v.* To trip and nearly fall over something; to come upon unexpectedly.

stump *n.* The part of a tree which remains after the top is cut down. *v.* To puzzle or be puzzled; to walk heavily; to campaign.

stun *v.* To render senseless by or as if by a blow.

stu•pid *adj.* Slow in apprehension or understanding. **stupidity** *n.*

stur•dy *adj.* Possessing robust strength and health. **sturdily** *adv.*

stut•ter *v.* To speak with involuntary repetitions of sound.

style *n.* A method, manner, or way of performing, speaking, or clothing; elegance, grace, or excellence in performance or appearance. **stylish** *adj.*

sub•ject *n.* The word in a sentence that defines a person or thing; a person who is under the control of another's governing power. *v.* To subdue or gain control over. **subjection** *n.*

sub•ma•rine *adj.* Operating or existing beneath the surface of the sea. *n.* A ship that travels underwater.

sub•merge *v.* To plunge under the surface of the water.

sub•mit *v.* To give into or surrender to another's authority. **submission**.

sub•side *v.* To move to a lower level or sink; to become less intense.

sub•sist *v.* To have continued existence.

sub•stance *n.* Matter or material of which anything consists.

sub•sti•tute *n.* Something or someone that takes the place of another.

sub•tract *v.* To deduct or take away from.

sub•urb *n.* A residential community near a large city. **suburban** *adj.*

sub•way *n.* An underground electrically powered train.

suc•ceed *v.* To accomplish what is attempted; to come next or to follow.

suc•cess *n.* Achievement of something intended or desired; attaining wealth, fame, or prosperity.

suc•ces•sion *n.* The act or process of following in order; sequence; series; the order, sequence or act by which something changes hands.

such *adj.* Of this or that kind or thing; a great degree or extent in quality. *pron.* Of a particular degree or kind; a person or thing of such.

suck *v.* To pull liquid in the mouth by means of a vacuum created by the lips and tongue. *n.* The action of sucking.

suc•tion *n.* The process or act of sucking.

sud•den *adj.* Happening very quickly without warning or notice; sharp; abrupt; marked by haste. **suddenly** *adv.*, **suddenness** *n.*

suede *n.* Leather with a napped finish.

suf·fer *v.* To feel pain or distress; to sustain injury, loss, or damage. **sufferer** *n.*

suf·fi·cient *adj.* As much as is needed or desired. **sufficiency** *n.*, **sufficiently** *adv.*

suf·fix *n.* A form affixed to the end of a word.

suf·fo·cate *v.* To kill by depriving something or someone of oxygen. **suffocation** *n.*

sug·ar *n.* A sweet, water-soluble, crystalline carbohydrate. *slang* A nickname.

sug·gest *v.* To give an idea for action or consideration; to imply, hint or intimate.

sug·ges·tion *n.* The act of suggesting; a slight insinuation; hint.

su·i·cide *n.* The act of taking one's own life. **suicidal** *adj.*

suit *n.* A set of articles, as clothing, to be used or worn together; in cards, one of the four sets: spades, hearts, clubs, and diamonds that make up a deck. *v.* To meet the requirements of; to satisfy.

sulk *v.*, To be sullenly silent.

sul·len *adj.* Ill-humored; melancholy; gloomy; depressing.

sul·try *adj.* Hot and humid.

sum *n.* The result obtained by adding; the whole amount, quantity, or number; summary.

sum·ma·ry *n.* The sum or substance; a statement covering the main points. **summarily** *adv.*

sum·mer *n.* The warmest of the four seasons, following spring and coming before autumn. **summery** *adj.*

sum·mit *n.* The top and highest point, degree, or level.

sum·mons *n.* An order or command to perform a duty; a notice to appear at a certain place.

sun *n.* The star around which other planets of the solar system orbit; the energy, light, and heat emitted by the sun; sunshine.

sun·down *n.* The time of day the sun sets.

sunk·en *adj.* Submerged or deeply depressed in.

su·per *adj.* Exceeding a norm; in excessive intensity or degree; surpassing most others; superior in rank, status or position; excellent.

su·perb *adj.* Of first-rate quality.

su·per·fi·cial *adj.* Pertaining to a surface; concerned only with what is not necessarily real.

su·pe·ri·or *adj.* Of higher rank, grade, or dignity. *n.* A person who surpasses another in rank or excellence. **superiority** *n.*, **superiorly** *adv.*

su·per·nat·u·ral *adj.* Beyond the natural world; pertaining to a divine power. **supernaturally** *adv.*

su·per·sti·tion *n.* A belief founded, despite evidence that it is irrational; a belief, resulting from faith in magic or chance. **superstitious** *adj.*

su·per·vise *v.* To have charge in directing the work of other people. **supervision**, **supervisor** *n.*

sup·per *n.* The evening meal of the day.

sup·ple·ment *n.* A part that compensates for what is lacking.

sup·ply *v.* To provide with what is needed; to make available. **supplier** *n.*

sup·port *v.* To bear or hold the weight of; to tolerate; to give assistance or approval.

sup·pose *v.* To think or assume as true; to consider probable. **supposed** *adj.*, **supposedly** *adv.*

su·preme *adj.* Of the highest authority, rank, or power.

sure *adj.* Firm and sturdy; being impossible to doubt; inevitable; not liable to fail. **surer, surest** *adj.*, **surely** *adv.*

surf *n.* The swell of the sea that breaks upon the shore. *v.* To ride on the crest of a wave; in computers, to browse randomly on an internet system.

sur·face *n.* The exterior or outside boundary of something; outward appearance.

surge *v.* To increase suddenly. *n.* A large swell of water:

sur·geon *n.* A physician who practices surgery.

sur·ger·y *n.* The branch of medicine in

which physical deformity or disease is treated by an operative procedure.

sur·name *n.* A person's family's last name.

sur·pass *v.* To go beyond the limits of; to be greater than. **surpassingly** *adv.*

sur·plus *n.* An amount beyond what is needed.

sur·prise *v.* To come upon unexpectedly or suddenly; to cause to feel amazed or astonished. **surprise, surpriser** *n.*, **surprisingly** *adv.*

sur·ren·der *v.* To give up or yield possession or power. *n.* The act of surrendering.

sur·round *v.* To extend around all edges of something; to enclose or shut in.

sur·vey *v.* To examine in detail; to determine area, boundaries, or position and elevation of a section of the earth's surface. **surveyor** *n.*

sur·vive *v.* To continue to exist; to outlast; to outlive. **surviving** *adj.*, **survival, survivor** *n.*

sus·pect *v.* To have doubt or distrust; to have a suspicion or inkling of someone or something. **suspect** *n.*

sus·pend *v.* To bar from a privilege for a certain time, as a means of punishment; to hang so as to allow free movement.

sus·pense *n.* The feeling of being insecure or undecided, resulting from uncertainty.

sus·pi·cion *n.* The instance of suspecting something wrong without proof. **suspicious** *adj.*, **suspiciously** *adv.*

swal·low *v.* To cause food to pass from the mouth to the stomach; to retract or take back, as words spoken. *n.* The act of swallowing.

swan *n.* A mostly pure white bird having a long neck and heavy body.

swap *v.* To trade something for something in return. **swap** *n.*

swarm *n.* A large number of insects, as bees; a large group of persons or things. **swarm** *v.*, **swarmer** *n.*

swat *v.* To hit with a sharp blow.

sway *v.* To move or swing from right to left or side to side; to exert influence or control.

swear *v.* To make an affirmation under oath. **swearer** *n.*

sweat *v.* To excrete a salty moisture from the pores of the skin; to perspire.

sweat·er *n.* A knitted or crocheted garment with or without sleeves attached.

sweep *v.* To touch very lightly; to remove or clear away with a brush or broom; to move with an even action.

sweet *adj.* Having a sugary, agreeable flavor; arousing pleasant emotions; *n.* A beloved or dear person.

swell *v.* To increase in size or bulk; to grow in volume. *n.* The process, effect, or act of swelling; a continuous wave that is long and billowing. *adj.* Fine; excellent; smart.

swel·ter *v.* To suffer from extreme heat.

swerve *v.* To turn aside from the regular course.

swift *adj.* Moving with great speed; accomplished or occurring quickly. **swiftly** *adv.*, **swiftness** *n.*

swim *v.* To move oneself through water by moving parts of the body.

swin·dle *v.* To cheat out of property or money; to practice fraud. **swindle, swindler** *n.*

swine *n.* A hoofed mammal with a snout, related to pigs and hogs; a low, despicable person. **swinish** *adj.*

swing *v.* To move freely back and forth; to hang or to be suspended. *n.* The act of a swing; a seat that hangs from chains or ropes; in music, jazz played by a larger band and developed by using simple harmonic patterns. **swinger** *n.*

swirl *v.* To move with a whirling, rotating motion. **swirl** *n.*, **swirly** *adj.*

switch *n.* A small, thin, flexible stick, twig or rod; in electronics, a device for opening or closing an electric circuit. *v.* To shift to another train track; to exchange.

sword *n.* A weapon with a long, pointed cutting blade.

syl·la·ble *n.* A word or part of one that consists of a single vocal impulse, usually consisting of one or more vowels or consonants.

syl•la•bus *n.* An outline of a course of study.

sym•bol *n.* Something that stands for or represents something else. **symbolic, symbolical** *adj.*, **symbolically** *adv.*

sym•met•ri•cal *adj.* Involving symmetry. **symmetricalness** *n.*

sym•me•try *n.* Balance in form, size, and position of parts on two sides of an axis.

sym•pa•thet•ic *adj.* Having or showing kindness or sympathy for others. **sympathetically** *adv.*, **sympathize** *v.*

sym•pa•thize *v.* To respond to someone or something with sympathy.

sym•pa•thy *n.* Mutual understanding or affection during a time of sadness or loss.

sym•pho•ny *n.* A large orchestra with wind, percussion and string sections. **symphonic** *adj.*

sym•po•si•um *n.* A gathering or meeting where several specialists give short speeches on a topic or on subjects related.

symp•tom *n.* A sign of change in a body's functions or appearance.

symp•tom•at•ic *adj.* Having the characteristics of a particular disease but arising from something else.

syn•chro•nize *v.* To operate or take place at the same time.

syn•di•cate *n.* An organization set up to carry out business transactions; a company that sells materials for simultaneous publication at a number of different locations. **syndication** *n.*

syn•drome *n.* A set of concurrent symptoms that indicate or characterize a disorder or disease.

syn•o•nym *n.* A word that means the same or nearly the same as another. **synonymous** *adj.*, **synonymy** *n.*

syn•op•sis *n.* A shortened statement or narrative. **synopses** *pl.*

syn•the•sis *n.* A production of a substance by the joining of chemical elements. **syntheses** *pl.*

syn•the•size *v.* To produce or to make with synthesis.

syn•thet•ic *adj.* Involving synthesis.

synthetically *adv.*

sy•ringe *n.* A medical instrument used to inject or draw fluids from the body.

syr•up *n.* A sticky, thick, sweet liquid, used as a topping for food.

sys•tem *n.* A method or way of doing something; the human body or related parts of the body that perform vital functions; an orderly arrangement. **systematic** *adj.*, **systematically** *adv.*

T

T, t The twentieth letter of the English alphabet.

tab *n.* A strip, flap, or small loop that projects from something.

ta•ble *n.* An article of furniture having a flat top, supported by legs; a collection of related signs, values, or items. *v.* To put off or postpone.

tac•it *adj.* Understood; expressed or implied nonverbally; implicit. **tacitly** *adv.*, **tacitness** *n.*

tack *n.* A small, short nail with a flat head; a sewing stitch used to hold something temporarily; the changing of a sailboat from one direction to another. *v.* To change the direction in which a sailboat is going.

tack•le *n.* Equipment used for fishing or other sports; an apparatus of ropes and pulley blocks for pulling and hoisting heavy loads. **tackled** *v.*, **tackler** *n.*

tack•y *adj.* Slightly sticky; shabby; lacking style or good taste; flashy.

tact *n.* Having the ability to avoid what would disturb someone. **tactful, tactless** *adj.*, **tactfully, tactlessly** *adv.*, **tactfulness, tactlessness** *n.*

tac•tic *n.* A way or method of working toward a goal; the art of using strategy to gain military objectives or other goals. **tactical** *adj.*, **tactician** *n.*

tad *n.* A small boy; an insignificant degree or amount.

tag *n.* A piece of plastic, metal, paper, or

other material that is attached to something in order to identify it; a children's game of running and tagging.

tail *n.* The posterior extremity, extending from the end or back of an animal. *pl.* The opposite side of a coin from heads.

tai•lor *n.* One whose profession is making, mending, and altering clothing.

taint *v.* To spoil, contaminate, or pollute. *n.* A blemish or stain.

take *v.* To seize or capture; to get possession of; to receive, swallow, absorb, or accept willingly; to attack and surmount; to choose or pick. *n.* The process of acquiring; the total receipts at an event.

tale *n.* A story or recital of relating events that may or may not be true; a malicious or false story; gossip.

tal•ent *n.* The aptitude, disposition, or characteristic ability of a person.

talk *v.* To communicate by words or speech; to engage in chatter or gossip. *n.* A speech or lecture.

tall *adj.* Of greater than average height; of a designated or specified height; imaginary.

tame *adj.* Not wild or ferocious; domesticated or manageable. *v.* To make docile or calm. **tamely** *adv.*, **tamer** *n.*

tam•per *v.* To change, meddle, or alter something; to use corrupt measures to scheme.

tan *v.* To cure a hide into leather by using chemicals. *n.* A brownish skin tone caused by exposure to the sun.

tang *n.* A sharp, distinct taste or smell; a slender shank that projects from a tool and connects to a handle. **tangy** *adv.*

tan•gent *n.* A line that touches a curved line but does not intersect or cross it; a sudden change to another course.

tan•gi•ble *adj.* Capable of being appreciated or felt by the sense of touch; capable of being realized.

tan•gle *v.* To mix, twist, or unite in a confused manner making separation difficult.

tank *n.* A large container for holding or storing a gas or liquid. **tankful** *n.*

tan•trum *n.* A fit; an outburst or a rage.

tap *v.* To strike repeatedly, usually while making a small noise; to strike or touch gently; to make secret contact with something; in medicine, to remove fluids from the body. **tapper** *n.*

tape *n.* A narrow strip of woven fabric; a string or ribbon stretched across the finish line of a race.

ta•per *n.* A very slender candle. *v.* To become gradually smaller or thinner at one end.

tar•dy *adj.* Late; not on time. **tardily** *adv.*, **tardiness** *n.*

tar•get *n.* An object marked to shoot at; an aim or goal.

tar•nish *v.* To become discolored or dull; to lose luster; to spoil.

tart *adj.* Sour; biting in tone or meaning.

task *n.* A bit of work, usually assigned by another; a job.

taste *n.* The ability to sense or determine flavor in the mouth; a personal liking or disliking. *v.* To test or sense flavors in the mouth.

tat•too *n.* A permanent design or mark made on the skin by pricking and inserting an indelible dye. **tattoo** *v.*, **tattooer** *n.*

taught *v.* Past tense of *teach*.

tav•ern *n.* An inn; an establishment or business licensed to sell alcoholic drinks.

tax *n.* A payment imposed and collected from individuals or businesses by the government.

tax•i *v.* To move along the ground or water surface on its own power before taking off.

tax•i•cab *n.* A vehicle for carrying passengers for money.

tea *n.* A small tree or bush which grows where the climate is very hot and damp; a drink made by steeping the dried leaves of this shrub in boiling water.

teach *v.* To communicate skill or knowledge; to give instruction or insight. **teacher** *n.*

team *n.* Two or more players on one side in a game; a group of people trained or organized to work together; two or more animals harnessed to the same implement.

tear *v.* To become divided into pieces; to separate; to rip into parts or pieces; to move fast; to rush. *n.* A rip or torn place.

tear *n.* A fluid secreted by the eye to moisten and cleanse.

tease *v.* To make fun of; to bother; to annoy; to tantalize. *n.* A person who teases. **teaser** *n.*, **teasingly** *adv.*

tech•ni•cal *adj.* Expert; derived or relating to technique; relating to industry or mechanics.

tech•nique *n.* A technical procedure or method of doing something.

teens *pl. n.* The ages between 13 and 19; the years of one's life between 13 and 19.

teeth *pl. n.* The plural of *tooth*.

tel•e•phone *n.* A system or device for transmitting conversations by wire. **telephone** *v.*, **telephoner** *n.*

tel•e•scope *n.* An instrument which contains a lens system which makes distant objects appear larger and nearer. **telescopic** *adj.*

tel•e•vi•sion *n.* Reception and transmission of images on a screen with sound; the device that reproduces television sounds and images.

tell *v.* To relate or describe; to command or order. **tellable, telling** *adj.*, **teller** *n.*

tel•net *n.* In computers, a protocol allowing users to log in and access files from any terminal.

tem•per *n.* The state of one's feelings. *v.* To modify something, making it flexible or hard.

tem•per•ate *adj.* Avoiding extremes; moderate.

tem•per•a•ture *n.* A measure of heat or cold in relation to the body or environment; an elevation in body temperature above the normal 98.6 degrees Fahrenheit.

tem•pest *n.* A severe storm, usually with snow, hail, rain, or sleet.

tem•ple *n.* A place of worship; the flat area on either side of the forehead.

tem•po•rar•y *adj.* Lasting for a limited amount of time; not permanent.

tempt *n.* To encourage or draw into a foolish or wrong course of action; to lure. **temptation, tempter** *n.*

tend *v.* To be inclined or disposed; to be directed; to look after.

ten•den•cy *n.* A disposition to act or behave in a particular way; a particular direction, mode, outcome, or direction.

ten•der *adj.* Fragile; soft; not hard or tough; painful or sore when touched. *n.* Something offered as a formal bid or offer; compassionate; a supply ship. *v.* To make an offer to buy or purchase; to present as a resignation.

ten•or *n.* An adult male singing voice, above a baritone.

tense *adj.* Taut or stretched tightly; nervous; under strain.

ten•sion *n.* The condition of stretching or the state of being stretched.

tent *n.* A portable shelter made by stretching material over a supporting framework.

ten•ta•cle *n.* A long, unjointed, flexible body part that projects from certain invertebrates, as the octopus.

term *n.* A phrase or word; a limited time or duration; a phrase having a precise meaning.

ter•mi•nal *adj.* Of, forming, or located at the end; final. *n.* A station at the end of a bus line, railway, or airline; in computers, the end location of the information network, where electronic signals can be encoded or decoded into readable text; a worksite dedicated to such activity, usually consisting of computer, monitor, and keyboard.

ter•mi•nate *v.* To bring to a conclusion or end; to finish. **termination** *n.*

ter•mite *n.* The winged or wingless insect which lives in large colonies feeding on wood.

ter•race *n.* An open balcony or porch; a level piece of land that is higher than the surrounding area; a row of houses built on a sloping or raised site.

ter•rif•ic *adj.* Terrifying; excellent; causing

terrify

amazement.

ter•ri•fy v. To fill with fear or terror; to frighten. **terrified, terrifying** adj.

ter•ri•to•ry n. An area, usually of great size, which is controlled by a particular government; a district or area assigned to one person or group.

ter•ror n. Extreme fear.

ter•ror•ist n. One who causes terror.

test n. An examination or evaluation of something or someone; an examination to determine one's knowledge, skill, intelligence or other qualities.

tes•ti•fy v. To give evidence while under oath; to serve as proof. **testifier** n.

text n. The actual wording of an author's work; the main part or body of a book. **textual** adj., **textually** adv.

tex•ture n. The look, surface, or feel of something; the basic makeup. **textural** adj., **texturally** adv.

than conj. In comparison with or to something.

thank v. To express one's gratitude; to credit.

thank•ful adj. Feeling or showing gratitude; grateful. **thankfully** adv., **thankfulness** n.

that adj. The person or thing present or being mentioned. conj. Used to introduce a clause stating what is said. **those** pl.

thaw v. To change from a frozen state to a liquid or soft state; to grow warmer; to melt.

the def. adj. or art. Used before nouns and noun phrases as a determiner, designating particular persons or things. adv. Used to modify words in the comparative degree; by so much; by that much.

the•a•ter or **the•a•tre** n. A building adapted to present dramas, motion pictures, plays, or other performances; a performance.

the•at•ri•cal adj. Extravagant; designed for show, display, or effect.

theft n. The act of stealing; larceny.

their adj. or pron. The possessive case of they; belonging to two or more things or beings previously named.

them pron. The objective case of they.

theme n. The topic or subject of something; in music, a short melody of a musical composition. **thematic** adj.

them•selves pron. Them or they; a form of the third person plural pronoun.

then adv. At that time; soon or immediately. adj. Being or acting in or belonging to or at that time.

the•o•ry n. A general principle or explanation which covers the known facts; an offered opinion which may possibly, but not positively, be true.

there adv. In, at, or about that place; toward, into, or to. **thereabouts, thereafter, thereby, therefore, therefrom, therein** adv.

the•sau•rus n. A book which contains synonyms and antonyms.

these pron. The plural of this.

the•sis n. A formal argument or idea; a paper written by a student that develops an idea or point of view. **theses** pl.

they pron. The two or more beings just mentioned.

thick adj. Having a heavy or dense consistency; having a considerable extent or depth from one surface to its opposite.

thief n. A person who steals.

thin adj. Having very little depth or extent from one side or surface to the other; not fat; slender.

thing n. Something not recognized or named; an idea, conception, or utterance; a material or real object.

things n. One's belongings.

think v. To exercise thought; to use the mind, to reason and work out in the mind; to visualize.

thirst n. An uncomfortably dry feeling in the throat and mouth accompanied by an urgent desire for liquids. **thirsty** adj.

this pron. The person or thing that is near, present, or just mentioned; the one under discussion. **these** pl.

thorn n. A sharp, pointed, woody projection on a plant stem.

thor•ough *adj.* Complete; intensive; accurate; very careful; absolute.

those *adj.* The plural of *that.*

though *adv.* Nevertheless; in spite of.

thought *n.* The process, act, or power of thinking; a possibility; an idea.

thou•sand *n.* The cardinal number equal to 10 x 100.

thread *n.* A thin cord of cotton or other fiber; the ridge going around a bolt, nut or screw. *v.* To pass a thread through, as to thread a needle.

threat *n.* An expression or warning of intent to do harm; anything holding a possible source of danger. **threaten** *v.,* **threatener** *n.,* **threateningly** *adv.*

threw *v.* Past tense of *throw.*

thrift *n.* The careful use of money and other resources. **thriftily** *adv.,* **thriftiness** *n.,* **thrifty** *adj.*

thrill *n.* A feeling of sudden intense excitement, fear, or joy.

thrive *v.* To prosper; to be healthy; to do well in a position.

throat *n.* The front section or part of the neck containing passages for food and air.

through *prep.* From the beginning to the end; in one side and out the opposite side; finished.

throw *v.* To toss or fling through the air with a motion of the arm; to hurl with force.

thrust *v.* To push; to shove with sudden or vigorous force. *n.* A sudden stab or push.

thumb *n.* The short first digit of the hand; the part of the glove that fits over the thumb. *v.* To browse through something quickly.

thun•der *n.* The loud explosive sound made as air is suddenly expanded by heat and then quickly contracted again.

tick *n.* One of a series of rhythmical tapping sounds made by a clock; a small bloodsucking parasite, many of which are carriers of disease.

tick•et *n.* A printed slip of paper or cardboard allowing its holder to enter a specified event or to enjoy a privilege.

tick•le *v.* To stroke lightly so as to cause laughter; to amuse or delight.

tid•al wave *n.* An enormous rise of destructive ocean water caused by a storm or earthquake.

tid•bit *n.* A choice bit of food, news, or gossip.

tide *n.* The rise and fall of the surface level of the ocean which occurs twice a day due to the gravitational pull of the sun and moon on the earth.

ti•dy *adj.* Well arranged; neat; orderly.

tie *v.* To secure or bind with a rope, line, cord or other similar material; to make secure or fasten with a rope; to make a bow or knot in; to match an opponent's score. *n.* A string, rope, cord or other material used to join parts or hold something in place; a necktie; a beam that gives structural support; [with *railroad*] a device, as timber, laid crosswise to support train tracks.

tier *n.* A layer or row placed one above the other.

ti•ger *n.* A large carnivorous cat having tawny fur with black stripes.

tight *adj.* Set closely together; bound or securely firm; not loose; taut; difficult. **tighten** *v.*

tile *n.* A thin, hard, flat piece of plastic, asphalt, baked clay, or stone used to cover walls, floors, and roofs. *v.* To cover with tile.

till *prep.* Until; unless or before. *v.* To cultivate; to plow. *n.* A small cash register or drawer for holding money.

tilt *v.* To tip, as by raising one end. *n.* The state of tilting or being tilted.

tim•ber *n.* Wood prepared for building; a finished piece of wood or plank.

time *n.* A continuous period measured by clocks, watches, and calendars; the period or moment in which something happens.

tim•id *adj.* Lacking self-confidence; shy.

tin *n.* A white, soft, malleable metallic element, symbolized by *Sn*; a container made of tin.

tin•gle *v.* To feel a stinging or prickling

tinny

sensation. **tingle** *n.*, **tingly** *adj.*

tin·ny *adj.* Pertaining to or composed of tin.

tin·sel *n.* Thin strips of glittering material used for decorations.

tint *n.* A slight amount or trace of color. *v.* To color.

ti·ny *adj.* Minute; very small.

tip *v.* To slant from the horizontal or vertical. *n.* Extra money given as an acknowledgment of a service; a helpful hint.

tire *v.* To become or make weary; to be fatigued; to become bored. *n.* The outer covering for a wheel, usually made of rubber.

tire·less *adj.* Untiring. **tirelessly** *adv.*

tis·sue *n.* Similar cells and their products developed by plants and animals; a soft, absorbent piece of paper, consisting of two layers.

ti·tle *n.* An identifying name of a book, poem, play, or other creative work; a name or mark of distinction indicating a rank or an office; in law, the evidence giving legal right of possession or control.

to *prep.* Toward, opposite or near; in contact with; as far as; used as a function word indicating an action, movement, or condition suggestive of movement; indicating correspondence, dissimilarity, similarity, or proportion.

toad *n.* A tailless amphibian, resembling the frog but without teeth in the upper jaw and having a rougher, drier skin.

toast *v.* To heat and brown over a fire or in a toaster. *n.* Sliced bread browned in a toaster. **toasty** *adj.*, **toaster** *n.*

to·bac·co *n.* A suspected carcinogenic tropical American plant containing nicotine, whose leaves are chewed and smoked.

to·day *adv.* On or during the present day. *n.* The present time, period, or day.

toe *n.* One of the extensions from the front part of a foot; the part of a stocking, boot or shoe that covers the toes.

to·geth·er *adv.* In or into one group, mass, or body; regarded jointly; in time with what is happening or going on. **togetherness** *n.*

toil *v.* To labor very hard and continuously. *n.* A difficult task. **toilsome** *adj.*

toi·let *n.* A porcelain apparatus with a flushing device, used as a means of disposing body wastes.

to·ken *n.* A keepsake; a symbol of authority or identity; a piece of imprinted metal used in place of money. *adj.* Done as a pledge or indication.

tol·er·ate *v.* To put up with; to recognize and respect the opinions and rights of others; to endure; to suffer.

toll *n.* A fixed charge for travel across a bridge or along a road. *v.* To sound a bell in repeated single, slow tones.

tom *n.* A male turkey or cat.

to·mor·row *n.* The day after the present day. *adv.* On the day following today.

ton *n.* A measurement of weight equal to 2,000 pounds.

tone *n.* A vocal or musical sound that has a distinct pitch, loudness, quality, and duration; the condition of the body and muscles when at rest.

tongue *n.* The muscular organ attached to the floor of the mouth, used in tasting, chewing, and speaking; anything shaped like a tongue, as the material under the laces or buckles of a shoe.

to·night *n.* This night; the night of this day; the night that is coming. *adv.* On or during the present or coming night.

too *adv.* Also; as well; more than is needed.

tool *n.* An implement used to perform a task; anything needed to do one's work. *v.* To make or shape with a tool. **tooling** *n.*

tooth *n.* One of the hard, white structures rooted in the jaw and used for chewing and biting; the small, notched, projecting part of any object, such as a gear, comb or saw. **toothed, toothless** *adj.*, **teeth** *pl.*

top *n.* The highest part or surface of anything; a covering or lid; the aboveground part of a rooted plant; the highest degree; a toy having a symmetric body with a tapered end upon which it spins.

torch *n.* A stick of resinous wood which is burned to give light; any portable device which produces hot flame.

tor•ment *n.* Extreme mental anguish or physical pain; a source of trouble or pain. *v.* To cause terrible pain; to pester, harass, or annoy.

ter•na•do *n.* A whirling, violent windstorm accompanied by a funnel-shaped cloud that travels a narrow path over land; a whirlwind; a cyclone.

tor•rent *n.* A swift, violent stream; a raging flood. **torrential** *adj*

tor•rid *adj.* Parched and dried by the heat.

tor•toise *n.* A turtle that lives on the land; a person or thing regarded as slow.

tor•ture *n.* The infliction of intense pain as punishment; something causing anguish or pain. *v.* To subject or cause intense suffering; to wrench or twist out of shape.

toss *v.* To fling or throw about continuously; to throw up in the air.

tot *n.* A young child; a toddler.

to•tal *n.* The whole amount or sum; the entire quantity. *adj.* Absolute; complete.

touch *v.* To allow a part of the body, as the hands, to feel or come into contact with; to hit or tap lightly; to eat or drink; to join; to come next to; to have an effect on; to move emotionally. *n.* An instance or act of touching; the feeling, fact, or act of touching or being touched; a trace; a tiny amount.

tough *adj.* Resilient and strong enough to withstand great strain without breaking or tearing; strong; hardy; very difficult; difficult to cut or chew. *n.* An unruly person; a thug.

tour *n.* A trip with visits to points of interest; a journey; a period or length of service at a single place or job. **tourism**, **tourist** *n.*

tour•na•ment *n.* A contest involving competitors for a title or championship.

tour•ni•quet *n.* A device used to temporarily stop the flow of blood through an artery.

tow *v.* To drag or pull, as by a chain or rope. *n.* The act of being pulled; a rope or line for pulling or dragging; coarse, broken flax, hemp, or jute fiber prepared for spinning.

to•ward *prep.* In the direction of; just before; somewhat before; regarding; with respect to.

tow•el *n.* An absorbent piece of cloth used for drying or wiping. **towel** *v.*

tow•er *n.* A very tall building or structure; a skyscraper; a place of security or defense.

town *n.* A collection of houses and other buildings larger than a village and smaller than a city.

toy *n.* An object designed for the enjoyment of children; any object having little value or importance; a small trinket; a bauble; a dog of a very small breed. *v.* To amuse or entertain oneself.

trace *n.* A visible mark or sign of a thing, person, or event; something left by some past agent or event. *v.* To follow the course or track of; to copy by drawing over the lines visible through a sheet of transparent paper.

track *n.* A mark, as a footprint, left by the passage of anything; a regular course; a set of rails on which a train runs; a circular or oval course for racing. *v.* To follow a trail of footprints.

trac•tor *n.* A diesel or gasoline-powered vehicle used in farming to pull another piece of machinery.

trade *n.* A business or occupation; skilled labor; a craft; an instance of selling or buying; a swap. **trade** *v.*, **tradeable** *adj.*, **trader** *n.*

tra•di•tion *n.* The doctrines, knowledge, practices, and customs passed down from one generation to another. **traditional** *adj.*

traf•fic *n.* The passage or movement of vehicles; trading, buying and selling; the signals handled by a communications system. **trafficker** *n.*

trag•e•dy *n.* An extremely sad or fatal event or course of events; a story, play, or other literary work which arouses terror or pity by a series of misfortunes or sad events.

trail *v.* To draw, drag, or stream along behind; to follow in the tracks of; to follow slowly behind or in the rear; to let hang so as to touch the ground. *n.* Something that hangs or follows along behind; a rough path through woods.

trail•er *n.* One who trails; a large vehicle that transports objects and is pulled by another vehicle.

train *n.* The part of a long gown that trails behind the wearer; a long moving line of vehicles or persons; a group of railroad cars. *v.* To instruct so as to make skillful or capable of doing something; to aim; to direct. **trainee, trainer** *n.*

trait *n.* A quality or distinguishing feature, such as one's character.

tramp *v.* To plod or walk with a heavy step. *n.* A homeless person or vagrant who travels about aimlessly.

trance *n.* A stupor, daze, mental state, or condition, such as produced by drugs or hypnosis.

tran•quil *adj.* Very calm, quiet, and free from disturbance. **tranquillity** *n.*, **tran-quilly** *adv.*, **tranquilize** *v.*

trans•fer *v.* To remove, shift, or carry from one position to another. **transferable** *adj.*

trans•form *v.* To change or alter completely in nature, form or function.

trans•late *v.* To change from one language to another while retaining the original meaning; to explain.

trans•lu•cent *adj.* Diffusing and admitting light but not allowing a clear view.

trans•mis•sion *n.* The act or state of transmitting; in mechanics, the gears and associated parts of an engine which transmit power to the driving wheels of an automobile or other vehicle.

trans•mit *v.* To dispatch or convey from one thing, person, or place to another. **transmissible, transmittable** *adj.*, **transmitter** *n.*

trans•par•ent *adj.* Admitting light so that images and objects can be clearly viewed; easy to understand; obvious.

trans•port *v.* To carry or move from one place to another. *n.* A vessel or ship used to carry military supplies and troops; the act of transporting. **transportation** *n.*

trap *n.* A device for holding or catching animals; a device which hurls clay pigeons, disks, or balls into the air to be fired upon by sportsmen; anything which deliberately catches or stops people or things. *v.* To catch in a trap; to place in an embarrassing position.

tra•peze *n.* A short horizontal bar suspended by two ropes, used for acrobatic exercise or stunts.

trau•ma *n.* A severe wound caused by a sudden physical injury; an emotional shock causing substantial damage to a person's psychological development.

tra•vail *n.* Strenuous mental or physical exertion; labor in childbirth. *v.* To undergo the sudden sharp pain of childbirth.

trav•el *v.* To journey or move from one place to another. *n.* The process or act of traveling. **traveler** *n.*

tray *n.* A flat container having a low rim used for carrying, holding, or displaying something.

treach•er•ous *adj.* Disloyal; deceptive; unreliable. **treachery** *n.*

tread *v.* To walk along, on, or over; to trample. *n.* The act or manner of treading; the part of a wheel which comes into contact with the ground.

trea•son *n.* Violation of one's allegiance to a sovereign or country, as giving or selling state secrets to another country or attempting to overthrow the government. **treasonous** *adj.*

treas•ure *n.* Hidden riches; something regarded as valuable. *v.* To save and accumulate for future use; to value.

treas•ur•er *n.* A person having charge and responsibilities for funds.

treas•ur•y *n.* A place where public or private funds are kept.

treat *v.* To behave or act toward, to regard

in a given manner; to provide entertainment or food for another at one's own expense or cost. *n.* A pleasant surprise; something enjoyable which was unexpected. **treatable** *adj.*, **treatment** *n.*

tree *n.* A tall woody plant, usually having a single trunk of considerable height; a diagram resembling a tree, as one used to show family descent.

trem·ble *v.* To shake involuntarily, as with fear or from cold; to feel anxiety.

tre·men·dous *adj.* Extremely huge; vast.

trem·or *n.* A quick, shaking movement; any continued and involuntary trembling or quavering of the body.

trench *n.* A ditch; a long, narrow excavation in the ground. *v.* To cut deep furrows for protection.

trend *n.* A general inclination, direction, or course; a fad, *v.* To have or take a specified direction. **trendsetter** *n.*

tres·pass *v.* To infringe upon another's property; in law, to invade the rights, property, or privacy of another.

tri·al *n.* In law, the examination and hearing of a case before a court of law in order to determine the case; an attempt or effort; an experimental treatment or action to determine a result.

tri·an·gle *n.* A plane figure bounded by three sides and having three angles. **triangular** *adj.*, **triangularity** *n.*

tribe *n.* A group of people composed of several villages, districts, or other groups which share a common language, culture, and name.

trick *n.* An action meant to fool, as a scheme; a prank; a feat of magic. *v.* To deceive or cheat. **tricky** *adj.*, **trickery** *n.*

trick·le *v.* To flow in droplets or a small stream.

tri·cy·cle *n.* A small vehicle having three wheels, propelled by pedals.

tried *adj.* Tested and proven reliable or useful.

tri·fle *n.* Something of little value or importance; a dessert made with cake, jelly, wine, and custard. *v.* To use or treat without proper concern.

trig·ger *n.* A lever pulled to fire a gun; a device used to release or start an action. *v.* To start.

trim *v.* To cut off small amounts in order to make neater; to decorate. *adj.* Neat.

trin·ket *n.* A small piece of jewelry.

tri·o *n.* A set or group of three.

trip *n.* Travel from one place to another; a journey; a loss of balance. *v.* To stumble.

trip·le *adj.* Having three parts. *v.* To multiply by three.

trip·let *n.* One of three born at the same time.

trip·li·cate *n.* A group of three identical things.

tri·pod *n.* A three-legged stand or frame.

trite *adj.* Used too often; common.

tri·umph *v.* To be victorious. *n.* A victory. **triumphant** *adj.*

triv·i·al *adj.* Insignificant; of little value.

trol·ley *n.* A streetcar powered by electricity from overhead lines.

troop *n.* A group or assembly of people or animals; a group of Boy Scouts or Girl Scouts having an adult leader; a military unit. **trooper** *n.*

tro·phy *n.* A prize or object, such as a plaque, awarded to someone for success, victory, or achievement.

trop·ic *n.* Either of two imaginary parallel lines which constitute the Torrid Zone. *pl.* The very warm region of the earth's surface between the Tropic of Cancer and the Tropic of Capricorn. **tropical** *adj.*

trot *n.* The gait of a horse or other four-footed animal, between a walk and a run, in which the hind leg and opposite front leg move at about the same time.

trou·ble *n.* Danger; affliction; need; distress; an effort; physical pain, disease or malfunction. *v.* To bother; to worry; to be bothered; to be worried.

truce *n.* An agreement to stop fighting; a cease-fire.

truck *n.* An automotive vehicle used to carry heavy loads; any of various devices with wheels designed to move loads;

trudge

garden vegetables for sale. **trucker** *n.*

trudge *v.* To walk heavily; to plod.

true *adj.* In accordance with reality or fact; not false; real; loyal; faithful.

trunk *n.* The main part of a tree; the human body, excluding the head, arms and legs; a sturdy box for packing clothing, as for travel or storage; the long snout of an elephant.

trust *n.* Confidence or faith in a person or thing; care or charge; the confidence or arrangement by which property is managed and held for the good or benefit of another person. *v.* To have confidence or faith in; to believe; to expect; to entrust; to depend on.

truth *n.* The facts corresponding with actual events or happenings; sincerity or honesty. **truthful** *adj.*, **truthfully** *adv.*

try *v.* To make an attempt; to make an effort; to strain; to hear or conduct a trial; to place on trial. **trying** *adj.*, **tryout** *n.*

tub *n.* A round, low, flat-bottomed, vessel with handles on the side.

tu•ba *n.* A large, brass wind instrument having a low range.

tube *n.* A hollow cylinder, made of metal, rubber, glass or other material, used to pass something through. **tubal** *adj.*

tug *v.* To strain and pull vigorously. *n.* A hard pull; a strong force.

tum•ble *v.* To fall or cause to fall; to perform acrobatic rolls, somersaults, and similar maneuvers; to mix up; to turn over and over. **tumbler** *n.*

tum•ble•down *adj.* Ramshackle; in need of repair.

tu•mor *n.* A swelling on or in any part of the body; an abnormal growth.

tu•na *n.* Any of several large food fish.

tun•dra *n.* A treeless area in the arctic regions having a subsoil which is permanently frozen.

tune *n.* A melody which is simple and easy to remember; agreement; harmony. *v.* To adjust. **tunable** *adj.*, **tunably** *adv.*, **tuner** *n.*

tun•nel *n.* An underground or underwater

passageway. **tunnel** *v.*

tur•bine *n.* A motor having one or more rotary units mounted on a shaft, which are turned by the force of gas or a liquid.

tur•bu•lent *adj.* Marked by a violent disturbance.

turf *n.* A layer of earth with its dense growth of grass and matted roots.

tur•key *n.* A large game bird of North America, having a bare head and extensible tail; the meat of this bird.

tur•moil *n.* A state of confusion or commotion.

turn *v.* To move or cause to move around a center point; to revolve or rotate; to transform or change; to move so that the bottom side of something becomes the top and the top becomes the bottom; to strain or sprain.

turn•o•ver *n.* The process or act of turning over; an upset; a change or reversal; the number of times merchandise is bought, sold, and restocked in a certain period of time; a piece of pastry made by putting a filling on one half of the dough and turning the other half over to enclose the filling.

tur•quoise *n.* A blue-green gemstone; a light bluish-green color. **turquoise** *adj.*

tur•tle *n.* A scaly-skinned animal having a soft body covered with a hard shell into which the head, legs, and tail can be retracted.

tusk *n.* A long, curved tooth, as of an elephant or walrus.

tus•sle *n.* A hard fight or struggle with a problem or person.

tu•tor *n.* A person who teaches another person privately. *v.* To teach, coach, or instruct privately.

tux•e•do A semiformal dress suit worn by men.

twice *adv.* Double; two times.

twig *n.* A small branch which grows from a larger branch on a tree.

twi•light *n.* The soft light of the sky between sunset and complete darkness.

twin *n.* One of two persons born at the

same time to the same mother; one of two similar persons or things. *adj.* Having two similar or identical parts.

twine *v.* To weave or twist together. *n.* A strong cord or thread made by twisting many threads together.

twinge *n.* A sudden, sharp pain; a brief emotional or mental pang.

twin•kle *v.* To gleam or shine with quick flashes; to sparkle.

twirl *v.* To rotate or cause to turn around and around.

twist *v.* To wind two or more pieces of thread, twine, or other materials together to make a single strand; to curve; to bend, to distort or change the meaning of; to injure and wrench.

twist•er *n.* A tornado; a cyclone; one that twists. In baseball, a ball batted or thrown in a twisting, spinning motion.

twit *v.* To tease about a mistake. *n.* A taunting reproach.

twitch *v.* To move or cause to move with a jerky movement. *n.* A sudden tug.

twit•ter *v.* To utter a series of chirping sounds; to chatter nervously.

two•bit *adj.* Insignificant.

two bits *n.* Twenty-five cents.

two-faced *adj.* Double-dealing.

two•fold *n.* Being double; as much or as many.

two•time *v.* To be unfaithful to.

ty•coon *n. slang* A business person of wealth and power.

tyke *n.* A small child.

type *n.* A class or group of persons or things; letters, numbers, and other symbols typewritten on paper or another surface; in printing, the piece of plastic, metal, or wood having the character or characters that are printed; a model or example of. *v.* To identify according to some sort of classification; to typewrite.

typ•i•cal *adj.* Exhibiting the characteristics of a certain class or group.

typ•i•fy *v.* To be characteristic or typical of; to show all the traits or qualities of.

typ•ist *n.* The operator of a typewriter.

ty•rant *n.* An absolute, unjust, or cruel ruler; one who exercises power, authority, or control unfairly.

U

U, u The twenty-first letter of the English alphabet.

ud•der *n.* The milk-producing organ pouch of some female animals, having two or more teats.

ug•ly *adj.* Offensive; unpleasant to look at.

u•ku•le•le *n.* A small, four-stringed musical instrument, originally from Hawaii.

ul•cer *n.* A festering, inflamed sore on a mucous membrane or on the skin that results in the destruction of the tissue. **ulceration** *n.*, **ulcerate** *v.*

ul•ti•mate *adj.* Final; ending; most extreme. **ultimately** *adv.*

ul•ti•ma•tum *n.* A final demand, proposal, or choice, as in negotiating.

ul•tra•vi•o•let *adj.* Producing radiation having wave-lengths just shorter than those of visible light and longer than those of X rays. **ultraviolet** *n.*

um•brel•la *n.* A collapsible frame covered with plastic or cloth, held above the head as protection from sun or rain.

um•pire *n.* In sports, the person who rules on plays. *v.* To act as an umpire.

un•a•ble *adj.* Not having the capabilities.

u•nan•i•mous *adj.* Agreed to completely; based on the agreement of all.

un•a•void•a•ble *adj.* Inevitable; unstoppable. **unavoidably** *adv.*

un•a•ware *adj.* Not realizing.

un•bear•a•ble *adj.* Not possible to endure; intolerable. **unbearably** *adv.*

un•be•liev•a•ble *adj.* Incredible; hard to accept; not to be believed.

un•cer•tain *adj.* Doubtful; not sure; not known; hard to predict.

un•changed *adj.* Having nothing new or different.

un•cle *n.* The brother of one's mother or father; the husband of an aunt.

uncomfortable

un•com•fort•a•ble *adj.* Disturbed; not at ease physically or mentally; causing discomfort. **uncomfortably** *adv.*

un•com•mon *adj.* Rare; odd; unusual. **uncommonly** *adv.*

un•con•di•tion•al *adj.* Without conditions or limits. **unconditionally** *adv.*

un•con•scious *adj.* Not mentally aware; done without thought; not on purpose.

un•con•sti•tu•tion•al *adj.* Contrary to the constitution of a state or country.

un•cov•er *v.* To remove the cover from something; to disclose. **uncovered** *adj.*

un•de•cid•ed *adj.* Unsettled; having made no firm decision; open to change.

un•der *prep.* Below, in place or position; in a place lower than another; less in degree, number, or other quality; inferior in rank, quality, or character.

un•der•brush *n.* Small bushes, vines, and plants that grow under tall trees.

un•der•grad•u•ate *n.* A college or university student studying for a bachelor's degree.

un•der•line *v.* To draw a line directly under something.

un•der•neath *adv.* Beneath or below; on the under side; lower. *prep.* Under; below.

un•der•pass *n.* A road or walk that goes under another.

un•der•stand *v.* To comprehend; to realize; to know the feelings and thoughts of. **understanding** *v.*

un•der•stand•a•ble *adj.* Able to sympathize or comprehend.

un•der•stood *adj.* Agreed upon by all.

un•der•take *v.* To set about to do a task; to pledge oneself to a certain job; to attempt. **undertaking** *n.*

un•der•tak•er *n.* A person who prepares the dead for burial.

un•der•wa•ter *adj.* Occurring, happening or used beneath the surface of the water.

un•de•sir•a•ble *adj.* Offensive; not wanted. **undesirably** *adv.*

un•do *v.* To cancel; to reverse; to loosen or unfasten; to open a package.

un•done *adj.* Not finished; unfastened; ruined.

un•eas•y *adj.* Feeling or causing distress or discomfort; embarrassed; uncertain. **uneasily** *adv.*, **uneasiness** *n.*

un•em•ployed *adj.* Without a job; without work. **unemployment** *n.*

un•e•qual *adj.* Not even; not fair; not of the same size or time; lacking sufficient ability. **unequaled** *adj.*

un•e•ven *adj.* Not equal; varying in consistency or form; not balanced.

un•ex•pect•ed *adj.* Surprising; happening without warning. **unexpectedly** *adv.*

un•fair *adj.* Not honest; marked by a lack of justice. **unfairness** *n.*

un•faith•ful *adj.* Breaking a promise or agreement; without loyalty.

un•fa•mil•iar *adj.* Not knowing; strange; foreign. **unfamiliarity** *n.*

un•fit *adj.* Not suitable; not qualified; in poor body or mental health.

un•fold *v.* To open up the folds of and lay flat; to reveal gradually.

un•for•get•ta•ble *adj.* Impossible or hard to forget; memorable.

un•for•tu•nate *adj.* Causing or having bad luck, damage, or harm. *n.* A person who has no luck.

un•grate•ful *adj.* Not thankful; showing no appreciation. **ungratefully** *adv.*

un•hap•py *adj.* Sad; without laughter or joy; not satisfied or pleased. **unhappily** *adv.*, **unhappiness** *n.*

un•heard *adj.* Not heard; not listened to.

u•ni•corn *n.* A mythical animal resembling a horse, with a horn in the center of its forehead.

u•ni•cy•cle *n.* A one-wheeled vehicle with pedals.

un•i•den•ti•fied fly•ing ob•ject *n.* A flying object that cannot be explained or identified, abbreviated as *UFO*.

u•ni•form *n.* Identical clothing worn by the members of a group to distinguish them. **uniformly** *adv.*

u•ni•fy *v.* To come together as one; to unite. **unifier** *n.*

un•in•hab•it•ed *adj.* Not lived in; empty.

un•in•ter•est•ed *adj.* Having no interest or concern in; not interested.

un•ion *n.* The act of joining together of two or more groups or things; a group of countries or states joined under one government; a marriage; an organized body of employees who work together to upgrade their working conditions and wages.

u•nique *adj.* Unlike any other; sole. **uniqueness** *n.*, **uniquely** *adv.*

u•nit *n.* Any one of several parts regarded as a whole; an exact quantity that is used as a standard of measurement; a special section or part of a machine.

u•nite *v.* To join or come together for a common purpose.

u•ni•ty *n.* The fact or state of being one; accord; agreement; harmony.

u•ni•ver•sal *adj.* Having to do with the world or the universe in its entirety.

u•ni•verse *n.* The world, stars, planets, space, and all that is contained.

u•ni•ver•si•ty *n.* An educational institution offering undergraduate and graduate degrees in a variety of academic areas.

un•just *adj.* Not fair; lacking justice or fairness. **unjustly** *adv.*

un•kempt *adj.* Poorly groomed; messy; untidy.

un•kind *adj.* Harsh; lacking in sympathy, concern, or understanding.

un•known *adj.* Strange; unidentified; not known; not familiar or famous.

un•like *prep.* Dissimilar; not alike; not equal in strength or quantity; not usual.

un•lim•it•ed *adj.* Having no boundaries.

un•load *v.* To take or remove the load; to unburden; to dispose or get rid of by selling in volume.

un•lock *v.* To open, release, or unfasten a lock; open with a key.

un•luck•y *adj.* Unfortunate; having bad luck; disappointing or unsuitable.

un•mis•tak•a•ble *adj.* Very clear and evident; understood; obvious.

un•nat•u•ral *adj.* Abnormal or unusual; strange; artificial. **unnaturally** *adv.*

un•nec•es•sar•y *adj.* Not needed; not appropriate. **unnecessarily** *adv.*

un•oc•cu•pied *adj.* Empty; not occupied.

un•pack *v.* To remove articles out of suitcases, boxes, or other storage places.

un•pleas•ant *adj.* Not agreeable; not pleasant. **unpleasantness** *n.*

un•pop•u•lar *adj.* Not approved or liked. **unpopularity** *n.*

un•pre•dict•a•ble *adj.* Not capable of being foretold; not reliable. **unpredictably** *adj.*

un•pre•pared *adj.* Not equipped or ready.

un•pro•fes•sion•al *adj.* Contrary to the standards of a profession; having no professional status.

un•prof•it•a•ble *adj.* Showing or giving no profit; serving no purpose.

un•qual•i•fied *adj.* Lacking the proper qualifications; unreserved.

un•rav•el *v.* To separate threads; to solve; to clarify; to come apart.

un•real *adj.* Having no substance or reality.

un•rea•son•a•ble *adj.* Not according to reason; exceeding all reasonable limits.

un•re•li•a•ble *adj.* Unable to be trusted; not dependable.

un•re•served *adj.* Done or given without reserve; unlimited.

un•re•strained *adj.* Not held back, forced, or affected.

un•ru•ly *adj.* Disorderly; difficult to subdue or control.

un•sat•is•fac•to•ry *adj.* Unacceptable; not pleasing.

un•scru•pu•lous *adj.* Without morals, guiding principles, or rules.

un•sel•fish *adj.* Willing to share; thinking of another's well-being before one's own. **unselfishly** *adv.*, **unselfishness** *n.*

un•sight•ly *adj.* Not pleasant to look at; ugly.

un•skilled *adj.* Having no skills or training in a given kind of work.

un•sta•ble *adj.* Not steady or firmly fixed; having the tendency to fluctuate or change.

un•stead•y *adj.* Not secure; unstable; variable. **unsteadily** *adv.*

un·suit·a·ble *adj.* Unfitting; not suitable; not appropriate.

un·tan·gle *v.* To free from entanglements.

un·ti·dy *adj.* Messy; showing a lack of tidiness. **untidily** *adv.*, **untidiness** *n.*

un·tie *v.* To unfasten or loosen; to free from a restraint or bond.

un·til *prep.* Up to the time of. *conj.* To the time when; to the degree or place.

un·told *adj.* Not revealed; not told; inexpressible; cannot be described or revealed.

un·true *adj.* Not true; contrary to the truth; not faithful; disloyal.

un·truth *n.* Something which is not true; the state of being false.

un·u·su·al *adj.* Not usual; uncommon. **unusually** *adv.*, **unusualness** *n.*

un·veil *v.* To remove a veil from; to uncover; to reveal,

un·war·y *adj.* Not cautious or careful; careless.

un·whole·some *adj.* Unhealthy; morally corrupt or harmful.

un·wor·thy *adj.* Not deserving; not becoming or befitting; lacking merit or worth; shameful. **unworthiness** *n.*

up *adv.* From a lower position to a higher one; on, in, or to a higher level, position, or place; to a greater degree or amount; in or into a specific action or an excited state.

up·hill *adv.* Up an incline. *adj.* Hard to accomplish; going up a hill or incline.

up·hol·ster *v.* To cover furniture with fabric covering, cushions, and padding. **upholsterer, upholstery** *n.*

up·keep *n.* The cost and work needed to keep something in good condition.

up·on *prep.* On.

up·per *adj.* Higher in status, position or location. *n.* The part of a shoe to which the sole is attached.

up·per case *n.* The large or capital case of letters.

up·stairs *adv.* Up one or more flights of stairs. *adj.* Situated on the upper floor.

up·ward *adv.* From a lower position to or toward a higher one. *adj.* Directed toward a higher position. **upwardly** *adv.*

ur·ban *adj.* Pertaining to a city or having characteristics of a city; living or being in a city. **urbanite** *n.*, **urbanize** *v.*

urge *v.* To encourage, push, or drive; to recommend persistently and strongly. *n.* An influence, impulse, or force.

ur·gent *adj.* Requiring immediate attention. **urgency** *n.*, **urgently** *adv.*

us·a·ble or **use·a·ble** *adj.* Fit or capable of being used. **usability** *n.*

u·su·al *adj.* Ordinary or common; regular; customary.

u·su·al·ly *adv.*, **usualness** *n.*

u·til·i·ty *n.* The state or quality of being useful; a company which offers a public service, as water, heat, or electricity.

ut·ter *v.* To say or express verbally; to speak. *adj.* Absolute; complete.

V

V, v The twenty-second letter of the English alphabet; the Roman numeral for 5.

va·cant *adj.* Empty; not occupied; without expression.

va·cate *v.* To leave; to cease to occupy.

va·ca·tion *n.* A period of time away from work for pleasure, relaxation, or rest.

vac·ci·nate *v.* To inject with a vaccine so as to produce immunity to an infectious disease. **vaccination** *n.*

vac·cine *n.* A solution of weakened or killed microorganisms, as bacteria or viruses, injected into the body to produce immunity to a disease.

vac·u·um *n.* A space absolutely empty; a void; a vacuum cleaner.

vag·a·bond *n.* A homeless person who wanders from place to place; a tramp.

va·grant *n.* A person who wanders from place to place. *adj.* Roaming from one area to another without a job. **vagrancy** *n.*

vague *adj.* Not clearly expressed; not sharp or definite. **vaguely** *adv.*

vain *adj.* Conceited; lacking worth or substance; having too much pride in

verbal

oneself.

val·e·dic·to·ri·an *n.* The student ranking highest in a graduating class, who delivers a speech at the commencement.

val·iant *adj.* Brave; exhibiting valor. **valiance, valor** *n.*

val·id *adj.* Founded on facts or truth.

val·ley *n.* Low land between ranges of hills or mountains.

val·u·a·ble *adj.* Of great value or importance; having a high monetary value.

valve *n.* The movable mechanism which opens and closes to control the flow of a substance through a pipe or other passageway.

van *n.* A large closed wagon or truck.

van·dal·ism *n.* The malicious anonymous defacement or destruction of private or public property.

vane *n.* A metal device that turns in the direction the wind is blowing; a thin rigid blade of an electric fan, propeller, or windmill.

van·ish *v.* To disappear suddenly; to drop out of sight; to go out of existence.

van·tage *n.* A superior position; an advantage.

va·por *n.* Moisture or smoke suspended in air, as mist or fog.

var·i·a·ble *adj.* Changeable; tending to vary; inconstant. *n.* A quantity or thing which can vary.

var·i·a·tion *n.* The result or process of varying; the degree or extent of varying; a different form of a given theme, with modifications in rhythm, key, or melody.

va·ri·e·ty *n.* The state or character of being varied or various; a number of different kinds; an assortment.

var·i·ous *adj.* Of different kinds.

var·nish *n.* A solution used to coat or cover a surface with a hard, transparent, shiny film. *v.* To put varnish on.

var·si·ty *n.* The best team representing a college, university, or school.

var·y *v.* To change; to make or become different; to be different; to make different kinds.

vast *adj.* Very large or great in size. **vastly** *adv.,* **vastness** *n.*

vault *n.* An arched structure that forms a ceiling or roof; a room for storage and safekeeping, as in a bank, usually made of steel; a burial chamber. *v.* To supply or construct with a vault; to jump or leap with the aid of a pole.

veg·e·ta·ble *n.* A plant, as green beans or lettuce, raised for the edible part.

veg·e·ta·tion *n.* Plants or plant life which grows from the soil.

ve·hi·cle *n.* A motorized device for transporting goods, equipment, or passengers; any means by which something is transferred, expressed, or applied.

veil *n.* A piece of transparent cloth worn on the head or face for concealment or protection; anything that conceals from view. *v.* To cover or conceal.

vein *n.* A vessel which transports blood back to the heart after passing through the body; one of the branching support tubes of an insect's wing; a long wavy, irregularly colored streak, as in marble, or wood.

ven·i·son *n.* The edible flesh of a deer.

ven·om *n.* A poisonous substance secreted by some animals, as scorpions or snakes, usually transmitted through a bite or sting. **venomous** *adj.*

vent *n.* A means of escape or passage from a restricted area; an opening which allows the escape of vapor, heat, gas, or liquid.

ven·ti·late *v.* To expose to a flow of fresh air for refreshing, curing, or purifying purposes; to cause fresh air to circulate through an area; to expose to public discussion. **ventilation, ventilator** *n.*

ven·ture *n.* A course of action involving risk, chance, or danger, especially a business investment. *v.* To take a risk.

verb *n.* The part of speech which expresses action, existence, or occurrence.

ver·bal *adj.* Expressed in speech; expressed orally; not written; relating to or derived from a verb. *n.* An adjective, noun, or other word based on a verb and retains some characteristics of a verb. **verbally**

215

adv., **verbalize** *v.*

verge *n.* The extreme edge or rim; margin; the point beyond which something begins. *v.* To border on.

ver•min *n.* A destructive, annoying animal harmful to one's health.

ver•sa•tile *adj.* Having the capabilities of doing many different things; having many functions or uses. **versatility** *n.*

verse *n.* Writing that has a rhyme; poetry; a subdivision of a poem or chapter of the Bible.

ver•sion *n.* An account or description told from a particular point of view; a translation from another language, especially a translation of the Bible; a form or particular point of view; a condition in which an organ, such as the uterus, is turned; manual turning of a fetus in the uterus to aid delivery.

ver•sus *prep.* Against; in contrast to; as an alternative of.

ver•ti•cal *adj.* In a straight up-and-down direction; being perpendicular to the plane of the horizon or to a primary axis; upright. **vertically** *adv.*

ver•y *adv.* To a high or great degree; truly; absolutely; exactly; actually; in actual fact.

ves•sel *n.* A hollow or concave utensil, as a bottle, kettle, container, or jar; a hollow craft designed for navigation on water, one larger than a rowboat.

vest *n.* A sleeveless garment open or fastening in front, worn over a shirt.

vet•er•an *n.* A person with a long record or experience in a certain field; one who has served in the military.

vet•er•i•nar•i•an *n.* One who is trained and authorized to give medical treatment to animals. **veterinary** *adj.*

ve•to *n.* The power of a government executive, as the president or a governor, to reject a bill passed by the legislature. *v.* To reject a bill passed by the legislature.

vi•a *prep.* By way of; by means of.

vi•a•duct *n.* A bridge, resting on a series of arches, carrying a road or railroad.

vi•brate *v.* To move or make move back and forth or up and down. **vibration** *n.*

vice *n.* An immoral habit or practice; evil conduct; second in command.

vi•ce ver•sa *adv.* With the order or meaning of something reversed.

vi•cin•i•ty *n.* The surrounding area or district; the state of being near in relationship or space.

vi•cious *adj.* Dangerously aggressive; having the quality of immorality.

vic•tim *n.* A person who is harmed or killed by another; a living creature slain and offered as sacrifice; one harmed by circumstance or condition. **victimize** *v.*

vic•tor *n.* A person who conquers; the winner.

vic•to•ri•ous *adj.* Being the winner in a contest.

vic•to•ry *n.* A defeat of those on the opposite side.

vid•e•o *adj.* Being, related to, or used in the reception or transmission of television; a videotape.

view *n.* The act of examining or seeing; a judgment or opinion; the range or extent of one's sight; something kept in sight. *v.* To watch or look at attentively; to consider.

vig•il *n.* A watch with prayers kept on the night before a religious feast; a period of surveillance.

vig•or *n.* Energy or physical strength; intensity of effect or action.

vil•lage *n.* An incorporated settlement, usually smaller than a town. **villager** *n.*

vil•lain *n.* An evil or wicked person; a criminal; an uncouth person.

vine *n.* A plant whose stem needs support as it climbs or clings to a surface.

vin•e•gar *n.* A tart, sour liquid derived from cider or wine.

vi•o•late *v.* To break the law or a rule; to disrupt or disturb a person's privacy.

vi•o•lence *n.* Physical force or activity used to cause harm, damage, or abuse.

vi•o•lin *n.* A small stringed instrument, played with a bow.

vir•tue *n.* Morality, goodness or

uprightness; a special type of goodness.
virtuous *adj.*, **virtuously** *adv.*

vi•rus *n.* Any of a variety of microscopic organisms which cause diseases; in computers, a program that automatically distributes itself along the web of online devices, usually malicious in nature.

vise *n.* A tool in carpentry and metalwork having two jaws to hold things in position.

vis•i•bil•i•ty *n.* The degree or state of being visible; the distance that one is able to see clearly.

vis•i•ble *adj.* Apparent; exposed to view.

vi•sion *n.* The power of sight; the ability to see; an image created in the imagination; a supernatural appearance.

vis•it *v.* To journey to or come to see a person or place. *n.* A professional or social call. **visitor, visitation** *n.*

vi•sor *n.* A brim on the front of a hat which protects the eyes.

vi•su•al *adj.* Visible; relating to sight.

vi•tal *adj.* Essential to life; very important. **vitally** *adv.*

vi•ta•min *n.* Any of various substances found in foods that are essential to good health.

vi•va•cious *adj.* Filled with vitality or animation; lively. **vivaciously** *adv.*

viv•id *adj.* Bright; brilliant; intense; having clear, lively, bright colors. **vividly** *adv.*

vo•cab•u•lar•y *n.* A list or group of words and phrases, usually in alphabetical order; all the words that a person uses or understands.

vo•cal *adj.* Of or related to the voice; uttered by the voice; to speak freely.

vo•ca•tion *n.* A career, occupation, or profession.

volt•age *n.* The amount of electrical power, given in terms of volts.

vol•ume *n.* The capacity or amount of space or room; a book; a quantity; the loudness of a sound.

vol•un•tar•y *adj.* Done cooperatively or willingly; from one's own choice.

vol•un•teer *n.* One who offers himself for a service of his own free will. *v.* To offer

voluntarily.

vote *n.* The expression of one's choice by voice, by raising one's hand, or by secret ballot. *v.* To express one's views. **vote-less** *adj.*, **voter** *n.*

vouch *v.* To verify or support as true; to guarantee. **voucher** *n.*

vow *n.* A solemn pledge or promise, especially one made to God; a marriage vow.

vow•el *n.* A sound of speech made by voicing the flow of breath within the mouth; a letter representing a vowel, as *a, e, i, o, u,* and sometimes *y.*

voy•age *n.* A long trip or journey.

vul•gar *adj.* Showing poor manners; crude; immoral or indecent. **vulgarity** *n.*

vul•ner•a•ble *adj.* Open to injury or attack. **vulnerability** *n.*, **vulnerably** *adv.*

W

W, w The twenty-third letter of the English alphabet.

wad *n.* A small crumpled mass or bundle; a soft plug used to hold shot or gunpowder charge in place.

wade *v.* To walk through a substance as mud or water which hampers one's steps.

waf•fle *n.* Pancake batter cooked in a waffle iron.

wag *v.* To move quickly from side to side or up and down. *n.* A playful, witty person. **waggish** *adj.*

wage *n.* A payment of money for labor or services. *v.* To conduct. **wa•ger** *v.* To make a bet. **wager** *n.*

wag•on *n.* A four-wheeled vehicle used to transport goods; a station wagon; a child's four-wheeled cart with a long handle.

wail *n.* A loud, mournful cry or weep. *v.* To make such a sound.

waist *n.* The narrow part of the body between the thorax and hips; the middle part or section of something narrower than the rest.

wait•er *n.* A person who serves food at a restaurant.

wake v. To come to consciousness, as from sleep. n. A vigil for a dead body; the surface turbulence caused by a vessel moving through water.

walk v. To move on foot over a surface; to pass over, go on, or go through by walking; in baseball, to advance to first base after four balls have been pitched. **walker** n.

wall n. A vertical structure to separate or enclose an area. v. To provide or close up, as with a wall.

wal·let n. A flat folding case for carrying paper money.

wal·nut n. An edible nut with a hard, light-brown shell; the tree on which this nut grows.

wand n. A slender rod used by a magician.

wan·der v. To travel about aimlessly; to roam; to stray. **wanderer** n.

wane v. To decrease in size or extent; to decrease gradually.

want v. To wish for or desire; to need; to lack; to fail to possess a required amount; to hunt in order to apprehend. n. The state of lacking a required or usual amount.

war n. An armed conflict among states or nations; a state of discord; the science of military techniques or procedures.

ward n. A section in a hospital for certain patients requiring similar treatment; a person under protection or surveillance.

warm adj. Moderate heat; neither hot nor cold; comfortably established; marked by a strong feeling; having pleasant feelings.

warn v. To give notice or inform beforehand; to call to one's attention; to alert.

warp v. To become bent out of shape; to deviate from a proper course. n. The condition of being twisted or bent; threads running down the length of a fabric.

war·ri·or n. One who fights in a war or battle.

war·y adj. Marked by caution; alert to danger.

wash v. To cleanse by the use of water; to remove dirt; to move or deposit as if by the force of water. n. A process or instance of washing; a group of soiled clothes or linens.

wash·er n. A small disk usually made of rubber or metal having a hole in the center, used with nuts and bolts; a washing machine.

wash·ing n. Clothes and other articles washed or to be washed; cleaning.

was·n't contr. Was not.

wasp n. Any of various insects, having a slim body with a constricted abdomen, the female capable of inflicting a sting.

waste v. To be thrown away; to be available but not used completely. n. A barren region; the instance of wasting; useless material produced as a by-product.

watch v. To view carefully; to guard; to keep informed. n. The act of staying awake to guard or protect; a small timepiece worn on the wrist, designed to keep the correct time of day.

wa·ter n. Two hydrogen atoms and one oxygen atom combined in a compound; the clear liquid making up oceans, lakes, and streams. v. To pour or spray water on something or someone; to give water to drink; to weaken or dilute with water.

wa·ter·proof adj. Capable of preventing water from penetrating. v. To make or treat in order to make waterproof. n. A material or fabric.

watt n. A unit of electrical power represented by current of one ampere, produced by the electromotive force of one volt.

wave v. To move back and forth or up and down; to motion with the hand. n. A swell or moving ridge of water; a curve or curl, as in the hair.

wa·ver v. To sway unsteadily; to move back and forth; to weaken in force.

wax n. A natural yellowish substance made by bees, solid when cold and easily melted or softened when heated. **waxy** adj.

way n. A manner of doing something; a tendency or characteristic; a habit or customary manner of acting or living; a direction; freedom to do as one chooses.

way·ward adj. Unruly; unpredictable.

we *pron.* First person plural of *I*, used to refer to the person speaking and one or more other people.

weak *adj.* Having little energy or strength; easily broken; having inadequate skills; not reasonable or convincing. **weakness** *n.*, **weakly** *adv.*

wealth *n.* An abundance of valuable possessions or property; all goods and resources having monetary value.

wealth•y *adj.* Having much wealth or money; abundant, rich.

weap•on *n.* A device used in fighting a war, a device which can be used to harm another person.

wear *v.* To have on or put something on the body; to display. *n.* The act of wearing out or using up; the act of wearing.

wea•ry *adj.* Exhausted; tired, feeling fatigued. *v.* To make or become tired; to become fatigued. **wearily** *adv.*, **weariness** *n.*

weath•er *n.* The condition of the air or atmosphere in terms of humidity, temperature, and similar features. *v.* To become worn by the actions of weather; to survive.

weave *v.* To make a basket, cloth, or other item by interlacing threads or other strands of material.

web *n.* A cobweb; a piece of interlacing material which forms a woven structure; something constructed as an entanglement; a thin membrane that joins the toes of certain water birds.

wed *v.* To take as a spouse; to marry.

we'd *contr.* We had; we should.

wed•ding *n.* A marriage ceremony; an act of joining together in close association.

wedge *n.* A tapered, triangular piece of wood or metal used to split logs, to add leverage, and to hold something open or ajar. *v.* To force or make something fit.

wed•lock *n.* Marriage; the state of being married.

weed *n.* An unwanted plant which interferes with the growth of grass, vegetables, or flowers.

week *n.* A period of seven days, beginning with Sunday and ending with Saturday; the time or days normally spent at school or work.

week•day *n.* Any day of the week except Saturday or Sunday.

week•end *n.* The end of the week from the period of Friday evening through Sunday evening.

weep *v.* To shed tears; to express sorrow, joy, or emotion by shedding tears; to cry.

weigh *v.* To determine the heaviness of an object by using a scale; to consider carefully in one's mind; to be of a particular weight; to oppress or burden.

weight *n.* The amount that something weighs; heaviness; a heavy object used to hold or pull something down; an overpowering force; the quality of a garment for a particular season. *v.* To make heavy.

weird *adj.* Having an extraordinary or strange character.

wel•come *v.* To extend warm hospitality; to accept gladly. *adj.* Received warmly. *n.* A greeting upon one's arrival.

wel•fare *n.* The state of doing well; governmental aid to help the disabled or disadvantaged.

well *n.* A hole in the ground which contains a supply of water; a shaft in the ground through which gas and oil are obtained. *adj.* Being in good health; in an agreeable state.

we'll *contr.* We will; we shall.

well-be•ing *n.* The state of being healthy, happy, or prosperous.

went *v.* Past tense of *go*.

wept *v.* Past tense of *weep*.

were *v.* Plural past tense of *to be*; conditional voice of *to be*.

we're *contr.* We are.

were•n't *contr.* Were not.

west *n.* The direction of the setting sun; the direction to the left of a person facing north.

whale *n.* A very large mammal resembling a fish which lives in salt water.

wharf *n.* A pier or platform at the edge of water where ships can load and unload.

what *pron.* Which one; which things; which type or kind. *adv.* In which way. *adj.* Which particular one.

what·ev·er *pron.* Everything or anything. *adj.* No matter what.

what's *contr.* What is.

wheat *n.* A grain ground into flour, used to make breads and similar foods.

wheel *n.* A circular disk which turns on an axle; an apparatus having the same principles of a wheel; something which resembles the motion or shape of a wheel. *v.* To move on or as if by wheels; to turn around a central axis; to rotate, pivot, or turn around.

when *adv.* At what time; at which time. *pron.* What or which time. *conj.* While; at the time that; although.

whence *adv.* From what source or place; from which.

when·ev·er *adv.* At any time; when. *conj.* At whatever time.

where *adv.* At or in what direction or place.

where·as *conj.* It being true or the fact; on the contrary.

where·by *conj.* Through or by which.

wher·ev·er *adv.* In any situation or place.

wheth·er *conj.* Indicating a choice; alternative possibilities; either.

whew *interj.* Used to express relief; or tiredness.

which *pron.* What one or ones; the one previously; whatever one or ones; whichever. *adj.* What one; any one of.

which·ev·er *pron.* Any; no matter which or what.

whiff *n.* A slight puff; a light current of air; a slight breath or odor.

while *n.* A length or period of time. *conj.* During the time that; even though; at the same time; although.

whim *n.* A sudden desire or impulse.

whine *v.* To make a squealing, plaintive sound; to complain in an irritating, childish fashion.

whin·ny *v.* To neigh in a soft gentle way.

whip *v.* To spank repeatedly with a rod or stick; to punish by whipping. *n.* A flexible stick or rod used to herd or beat animals; a dessert made by whipping ingredients; the utensil used to do so.

whirl *v.* To rotate or move in circles; to twirl; to move, drive, or go very fast. *n.* A rapid whirling motion. **whirler** *n.*

whisk *v.* To move with a sweeping motion; to move quickly or lightly. *n.* A sweeping movement; a utensil used in cooking; to stir.

whisk·er *n.* The hair that grows on a man's face; the long hair near the mouth of dogs, cats, and other animals. *pl.* A man's beard.

whis·per *v.* To speak in a very low tone; to tell in secret. *n.* A low rustling sound; the act of whispering.

whis·tle *v.* To make a clear shrill sound by blowing air through the teeth, through puckered lips, or through a special instrument. *n.* A device used to make a whistling sound. **whistler** *n.*

white *n.* The color opposite of black; the part of something white or light in color, as an egg or the eyeball; a member of the Caucasian group of people. *adj.* Having a light color; pale; pure; without sin.

white·cap *n.* A wave having a top of white foam.

white-col·lar *adj.* Relating to an employee whose job does not require manual labor.

who *pron.* Which or what certain individual, person, or group; referring to a person previously mentioned.

who'd *contr.* Who would; who had.

who·ev·er *pron.* Whatever person; all or any persons.

whole *adj.* Complete; having nothing missing; not divided or in pieces; a complete system or unity; everything considered; in math, not a fraction.

who'll *contr.* Who shall; who will.

whol·ly *adv.* Totally; exclusively.

whom *pron.* The form of who used as the direct object of a verb or the object of the preposition.

whop•per *n.* Something of extraordinary size.

who's *contr.* Who is; who has.

whose *pron.* Belonging to or having to do with one's belongings. *adj.* Relating to *which* or *whom.*

why *adj.* For what reason or purpose. *conj.* The cause, purpose, or reason for which. *inter.* Expressing surprise or disagreement.

wide *adj.* Broad; covering a large area; completely extended or open. *adv.* Over a large area; full extent.

wide•spread *adj.* Fully spread out; over a broad area.

wid•ow *n.* A woman whose husband is no longer living.

wid•ow•er *n.* A man whose wife is no longer living.

width *n.* The distance or extent of some thing from side to side.

wield *v.* To use or handle something skillfully; to employ power effectively.

wife *n.* A married female.

wig *n.* Artificial or human hair woven together to cover baldness or a bald spot on the head.

wig•gle *v.* To squirm; to move with rapid side-to-side motions.

wild *adj.* Living in a natural, untamed state; not occupied by man; not civilized; strange and unusual. *n.* A wilderness region not cultivated or settled by man.

wil•der•ness *n.* An unsettled area; a region left in its natural state.

wild•life *n.* Animals and plants living in their natural environments.

will *n.* The mental ability to decide or choose for oneself; strong desire or determination; a legal document stating how one's property is to be distributed after death. *v.* To bring about by an act of a will; to decide as by decree; to give or bequeath something in a will.

win *v.* To defeat others; to gain victory in a contest; to receive. *n.* Victory; the act of winning. **winner** *n.*

wind *n.* A natural movement of air. *v.* To become short of breath. **windy** *adj.*

wind *v.* To wrap around and around something; to turn, to crank. *n.* A turning or twisting.

wind in•stru•ment *n.* A musical instrument which produces sound when a person forces breath into it.

wind•mill *n.* A machine operated or powered by the wind.

win•dow *n.* An opening built into a wall for light and air; a pane of glass.

wine *n.* A drink containing 10-15% alcohol by volume, made by fermenting grapes.

wing *n.* One of the movable appendages that allow a bird or insect to fly; one of the airfoils on either side of an aircraft, allowing it to glide or travel through the air.

wink *v.* To shut one eye as a signal or message; to blink rapidly. *n.* The act of winking; a short period of rest; a nap.

win•ning *adj.* Defeating others; captivating. *n.* Victory.

wipe *v.* To clean by rubbing; to take off by rubbing.

wire *n.* A small metal rod used to conduct electricity; thin strands of metal twisted together to form a cable; the telephone or telegraph system; the finish line of a race. *v.* To equip with wiring.

wis•dom *n.* The ability to understand what is right, true, or enduring; good judgment; knowledge.

wise *adj.* Having superior intelligence; having great learning; having a capacity for sound judgment marked by deep understanding.

wish *v.* To desire or long for something; to command or request. *n.* A longing or desire.

wit *n.* The ability to use words in a clever way; a sense of humor.

with *prep.* In the company of; near or alongside; having, wearing or bearing; in the judgment or opinion of; supporting; among; occurring at the same time.

with•draw *v.* To take away; to take back; to remove; to retreat.

with·er *v.* To dry up or wilt from a lack of moisture; to lose freshness or vigor.

with·hold *n.* To hold back or keep.

with·hold·ing tax *n.* The tax on income held back by an employer in payment of one's income tax.

with·in *adv.* Inside the inner part; inside the limits; inside the limits of time, distance, or degree.

with·out *adv.* On the outside; not in possession of. *prep.* Something or someone lacking.

with·stand *v.* To endure.

wit·ness *n.* A person who has seen, experienced, or heard something; something serving as proof or evidence. *v.* To see or hear something; to give proof or evidence of; to give testimony.

wit·ty *adj.* Amusing or cleverly humorous.

woe *n.* Great sorrow or grief; misfortune.

woke *v.* Past tense of *wake.*

wolf *n.* A carnivorous animal found in northern areas; a fierce person. *v.* To eat quickly and with greed.

wo·man *n.* The mature adult human female; a person who has feminine qualities.

wo·man·hood *n.* The state of being a woman.

won *v.* Past tense of *win.*

won·der *n.* A feeling of amazement or admiration. *v.* To feel admiration; to feel uncertainty. **wonderful** *adj.*

won·drous *adj.* Wonderful; marvelous.

won't *contr.* Will not.

wood *n.* The hard substance which makes up the main part of trees. *pl.* A growth of trees smaller than a forest.

wood·en *adj.* Made of wood; resembling wood; stiff; lifeless; lacking flexibility.

wool *n.* The soft, thick hair of sheep and other such mammals; a fabric made from such hair.

word *n.* A meaningful sound which stands for an idea; a comment; a brief talk; an order or command *v.* To express orally. **wording** *n.*

word proc·ess·ing *n.* A system which produces typewritten documents with automated type and editing equipment.

work *n.* The action or labor required to accomplish something; employment; a job; a project or assignment; something requiring physical or mental effort. *v.* To engage in mental or physical exertion; to labor; to have a job; to arrange.

work·book *n.* A book designed to be written in, containing exercises and problems, usually advancing in difficulty from kindergarten through grade 6, ranging in subjects such as math and reading.

work·er *n.* A person who works for wages; an employee; a bee or other insect which performs special work in the colony in which it lives.

work·ing *adj.* Adequate to permit work to be done; assumed to permit further work.

world *n.* The planet Earth; the universe; the human race; a field of human interest.

world·ly *adj.* Interested in the physical world rather than religious or spiritual matters; well-educated, broadly traveled.

worm *n.* A small, thin animal having a long, flexible, rounded or flattened body.

worn *adj.* Made weak or thin from use; exhausted.

wor·ry *v.* To be concerned or troubled; to tug at repeatedly; to annoy; to irritate. *n.* Distress or mental anxiety.

wor·ship *n.* Reverence for a sacred object; high esteem or devotion for a person. *v.* To revere; attend a religious service. **worshiper** *n.*

worst *adj.* Bad; most inferior; most disagreeable.

would *v.* Past tense of *will.*

wound *n.* A laceration of the skin. *v.* To injure by tearing, cutting, or piercing the skin.

wrath *n.* Violent anger or fury.

wreath *n.* A decorative ring-like form of intertwined flowers, bows, and other articles.

wres·tle *v.* To struggle with an opponent in order to pin him down. **wrestler** *n.*

wretch *n.* An extremely unhappy person; a

miserable person. **wretched** *adj.*

wrig•gle *v.* To squirm; to move by turning and twisting.

wring *v.* To squeeze and twist by hand or machine; to press together.

wrin•kle *n.* A small crease on the skin or on fabric. *v.* To have or make wrinkles.

wrist *n.* The joint of the body between the hand and forearm; the part of a sleeve which encircles the wrist.

write *v.* To form symbols or letters; to form words on a surface; to communicate by writing; to earn a living by writing books.

wrote *v.* Past tense of *write.*

wrought *adj.* Fashioned; formed; beaten or hammered into shape.

wrung *v.* Past tense of *wring.*

WWW *abbr.* World Wide Web; In computers, a system of linked documents connected by hypertext, allowing access to many information sources from one site.

X, x The twenty-fourth letter of the English alphabet.

Xan•a•du *n.* A place having idyllic beauty.

xan•thic *adj.* The color yellow or all colors that tend toward the color yellow when relating to flowers.

X chro•mo•some *n.* The sex female chromosome, associated with female characteristics; occurs paired in the female and single in the male chromosome pair.

xe•non *n.* The colorless, odorless gaseous element found in small quantities in the air, symbolized by *Xe.*

xe•no•phile *n.* One attracted to foreign people, styles, or manners.

xen•o•phobe *n.* A person who dislikes, fears, and mistrusts foreigners or anything strange. **xenophobia** *n.*

xe•ric *adj.* Relating to or requiring only a small amount of moisture.

X ray *n.* Energy radiated with a short wavelength and high penetrating power; a black and white negative image or picture

of the body.

x-sec•tion *n.* A cross section of something.

xy•lo•phone *n.* A musical instrument consisting of mounted wooden bars which produce a ringing musical sound when struck with two small wooden hammers.

Y, y The twenty-fifth letter of the English alphabet.

yacht *n.* A small sailing vessel powdered by wind or motor, used for pleasure cruises. **yacht** *v.*

yak *n.* A longhaired ox of Tibet and the mountains of central Asia.

yam *n.* An edible root; a variety of the sweet potato.

Yan•kee *n.* A native of the northern United States.

yap *v.* To bark in a high pitched, sharp way.

yard *n.* A unit of measure that equals 36 inches or 3 feet; the ground around or near a house or building.

yard•stick *n.* A graduated measuring stick that equals 1 yard or 36 inches; standard of measurement.

yarn *n.* Twisted fibers, as of wool, used in knitting or weaving; an involved tale.

yawn *v.* To inhale a deep breath with the mouth open wide, indicating fatigue.

Y chro•mo•some *n.* The sex male chromosome, associated with male characteristics; occurs paired with the X chromosome in the male chromosome pair.

year *n.* A period of time starting on January 1st and continuing through December 31st, consisting of 365 days or 366 days in a leap year; one circumlocution of the sun by the planet Earth.

year•book *n.* A book printed each year giving facts about the year; a book printed each year for a high school or college.

year•ling *n.* An animal that is one year old.

year•ly *adj.* Pertaining to something that happens, appears, or comes once a year; every year.

yearn *v.* To feel a strong craving; deep desire; a wistful feeling. **yearner, yearning** *n.*

yeast *n.* Fungi or plant cells used to make baked goods rise or fruit juices ferment.

yell *v.* To cry out loudly. *n.* A loud cry; a cheer to show support for a team.

yel·low *n.* The bright color of a lemon; the yolk of an egg. *v.* To make or become yellow. *adj.* Of the color yellow.

yelp *n.* A quick, sharp, shrill cry, as from pain.

yes *interj.* An expression of agreement.

yes·ter·day *n.* The day before today; a former or recent time. *adv.* On the day before the present day.

yet *adv.* Up to now; at this time; even now; more so. *conj.* Nevertheless; but.

yield *v.* To bear or bring forward; to give up the possession of something; to give way to. *n.* An amount that is produced.

yield·ing *adj.* Ready to yield, comply, or submit; unresisting. **yieldingly** *adv.*

yo·ga *a.* A system of exercises which helps the mind and the body to achieve tranquillity and spiritual insight.

yo·gurt *n.* A thick custard-like food made from curdled milk.

yolk *n.* The yellow nutritive part of an egg.

you *pron.* The person or persons addressed.

you'd *contr.* You had; you would.

you'll *contr.* You will; you shall.

young *adj.* Of or relating to the early stage of life; not old. *n.* The offspring of an animal. **youngster** *n.*

your *adj.* Belonging to you, yourself, or the person spoken to.

you're *contr.* You are.

your·self *pron.* A form of you for emphasis when the object of a verb and the subject is the same.

youth *n.* The appearance or state of being young; the time of life when one is not considered an adult; a young person.

youth·ful *adj.* Being of a young age or early stage in life. **youthfully** *adv.*, **youthfulness** *n.*

you've *contr.* You have.

Z

Z, z The twenty-sixth letter of the English alphabet.

za·ny *n.* A clown; a person who acts silly or foolish. *adj.* Typical of being clownish.

zap *v.* To destroy; to do away with.

zeal *n.* Great interest or eagerness.

zeal·ot *n.* A fanatical person; a deeply committed follower.

zeal·ous *adj.* Full of interest; eager; passionate. **zealously** *adv.*

ze·bra *n.* An African mammal of the horse family having black or brown stripes on a white body.

ze·ro *n.* The number or symbol 0; nothing; the point from which degrees or measurements on a scale begin; the lowest point; the symbol used to multiply by ten.

zest *n.* Enthusiasm; a keen quality.

zip *v.* To act or move with vigor or speed; to move with energy, speed, or facility; to open or close with a zipper; zero; nothing.

zip·per *n.* A fastener consisting of two rows of plastic or metal teeth that are interlocked by means of sliding a tab. **zippered** *adj.*

zo·di·ac *n.* The celestial sphere; the unseen path followed through the heavens by the moon, sun, and most planets; this path divided into twelve parts or twelve astrological signs, each bearing the name of a constellation. **zodiacal** *adj.*

zom·bie *n.* A person who resembles the walking dead; a person who has a strange appearance or behavior.

zone *n.* An area or region set apart from its surroundings by some characteristic.

zoo *n.* A public display or collection of living animals.

zo·ol·o·gy *n.* The science that deals with animals, animal life, and the animal kingdom. **zoologist** *n.*

zoom *v.* To move with a continuous, loud, buzzing sound; to move upward sharply; to move toward a subject with great speed.